Andreas Heinemann-Grüder (ed.)

WHO ARE THE FIGHTERS?
Irregular Armed Groups in the Russian-Ukrainian War since 2014

Bibliografische Information der Deutschen Nationalbibliothek

Die Deutsche Nationalbibliothek verzeichnet diese Publikation in der Deutschen Nationalbibliografie; detaillierte bibliografische Daten sind im Internet über http://dnb.d-nb.de abrufbar.

Bibliographic information published by the Deutsche Nationalbibliothek

Die Deutsche Nationalbibliothek lists this publication in the Deutsche Nationalbibliografie; detailed bibliographic data are available in the Internet at http://dnb.d-nb.de.

Cover picture: Soldiers practice during urban warfare drills on Dec. 26, 2021 in Kyiv. (Kyiv's 130th Territorial Defense Brigade).
https://kyivindependent.com/defense-ministry-to-create-150-reservist-battalions/

ISBN-13: 978-3-8382-1777-2
© *ibidem*-Verlag, Hannover • Stuttgart 2024
Alle Rechte vorbehalten

Das Werk einschließlich aller seiner Teile ist urheberrechtlich geschützt. Jede Verwertung außerhalb der engen Grenzen des Urheberrechtsgesetzes ist ohne Zustimmung des Verlages unzulässig und strafbar. Dies gilt insbesondere für Vervielfältigungen, Übersetzungen, Mikroverfilmungen und elektronische Speicherformen sowie die Einspeicherung und Verarbeitung in elektronischen Systemen.

All rights reserved. No part of this publication may be reproduced, stored in or introduced into a retrieval system, or transmitted, in any form, or by any means (electronic, mechanical, photocopying, recording or otherwise) without the prior written permission of the publisher. Any person who commits any unauthorized act in relation to this publication may be liable to criminal prosecution and civil claims for damages.

Printed in the EU

Contents

The War in Ukraine and Irregular Armed Groups
Andreas Heinemann-Grüder 7

Organizations of Russian Nationalists in the Russia-Ukraine Conflict
Nikolay Mitrokhin 15

Pro-Russian Irregular Armed Groups
Natalia Savelyeva 47

The Far-Right Predecessor Organizations of the Ukrainian Irregular Armed Units
Anton Shekhovtsov 89

Irregular Armed Groups in Ukraine: State Savior or State-Capture?
Andreas Heinemann-Grüder 117

Between Frontline and Parliament: Ukrainian Political Parties and Irregular Armed Groups since 2014
Kostiantyn Fedorenko, Andreas Umland 189

Ukrainian Volunteer Groups: Oversight by the Government
Leonid Poliakov 229

The Long Shadow of the War: Return and Reintegration of War Veterans
Julia Friedrich, Theresa Lütkefend 255

Between Two Worlds: Internally Displaced Persons
Vyacheslav Likhachev 285

Media Policy of Armed Groups in Ukraine
Kostiantyn Fedorenko 309

Russia's Corporate Warriors
Andreas Heinemann-Grüder 333

Contributors 355

Soviet and Post-Soviet Politics and Society (SPPS) Vol. 261
ISSN 1614-3515

General Editor: Andreas Umland,
Stockholm Centre for Eastern European Studies, andreas.umland@ui.se

Commissioning Editor: Max Jakob Horstmann,
London, mjh@ibidem.eu

EDITORIAL COMMITTEE*

DOMESTIC & COMPARATIVE POLITICS
Prof. **Ellen Bos**, *Andrássy University of Budapest*
Dr. **Gergana Dimova**, *Florida State University*
Prof. **Heiko Pleines**, *University of Bremen*
Dr. **Sarah Whitmore**, *Oxford Brookes University*
Dr. **Harald Wydra**, *University of Cambridge*

SOCIETY, CLASS & ETHNICITY
Col. **David Glantz**, *"Journal of Slavic Military Studies"*
Dr. **Marlène Laruelle**, *George Washington University*
Dr. **Stephen Shulman**, *Southern Illinois University*
Prof. **Stefan Troebst**, *University of Leipzig*

POLITICAL ECONOMY & PUBLIC POLICY
Prof. **Andreas Goldthau**, *University of Erfurt*
Dr. **Robert Kravchuk**, *University of North Carolina*
Dr. **David Lane**, *University of Cambridge*
Dr. **Carol Leonard**, *University of Oxford*
Dr. **Maria Popova**, *McGill University, Montreal*

FOREIGN POLICY & INTERNATIONAL AFFAIRS
Dr. **Peter Duncan**, *University College London*
Prof. **Andreas Heinemann-Grüder**, *University of Bonn*
Prof. **Gerhard Mangott**, *University of Innsbruck*
Dr. **Diana Schmidt-Pfister**, *University of Konstanz*
Dr. **Lisbeth Tarlow**, *Harvard University, Cambridge*
Dr. **Christian Wipperfürth**, *N-Ost Network, Berlin*
Dr. **William Zimmerman**, *University of Michigan*

HISTORY, CULTURE & THOUGHT
Dr. **Catherine Andreyev**, *University of Oxford*
Prof. **Mark Bassin**, *Södertörn University*
Prof. **Karsten Brüggemann**, *Tallinn University*
Prof. **Alexander Etkind**, *Central European University*
Prof. **Gasan Gusejnov**, *Free University of Berlin*
Prof. **Leonid Luks**, *Catholic University of Eichstaett*
Dr. **Olga Malinova**, *Russian Academy of Sciences*
Dr. **Richard Mole**, *University College London*
Prof. **Andrei Rogatchevski**, *University of Tromsø*
Dr. **Mark Tauger**, *West Virginia University*

ADVISORY BOARD*

Prof. **Dominique Arel**, *University of Ottawa*
Prof. **Jörg Baberowski**, *Humboldt University of Berlin*
Prof. **Margarita Balmaceda**, *Seton Hall University*
Dr. **John Barber**, *University of Cambridge*
Prof. **Timm Beichelt**, *European University Viadrina*
Dr. **Katrin Boeckh**, *University of Munich*
Prof. em. **Archie Brown**, *University of Oxford*
Dr. **Vyacheslav Bryukhovetsky**, *Kyiv-Mohyla Academy*
Prof. **Timothy Colton**, *Harvard University, Cambridge*
Prof. **Paul D'Anieri**, *University of California*
Dr. **Heike Dörrenbächer**, *Friedrich Naumann Foundation*
Dr. **John Dunlop**, *Hoover Institution, Stanford, California*
Dr. **Sabine Fischer**, *SWP, Berlin*
Dr. **Geir Flikke**, *NUPI, Oslo*
Prof. **David Galbreath**, *University of Aberdeen*
Prof. **Frank Golczewski**, *University of Hamburg*
Dr. **Nikolas Gvosdev**, *Naval War College, Newport, RI*
Prof. **Mark von Hagen**, *Arizona State University*
Prof. **Guido Hausmann**, *University of Regensburg*
Prof. **Dale Herspring**, *Kansas State University*
Dr. **Stefani Hoffman**, *Hebrew University of Jerusalem*
Prof. em. **Andrzej Korbonski**, *University of California*
Dr. **Iris Kempe**, *"Caucasus Analytical Digest"*
Prof. **Herbert Küpper**, *Institut für Ostrecht Regensburg*
Prof. **Rainer Lindner**, *University of Konstanz*

Dr. **Luke March**, *University of Edinburgh*
Prof. **Michael McFaul**, *Stanford University, Palo Alto*
Prof. **Birgit Menzel**, *University of Mainz-Germersheim*
Dr. **Alex Pravda**, *University of Oxford*
Dr. **Erik van Ree**, *University of Amsterdam*
Dr. **Joachim Rogall**, *Robert Bosch Foundation Stuttgart*
Prof. **Peter Rutland**, *Wesleyan University, Middletown*
Prof. **Gwendolyn Sasse**, *University of Oxford*
Prof. **Jutta Scherrer**, *EHESS, Paris*
Prof. **Robert Service**, *University of Oxford*
Mr. **James Sherr**, *RIIA Chatham House London*
Dr. **Oxana Shevel**, *Tufts University, Medford*
Prof. **Eberhard Schneider**, *University of Siegen*
Prof. **Olexander Shnyrkov**, *Shevchenko University, Kyiv*
Prof. **Hans-Henning Schröder**, *SWP, Berlin*
Prof. **Yuri Shapoval**, *Ukrainian Academy of Sciences*
Dr. **Lisa Sundstrom**, *University of British Columbia*
Dr. **Philip Walters**, *"Religion, State and Society"*, Oxford
Prof. **Zenon Wasyliw**, *Ithaca College, New York State*
Dr. **Lucan Way**, *University of Toronto*
Dr. **Markus Wehner**, *"Frankfurter Allgemeine Zeitung"*
Dr. **Andrew Wilson**, *University College London*
Prof. **Jan Zielonka**, *University of Oxford*
Prof. **Andrei Zorin**, *University of Oxford*

While the Editorial Committee and Advisory Board support the General Editor in the choice and improvement of manuscripts for publication, responsibility for remaining errors and misinterpretations in the series' volumes lies with the books' authors.

Soviet and Post-Soviet Politics and Society (SPPS)
ISSN 1614-3515

Founded in 2004 and refereed since 2007, SPPS makes available affordable English-, German-, and Russian-language studies on the history of the countries of the former Soviet bloc from the late Tsarist period to today. It publishes between 5 and 20 volumes per year and focuses on issues in transitions to and from democracy such as economic crisis, identity formation, civil society development, and constitutional reform in CEE and the NIS. SPPS also aims to highlight so far understudied themes in East European studies such as right-wing radicalism, religious life, higher education, or human rights protection. The authors and titles of all previously published volumes are listed at the end of this book. For a full description of the series and reviews of its books, see www.ibidem-verlag.de/red/spps.

Editorial correspondence & manuscripts should be sent to: Dr. Andreas Umland, Department of Political Science, Kyiv-Mohyla Academy, vul. Voloska 8/5, UA-04070 Kyiv, UKRAINE; andreas.umland@cantab.net

Business correspondence & review copy requests should be sent to: *ibidem* Press, Leuschnerstr. 40, 30457 Hannover, Germany; tel.: +49 511 2622200; fax: +49 511 2622201; spps@ibidem.eu.

Authors, reviewers, referees, and editors for (as well as all other persons sympathetic to) SPPS are invited to join its networks at www.facebook.com/group.php?gid=52638198614
www.linkedin.com/groups?about=&gid=103012
www.xing.com/net/spps-ibidem-verlag/

Recent Volumes

252 *Eduard Baidaus*
An Unsettled Nation
State-Building, Identity, and Separatism in Post-Soviet Moldova
With forewords by John-Paul Himka and David R. Marples
ISBN 978-3-8382-1582-2

253 *Igor Okunev, Petr Oskolkov (Eds.)*
Transforming the Administrative Matryoshka
The Reform of Autonomous Okrugs in the Russian Federation, 2003–2008
With a foreword by Vladimir Zorin
ISBN 978-3-8382-1721-5

254 *Winfried Schneider-Deters*
Ukraine's Fateful Years 2013–2019
Vol. I: The Popular Uprising in Winter 2013/2014
ISBN 978-3-8382-1725-3

255 *Winfried Schneider-Deters*
Ukraine's Fateful Years 2013–2019
Vol. II: The Annexation of Crimea and the War in Donbas
ISBN 978-3-8382-1726-0

256 *Robert M. Cutler*
Soviet and Post-Soviet Russian Foreign Policies II
East-West Relations in Europe and the Political Economy of the Communist Bloc, 1971–1991
With a foreword by Roger E. Kanet
ISBN 978-3-8382-1727-7

257 *Robert M. Cutler*
Soviet and Post-Soviet Russian Foreign Policies III
East-West Relations in Europe and Eurasia in the Post-Cold War Transition, 1991–2001
With a foreword by Roger E. Kanet
ISBN 978-3-8382-1728-4

258 *Pawel Kowal, Iwona Reichardt, Kateryna Pryshchepa (Eds.)*
Three Revolutions: Mobilization and Change in Contemporary Ukraine III
Archival Records and Historical Sources on the 1990 Revolution on Granite
ISBN 978-3-8382-1376-7

259 *Mykhailo Minakov (Ed.)*
Philosophy Unchained
Developments in Post-Soviet Philosophical Thought
With a foreword by Christopher Donohue
ISBN 978-3-8382-1768-0

260 *David Dalton*
The Ukrainian Oligarchy After the Euromaidan
How Ukraine's Political Economy Regime Survived the Crisis
With a foreword by Andrew Wilson
ISBN 978-3-8382-1740-6

The War in Ukraine and Irregular Armed Groups

Andreas Heinemann-Grüder

The sequence of revolt and organized violence in and around Ukraine since late 2013 culminated in a watershed first in European, then in global politics, following the beginning of Russia's fully fledged war against Ukraine from 24 February 2022 onwards.[1] The violent conflict that escalated over the last ten years represents a multi-causal and multi-dimensional series of events that were not pre-ordained by any master plan. Structural prerequisites and critical junctures created their own path dependencies. Ukraine's post-Soviet nation- and state-building was incomplete and evidenced many vulnerabilities, which turned into entry points for Russia's imperial interference. The crisis of legitimacy, the repeated frustration of popular hopes to overcome kleptocracy, corruption and oligarchic clientelism provided fertile grounds for Russia's aggression and its mobilization of discontent. However, without Russia's military intervention the internal fractures would have remained a domestic affair of Ukraine.

The irregular armed groups that mushroomed in Ukraine as a result of the turn of the originally peaceful Maidan protests into violent insurgency and counter-insurgency were and are critical actors in the conduct of war. Originally, the conflict derived its explosiveness from the deep crisis of legitimacy of the Ukrainian government under the then President Viktor Yanukovich, a crisis that grabbed the center, epitomized by the demonstrations and the insurgency on Ukraine's main square, the Maidan, but extended to the regions as well. Anti-government sentiments were fueled by

---

1   This publication is the result of a joint project by the Bonn International Centre for Conflict Studies (BICC), the St. Petersburg based Centre for Independent Social Research (CISR) and the Kyiv based Institute for Euro-Atlantic Cooperation (IEAC), which was generously funded by the Volkswagen Foundation. I would like to particularly thank Olena Shevchyk for her diligent research assistance over the years and Heike Webb for her help with editing the English translation.

frustrations over rampant kleptocracy, patronage, clientelism and corruption, as well as the erosion of the state monopoly of violence. The violent conflict was not pre-ordained or over-determined by historical or geopolitical forces or allegedly polar ethnic identities. The organized violence, the experience of massive destruction, harm, torture, repression, pain, trauma and displacement polarized, antagonized and hardened identities. From December 2013 onwards, the use of violence by Ukraine's special forces and right-wing extremist groups was the key trigger for turning the peaceful protest movement on Kyiv's Maidan square into a radical quest for changing the regime, which ultimately led to the ouster of President Yanukovich on 22 February 2014. Latent tensions between pro-European, pro-Russian, nationalist and regionalist as well as Soviet-oriented forces manifested themselves in the course of events.

This volume focuses on irregular armed groups as force multipliers, agents of illicit warfare and self-interested actors of violence. In a project conducted from 2016 onwards and funded by the Volkswagen Foundation, teams from the St. Petersburg-based Centre for Independent Social Research (CISR, one of the few remaining independent social science institutes in Russia), the Institute for Euro-Atlantic Cooperation (IEAC) in Kyiv and the Bonn International Centre for Conflict Studies (BICC) in Germany collaborated on the collective action of irregular armed groups.[2] The war in and against Ukraine provides fertile ground for the study of collective actors formed in the course of violent action.

Why Irregular Armed Groups?

After the change of government in Kyiv in February 2014, and in the course of the Russian intervention in Ukraine's south and east,

---

2   The CISR team consisted of Natalia Savaleva, Oleg Zhuravlev, Maksim Alyukov, Svetlana Erpyleva, Andrey Nevskij. Particular thanks go to Viktor Voronkov from CISR. The IEAC team consisted of Andreas Umland, Anton Shekhovtsov, Anton Pisarenko, Kostiantyn Fedorenko, Volodymyr Kopchak, Leonid Poliakov and Andrey Matiukhanov. The BICC team included Andreas Heinemann-Grüder and Olena Shevchyk, who built up the project's data bank and contributed to fact-checking, project management, and editing.

the Ukrainian government lost control over parts of its security sector. State-controlled services were defunct or switched sides — a sign of state erosion or even state capture before the Maidan protests. Pro-state militias in turn began to compensate for the paralysis or defection of the Ukrainian security sector. Russia sponsored pro-Russian militias and sent its own armed forces, although under disguise, to the Crimea and eastern Ukraine.

The study of irregular armed groups usually focuses on conducive or enabling conditions, among them political or economic grievances, greed, access to weapons or lootable resources, opportunities such as weak statehood or on onset conditions and conflict triggers such as political murder, terror attacks, pogroms or excessive state violence. A perspective on micro-dynamics looks instead at factors that transform opportunities into action, among them incentives to join an armed group, legitimizing strategies, interaction patterns between state and non-state actors and among irregular groups. Studying micro-dynamics is about the transformation of irregular groups into political or civil society organizations.

Any military is characterized by a defined and known hierarchy, by internalized command structures. None of this was a given in the irregular armed groups. Often, the groups were lumped together on an ad hoc basis; the men fighting together barely knew each other. What characterized their groupness? One of the key capabilities for survival in a combat group is mutual trust, based on a shared sense of purpose and reliable communication. In this respect, the irregular armed groups proved highly vulnerable. Loosely formed groups around a self-declared or chosen leader converted over time into more or less professional combat units with hierarchical structures and command and logistic chains, i.e., into battalions. The term battalion pertains to a military group of the infantry with a size varying between 300 to 1,200 people.

Armies worldwide have used this term differently, but as a rule, a battalion consists of a couple of companies or rotes. In the context of the violent conflict in Ukraine, the term "volunteer battalion" pertains to a distinct military unit with a name, a commander, a headquarters and distinct location, which was mobilized for the specific purpose of enacting or resisting the Russian annexation of Crimea and the separatism in Donbas. Groups were often summarily called battalions, regardless of their size. The term, therefore, has a broad meaning, and at times battalions were relabeled into regiments or brigades. A battalion consisted, as a rule, of infantry rotes, stormtroopers, reconnaissance, artillery, communication units, a medical unit, and logistics. A rote is made up of up to a hundred persons, these rotes were composed in turn of platoons (взвод). The battalions often fought together with brigades, a brigade usually consisting of 1,500 to 5,000 men. Brigades and battalions are characterized by their capability to act flexibly and autonomously.

The key findings of our project can be summarized as follows: The battalions in the Ukrainian conflict were irregular, but by no means non-state—they represented pro-state militias, either for the Russian de facto regimes in Donbas or the Ukrainian state. Among the pro-Ukrainian battalions, we identified three types: Volunteer battalions that built on right-wing paramilitary organizations; battalions created "from above" by state security apparatuses; and battalions created and sponsored by oligarchs. In comparison, the pro-Russian battalions were either continuations of existing nationalist organizations in eastern Ukraine or were established directly by the Russian state and semi-state sponsors in Russia. The irregular battalions on the Russian and Ukrainian sides were predominantly established by state agencies, i.e., they did not emerge autonomously "from below" but were created and maintained for hybrid warfare or to compensate for the weakness of regular forces.

The relative success (or failure) of battalions was determined by the organizational qualities of the commanders, connections to political, economic and social support groups and their ability to include diverse strata. From 2015 onwards, the vast majority of battalions was transferred to (quasi-)state structures in the areas controlled by Russia and those under the control of Ukraine. Only a few radical right-wing battalions in Ukraine remained beyond state control, while Russian "security agents" brought autonomous battalions and their commanders under hierarchical control too.

A novelty of the irregular battalions in the violent conflict in Ukraine was the recruitment, fundraising and legitimization through social media. For several battalion commanders, participation in the war became a source of social capital to launch a career as a politician. In an environment that was and still is permeated by the presence of irregular battalions, the popular interactions with irregular actors of violence are dynamic, complex and characterized by insecurity, fear and opportunism.

The importance of irregular armed groups for Russia has been increasing since it began its war against Ukraine in 2014/15. These irregular armed groups act in coordination with the Russian Ministry of Defense, the Federal Security Service (FSB), the foreign intelligence service and the presidential administration. Russia's mercenaries practice exterminatory warfare and operate as parallel or shadow armies, which can rarely be held accountable.

Russia's infamous Wagner group and its successor organizations are one of the remnants of the war in 2014/15. Its combatants specialize in capturing cities, they provide agile ground forces for reconnaissance, sabotage operations and the indiscriminate liquidation of people attributed to the opposing side. The relationship between regular and irregular groups is strenuous. There are repeated complaints from irregular combatants that Russia's regular army puts them at a disadvantage when providing them with weapons, ammunition, vehicles, food and other supplies or sends them on high-risk missions without support—the main reason for the mutiny of the Wagner group against the Ministry of Defense in Russia.

Beyond the war in Ukraine, Russia`s irregular armed groups turned into an instrument of Russia's foreign and security policy. They can be deployed flexibly and covertly and cannot be held accountable for crimes—or only to a limited extent. Within their missions, business interests and military objectives are intertwined. Beyond Ukraine, Russia's military companies serve to destabilize pro-Western and stabilize anti-Western governments, for example, in Syria, Libya, Mali, Sudan or the Central African Republic. They prepare for, support and complement the deployment of regular forces and are likely to operate at a lower overall cost than regular forces.

Deaths and injuries among irregular combatants are officially invisible. The exploitation of lucrative gold, diamond, oil or gas deposits is an expression of the economic and political fusion of oligarchic and military interests that lie behind these private military companies. Russian irregular armed groups interact with the Russian Ministry of Defense, especially the military intelligence (GRU), as well as the FSB, the foreign intelligence service (SVR) and the presidential administration. They complement but do not replace regular security organs.

The term "armed conflict in Donbas" or "war in Donbas" has been common since 2014. However, the region of violent conflict is not identical with "Donbas" — Donbas is linked to the Donetsk coal basin, which includes part of the territory of Donetsk and Luhansk regions, but also parts of Dnipropetrovsk region and Rostov region of Russia. On the other hand, the northern parts of Luhansk and Donetsk oblasts (historically belonging to *Slobozhanshchyna*) and the southern part of Donetsk oblast (Azov region) are not included in Donbas. The label "armed conflict in Donbas", frequently in use until February 24, 2022, incorrectly excluded Russia's annexation of Crimea and the later ambition to undermine Ukraine's existence as an independent nation-state. With Russia's launch of a war of annihilation of Ukraine as a sovereign state, the term "Donbas conflict" is even more misleading — the war results from Russia's aggression, not internal strife.

The war in Donbas is part of the overarching Russian–Ukrainian inter-state armed conflict that began with the Russian aggression in Crimea in February 2014. The organized violence shifted from violent clashes between Maidan and anti-Maidan forces in early 2014 to separatism sponsored and conducted by Russian-controlled military from March/April 2014 onwards to an enduring rivalry between February 2015 to 2022 and the resumption of a fully-fledged war by Russia against Ukraine on February 24, 2022. The violence polarized and antagonized identities which in turn provided feedback loops to further violence.

Starting with the war against Ukraine in 2014, the irregular armed groups have become agents of influence of the Russian autocratic regime, war profiteers and auxiliary forces for state security agencies. Russia's irregular armed groups reflect the Russian regime's aggressive, criminal and oligarchic nature, the privatization and commercialization of organized violence, the coexistence of regular security agencies and state-terrorist shock troops and the competition of various security agencies over resources and access to political power.

No war ends with a return to the status quo ante, each war transforms the role images and the behavior of adversaries. Wars undermine trust in agreements and common goods. Communicative ties dissolve, intermingled societies fracture and split apart. War fosters enmities which were not present in the first place. Latent resentments turn into manifest enmity, and any outlook at future peace and reconciliation will have to take long periods of emotional demobilization and recognition of inflicted pain into account.

Organizations of Russian Nationalists in the Russia-Ukraine Conflict

Nikolay Mitrokhin

Why did Russian nationalist organizations exist outside Russia and particularly in Ukraine? What role did they play in the occupation of Crimea and the Donbas region? Were they agents of the Russian state or autonomous actors? In this chapter, I will provide an analysis of the organizations of Russian nationalists in the post-Soviet area and their relations with the authorities of the Russian Federation. These organizations are frequently of a paramilitary nature, armed Russian nationalism has access to firearms and explosives.[1] Depending on the situation, they can be supplied by the black market or government agencies, or they may be the spoils of war. "Armed Russian nationalism" refers to the non-governmental and network organizations based on ideas of Russian nationalists, including those that are fully or partially under state control.

The utmost mobility of Russian national3ists and their willingness to participate in the paramilitary activities and the real war, as well as their exceptional brutality and determination, came as a complete surprise to external observers of the war in Donbas starting in spring 2014. Small groups of pro-Russian "volunteers" reinforced by local militia were able to fight the divisions of the Ukrainian Army and special forces for months. This raised the question of whether this was a war with "volunteers" or with a professional army (Mitrokhin 2015a; Mitrokhin 2015b; Mitrokhin 2017).

The following analysis is based on publications in the media, on websites of socio-political organizations and social networks as well as interviews conducted by the author from 2015 to 2018 in Ukraine and Russia. A peculiar source of information is the correspondence between a whole string of "masterminds" behind the acts of aggression in Ukraine, which was hacked by Ukrainians and

---

1 http://www.nz-online.ru/index.phtml?aid=20010661.

published by the Ukrainian media or phone calls of the same individuals which were intercepted by the Security Service of Ukraine (SBU) and made public.²

The movement of Russian nationalists already existed in the last decades of the USSR as an independent social movement (Mitrokhin 2003). The first legal organizations of Russian nationalists were founded in 1987 and by the end of perestroika, they were already in the hundreds. It is widely assumed that all of them were or are run from Moscow and that they, as well as the Russian Orthodox Church, are directly supervised by the Russian secret service. However, even a brief look at the history of Russian nationalism from 1987 to 2017 reveals that the matter is not quite that simple. Russian nationalists both in Russia and abroad were in opposition to the executive power first of the Soviet Union and later of Russia. The umbrella organizations of those in favor of keeping the empire in the republics of USSR, such as the International Fronts and the United Works Councils that closely collaborated with Russian nationalists, criticized Moscow for the absence of real support and later on suspected a "betrayal" of Russian speakers abroad. Russian nationalists inside Russia were skeptical about democratic reforms; they supported the dissolution of the USSR (i.e. they opposed Mikhail Gorbachev) and then, just as consistently, opposed Boris Yeltsin (Laruelle 2003), the new president of the Russian Federation. They not only criticized Boris Yeltsin vigorously and persistently on various occasions but also his successor Vladimir Putin, remaining in opposition to both of them (Smith 2002). In the late 2000s, the Russian authorities started to pursue repressive policies against the oppositional part of the movement of Russian nationalists. Some of their radical leaders and ordinary activists ended up behind bars, while others were forced to immigrate (Pribylovski 2015). A considerable number of Russian nationalists supported the mass protests against electoral fraud in big cities of Russia in the

---

2   A substantial amount of data concerning the involvement of Russian nationalists in the events in question has been published. Hundreds of Russian nationalists have given interviews to the media, some have published their memoirs. Dozens of Russian nationalists' organizations are proud to be part of the intervention in Ukraine and publish relevant information about their involvement.

winter of 2011/2012. Indeed, some radicals from these backgrounds became part of Ukrainian volunteer battalions in 2014 to 2015.

Despite their public criticism of Putin the radical nationalists were keen to contribute to the development of the "Russian World" project, promoted by Russian ideologists. This resulted in the active participation of Ukrainian and other post-Soviet states' Russian nationalists (foremost in Belarus and Latvia) in the so-called *Russian Spring,* a series of public protests and riots in eastern and southern Ukrainian cities from November 2013 to May 2014 leading to Russia's occupation of Crimea and the war in the Donbas region.

Social Framework of the Russian Nationalist Movement

The dissolution of the USSR left a huge number of people unemployed. In Russia, various members of the formerly privileged classes who had been serving the empire (foremost the military, Party officials, and low-level propagandists) felt humiliated and debased. After the defeat of the "national patriotic" forces in October 1993 — the coup attempt in Moscow —, some became activists of the Russian Orthodox Church. The Russian Orthodox Church has evolved into a major, though not parliamentary, party of Russian nationalists and has influenced both Russia's domestic and international po9licy (Mitrokhin 2006). Even though the USSR ceased to exist more than thirty years ago, these groups of the debased in Russia and in the post-Soviet states alike underpin the movement of Russian nationalists. The analysis of such activists' biographies (the author studied no fewer than 200 of them) leads us to the following social strata: Military and law enforcement personnel, engineers on the payroll of large enterprises belonging to the military–industrial complex, teachers of the Russian language and culture or Cossack culture (for instance, directors of choirs and dance groups), highly qualified human sciences scholars, studying Russian history or philosophy, specializing in Slavic studies or clergy and monkhood of the Russian Orthodox Church. In the 1980s, a considerable part of the heads of Russian nationalist organizations were political officers in the Soviet Army, military reporters, policemen and local Komsomol officials. The family members of the representatives of the aforementioned social groups (wives, children) play an active part in the Russian nationalist movement as well.

Types of Organizations and Their Coordination

Russian nationalists belong to a wide range of ideological platforms. Apart from Russian nationalists proper, there are "protectors" of the interests of the white race, Slavs, Cossacks, Orthodox Christianity, Russian culture and language, "the traditions of our ancestors" (Russian neo-Paganism), of the USSR, of "the honor" of the Russian (Soviet) officers, "the commemoration of the feats of the Soviet people in the Great Patriotic War", defenders of the honor and dignity of specific Russian football and hockey teams, supporters of the National-Bolshevik as well as Eurasian ideologies (Bassin; Pozo 2017), and also communists. The contemporary communists represent a highly blurred ideology and practice, they are primarily united by the idea of reviving the USSR. Regardless of the differences in publicly announced concepts, the ideology of Russian nationalism, namely the idea of defending Russians ("our people", "Slavs") from external and domestic enemies, is predominant and serves as the basis for their cooperation and consolidation. These movements are also characterized by a high level of anti-Semitism, intense anti-Islamic and anti-immigrant sentiments, as well as anti-Americanism and anti-Westernism.

Russian nationalist organizations employ two main types of communication and cooperation. On the one hand, they maintain contacts at the local level within their city or region; on the other hand, the majority of them is incorporated into the network of organizations of the same ideological line that have vertical links to the headquarters, usually in Moscow. A considerable number of these organizations' activists could, in fact, simultaneously represent a variety of vertical network organizations and be at the same time an Orthodox activist, a monarchist, a biker from the *Night Wolves* (biker club), a re-enactor (i.e. a constant participant in the games recreating specific battles of the past), a veteran of the air borne forces or of the Afghanistan war and have a wealth of previous experience in being part of some other organizations.[3] The permanent squabble, i.e. hostile competitiveness and unconstructive criticism, inside the community of Russian nationalists, allows its members to be well acquainted with all the other activists, at least in their own city. Often the major tactics of nationalist organizations do not coincide with the declared principles of action. An Orthodox parish, for example, could function either as a mere religious community or as a center for political and cultural propaganda or it can also serve as a center of paramilitary units. The latter is true for many so called "Cossack" parishes, where one of the priests is a confessor of the Cossack community and they consider this temple "their own".

The following types of organizations can be distinguished: cultural and subcultural (for instance, bikers and re-enactors), religious, propagandistic, lobbying and sports organizations, political parties, mass media, commemoration communities (some real and some to be found only online, from the organizations of the "Afghanistan veterans" to websites such as "we lived in the USSR" in social networks), organizations of "actionists" (holding actions for the mass media and spectators), paramilitary groups (i.e. uniformed members , official headquarters, weaponry), including some private security companies, and armed underground units.

Armed Russian Nationalism

The armed underground movement of Russian nationalists emerged during the Transnistrian conflict at the end of 1991 – beginning of 1992. It was based on the blending and joint activities of Russian nationalists with a common social background – former veterans of the Afghanistan war, mostly soldiers of various special forces (air borne forces, GRU special forces, airborne assault units). After the war, many of them served as low-ranking personnel in the law enforcement. Those were former low enforcement agents

---

3   http://petrimazepa.com/ru/nonwhite.html.

who formed the Riga OMON, Cossacks from Southern Russia and members of political organizations of Russian nationalists from big cities (some of them were young people who had not yet served in the army).[4] The crucial factor for establishing the underground network was the ability to get hold of unregistered firearms.

Former members of the Riga OMON, a special police unit, became the core of the armed underground movement of Russian nationalists. OMON squads were established in 1988 and were officially pronounced to be detachments of the Ministry of Internal Affairs for the armed support in the fight against organized crime. But in fact, they were used to disperse public meetings and other forms of mass protests. Initially, OMON squads were controlled by the KGB and GRU and were composed of former members of such elite units of the Soviet Army as air borne GRU special forces, airborne assault units, border guards and marine corps. Many of them served and fought in Afghanistan. In the former USSR republics, their main task became the fight against separatism and ethnic conflicts. After the failed putsch of August 1991 against Gorbachev, a considerable part of the Riga OMON along with their families and vast amounts of unregistered weapons confiscated from the local republican police were evacuated to the City of Tyumen, Russia.[5]

However, shortly thereafter, part of the unit led by its commander Cheslav Mlynnik moved to Transnistria, where they assumed leading positions in the detachments fighting against the Moldovan authorities to establish control over the rebel enclave on the left bank of the river Dniester. It was these armed groups, founded by the former OMON members (and some of their mentors from the Ministry of Internal Affairs of the Latvian SSR), that attracted volunteers from among Cossacks and other Russian nationalists. In the aftermath of the armed part of the conflict in the Transnistrian Moldavian Republic, some Russian nationalists were

---

4   OMON = in Russian Отряд мобильный особого назначения (mobile special purpose unit of the Russian National Guard).
5   Aleksandr Petrushin Tyumen Secrets of Riga OMON, Tyumen Courier 16 September 2006, (No. 124-125); Tyumen Courier 25 September 2006 (No. 128); Tyumen Courier 30 September 2006 (No. 131), http://svpressa.ru/society/article/41768/.

willing to carry the war on, frequently under the leadership of that same Mlynnik, who turned into the main recruiter of volunteers and mercenaries. "His" combatants were engaged in combat operations in Abkhazia (1992-1993), in Moscow (October1993), in the former Yugoslavia (1993-1995) and in Chechnya (1993-1996).[6]

Mlynnik and some members of his unit moved to Saint Petersburg in early 1992. There, Mlynnik and Roman Tsepov, the owner of a private security company providing security services to Anatoly Sobchak, the Mayor of Saint Petersburg, had business together.[7] Tsepov was the key middleman between the criminal underworld of the city, law enforcement authorities and the Mayor's office. In the following years, right up to the day he was poisoned in 2004, Tsepov managed to retain his authority in the underworld relying on his relationship with Vladimir Putin.[8] In the 2000s, Mlynnik was the representative of the President of the Russian Federation for the settlement in Abkhazia and held the rank of colonel in the Ministry of Defence of the Russian Federation.[9] No information is available concerning his activities after 2008. In one of the interviews, he stated that he "serves his country" but offered no further details.[10]

The impact of the Transnistrian region of Moldova and the Riga OMON on the war in the Donbas region is quite tangible. Vladimir Antiufeyev, the former mentor of the Riga OMON at the Ministry of Internal Affairs of the Latvian SSR (and afterwards the Minister of Public Security in the self-proclaimed Transnistrian Moldavian Republic in 1992-2011), became the Deputy Prime Minister for Security Issues of the Donetsk People's Republic (DPR) in summer of 2014.[11] Aleksandr Boroday and Igor Girkin, the future Prime Minister and chargé d'affaires for security and defense of the Donetsk People's Republic respectively, began their political careers

---

6   http://www.rosbalt.ru/world/2016/11/12/1566341.html.
7   http://konkretno.ru/2010/03/19/aleksandr-nevzorov-nazval-strashnuyu-cenu.html.
8   http://www.compromat.ru/page_16478.htm.
9   He was referred to as a retired colonel in an interview: http://www.rosbalt.ru/world/2016/11/12/1566341.html.
10 https://www.fontanka.ru/2016/10/28/156/.
11 http://zavtra.ru/blogs/pyat-vojn-generala-antyufeeva-.

as combatants in the Black Sea Cossack Host in the Transnistrian Moldavian Republic.[12]

The network of armed Russian nationalists began to grow exceedingly after 1992, escaping the direct control of one single person or even a group of individuals. Several substantive factors affected its development. A considerable number of Russian nationalists was engaged in the armed confrontation with the pro-government forces in October 1993 in Moscow, and most of them were obviously radicalized. The First Chechen War gave Russian nationalists an opportunity to acquire combat experience either in the army or in various police and even Cossack divisions. Russian nationalists got access to unregistered firearms and provided the underground movement with fresh manpower from the former military who felt frustrated and willing to fight their unfinished battles.[13]

On the background of these episodes of violence, the neo-Nazi organization Russian National Unity started to grow rapidly. It had numerous regional units (even in the countries of the Commonwealth of Independent States), which incorporated former military into their political structures and in private security companies. The sustained armed hostilities in Yugoslavia were instrumental for recruiting armed nationalists and to establish contacts with radical Serbian nationalists. The Russian National Unity became the first fully-fledged, long-lived and full-scale paramilitary organization of Russian nationalists in the modern Russian history (Likhachev 2005). Despite its internal crisis and de facto break-up in the early 2000s, its former members, first of all Ukrainian nationals, played a significant role in Russia's aggression against Ukraine in 2014. Cossack organizations became another essential element in armed Russian nationalism. Like the Russian National Unity, they combined radical forms of Russian nationalism (and occasionally neo-Nazism

---

12   http://strelkov-i-i.livejournal.com/9119.html.
13   In 2005, a former commander of a GRU brigade, Vladimir Kvachkov and his former subordinates were accused of arranging an attempted murder of Anatoly Chubais, a famous Russian politician of the Yeltsin years. Though Kvachkov was acquitted of the attempted assassination of Chubais, he was shortly afterwards arrested and convicted of creating an underground organization consisting of former military who were preparing an armed insurrection, https://ria.ru/society/20091020/189647285.html.

as well) with commercial (private security companies) and criminal activities.

In the 2000s, new characters with no combat experience but with membership in radical neo-Nazi organizations were continuously joining the armed underground movement. They were looking for firearms to use in terrorist activities against their political opponents and their number one enemy—labor migrants. Two of them became the most notorious. The Fighting Force of Russian Nationalists in the mid-2000s committed several high-profile political murders in Moscow.[14] The gang's main hit man was a former marine from Sevastopol and an FSB warrant officer.[15] Another gang, the *Savior*, organized a series of explosions, including the massive terrorist attack on August 21, 2006 at the Cherkizovsky market in Moscow, which entailed a significant number of victims (14 people died, 61 were wounded). It was founded by an "Old-Believer", a hand-to-hand and knife combat instructor and yet another FSB warrant officer.[16]

The so called archaeological looters, who searched the battlefields of World War II for weaponry and artefacts with the intent of selling them, supplied these gangs with firearms and explosives. Re-enactment movement became the legal part of this fairly common business. On certain commemorative dates, reenactors staged mass performances dressing up in the uniforms of the armies of various historical epochs. In the 2000s, the re-enactment movement started to enjoy the authorities' special attention. It was seen as a great opportunity to be utilized for patriotic education, since re-enactment was genuinely popular among a broad audience.[17]

Knife combat clubs and sports clubs for various "Russian" martial arts (such as "slavjano-gorickaja borba", "Russian" and "Cossack" fighting style) served as a cover for neo-Nazi armed gangs. In these clubs, teenagers were introduced to the world of right radicalism and neo-Nazism and taught how to kill with a knife quickly and effectively, knives designed to kill were sold. In

---

14 https://batenka.ru/protection/born/.
15 https://theins.ru/politika/8873.
16 http://www.newsru.com/russia/08aug2007/vzryv_4erkiz.html.
17 https://graniru.org/opinion/mitrokhin/m.238381.html.

general, the whole network of the armed underground movement, including communities of local war veterans, Cossacks and neo-Nazis, was not very expanded – probably around one hundred individuals all over Russia. It was mainly controlled by the Russian secret services, monitoring the radical elements.[18] However, the network was substantially assisted by support groups and therefore stayed operational.

This milieu split over the events in Ukraine. Those who served in the Soviet and Russian armies unequivocally adopted the official interpretation, which was declared by the Russian authorities. Although they were right-wing extremists and Russian nationalists, their main idea was the protection of the Russians and Russia. Persons who did not have such military experience, rather took the Ukrainian side, since their political ideal was a white supremacist state and not a state of exclusively Russian people. They were not ready to go into battle against their brothers-in-race. They perceived contemporary Russia as a country where ethnic minorities and migrants would receive too much support from the state. At the same time, they saw Ukraine as still a Slavic land. Ukraine's official support of the openly right-wing extremists batallions (first and foremost the Azov Regiment) provided neo-Nazis with opportunities for self-expression, obtaining legal weaponry and realization of their own political significance. Both parts of the movement eventually came together on the Donbas battlefields.

New Techniques of Controlling Russian Nationalists

In the 1990s, the organizations and parties of Russian nationalists were constantly in conflict with Russia's acting executive branch. In the 2000s, the situation changed dramatically. At that time, the presidential administration of the Russian Federation began to establish a management system for controlling all significant segments of the Russian political scene and began to actively cooperate with the Russian leader's potential allies abroad (Laruelle 2012).

---

18 For instance, Igor Girkin, an FSB colonel, was also a moderator of the Forum of Collectors, where far-right groups could buy weaponry; he was also a coordinator for part of the volunteers willing to participate in combat operations.

The new publicly announced ideology was based on the idea of Russia "getting up from her knees", strengthening herself, punishing her numerous domestic and external enemies and, de facto, beginning to rebuild the lost USSR.

Already in the early 2000s, a network of semi-official organizations was established in order to manage social and political "projects". Through these organizations, official communication was carried out and public funds were distributed. One of these organizations was the *Civic Chamber*, founded in 2005 for supervising the "third sector". Another example is the Council for Matters of Cossack Communities by the Presidential Administration of the Russian Federation founded in 2009. The outsourced employees of political funds close to the Kremlin monitored such projects directly. They practically acted as civil servants without being officially on the governmental payroll.[19] This allowed the governmental authorities to hire experts specializing in political and dubious criminal activities. At the same time, private organizations which officially had nothing to do with the presidential administration of the Russian Federation could always be held responsible for the actions of these experts (Wilson 2005). This is how, through the "Institute of Commonwealth of Independent States Countries", the so called "Russian Spring" in Ukraine was coordinated.

In the 2000s, the cooperation with internet activists and social networks became a significant part of the activities of the presidential administration of the Russian Federation. In 2013-2014, pro-Kremlin internet communities turned into an important propaganda and mobilization tool in the Russia-Ukraine conflict, but the major communities and groups had been created long before the conflict started (Mitrokhin 2015).[20] The revival of the "USSR victory in the Great Patriotic War" mythology along with the respective symbolic connotations and projections into the modern age proved to be one of the key unifying ideas for these activists (Demmel 2016). According to this mythology, the war between "our people"

---

19 Author's facebook interview with one of the former members of such an organization. March 2018.
20 On the organizational structures of such societies see: http://www.nlobooks.ru/node/8848.

and "fascists", which included all kinds of "Russia's adversaries", was not over yet (Jablokov 2016). Accordingly, every supporter of Russia should be an anti-fascist and prepare himself for the upcoming imminent battles. Numerous on-line activists understood this message as an invitation to by ready for guerrilla warfare. This virtual support was quickly transformed into a real one thanks to the sport and military-patriotic clubs as well as to an active distribution of various educational and guidance materials such as the ones promoting the actions of GRU saboteurs.[21]

The Rodina political party, one of the Kremlin key political agents, who supervised the pro-Russia actions in Ukraine in the winter and spring of 2014, issued a triumphant manifesto after the annexation of Crimea and stated:

> "Social patriots from Rodina were the first to utilize anti-Nazism in combat against both external enemies of Russia and corrupt pro-Western liberals inside the country, who forever disgraced themselves by supporting the anti-Russia powers in Ukraine and, therefore, committing treason."[22]

Eventually, the pro-Russian organizations, first of all the ones supporting Russian nationalism in former Soviet Republics and in exile, were integrated into a hierarchical, central management scheme in Moscow. The leaders and activists of these organizations relied on "credible" information channels usually broadcasting from Moscow, such as TV channels, newspapers, on-line publications, renowned bloggers or internet communities. They were able to create a specific discourse environment for their readers, which allowed them to manipulate the readers extensively and was ultimately aimed at stimulating the desire to move from reading and sympathizing to real actions.[23] Thirdly, the organizations with no vertical subordination structure were offered horizontal schemes of including them into the mission of serving Russia. In order to do

---

21 http://www.css.ethz.ch/content/dam/ethz/special-interest/gess/cis/center-for-securities-studies/pdfs/RAD_207.pdf.
22 http://www.rodina.ru/novosti/slovo-i-delo/RODINA-Krymskaya-pobeda-2014.
23 For a detailed review see http://www.nlobooks.ru/node/8848.

so, the whole system of cooperation with the so called "compatriots", i.e. the pro-Russian sympathizers abroad, was restructured. In 2001-2012, with the use of Russian budgetary funds and some private investments, a framework of foundations and organizations focusing exclusively on promoting Russia's positive image was established; it connected local Russian-speaking organizations to funding from Moscow and politically influenced local Russian-speaking communities. This framework consists of the following organizations and foundations: World Congress of Compatriots (founded in 2001), Moscow House of the Compatriot (2002), Foundation for Exploring the Historical Perspective (2004), Russian World Foundation (2007), Foundation for Support of Public Diplomacy named after Gorchakov (2010), Fund for Support and Protection of Compatriots' Rights (2012).

Each of these organizations has its own field of expertise and area of responsibility. For instance, the Foundation for Support of Public Diplomacy named after Gorchakov works with young people and academic elite; the Fund for Support and Protection of Compatriots' Rights provides financial support for organizations and law offices who defend the rights of Russians and "compatriots" against the countries they live in. However, the only organization with regional offices was the World Congress of Compatriots (Kotkina 2017, 64-65; Gasimov 2012).

Other forms of cooperating with the Russian cultural diaspora included the Congresses of Compatriots, congresses of the Russian Press as well as events organized by regional administrations in Russia. Since 2001, the Moscow city government has established a special department for cooperation with compatriots and since 2002, the Moscow House of Compatriot has been active, it facilitates such programs as "Russians abroad in the fight against fascism".[24] Its branch in Sevastopol has been the center of pro-Russian activities over many years and the main rallies in 2013-2014 were held in front of this building.

---

[24] http://pravfond.ru/?module=articles&action=view&id=2134.

Reasons for the Anti-Ukrainian Campaign

Obviously, Russia's political class in general did not accept or acknowledge Ukraine as a state independent from Russia and was not ready to recognize the Ukrainian national borders. The concept of Russia as a "liberal empire" supervising Ukraine's sovereignty was extremely popular at the highest level of Russia's executive branch. This resulted in the active engagement of Russia's government on Crimea and especially in Sevastopol in the 1990s and 2000s. Another obvious example is the flagrant interference in the internal policy of Ukraine, beginning at least with the presidential election of 2004.

Russia's leadership placed their stakes on Viktor Yanukovych, a pro-Russian politician, and received an ambivalent outcome. Yanuckovich did not defy Russia's interests but did not promote them either. He was building up his own networks of influence in the government, while giving priority to his own criminal family clan. As long as Yanukovich was president of Ukraine, it was impossible to implement Russia's plans of including Ukraine in a joint Union State with Russia and Belarus.

After losing the support of the Ukrainian people in 2004 during the "Orange Revolution", the Russian authorities decided to seriously fight for Ukraine. As a result, the whole framework for cooperation and dealing with Ukraine was restructured. If previously Ukraine was dealt with on an ad hoc basis, when challenges emerged, since 2005, persons holding ranks as high as Head of the Presidential Administration of the Russian Federation or his deputies started to deal with Ukraine-related issues on a regular basis.[25] Ukraine was taken care of by the assistants to the Russian president (S. Glazyev and V. Surkov) and some staff members of the presidential administration of the Russian Federation. One such staff member was Vladimir Chernov (born 1951), who in 2012 was appointed as head of the Office for Interregional and Cultural Relations with Foreign Countries of the presidential administration of

---

25 Author's interview with a former consultant of the presidential administration of the Russian Federation, Moscow, June 2018.

the Russian Federation and, according to the hacked letters of Kirill Frolov, was given the role as "supervisor of Ukraine".[26] In the internet, there are numerous references to Chernov's work for the Soviet foreign intelligence (as rank of colonel), including his deportation from the United Kingdom in 1983.[27] Before Chernov joined the staff of the presidential administration of the Russian Federation, he was an adviser to Sergey Ivanov, the Minister of Defense of the Russian Federation between 2001-2007, who in turn was appointed as head of the Presidential Administration of the Russian Federation in December 2011. Ivanov (born 1953), who had worked with Chernov as far back as in Finland's KGB station, assigned the essential task of supervising Ukraine to one of his very few associates. In March 2014, Oleg Belaventsov (born 1953) was appointed as plenipotentiary representative of the Russian president to the Crimean Federal District. He must have met Chernov personally in the United Kingdom, where he spent the years between 1982 and1985 as a counsellor of the embassy and was deported for espionage in 1985.[28] Old KGB acquaintances were thus in charge of managing Ukrainian affairs.

In the 2010s, Vladimir Putin decided to establish the Eurasian Economic Union and concluding a customs agreement with its members. This opened new perspectives for creating a strong economic alliance under Moscow's supervision. However, this alliance clearly was not complete without Russia's largest neighbor — Ukraine. The long-planned EU-Ukraine Association Agreement, which would have opened the Ukrainian market to European products, competed with the integration of the former Soviet Republics

---

26 https://informnapalm.org/31475-frolovleaks-pussy-riot-epizod-v/ with the link to the letter of K. Frolov to M. Kuksov dated 5 June 2012).
27 https://ruspekh.ru/people/item/chernov-vladimir-aleksandrovich; http://anticompromat.org/ivanov01/litv_ivanov-s.html; the most detailed version of his personal history with the intelligence service was published in 2004, see http://modernlib.net/books/grechenevskiy_oleg/istoki_nashego_demokraticheskogo_rezhima/read_9/.
28 On Oleg Belaventsev see Kommersant. No. 48, 22 March 2014, http://modernlib.net/books/grechenevskiy_oleg/istoki_nashego_demokraticheskogo_rezhima/read_9/. It might be that Ivanov, Belaventsov, Chernov and Bratchikov (who will be discussed below) — three of them were born in 1953 and one in 1954 — first met in the KGB School.

under Moscow's auspices. Thus, a common customs and economic regime of Ukraine with the EU and with the Eurasian Economic Union would have been impossible (Pozo 2017). Vladimir Putin therefore increased the pressure on Ukraine.

Common Framework and Multiplicity of Actors

In the public space, there is no information available about the co-ordination of the actions of Russian authorities regarding Ukraine in 2013-2014. The Russian Spring covered at least 10 regions of eastern and southern Ukraine. Dozens of organizations and Russian governmental structures were engaged. On September 13, 2013 the overall coordination of the anti-Ukraine campaign was transferred to Vladislav Surkov, who was appointed as assistant to the Russian president for relations with Abkhazia and South Ossetia, the Georgian separatist regions occupied in 2008.[29] Surkov probably inherited this task from Sergey Glazyev, who had previously supervised the incorporation of Ukraine into the Eurasian Economic Union, and from Chernov, who supervised the domestic policy of the country. Boris Rappoport, Surkov's long-time associate and staff member of the presidential "Office for Social and Economic Cooperation with Commonwealth of Independent States (CIS) Countries, Abkhazia and south Ossetia", became his main assistant for the liaison with non-governmental organizations.

After his resignation, Rappoport described the world view of his boss: "He has always been and remains a supporter of the doctrine "Moscow is the third Rome". He believes that every state begins to degrade the moment it stops to expand its influence. He assumes that expansion is a natural state of a healthy country."[30] It was Surkov, who in 2005 coined the expression "Russian World" and introduced it to the political discourse. Surkov's ideas were im-

---

29 Report by Gazeta.ru, which was not officially confirmed but subsequently supported by a variety of sources, https://www.gazeta.ru/politics/news/2013/09/13/n_3181753.shtml.

30 http://www.mk.ru/politics/2014/12/15/boris-rapoport-uzhe-v2013m-v-priemnoy-surkova-visela-karta-na-kotoroy-krym-byl-chastyu-rossii.html.

plemented through the headquarters of the southern military district in Rostov-on-Don. The troops of this military district were mainly engaged in the occupation of Crimea and in supplying the Donbas separatist militias with weaponry, ammunition and military equipment. The bulk of the pro-Russian "volunteers" was transferred through Rostov-on-Don to Crimea and the Caucasus and, according to the Russia's official version, this was the city where the former president of Ukraine, Viktor Yanukovych, was moved to. It is here that the main monument to Russia's "volunteers", who were fighting in the Donbas region, was unveiled in the presence of Surkov in October 2017.[31]

That said, a considerable number of organizations and individuals were authorized directly by Surkov and Putin to act at their own discretion within the framework of common goals and objectives. All of this can be described by the term "public-private partnership" typical for the whole Putin's system. In may be assumed, that all those activities were mainly monitored by the secret service FSB and other special forces, which occasionally "peered from behind the curtains".

Pro-Russian Agents in Ukraine

The political influence of a given organization of Russian nationalists depended directly on whether it could curry favors with the presidential administration of the Russian Federation (Mantschurjan 2016). The degree of political influence was also subject to the popularity of an organization, their ability to find associates, to set up own networks and enter into alliances with like-minded people. Two Russian political parties, the Liberal Democratic Party of Russia (LDPR, then led by Vladimir Zhirinovsky) and the Communist Party (CPRF), generally share nationalist views, but chose diametrically opposed policies. The LDPR ignored potential allies and rivals and, paradoxically, paid hardly any attention to the organizations of "compatriots" outside Russia. De facto, the LDPR had no allies or "clienteles" in Ukraine during Russia's aggression.

---

31   https://www.gazeta.ru/social/news/2017/10/19/n_10711940.shtml.

Throughout the conflict, it was not able to establish a single paramilitary unit under its own auspices, although it did donate some money and military equipment to the "volunteers".[32] The CPRF, on the contrary, actively collaborated with various "national-patriotic" coalitions. The revival of the USSR as the main goal of the post-Soviet communist parties coincided with the neo-imperial goals of Russian nationalists and made both forces reliable allies. The Communist party of Ukraine was one of the participants of the anti-Maidan demonstrations in winter 2013-2014 and was actively engaged with the *Russian Spring* movement, although it did not play a leading role.[33] In Russia, the CPRF was actively gathering supporters and financial help for "the people of the Donbas" but did not make a decisive difference.[34]

Within the *United Russia* party, which generally cannot be classified as an organization being deeply motivated by Russian nationalism, a separate fraction called the *Patriotic Platform* existed. It embraced the ideology of the post-imperial Russian nationalism.[35] Dmitri Sablin, the leader of the *Patriotic Platform*, and some other deputies played an active role in the occupation of Crimea and in unleashing the war in the Donbas.[36] However, it is difficult to establish the degree of cooperation of the *Patriotic Platform* or *United Russia* as a whole with partner organizations in Ukraine.

On the operational level, the key role in the Russia-Ukraine conflict was played by Dmitri Rogozin, Sergey Glazyev and Konstantin Zatulin, i.e., the former leaders of *Rodina*, which was only

---

32 https://www.gazeta.ru/auto/2014/05/08_a_6022997.shtml.
33 In anti-Maidan publications, the Communist Party of Ukraine has been criticized for its conciliatory position towards the new Ukrainian government. Nevertheless, the pro-Russian and anti-Maidan activities of its regional offices have been also vividly depicted, http://rabkor.ru/columns/left/2015/02/11/year-after-maidan/. On the financing and organization of pro-Russian demonstrations in the Luhansk region see https://news.online.ua/743660/vladimir-landik/. On the attempt of the Kyiv City Committee of the Communist Party of Ukraine to lead the Maidan opposition, see https://riss.ru/analitycs/24338/.
34 https://www.nakanune.ru/articles/113674/; http://rusvesna.su/news/1474 188476; http://uralpolit.ru/article/chel/05-02-2015/55451.
35 http://xn--b1adccaencl0bewna2a.xn--p1ai/index.php/arhiv/11886-2012-10-18-07-19-19.
36 http://www.vedomosti.ru/politics/characters/2015/03/16/esli-eto-imelo-o predelennuyu-rezhissuru---rezhisseru-nuzhno-postavit-pyat-s-plyusom.

once elected to the Duma, Russia's parliament. This party had emerged from a social and political project called "Congress of Russian Communities" that, from the mid-1990s onwards, strived to represent in Russia the interests of the Russian-speaking communities in the post-Soviet area as well as of those Russian speakers who had emigrated to Russia. The *Congress of the Russian Communities* was closely related to the leadership of the Transnistrian Moldavian Republic and promoted their interests in Russia. The *Congress of the Russian Communities* was reorganized as a party and incorporated a vast number of members of right groups and right-wing extremist gangs (Titkov 2016, pp. 18-19). The party nominated former air borne officers as deputies and started to represent the air assault forces veteran communities. In 2003, the *Congress of the Russian Communities* was transformed first into an electoral bloc and then into the *Rodina* political party. Thanks to the updated image and public utilization of xenophobic rhetoric, *Rodina* achieved a decent result in the 2004 election (9 percent) and got into the parliament. However, in 2005, an anti-Semitic scandal, known as the "Letter of 500", in which it was demanded to dissolve all the Jewish organizations in Russia on account of extremism charges, the Kremlin pressed to disband the party (Titkov 2016, pp. 48-53).

The loyalty of Dmitri Rogozin and Sergey Glazyev was rewarded—they received high bureaucratic positions. Rogozin was first appointed as representative of the Russian Federation to NATO and afterwards he was promoted to the post of Deputy Prime Minister for Defense. Sergey Glazyev became the Assistant to the President of the Russian Federation for the Eurasian Economic Union. Konstantin Zatulin kept his deputy seat in the State Duma. Therefore, the former leaders of the *Rodina* party became high-ranking officials of the executive branch. On the other hand, through the private Institute of CIS Countries owned by Zatulin and the closely affiliated State Russian Institute for Strategic Studies, they were able to coordinate organizations as well as individuals in many regions of the former USSR. The purpose of the State Russian Institute for Strategic Studies is to serve the interests of the

Foreign Operations Directorate as well as other Russian secret services. In the first half of the 2010s, it was headed by General Leonid Reshetnikov, an open Russian nationalist and monarchist.

A pool of pro-Russian parties cooperated with the former Rodina leaders in Ukraine. Most of these parties were not represented in the Verkhovna Rada but had parliamentary factions in regional parliaments, especially in the south of Ukraine, among them *Ukrainian Choice, the Progressive Socialist Party of Ukraine, the Russian Bloc, Russian Unity, Rodina* in Odesa and numerous less significant organizations, which, nevertheless, were actively participating in the "Russian Spring". Politicians of these parties legitimized the invasion of Crimea and the attempts to establish "People's Republics" in eastern and southern regions of Ukraine. Since mid-2000s, the mobilization and coordination of the pro-Russian nationalist associates was carried out through various forums and conferences as well as on the streets during the demonstrations against Ukrainian nationalists, the Ukrainian state, NATO, against Crimean Tatars or prospective shale gas production in the Donbas region. This campaign was organized by the pro-Russian groups in Ukraine in 2012-2013 and was based on anti-American slogans, since American companies were the ones to produce shale gas. The campaign was probably inspired by Gazprom, that feared a weakening of its influence in the country. Many activists of this campaign, especially in the Donbas, where the production was to be launched, later on became local leaders of the "Russian Spring". Slogans against the shale gas production were further on utilized in some cities and in the protests in the winter and spring of 2014.

Almost all the key pro-Russian activists in Ukraine had personal contacts with just two persons. Zatulin was one of them. He personally supervised Crimea and acted as a field coordinator for pro-Russian "public" organizations in Ukrainian regions. Sergey Glazyev said:

> "there is a war ongoing ... this is why Zatulin is the boss over there, he coordinates this war on the social and political front, where we keep failing."[37]

---

37 https://censor.net.ua/resonance/3047400/esli_my_zablokiruem_zaporoje_my_vyigraem_eto_plotina_mosty_i_energetika_bez_energetiki_krym_nejiz nesposoben.

Another key coordinator was Kirill Frolov, the head of the Ukraine department at the Institute of CIS Countries owned by Zatulin and, since 2013, the head of the Department for Relations with the Russian Orthodox Church.[38] Some documents from his correspondence indicate that he coordinated the pro-Russian combatant units in Ukraine in 2006 (probably even earlier), in particular during the blocking of roads in Crimea as well as combatant units from Odesa. In 2012, Frolov suggested to use the pro-Russian full-time militia groups from Kharkov (assault forces veterans), whom he was supervising, for the suppression of anti-Putin protests in Moscow.[39] Frolov was a leading staff member of the "Department for Cooperation between the Church and Society" of the Moscow Patriarchate, too. At least since 2012, he worked for Sergey Glazyev, the third and main coordinator of the Russian nationalists in Ukraine, who was permanently based in Moscow.

Frolov's correspondence, which has been hacked by Ukrainians, reveals that already in the early 2010s, he assisted staff members of the presidential administration of the Russian Federation, as high-ranking as its head Sergey Naryshkin, in organizing meetings with the representatives of social and political organizations as well as with the Ukrainian Orthodox Church of eastern and southern Ukraine. They visited Odesa to conduct negotiations with public and church leaders. Frolov had about 50 confidants in Ukraine — a dozen of Ukrainian Orthodox Church priests and the Metropolitan of Odesa Agathangelos (Savvin), about fifteen politicians and approximately 20 to 25 activists of public organizations as well as journalists, mainly in Kyiv, Kharkiv, Odesa, on Crimea and in the Donetsk region. With their help he was able to establish contacts with potential allies of Russia wishing, through him, to be received by government agencies in Moscow. Amongst them was Hryhoriy Pedchenko, Chief of the General Staff of Ukraine.[40]

---

38 http://www.portal-credo.ru/site/print.php?act=rating&id=28.
39 FrolovLeaks, https://informnapalm.org/31142-frolovleaks-4/.
40 Some extracts of this correspondence, which counts approx. 10,000 letters amounting to18 GB, were published in 8 parts on the Ukrainian website Informnapalm; see FrolovLeaks VIII, https://informnapalm.org/33340-frolovleaks-viii-pravoslavnaya-elegiya/.

On September 13, 2013 in a letter to Frolov, Glazyev offered him to work directly for Vladislav Surkov, the assistant to Putin for relations with Abkhazia and South Ossetia, who, as it has been mentioned above, on that very day became the chief supervisor of Ukrainian matters and preparations for the invasion.[41] On the first days of March 2014, "after meeting with big bosses", Frolov became the "supervisor of Odesa and Nikolaev". A little bit earlier, on February 27, 2014, he flew to Odesa with a budget of almost 800,000 dollars for organizing "ideological activities", purchasing weaponry and conducting "special operations". His partner was Aleksandr Zaldostanov, the leader of the *Night Wolves*, a nationalist biker club.[42]

After the appointment of Surkov, Glazyev was playing supporting roles but remained the key coordinator of the actions of Ukrainian pro-Russian public figures and the boss of Zatulin and Frolov. In winter and spring 2014, he stayed in permanent contact with them, coordinated the information flow and formulated new instructions. Glazyev was personally responsible for the supervision and organization of the Luhansk region, where he played a decisive role in convincing the local oligarchic groups to take Russia's side.[43]

These activities were financed (at least partially) by Sergey Batchikov (born in 1953) — a member of the Russian nationalist *Izborsk Club*, Glazyev's campaign chief in 2004, a businessman and a former Soviet spy in Latin America.[44] Batchikov (like Chernov,

---

[41] FrolovLeaks VI, https://informnapalm.org/32111-frolovleaks-vi-zavtra-byla-vojna/; letter from S. Glazyev to K. Frolov dated 13 Sept. 2013.

[42] FrolovLeaks VII, https://informnapalm.org/32451-frolovleaks-smeta-rusvesna/; with the link to the letter from Frolov to Aleksandr Zaldostanov dated 27 February 2014.

[43] https://news.online.ua/743660/vladimir-landik/. See also the abstract from a telephone conversation of Glazyev, Zatulin and Ukrainian regional politicians primarily from the Luhansk region, which was intercepted by the Ukrainian intelligence service SBU on March 1, 2014 and handed over to the Ukrainian press, https://censor.net.ua/resonance/3047400/esli_my_zablokiruem_zaporoje_my_vyigraem_eto_plotina_mosty_i_energetika_bez_energetiki_krym_neji znesposoben.

[44] He was the one who paid Frolov his salary during that period. FrolovLeaks VII, https://informnapalm.org/32451-frolovleaks-smeta-rusvesna/] (with the link to the letter from Frolov to Glazyev dated 21/04/2014.

Ivanov and Belaventsev) was another representative of the Soviet foreign intelligence engaged in the Ukrainian conflict. It is remarkable, that, according to the available sources, after Latin America, he worked at the KGB Information Analysis Department for General Nikolay Leonov, who became one of the key figures in the movement of Russian nationalists in the 1990s.[45] Sergey Tkachuck, Glazyev's secretary, was apparently the fourth significant coordinator of the pro-Russian "public" activities in Ukraine. As early as in February 2013, Tkachuck independently negotiated with Viktor Medvedchuk from the *Ukrainian Choice* party about the activation of the pro-Russian forces in Ukraine shortly before the planned signing of the EU-Ukraine association agreement.[46]

The pool of key public organizations in Moscow organizing the invasion included the businessman Konstantin Malofeyev and organizations under his jurisdiction, first of all the company "Marshall Capital" and the "Tsargradtelevision" company.[47] Malofeyev had close contacts with Igor Shchegolev, Putin's advisor for information technologies.[48] He conducts his public activities through his Foundation of Saint Basil the Great which supports orthodox projects (mainly information websites). Apart from Shchegolev, such ideologists of modern Russian nationalism as bishop Tichon (Shevkunov) and the film director Nikita Mikhalkov, who are both close to Vladimir Putin, were among the members of the foundation's board.[49] After the meeting with Glazyev on September 16, 2013 in the office of the "Marshall Capital" company on Novinski Boulevard in Moscow, Malofeyev was responsible for financing the ac-

---

45 About his work for the intelligence service seehttp://modernlib.net/books/grechenevskiy_oleg/istoki_nashego_demokraticheskogo_rezhima/read_9/.
46 FrolovLeaks VI, https://informnapalm.org/32111-frolovleaks-vi-zavtra-byla-vojna/; https://censor.net.ua/resonance/3047400/esli_my_zablokiruem_zaporoje_my_vyigraem_eto_plotina_mosty_i_energetika_bez_energetiki_krym_nejiznesposoben.
47 http://ruscharity.ru/articles/45.htm.
48 http://comnarcon.com/444.
49 http://fondsvv.ru/about/council/.

tivities of the Russian nationalists controlled by Glazyev and Zatulin in Moscow and in Ukraine.[50] Malofeyev had at his disposal a team for carrying out "active operations". His employees, Igor Girkin (Strelkov), the head of security of "Marshall Capital" since February 25, 2013, and Aleksandr Boroday, a political strategist, became both the leading figures in the Crimea occupation and afterwards in unleashing the war in the Donbas region.[51] In summer 2014, Boroday became acting "Prime Minister" in the Donetsk People's Republic.

The Russian Orthodox Church, the Eurasian Youth Union and Other Networks

One of the supporting roles in the mobilization and coordination of pro-Russian nationalists during the invasion in Ukraine was played by the Russian Orthodox Church. In Russia, it promoted itself as a counsellor to the state on how to govern the society, especially with respect to the confrontation with the West (Hagemeister 2015). Its branch in Ukraine, the Ukrainian Orthodox Church, is the largest religious institution in this country (about 12,000 communities). The Moscow Patriarchate, being the main administrative body of the Russian Orthodox Church, counted on the support from the pro-Russian priests and bishops of the Ukrainian Orthodox Church (Bremer 2016). Numerous prospective supporters of the "Russian World" (a concept promoted by future patriarch Kirill and his associates from the mid-2000s onwards) were found especially in

---

50 FrolovLeaks VI, https://informnapalm.org/32111-frolovleaks-vi-zavtra-byla-vojna/, this includes the link to the correspondence between Frolov and Aleksey Komov, assistant of Malofeyev, dated 12 September 2013.

51 In the hacked letters of Girkin, he introduced himself as the head of security of the Marshal Capital company owned by Malofeyev. Alexandr Boroday turned out to be Malofeyev's freelance consultant in an area as delicate as risk management. His services included being present during the police searches in late 2012 – early 2013 that were carried out in the offices of Malofeyev's company, his houses and the houses of his business partners, http://www.vedomosti.ru/politics/news/26607741/premerom-doneckoj-respubliki-izbran-aleksandr-borodaj. Malofeyev's (junior) partners were suspected of fraud and embezzlement of a VTB Bank loan in excess of 200 million dollars and he himself was a witness in that case. But the case was closed with no consequences, http://m.forbes.ru/article.php?id=215436.

eastern and southern dioceses of Ukraine (first of all in Donetsk, Zaporozhye, Luhansk, Odesa and Simferopol).

Patriarch Kirill and archpriest Vsevolod Chaplin, the head of the "Department for External Church Relations", were ardent supporters of Russia's aggression. This was due to their long-time engagement in the movement of Russian nationalists. In particular, patriarch Kirill, beginning with his time as a metropolitan in the early 1990s and up to the present time has been the co-chairman of the World Russian People's Council, a large Russian nationalist organization. During Viktor Yanukovich presidential term in office, the above mentioned Frolov permanently sent memos to the head of the Russian Orthodox Church and to the members of his inner circle, including the head of "Department for External Church Relations", metropolitan Illarion (Alfeev). The memos contained arguments to be raised before the President of Ukraine during personal meetings, in order to put pressure on this high-ranking active parishioner and, using his homophobia, to convince him to reject the European integration as well as to increase Russia's influence in the country and, as a long term objective, to unite Russia, Ukraine and Belarus into one state.[52]

However, it would be erroneous to conclude that the Ukrainian Orthodox Church was vertically subordinated to the Moscow Patriarchate. In the 2010s, the leadership of the Ukrainian Orthodox Church and most dioceses in eastern and southern Ukraine supported to a large extent the sovereignty of Ukraine and, whilst paying a tribute to Moscow, were definitely not in favor of the "Russian World". Pro-Russian priests and bishops in the Ukrainian Orthodox Church were part of the horizontal networks that frequently supported even more radical religious or Russian-nationalistic views than the leadership of the Russian orthodox church. These networks are controlled by spiritual leaders ("startsy"), only some of whom were based in Russia.[53] Some of the "startsy" and their

---

52 Note from Frolov to Zatulin meant for the patriarch, dated 03 February 2010; a letter from Frolov to metropolitan Illarion dated 17 March 2010 containing the "General Plan on Ukraine", FrolovLeaks, https://informnapalm.org/30831-frolovleaks-part3/.
53 http://www1.ku-eichstaett.de/ZIMOS/forum/inhaltruss17.html.

followers (about 10-14 percent of the clergy and active believers and no less than 50 percent of the monks) were very critical of the leadership of the Moscow Patriarchate and its head, Patriarch Kirill, as well as of some members of his inner circle.[54] The patriarch and his inner circle were thus forced to resort to intermediaries to connect with low-ranking pro-Russian activists in the Ukrainian church.[55] The aforementioned Kirill Frolov and archpriest Andrey Novikov, the secretary of the Odesa Diocese, who, according to the hacked correspondence, was close to Patriarch Kirill were among these intermediaries.[56] Frolov's notes to patriarch Kirill reveal that in the late 2000s and early 2010s he understood that the Moscow Patriarchate could have counted upon the support and understanding of no more than one fourth of Ukrainian episcopate, mainly from Odesa and Donetsk clans. He hoped to bribe or convince at least those to participate in concrete actions.[57]

However, the influence of Russian nationalists in the Ukrainian Orthodox Church was clearly overestimated in Moscow. Despite their activism in some dioceses in the west and south of the country and their monopoly on maintaining communication between the Ukrainian Orthodox Church and the Cossacks, they were overall a minority and their influence in the 2000-2010s consistently decreased. Most calculations of Frolov and the Moscow Patriarchate did not work out. The pro-Moscow party was able to block some of the corporation's "pro-Ukrainian" decisions but did not manage to impose their own. The disunity of the church radicals

---

54 The assessment is based on 20 years of research on the Ukrainian Orthodox Church conducted by the author; it was underpinned by the results of the field studies in several regions of the country (western and southern Ukraine, Kyiv).
55 Patriarch Kirill in his correspondence with Frolov is personally trying to convince some bishops of the Ukrainian Orthodox Church to take the necessary steps, i.e., reaching out to them through the Moscow based priests and bishops, FrolovLeaks VII, https://informnapalm.org/32451-frolovleaks-smeta-rusvesna/; Frolov's letter tom.birskiy@list.ru dated 09 January 2014; Frolov's letter to Tretjakov dated 26 July /2014.
56 FrolovLeaks VI, https://informnapalm.org/32111-frolovleaks-vi-zavtra-byla-vojna/. The same was confirmed by a high-ranking informant of the Ukrainian Orthodox Church. (correspondence with the author on Facebook, 14 August 2018).
57 FrolovLeaks, https://informnapalm.org/30831-frolovleaks-part3/.

and Russian nationalists, their relatively marginal status in the eyes of the "common" clergy were the very reasons for the lack of mass support for Russia's aggression by the dioceses of the Ukrainian Orthodox Church. Nevertheless, there are some examples of Russian nationalist support. This holds particularly true for the Donbas region, some dioceses in Crimea and Odesa.[58] According to the data of Ukrainian researchers, the biographical details of only 30 priests of the Ukrainian Orthodox Church were registered in the "Myrotvorets" database, containing the CVs of individuals actively supporting separatism (Dernoviy 2017, p. 331). This number is extremely negligible as compared to more than 10,000 priests of the Ukrainian Orthodox Church.

Another important organization which assisted Russia's invasion of Ukraine was Aleksandr Dugin's "Eurasian Youth Union". This small-sized organization adopted the post-imperial ideology and utilized an "actionists" approach. It worked with young people in various regions of the post-Soviet area, who were Putin's followers, hated the political order of their own countries and were ready to contribute to their reunification with Russia. In 2006, the "Eurasian Youth Union" organized a summer school in the Vladimir region, where numerous activists participated. These activists became leaders of the anti-Ukraine protest movements in winter and spring 2014 in southern and eastern Ukraine. Amongst them was also Pavel Gubarev, the prospective "people's governor" of the Donetsk region. In the midst of the invasion, the "Eurasian Youth Union" was engaged in the organization of the so called "people's republics" in the Ukrainian regions, designing their paraphernalia and promoting its activists for leading positions (Shekhovtsov 2017, pp. 181-200).

---

58 An extensive list of grievances against the clergy and the episcopate of the Ukrainian Orthodox Church was published by a patriotic Ukrainian journalist in a series of 15 articles in the Petr i Mazepa periodical, https://petrimazepa.com/kazaki_razboiniki_cvk_na_sluzbe_u_upc_mp_cast_15_doneckaa_eparhia_heppi_end. The duties of the priests in the Luhansk and Donetsk People's Republic included the consecration of the flags of separatists units and memorials to their fallen companions, marrying combatants and participation in official events of the Luhansk and Donetsk People's Republic.

A whole range of Russia's political and public organizations, which had branch offices in Ukraine, was engaged in pro-Russian actions during the military aggression. Amongst them were Slavic Unity, the Odesa office of the Russian National Unity and the Almighty Don Cossack Army (with headquarters in Rostov-on-Don), which had a network of offices in the Luhansk and Donetsk regions. Other Cossack organizations also worked in Ukraine, as did societies of monarchists, air assault forces veterans and veterans of the Afghanistan war.

Conclusions

In the 2000s and the early 2010s, the independent movement of Russian nationalists in post-Soviet countries was domesticated by the presidential administration of the Russian Federation with sticks and carrots. The sticks included deprivation of funding, restrictions of radical propaganda and the selective imprisonment of perpetrators of crimes. The carrot involved the integration of their "adequate" representatives into government agencies, governmental funding of social groups such as parishes of the Russian Orthodox Church, veterans or Cossacks. The rhetoric of Russian nationalists was shared by public officials—from the "protection of Orthodox Christianity" to imperial militarism. For the Russian nationalists outside Russia the carrot sufficed, i.e., moderate funding, some gifts and attention by Russia's officials and politicians.

Russia's political authorities were able to use Russian nationalists for their own purposes. Russia's political authorities were able to control the armed underground movement of Russian nationalists. Nationalists like Mlynnik and Girkin were one the one hand critical of the government while accomplishing dangerous missions on its behalf on the other hand. As "advocates of a strong state" they were fighting for Russia's strategic interests (whatever they thought those were).

In order to ensure a stable pro-Russian political course in Ukraine, especially after the 2004 Orange Revolution, a multi-level system was established. It included a group of government officials in Russia, who made political decisions, and a group of Moscow based operators with extensive networks. They had media resources and coordinators of pro-Russia (and pro-Putin) activities in Russia as well as in Ukraine. The operational efficiency of these networks was guaranteed by four key factors. Firstly, many networks were designed for coordinating the communities in Russia and in Ukraine (Cossacks, airborne assault forces veterans, veterans of the Afghanistan war and bikers). In times of crisis, it allowed to mobilize a considerable force coming from Russia to help "our people". Secondly, these networks utilized already existing forms of paramilitary organizations, armed underground groups, private security companies, or militarized political organizations (Russian National Unity, Eurasian Youth Union, National Bolshevik Party, Cossack villages). Thirdly, these paramilitary organizations consisted primarily of military professionals and retired veterans. A considerable part of them were special forces veterans, i.e., experienced personnel that knew how to use firearms, had combat experience, including unconventional war and mercenary activities, was skilled in guerrilla and irregular warfare and shared one or the other form of radical Russian nationalism. These paramilitary forces were standby and ready for new adventures. All these features interacted with the fact that there are regions and cities with ethnic Russian majorities in Ukraine. The larger such social strata were — they were especially sizable in the central cities of military and navy force districts or in the Donbas urban complexes — the more success the Kremlin could count on.

Over time, Russian nationalists were integrated into Russia's governmental agencies, their network coordinators and even low-ranking activists began to influence the decision-making processes. The low-ranking activists overstated their own significance, inflating the number of organizations' members and the "stock price" of their organizations, in order to receive more funding from Moscow and its coordinators. The coordinators presented the situation to their bosses in an even better light, both out of materialistic concerns — expecting an increase of funding and of their own standing — and idealistic reasons. The hacked correspondence of Kirill Frolov and Igor Girkin (Strelkov), who tried to achieve their own goals during the campaign in Ukraine, and the intercepted conversations of Glazyev and Zatulin, where the latter demanded to organize a takeover of his home city of Zaporozhye with no resources of his own at hand, are tangible evidence of this point.[59] Consequently, Russia's political leaders received an unrealistic picture of the situation in Ukraine. This contributed to the creation of megalomaniac projects on redrawing the political map of Ukraine, including the idea of establishing Novorossiya.

Yet, Russia's political leadership did not fully trust the "public figures" among the nationalists and limited its support in case of doubt. The Russian government moved its own military units to the Donbas regions of Ukraine instead of solely relying on local militants. In spring 2014, the Russian army supported the "public figures" among the separatists and pro-Russian sympathizers only if they undoubtedly dominated the streets of big cities over the pro-Ukrainian community and in case that their success was threatened by the Ukrainian army. In such cases, the Russian army was there to protect their proxies, committing an act of direct aggression.

The analysis of the intercepted conversations between the Moscow coordinators of Russia's invasion and their local representatives does not give any reason to believe that the actions of Russia's authorities were planned in advance and their local counteragents were utilized according to a Master plan. On the contrary, in many cases, they were forced to improvise, since much of the old and trusted personnel turned out to be incapacitated or arrested by the Ukrainian intelligence service SBU while new figures took their place.

References

Bremer, Thomas (2016), Diffuses Konzept. Die Russische Orthodoxe Kirche und die „Russische Welt", in: Osteuropa 03, pp. 4-6.

Demmel, Vera (2016), Das Georgsband: Ruhmesorden, Erinnerungszeichen, Pro-Kreml-Symbol, in: Osteuropa 03, pp. 19-31.

---

59 https://censor.net.ua/resonance/3044974/v_harkove_vzyali_uje_oblsovet_v
    _donetske_vzyali_nujno_brat_v_odesse_proslushka_sovetnika_putina_chas.

Dernoviy, Vitaliy (2017), Religious Factor in the Russian Spring project 2.0 // 25th Anniversary of the Independence of Ukraine as a History of Religious Freedoms and Pluralistic World View: State Institutions and Religious Organisations in Search of Partnership Models, Kyiv.

Gasimov, Zaur (2012), Idee und Institution. „Russkij mir" zwischen kultureller Mission und Geopolitik, in: Osteuropa 05, pp. 69-80.

Hagemeister, Michael (2016) "Bereit für die Endzeit". Neobyzantismus in Russland, in: Osteuropa 11-12, pp. 15-44.

Jablokov, Il'ja (2015), Feinde, Verräter, Fünfte Kolonnen. Verschwörungstheorien in Russland, in: Osteuropa 04, pp. 99-114.

Kotkina, Irina (2017): Geopolitical Imagination and Popular Geopolitics between Eurasian Union and Russky Mir, in: Mark Bassin; Gonsalo Pozo (eds.), The Politics of Eurasianism. Identity, Popular Culture and Russia's Foreign Policy, London; New-York, pp. 64-65.

Laruelle, Marlene (2009), In the Name of the Nation. Nationalism and Politics in Contemporary Russia, New York.

Laruelle, Marlene (2012), Russian Nationalism, Foreign Policy and Identity Debates in Putin's Russia. New Ideological Patterns after the Orange Revolution, Stuttgart.

Likhachev, Vyacheslav; Vladimir Pribylovsky (2005), Russkoe Natsional'noe Edinstvo, 1990-2000. V 2-kh tomakh: Russkoe Natsional'noe Edinstvo, vol.1. Istoriya i ideologiya, 1990-2000, Stuttgart.

Manutscharjan, Aschot (2016), Die Heimat ist in Gefahr. Außenpolitik im Isborsker Klub, in: Osteuropa 11, pp. 45-56.

Mitrokhin, Nikolay (2017), Diktaturtransfer im Donbass: Gewalt und „Staatsbildung" in Russlands „Volksrepubliken", in: Osteuropa 3-4, pp. 41–55.

Mitrokhin, Nikolay (2006), Russian Orthodox Church: Contemporary Condition and Actual Problems, Moscow.

Mitrokhin, Nikolay (2015), Infiltration, Instruction, Invasion: Russia's War in the Donbass, in: Journal of Soviet and Post-Soviet Politics and Society 01, pp. 219-249.

Mitrokhin, Nikolay (2015b), Bandenkrieg und Staatsbildung. Zur Zukunft des Donbass, in: Osteuropa 1, pp. 5-22.

Mitrokhin, Nikolay: N (2003), "Russian Party". The Russian Nationalist Movement in the USSR. 1953-1985. Moscow (in Russian).

Pozo, Gonzalo (2017), Eurasianism in Russian Foreign Policy: The Case of Eurasian Economic Union, in: Mark Bassin; Gonzalo Pozo (eds.), The Politics of Eurasianism. Identity, Popular Culture and Russia's Foreign Policy, London, New-York, pp. 161-180.

Pribylovski, Vladimir (2015): Chieftains and Leaders of Russian Nationalism and Russia's National Imperialism, Moscow (in Russian).

Shekhovtsov Anton (2017), Alexander Dugin's neo-Eurasianism and the Russian-Ukrainian war, in: Mark Bassin; Gonzalo Pozo (eds.), The politics of Eurasianism. Identity, Popular Culture and Russia's Foreign Policy, London, New-York, pp. 181-200.

Smith, Kathleen E. (2002), Mythmaking in the New Russia. Politics and Memory during the Yeltsin Era, Ithaca.

Titkov, Alexei (2006), Party No.4. "Motherland" and its Neighbourhood, Moscow, pp. 18-19.

Wilson, Andrew (2005), Virtual Politics: Faking Democracy in the Post-Soviet World, New Haven.

Pro-Russian Irregular Armed Groups

Natalia Savelyeva

The following chapter investigates the formation and evolution of the irregular armed groups in the territories of the Luhansk and Donetsk separatist regions (LPR and DPR) between winter 2014 and winter 2016, when they were merged into the People's Militia, which directly answered to the LPR and DPR Ministries of Defense.[1] Only those irregular armed groups which were formed during the conflict will be dealt with, I will thus not look into the activities of private military companies. Even though a considerable amount of information can be found in open sources, it often tends to be contradictory and insufficient. Our interviews with participants of the anti-Maidan actions since spring 2014 and the subsequent mobilization in the Donbas do not give a full picture either. I will therefore concentrate on specific cases, for the analysis of which it has been possible to collect more or less detailed information.

Over the course of roughly a year, from early spring 2014 to May 2015, disparate small paramilitary formations were transformed into effective battalions, operating in the territories of the Luhansk and Donetsk regions from May 2014 onwards, and were later fused into the People's Militia, an equivalent of regular armed forces. The major criteria for the following singling out of three stages of their evolution were the degree of institutionalization, the leadership type and the dependence on the unrecognized republics' government structures. The boundaries between these stages are not clear cut, since for each group, moving from one stage to another was associated with its location, history, connections with other groups, existing political forces, and other agents. I see these stages as follows:

---

[1] I would like to express my acknowledgements to Aliona Babkina and Oleg Zhuravliov for their commentaries.

1) The pre-war stage (February to May/June 2014). In that period, small groups with a leader were formed according to territorial (dwellers of one district or neighborhood), professional (members of veteran organizations, law enforcement officers, former military) or ideological (former members of political organizations) characteristics. The future battalions evolved from these initial formations.

The duration of the pre-war stage is different for each battalion. In the following, battalions are understood as armed groups headed by a specific leader, having a name, insignia (flags and chevrons) and being deployed in a specific location. Evidently, for the First Slavyansk Battalion, deployed in Slavyansk and operating under Igor Girkin's (nom de guerre: Strelkov) leadership, it started much earlier — as early as in May 2014 — than for the battalions deployed in Donetsk.[2] These battalions began to participate in the clashes with the troops of the Armed Forces of Ukraine and Ukrainian volunteer battalions only in June to July 2014, after Strelkov abandoned Slavyansk and retreated to Donetsk.

2) The combat stage (May/July 2014 to September 2014/February 2016). The beginning of the combat stage may be dated from the first days of May when warfare in Slavyansk began. On May 2, the third assault of Slavyansk took place during which helicopters and armored vehicles were used. From this time on, the battalions began to participate in the military operations, but they acted as individual armed groups forming then alliances. The battalions' leadership relied on personal loyalty and recognition.

3) The transitional period. The irregular armed groups transformed into the People's Militia (September 2014 to February 2016). In this period, the integration of individual battalions and their

---

2   Girkin is an officer of the Russian military reserves allegedly served for the Russian secret service FSB. He has fought against separatists in Chechnya, in Moldova's breakaway region of Transnistria, in Bosnia and Hercegovina, and as commander of the Russian "self-defence" on Crimea in March 2014. On 12 April 2014, Girkin led a group of militants who seized the administration, the police department, and the Security Service of Ukraine (SBU) offices in Sloviansk. Girkin claimed that his militia was formed in Crimea and consisted of volunteers from Russia, see https://en.wikipedia.org/wiki/Igor_Girkin.

leaders into a consolidated military structure named People's Militia took place. This transition included a change in the chain of command, based on recognition and personal loyalty, official subordination, regrouping, and disbandment of some battalions, and the disarmament of the battalions that refused to join People's Militia.[3] After this stage, the irregular armed groups evolved into a vertically integrated military structure. A considerable number of those who had originally joined the battalions in spring-summer 2014 did not participate in this transformation to a professional security apparatus, but left the irregular groups. The new military structure was then manned with younger people who did not participate in the violent clashes of the previous years.

Pre-war Stage: Recruitment Channels, Ties and Predecessor Organizations

The history of the formation of irregular armed groups, operating in the territory of the Luhansk and Donetsk Regions and subsequently becoming the core of People's Militia—the official military structure of the two unrecognized people's republics—began in spring 2014. At this time, Anti-Maidan rallies took place in big cities of the Donetsk and Luhansk Regions. They were supported by various political organizations, mostly left-wing parties and associations (e.g. the Progressive Socialist Party of Ukraine, Ukrainian Choice, Communist Party of Ukraine),[4] pro-Russia local political movements ("Donetsk Republic" headed by A. Ye. Purgin, who later became First Deputy Chairman of the DPR Council of Ministers, and the followers of Anti-Maidan leader Pavel Gubarev[5]); patriotic clubs, veteran associations, Cossacks as well as a few Russian

---

3   The cause of unnatural death of some battalion leaders are not clear. Among them are: Aleksei Mozgovoi (Prizrak), Pavel Driomov (Stakhanovsk Cossack Self-Defense), and Aleksander Bednov (Batman), see: https://www.rbc.ru/ph otoreport/08/02/2017/589ad2099a794713d13e6c5d.
4   https://gordonua.com/news/war/v-2014-godu-na-prorossiyskie-mitingi-v-luganske-vyhodili-predstaviteli-progressivnoy-socpartii-ukrainskogo-vybora-kpu-i-pr-eks-glava-luganskogo-sbu-petrulevich-191966.html.
5   Pavel Gubarev, one of the Anti-Maidan leaders, started to criticize the Ukrainian government in February 2014 and later created the People's Militia of Don-

nationalists organizations (National Liberation Movement, The Other Russia, Russian National Unity, Eurasian Youth Union, Essence of Time and others). The leaders of the nationalist and Cossack organizations urged to "defend the Russian population" in the Donbas before the Anti-Terror-Operation (ATO) was announced and the violent phase of the conflict began. At a press-conference of March 17, 2014, the day after the Crimean referendum, Nikolay Kozitsin, the future commander of the Almighty Don Army, spoke about the decision taken by the Chieftains' Extended Board of February 23, 2014. According to that decision, "they shall stand up for either the Cossacks or the Russian-speaking population living in the territory of Ukraine," and "today, 3,000 Cossacks have headed for the city of Donetsk."[6]

At the early stages of the Anti-Maidan, a division occurred between political organizations (led by the Communist Party of Ukraine, "Donetsk Republic" in Donetsk and Pavel Gubarev with his followers) and paramilitary organizations consisting of disparate groups that partly coordinated their actions and various coordination councils which appeared as a result of the protests. The anti-Maidan paramilitary organizations included members of local veteran organizations, patriotic and sports clubs, Russian members of few nationalist and Cossack organizations as well as associations that had emerged during the protests. Some leaders or ordinary members of these organizations had been connected with opposition political parties or had worked in local administrations.[7]

For a long time, veteran organizations, patriotic and sports clubs, pro-Russia nationalist and Cossack organizations main-

---

bas, he was arrested on March 6, 2014 by Ukrainian SBU agents. His wife, Yekaterina Gubareva, was the first DPR Minister of Foreign Affairs in summer 2014.

6   https://www.youtube.com/watch?v=yBsHDvD2qRU. The number is most likely very exaggerated. According to the media, on that same day, several hundred fully armed Russian Cossacks came into the Donetsk Region, https://tiras.ru/voennoe/39791-donskie-kazaki-prorvalis-v-doneck.html.

7   For instance, Aleksandr Kharitonov, the secretary of the Luhansk branch of the Regional Progressive Socialist Party of Ukraine, became head of the "Luhansk Guard", formed in January 2014.

tained connections which turned out to be critically important during the pre-war stage. They helped the formation of certain dispositions such as pro-Russian values, commitment to military discipline, nostalgia for the USSR as well as of skills necessary to join paramilitary groups. Such organizations and associations facilitated the establishment of small paramilitary groups. An important role in unleashing the military confrontation was played by the Berkut special police personnel who had suppressed the Maidan demonstrations and were fired after the power changeover in Kyiv.[8] However, even though many of them later joined the irregular armed groups, a critical role at the pre-war stage cannot be confirmed.

In contrast to Kyiv, the local law enforcement authorities in the Donbas did not confront the Anti-Maidan protesters. Berkut and the local law enforcement officers refused to disperse the demonstrations, and some of them took the protesters' side.[9] Some video recordings of the siege of the administration buildings (e.g. of the Donetsk secret service SBU or the Gorlovka Police Department) show the absence of resistance on the part of the civil servants and their support of the anti-Maidan protesters.[10]

The readiness for war by some leaders of the future armed groups stood in sharp contrast to the expectations of ordinary people who participated in anti-Maidan meetings at that time.[11] The

---

[8] Tatyana Malyarenko: Playing a Give-Away Game? The Undeclared Russian-Ukrainian War in Donbas, http://smallwarsjournal.com/jrnl/art/playing-a-give-away-game-the-undeclared-russian-ukrainian-war-in-donbas#_edn1.

[9] https://www.rferl.org/a/ukraine-police-berkut-forces-crimea/25295633.html
https://www.youtube.com/watch?v=y8WkwZtYUcw

[10] In a video of the capture of the Donetsk SBU on April 7, 2014, it can be seen that both parties are trying to come to an agreement, avoiding any clashes, and the SBU agents, overall, are expressing their solidarity with the protesters and are asking "not to beat the cops", as "they have had enough trouble in Kyiv already", https://www.youtube.com/watch?v=Ir_u2B-VUwc. The occupation of the Gorlovka Police Department on April 14, 2014, despite the aggressiveness of some participants, was supported by the crowd; when the police came to confront the occupiers, they went back to their bus followed by cries as "Police and people are one", https://www.youtube.com/watch?v=KEGnpKASFZE.

[11] During a rally in Donetsk on February 23, 2014, people expressed concerns that the government did not take their interests into account or that the Russian lan-

members of paramilitary, nationalist and pro-Russia organizations cared about the "Russian World" rhetoric[12] and the fight against the "fascist invaders", whereas ordinary people of Donetsk and Luhansk, who participated in the rallies, were concerned about the "coup d'état" in Kyiv, the "Law On the Language" and the deterioration of the economic situation. As early as in February 2014, before president Yanukovich`s resignation, the Donetsk and Luhansk regions took the second and third place respectively (the first place was taken by Crimea) as far as the level of support of the idea of joining Russia was concerned (33 percent of the respondents in the Donetsk region and 24 percent in the Luhansk region were in favor of it) (Melnyk 2014). In Donetsk and Luhansk, the majority of people (70.5 percent and 61.3 percent respectively) considered the Euro-Maidan protests to be a coup d'état, which was supported by Western governments. 63 percent in the Donetsk region and 63 percent in the Luhansk region were in favor of the forcible dispersion of the Euro-Maidan. In other regions, including Kharkov, Odesa and Mykolaiv, where numerous anti-Maidan rallies took place, these views were only shared by a minority of respondents.

Fear of violent actions by the new Kyiv government that had replaced president Yanukovich and the former ruling Party of Regions stimulated counter-mobilization as well as the feeling of being politically excluded. Initially, the fear in the Donetsk region was associated with the clashes in Kyiv, which had led to numerous casualties on the Maidan square in February 2014, and with the anti-Russian rhetoric of nationalist pro-Ukrainian organizations. Later, these fears grew in view of the violent clashes that took place in Kramatorsk and Mariupol in April, by the fire in the Trade Unions Building in Odesa in May 2014, as a result of which more than 40 anti-Maidan activists lost their lives, and by the fighting in the city

---

guage would no longer be one of the state languages or that their benefit payments were delayed. To the straight question whether they were ready to resort to arms, they replied that they were ready to stand their ground by "peaceful means," https://www.youtube.com/watch?v=2aklurujd9A.

12 The "Russian world" (*Russkiy mir*) is an ambiguous concept of a distinct Russian civilization based on traditions, history, the Russian language and the Russian Orthodox Church, including Russian-speakers outside Russia too.

of Slaviansk. The use of heavy armor by the Armed Forces of Ukraine after the beginning of the anti-terrorist operation (ATO) on April 14 served for many locals as a confirmation of Kyiv's military aggression against the Donbas. The ousted president Yanukovich, despite his low popularity, was perceived as someone who had protected the interests of the Donbas, whereas the Maidan protest with its Euro-integration agenda did not particularly appeal to a substantial segment of the local population.

Our interviews with local people and some members of the armed groups allow us to understand some of the sentiments of the spring of 2014 (though it is worth remembering that this is only a retrospective picture). Those who did not support the Euro-Maidan asked why the government in Kyiv had changed without their knowledge or approval. Fear among the local population and feelings of isolation created a perception that "Kyiv" did not want to listen to the Donbas and would start killing its people. Political and military leaders then emerged who managed to convert disparate grass-root groups into effective combat units, transforming the conflict subsequently into a war. Leaders as Igor Girkin (Strelkov), Aleksander Khodakovski, Igor Bezler or Aleksei Mozgovoi were decisive, i.e., people with a military background who had begun to form armed groups before (some of them long before) the announcement of the ATO.[13] Their rhetoric as well as their actions were dramatically different from the actions of ordinary anti-Maidan demonstrators. They believed that war was not only possible but inevitable and they helped to start it.[14] Leaders, who were associated with vet-

---

13 Khodakovski said in an interview: "We or I did not take the side of the people. We led the people", https://tsargrad.tv/articles/aleksandr-hodakovskij-my-poveli-narod-za-soboj_91307.
14 One of the Anti-Maidan participants described the sentiment in spring 2014 in a town close to Slaviansk: "At that moment (May 2014), at that moment, we were not ready for the armed confrontation, though the weapons were already there, they were there... When Strelkov appeared, with his tough attitude, he immediately added, let us say, some tension; he showed that if we go to war — and there was a war — Ukraine was really getting ready for war — then we fight and not get soft" (interview 37, male, born 1979).

eran organizations, law enforcement agencies, semi-criminal networks or military-patriotic clubs helped, with their skills and access to weapons, to militarize discontented but rather passive people.

After the Crimea referendum, some mobilized individuals moved from Crimea to the Donbas, where they organized their own battalions or joined existing ones. Russia's recognition of the Crimean referendum inspired hopes among the anti-Maidan supporters in the south-east of Ukraine that Russia would get actively involved here in the future too. In a certain sense, the actions of Ukrainian leaders, of the commanders of irregular armed groups and the Russian authorities reinforced each other: Part of the local people felt scared by the new Ukrainian leaders and the future separatist leaders exploited these fears in order to create paramilitary formations while the Russian authorities inspired hopes for a favorable outcome. All this was happening at a moment when law enforcement in the region had already considerably weakened.

The Pre-war Stage and the Formation of Battalions: The Vostok Battalion

The examples of the battalions Vostok and Russian Orthodox Army illustrate how the activation of pre-existing networks aided the formation of paramilitary groups. We observe a transition from participation in rallies to the setting up of road check-points or the occupation of administrative buildings to the ultimate formation of a battalion. At the lower level, ordinary people connected by personal or territorial ties started to interact. At the second level, already existing networks of former military men or members of a political organization began to mobilize. At the third level, this mobilization was picked up by the leaders who turned the disparate groups into paramilitary formations.

Aleksandr Khodakovsky, the commander of the Vostok battalion in spring 2014, was one of those spearheading the mobilization. Previously, he had been the commander of the Alfa special operations unit of the Donetsk Regional SBU Department and had taken part in dispersing the Euro-Maidan protests in Kyiv. On

March 1, 2014, during a rally in front of the Donetsk Regional Administration, he said that "he had come home" (he was born in the Donbas) "together with the combatants of Berkut, internal troops."[15] Possibly, it was these people whom he refers to as the "core", and it was with them that he would occupy the building of the youth branch of the Party of the Regions and would start to create his organization "Patriotic Forces of Donbas", the activists of which would join the Vostok battalion.[16]

It is difficult to say what the "Patriotic Forces of Donbas" was like at the beginning of the Donbas conflict. At a rally on March 1, 2014, Khodakovsky had asked the participants whether they were ready to separate from Ukraine (receiving a chorus of 'yes' as an answer) and who was ready to "give their lives for it". However, on March 7, he already doubted in an interview that the majority of the Donbas population would speak out in favor of separation from Ukraine, he insisted on negotiations with Kyiv, at the same time warning Russia against any intrusion.[17] Retrospectively describing the events of spring 2014, he says that "when it became clear as early as in spring that they [Kyiv – N. S.] would use force," he and his allies began to create clandestine combat groups of 90 to 120 people. Khodakovsky believed that the imminent war was a continuation of the global confrontation between Russia and the West.[18]

The official date of the creation of the Vostok battalion is May 6, 2014, even though the mobilization of former military and paramilitary networks, i.e., sports and patriotic clubs promoting pro-Russia and pro-Soviet values, who subsequently joined the Vostok battalion, had begun already at the end of February 2014, when Khodakovsky had returned to Donetsk. Three social backgrounds contributed to the formation of the Vostok battalion – the activation of veterans of the Afghanistan war, of former military men, who

---

15 https://www.youtube.com/watch?v=Bqewwq2kMss
16 https://tsargrad.tv/articles/aleksandr-hodakovskij-my-poveli-narod-za-soboj_91307; http://patriot-donetsk.ru/history.html.
17 https://www.youtube.com/watch?v=Yv9SDG9mgOY.
18 https://www.youtube.com/watch?v=DSSup7zmseM.

were engaged in criminal activities in the 1990s or in private security companies, and anti-Maidan followers from one of the towns in the Donetsk Region that was occupied by the Ukrainian Army after Igor Girkin (Strelkov) had retreated in June 2014. Before 2014, veteran organizations had existed in the whole of Ukraine. Afghan veterans from the former Soviet Union met once a year in Kharkov. In the city of Donetsk, several organizations united former brothers-in-arms. These organizations were mostly self-organized associations. One of the members said about their chairman (let us call him M), that he was "the facilitator here, the chairman, and that was his unofficial position. But we all respected him" (interview 58, male, born around 1970).[19] When, after Yanukovich's resignation, the anti-Maidan rallies turned into a mass movement, M began "to visit his brothers-in-arms." It appears that initially, during these personal meetings, they talked about some abstract readiness for combat actions, "if necessary" (the content of these meetings could not be independently verified). Allegedly, the majority of the veterans refused to participate in one way or another in the current or forthcoming "events" (interview 52, male, born around 1970). Yet, the 'Afghans', roughly 25 men, gradually formed the core of the future Vostok battalion. Before May 2014, their joint activities were limited to attending the anti-Maidan rallies and to discussing the ongoing events. Though the major part of "group M" consisted of former military men, some had not served in the army. A former university friend of one of the Afghanistan war veterans recalls:

> "Then [on May 3] the order came. It will take place tomorrow, right on Sunday. "We are getting together at 3 o'clock."[20]
> Interviewer: Where did the order come from?
> Respondent: C. [his old 'Afghan' friend—N. S.] phoned. He says: we have spoken to M. We are on the move. Where we are moving—who knows? So, here we are. We arrived, got together, sat down. There was a chap there. ...So we got together. So a platoon was formed by M. ... 12 people. Maybe,

---

19 In order to ensure the informants' confidentiality, no further information is indicated about the interviews. All the interviews took place in 2016-2017 in Moscow, Saint-Petersburg, Donetsk and the Donetsk Region, Lugansk and the Lugansk Region.
20 The "order" came on May 3, 2014, the day after the fire in the Trade Unions Building in Odesa.

fewer. There were two platoons, and B. [an 'Afghan' whom he met during the rallies—N S.] came. Well, 28 people, two platoons.[21] Khodakovsky spoke. We listened to him, we liked what he was saying. ... I saw enough for myself to want to carry on" (interview 52, male, born around 1970).

Apparently, social ties ensured M's and later Khodakovsky's credibility. The opportunity to identify people with similar views and objectives among the initial leaders of the armed groups was important. For the professional military and former mercenaries, the rhetoric of fighting against the West also mattered, whereas ordinary civilians felt appealed by the patriotic discourse, especially references to the Great Patriotic War. Former military men were additionally recruited to the Vostok battalion through the networks of private security companies of the 1990s as well as through patriotic or sports clubs. A similar habitus played an important role for the mobilization, because it allowed to easily identify like-minded people and to trust them.

The clashes between the Euro-Maidan demonstrators and the Berkut special forces in Kyiv triggered the coming together of future Vostok combatants. Fifty-seven people attended the first meeting on February 22, 2014, they began to form "mobile fives" that patrolled the city. The mission of these groups of fives was, in their view, to prevent "acts of sabotage on the part of Ukrainian nationalists" that were feared at that time. At the end of February 2014, the leader of this group contacted Khodakovsky. Straight after their first meeting, he decided to join ranks with him. Khodakovsky's narrative, according to this interview partner, coincided with his own. This respondent, similar to many professional military men, considered Khodakovsky's commitment to the use of "controlled force" important, i.e., his claim of being able to organize and control masses. Another agreeable factor at the end of February 2014 was the ability by Khodakovsky to coordinate action. One of our re-

---

21 Vladimir Savelov, who till 2014 had been the head of the organization of the Afghan war veterans in the Kyiv District of Donetsk for about 10 years, said that only a few people from their organization joined Vostok, see http://zavtra.ru/blogs/afgantsyi-na-zaschite-a.

spondents pointed out that the future battalion members were recruited through the spread of word among friends and acquaintances, noting that none of them were younger than 40.

The first wave of those who had joined Khodakovsky, before the Vostok battalion was actually established, consisted of former military men, some of whom had fought in violent conflicts in the post-Soviet republics, and their friends. These were people of roughly the same age and with similar views. They identified with the concept of 'Soviet people'. Part of them felt solidarity with the Berkut special forces officers in Kyiv and considered themselves as upholders of order. For others, the historical memory of the Great Patriotic War served as an identity marker.

Most future combatants had had more or less successful careers (in some cases, they had a semi-criminal past), families, and a stable financial position. These networks of former military men and their friends became active as early as in February 2014, long before the mass social movements came to life in the Donbas and violent clashes began in Slaviansk. Some of those who had joined Khodakovsky went to Russia and former Soviet republics to recruit people with recent combat experience, first and foremost, those who had participated in the military conflict in South Ossetia.[22]

Below, I will focus on the example of one of the towns in the Donetsk Region (let us refer to it as D) situated not far from Slaviansk. At the pre-war stage, the formation of primary irregular armed groups in this town was rather chaotic. Groups formed around the most active anti-Maidan activists, who were also officials of the local administration. In D the anti-Maidan rallies began in March 2014. The members of the local branch of the Afghan veteran organization took an active part in them. Gradually, a core of around 50 people was organized, which included local businessmen and administration officials.[23] They regularly met with each

---

22   Oleg Mamayev (Mamai) recalls meeting Khodakovsky's people who went to Vladikavkaz through Chechnya and Dagestan and persuaded him and other Ossetians to join Khodakovsky. https://ukraina.ru/interview/20151022/1014617230.html.
23   As far as we can judge, part of the town administration openly supported the pro-Russian (also called "Russian Spring"). In the session of the Municipal

other, interacted with the local leader and municipal council, spoke in its sessions and participated in holding the referendum. The municipal administration that was mainly against the new Kyiv authorities supported the anti-Maidan demonstrators. The turning point was between April 7, 2014, when the ATO was announced, and April 12, when Igor Girkin's group entered Slaviansk.

Local paramilitary structures were supposed to enforce public order and to resist the Ukrainian Army and the ultra-nationalist Right Sector which were perceived as a threat to the lives and safety of the town dwellers. The situation in the Donetsk Region was dangerous in itself: The administration buildings were seized, checkpoints were created, people turned up with arms which were not controlled at that time. At that time, Oleg Protsenko, vice chairman of the local Afghan veteran association, codenamed Dushman (Mujahid), was in Slaviansk. On April 7, 2014, he and his group took part in assailing the SBU (Ukraine's secret service) in Donetsk, then they disarmed the security staff of the Municipal Department in Slaviansk. According to one of his interviews, Protsenko had created his group already in 2013.[24] On April 13, the day after Igor Girkin's arrival at Slaviansk and a week after the ATO was announced, checkpoints began to be established in D. At the same time, the anti-Maidan activists, taking advantage of the inactivity of the local administration and the absence of any resistance, assumed the role of local law enforcement.

> "We started ... to set up the checkpoint, bring the wheels in, put up sand and logwood barriers, arranging things somehow. It was a day and night duty. It turned out that we controlled two roads leading to the town.
> Interviewer: Did many people form D take part in the defense, in the checkpoints?
> Respondent: At the beginning, there were many.
> Interviewer: How many?
> Respondent: You know, some came because they had nothing better to do. One was bored sitting at home with his wife, kids or in front of the television, so there he came. Hung around till 11-12 in the evening and then left.

Council on March 16, 47 out of 52 deputies supported the idea of the creation of the Donetsk People's Republic.

24   https://topwar.ru/78732-dushman-moy-dom-nahoditsya-na-okkupirovannoy-territorii.html.

Such people sifted out. But maybe by the end of June, beginning of July, 100 or more people were actually involved and could be relied upon. They served at military stations, patrolled, served at the checkpoints and all the rest of it. Even the cops. We helped them, we helped the Ukrainian police, well, the [town] administration just withdrew from everything. They, sort of, turned up for work but did not take any measures or decisions. We assumed all these responsibilities ourselves. The only ones who helped were the patrol guard police" (interview 37, male, born in 1979).

The connections between various groups extended and strengthened, including the groups that were already participating in armed clashes and occupied different towns. It is safe to assume that at the initial stage, interaction and coordination were more unofficial and relied on personal ties. After establishing the checkpoints and creating more or less organized groups that patrolled them, interaction and coordination became more orderly. For instance, delegates from D went to Slaviansk to establish contacts after Girkin took over control of the city.[25] Due to the territorial vicinity of the places, interaction with other groups became inevitable, which helped the spread of weapons:

"Then, we started to gradually get hold of some short rifles, the first sub-machine gun was given to me by Dushman when he was leaving for Donetsk. Then sub-machine guns, machine guns followed.
Interviewer: Where did it all come from?
Respondent: Partly, around 10-15%, not more, from Strelkov; all the rest came from Khodakovsky and Bezler.
Interviewer: And how did you actually liaise with them at that moment, when you were still at D.?
Respondent: We contacted Khdakovsky through Dushman. Dushman was bringing the guns in from Vostok. As for Gorlovka, we had the Gorlovka military station commander Vassilyevitch. We found him. And this is how we found him: The guys from Gorlovka lost their way and came here. They were going on a mission in Oktiabrski and ended up at my checkpoint. And I only had one sub-machine gun to go around for the whole checkpoint. Oh no! We already had a Mukha [a Russian rocket-propelled grenade]. A good job that they sent someone forward with the Soviet red flag. ... And they were coming with Grads [rocket launchers]. And it was through them that I

---

25 Interview with a militia man, codename Mitiai, https://polynkov.livejournal.com/1530974.html.

met Bezler.[26] And then we began to establish contacts" (interview 37, male, born in 1979).

Thanks to closer cooperation, arms were distributed and self-organized groups transformed into more orderly and effective combat units. For instance, thanks to meeting Igor Bezler at D, someone with the code name Vassilyich, a former marine from Crimea, arrived. "Vassilyich" became the commandant at D, as a result of which the military station changed from an unorganized crowd to an organized armed unit.

> "The military station was just a shapeless mass of 70 armed people. There, sort of, were checkpoints, sort of, everything. And then he came and literally within a week, he turned it into an armed unit (interview 37, male, born in 1974).

Girkin was recognized by the local leaders as someone who could give orders, he was perceived as a hero and a potential defender of the Russian population in the Donbas from the 'Kyiv threat.' Before the withdrawal of Girkin and his combatants from town, the checkpoint commanders received the order form Sloviansk to "leave the position" and retreat to Donetsk; they obeyed this order despite their unwillingness to abandon the town.[27] Besides, it was dangerous to stay at D because of the advance of the Ukrainian army. Although there had been a certain coordination between the armed groups, it was rather weak and depended on personal ties. Those who retreated to Donetsk joined the Vostok battailon when the confrontation began between Girkin and Khodakovsky (and their respective supporters). This confrontation was to become even more dramatic. The armed groups from D

---

26 Igor Bezler, son of an ethnic German father and a Ukrainian mother, was a Russian national who lived in Ukraine. He served in the Soviet Army in Afghanistan (1983–84) and fought against the separatist forces in Chechnya. In 1994-1997, he studied at the Moscow Military Academy, he retired from the Russian army with the rank of lieutenant colonel. After moving to Gorlovka, he headed the veteran organization of airborne troopers, see: https://ria.ru/20140828/1021803991.html.
27 Girkin and his combatants fled from Sloviansk on 4–5 July 2014, during an offensive by the Ukrainian military. Sloviansk was recaptured by Ukrainian forces, thus ending the separatist control.

joined Vostok, but only because Oleg Protsenko (Dushman) joined Vostok; "everyone in town knew him" because of his work in the veteran council, and he had gained a certain reputation of a hero participating in the clashes in Slaviansk (interview 37, male, born in 1974).

Summing up, we observe a pattern of mobilization. First, people joined those whom they already knew or whom they had met during the protests, and then the leaders of these primary groups helped them to join the battalion. The mobilization and militarization were carried out by experienced people, including those who had (unidentified) relations with Russia's security services.

The Pre-war Stage and Formation of the Russian Orthodox Army Battalion (ROA)

One of the future battalion leaders (let us refer to him as V) came to Donetsk in February 2014 for family reasons.[28] His father had served in the military, but he did not have any military service background. He was constantly on the move: He went from one city to another, often changed jobs (eventually, he became a businessman and constantly switched from one business to another), he changed places of study, and he had been married several times. He had never been a member of political organizations or associations. In his interviews, he made the impression of a person who is not able to clearly articulate his political views and convictions, let alone defend; he only had vague and intuitive preferences and initially no ultimate power ambitions. His rhetoric dramatically differed from that of Khodakovsky or Strelkov. If the former strove to emphasize their leading and organizing role in the conflict development, he, on the contrary, often said that he was only there for a short period of time "to help the people of the Donbas."

At the end of February, those who had participated in the Anti-Maidan rallies in Kyiv started to come back to Donetsk and the Donetsk Region. V had much time to spare, which he wanted to

---

28 To keep the informants' confidentiality, we have not included any details that may help to identify them. In this section, the references to the interviews will be most general.

spend at home, and after Yanukovich's resignation, he started going to rallies and tried to meet their organizers. He met Robert Donia, the self-appointed deputy of Pavel Gubarev, and offered his help.[29] V met active participants of the rallies, he began to socialize with them regularly, gradually extending his network while perceiving his participation in rallies and meeting the activists as entertainment, an enjoyable pastime-playing

Gradually, V extended his network, including people from Pavel Gubarev's inner circle. His contact network was filled with members of street gangs, self-organized groups and former members of pro-Russia organizations, such as the National Liberation Movement; he looked for these contacts and got in touch with them by himself. At the end of February, beginning of March 2014, V met people who had established a checkpoint on the road from Donetsk to his relatives` house and joined them. The combat alerts at the checkpoints led to new connections between the anti-Maidan supporters from different cities and towns: they met each other, shared their contacts and information.

We can see both similarities and differences between how the two battalions, Vostok and the Russian Orthodox Army, were formed. Both used strong public discontent with the Maidan protest and its consequences and mobilized people from below — initially disparate and uncoordinated groups. Vostok, however, had already established networks of comrades-in-arms, mercenaries, veterans, and law enforcement officers. The similarity in habitus — the core of the battalion consisted of former members of the Soviet military —, and they shared some ideology with diverse components such as the memory of the Great Patriotic War and the idea of an antagonism between Russia and the West. In the ROA case, a clear ideology and a common network were rather missing. In effect, V created this network himself, picking out people who shared

---

29 Gubarev was a pro-Russian activist for the Progressive Socialist Party of Ukraine, he proclaimed himself the "People's Governor" of the Donetsk Region on 3 March 2014, after separatists seized the building; he had earlier declared himself leader of the Donbas People`s Militia. Gubarev was arrested by the Security Service of Ukraine (SBU) on 7 May 2014, he was freed in exchange for SBU officers detained earlier by the Donbas People's Militia.

his views (vaguely nationalistic) and had similar dispositions (unstable position, inclination to change and adventures) or belonged to street gangs, neighborhood groups or were members of Russian nationalist organizations.

Thanks to his ability to make and maintain contacts, V gathered those who were ready to act, he became the middleman between the small disparate groups and the movement's political leadership, i.e. Pavel Gubarev and his associates. On April 6, they participated in the seizure of the Donetsk Regional State Administration. In order to maintain the hold of the regional administration building, the most active participants, using Zello radios and the Internet, called people to come to administration building— "there is where to sleep, there is food, just come here, your will is what matters" [author's archive]). Among those, who followed the call were many people who were "not settled in society", under 30, with no higher education and only irregular income. Thanks to the increase of the number of participants, it became possible to hold the building; people from other regions started to join, and so did Russian citizens, though in small numbers.

> "We had the floors organized by regions, who sleeps where. The guys from Russia, of course, came. This was when people from Russia turned up, when we seized the Regional Administration. They were coming because they saw that if the Regional Administration in Donetsk was held, then that was, sort of, it. And we were joined by the organized groups, well, what I mean by organized, two or three people, five people". As a result, according to one of the active participants of the events, within a week, they "accumulated enough personnel to defend the Regional Administration." (author's archive).

At the time, around thirty separate groups and their leaders were in the building of the regional administration, not only from Donetsk but also from the neighboring regions. Twenty or twenty-five of them occupied the, the others controlled the street. Judging by the available information, those were rather disparate groups, not answering to any single leadership, and they were at odds with each other ("we could not organize ourselves properly since everyone had ambitions"). Still, staying in the building strengthened existing ties:

"We knew more or less all the leaders, we got to know each other even better in the Regional Administration, because before the Regional Administration, we had been scattered around the region, and there, we finally got together. We looked each other in the eye, had a couple of meetings regarding the defense". (author's archive)

The distinction between "activists" who would later join the battalions and who did not have leadership ambitions and the "politicians' community", i.e. those who subsequently, when the war began, would stay apart and take administrative posts, became apparent. Khodakovsky originally tried to combine the role of a politician and activist, creating both a political movement and a battalion. In the case of the Russian Orthodox Army (ROA), the political and ideological leadership was outsourced instead, it was represented by Pavel Gubarev and his associates who did not belong to any of the groups that formed the ROA battalion, but still coordinated their actions at the initial stages. One of the informants refers to this division in the ROA between the "politicians" and "activists," as "tacit collusion".

The future core participants of the ROA avoided taking part in the political meetings—they had no political ambitions and still perceived the unrest as a temporary state of affairs and waited for some decisive actions either from Russia or from Ukraine. It is quite symptomatic that Girkin (Strelkov) describes the situation quite similarly, seeing it as a temporary war that may follow the Crimean scenario:

"At that moment, we all hoped that the will of the people of the Donetsk Republic would be supported by Russia in the same way as it had been earlier supported in Crimea. Everything that is happening now was not part of our plans and could not have possibly been. Russia had all the possibilities to implement the Crimean scenario in the Donbas. The acts of force, in this respect, are not perceived as an expression of some political will, but as a means of leverage towards those who have this will and power to deliver.[30]

The local authorities were paralyzed, the activists seized administration buildings, and there was no single command center. It was the "security" division and not the "political" one that took the

---

30 Interview with Igor Girkin (Strelkov) from 7 Nov. 2014, http://kolokolrussia.ru/russkiy-mir/igor-strelkov-menya-vynudili-uehat-iz-donecka.

decision to seize the other administration buildings, i.e. the treasury, local ministries and departments — everything, except the regional police building, military bases and prisons, since they were better fortified, and their personnel were armed. At least some of the future ROA battalion combatants reasoned that seizing the buildings could provoke the Kyiv government to hold a referendum in the Donetsk region. By seizing many buildings one could coerce Kyiv into negotiations, it was hoped.

After having seized the regional administration, the future ROA members occupied the 5th floor of the building. New people poured into the building and joined those who had come there earlier, joining already existing groups. Among these groups were the Russian Volunteer Army that was led by someone under the codename Mongol and which consisted of former police officers of Donetsk, a group called Orthodox Donbas (an association of Krasoarmeisk orthodox activists headed by Aleksander Nilolayevski from Nikolayevka), the Sarmat group, an association of small street groups from Makeyevka, and finally Shchit (Shield), an association of the Donetsk youth patriotic movement.[31]

The Leaders and the Command Structures

From the very beginning, the Vostok proto-battalion was well-integrated by an unchallenged leader, a clear ideology, a set of rules and army discipline. Khodakovsky was the leader of both the battalion and the political organization, thus combining two functions, first and foremost, he was able to arm the battalion.[32]

The formation of the ROA differs significantly from that of Vostok. The ROA was in comparison a loose alliance of disparate groups, each of which had its own leader. Up until June 2014, when the battalion moved to the occupied building of the Ukrainian secret service SBU, several people were fighting for leadership. The

---

31 http://rusvesna.su/recent_opinions/1417451815;
http://www.forbes.ru/sobytiya/obshchestvo/261679-donetskii-spetsnaz-portrety-na-fone-sovremennogo-iskusstva; https://stopterror.in.ua/info/2015/10/batalon-spetsialnogo-naznacheniya-nikolaevskogo-vympel/.

32 According to multiple sources, Vostok was one of the best armed battalions, even before it was officially established.

council was a compromise in order to delay decisions on a centralized battalion command. At the early stages of its existence, the battalion was divided. The one who eventually became the leader (I called him V), despite his support of Russian nationalist organizations, did not articulate any clear ideology; he only used the rhetoric of "helping the Donbas people." He was an entirely different type of leader, more of an entrepreneur.

Apart from their obvious function (to defend and attack), weapons and weapons distribution played an important role for the group formation. Possessing weapons guaranteed some trustworthiness of a paramilitary group and their leaders; having weapons affected the attractiveness of the military group. Khodakovsky may serve as an example. He inspired trust in those who had joined him not only thanks to his experience and ideas but also because of his ability to create an efficient combat organization and to supply it with weapons. The narrative of one of the ROA leaders confirmed that

> "the weapons tend to accumulate" and create a certain atmosphere around those who have them. "... People would follow any force. They saw that since we held weapons in our arms, it meant that we had power. It means, they should stick with us. And quite a few good and robust guys joined our movement." (authors archive)

The lack of weapons in some formations and abundance of weapons in others created the conditions for subordination and coalitions, the inevitability of which was also determined by territorial vicinity. People contacted each other in order to get arms; therefore. Having access to weapons gave some leaders an opportunity to subjugate other leaders, not by force but through the relationship of exchange. As we were able to see in the case of the irregulars in town A., Bezler, who "shared" weapons with them, appointed a person from his circle as the commandant who, apparently, reported to him. Therefore, weapons were exchanged for loyalty.

Relationships of subordination, strengthened by the weapon exchange, existed on the level of entire battalions. It was the insufficient number of weapons that made the independence of one battalion from another questionable. A good example of this role of weaponry is the ROA battalion. Since the battalion did not have enough weapons, one of its leaders decided to ask Girkin (Strelkov), who was at Slaviansk at the time, for help (June 2014). Strelkov rejected his request, saying that they did not have enough weapons either. Then he went to Bezler, who had more weapons and who was deployed closer to Donetsk. He went to Gorlovka, met with Abver who was Bezler's deputy at the time.[33] They managed to reach an agreement, and the ROA received several dozen rifles. However, "helping" with weapons was not for free and implied that those who had received help would subsequently coordinate their actions with those who had helped them.

Finally, the role of the leaders was not limited to the top or mid-level. The primary groups that were formed as early as between February to April 2014, such as those that one of the ROA leaders established connections with, or those that were organized at the checkpoints, in the neighborhoods or during rallies, or the "M group" which joined Vostok—all had leaders. Surely, after the battalions were formed, they received names, chevrons, and deployments; individuals who did not belong to any group started to join the battalions. At the first stage, it was important that the future battalions were composed of such groups, and these groups had their own leaders. Usually, the latter kept their leading positions after they became part of some battalion. They could become platoon or detachments commanders, depending on the number of people that had come with them; the group members remained under their official command. This pattern had three outcomes. The power of the battalion, group or detachment leader relied more on the subordinates' recognition than on the official hierarchy. At the initial stages, the leading positions were taken by those whom the group was ready to follow and not those who had been appointed. And when a group officially became part of the battalion, this attitude remained unchanged. This could lead to conflicts between small group leaders or between group leaders and the battalion

---

33 Sergei Zdriliuk Abver, born in Vinnitsa, lived in Crimea before the conflict and served in the SBU counter-intelligence. He came to Slaviansk together with Strelkov. The relationship between Bezler and Strelkov was unstable, see http://www.c-inform.info/interviews/id/73.

leader. The ROA leadership was thus constantly contested by a multitude of disparate groups. The existence of a large number of "internal leaders," the loyalty to whom may have been much stronger than to the battalion commander led to whole groups often moving from one battalion to another in the summer of 2014. Groups could also join other battalions when the leader withdrew from further participation. Finally, many commanders delegated their authorities to someone, because they did not want to fight; they were commanders in name only, they coordinated some groups of people at best.

Mobilization

In the pre-war stage the mobilization involved various population strata — participants of political movements or organizations, professional, territorial or friendship networks. The primary groups consisted of former comrades-in-arms, colleagues, friends, people living in the same neighborhood, in the same settlement, members of pro-Russia organizations. Four components contributed to the mobilization: Absence of resistance; Kyiv's policy; growing fears after the ATO was announced; and the fire in the Trade Unions Building in Odesa as well as clashes in Slaviansk, Mariupol, and Kramatorsk. Those who represented the political top echelon of the protests and represented its militant component often took the lead.

The formation of primary groups was supported by joint activities such as participation in rallies, patrolling and setting up checkpoints. At the next stage, the militarization of these groups and their transformation into combat units took place — thanks to people who assumed leadership, united disparate groups and who had access to weapons and a military background. Leaders — many of them former military, security and special forces officers — turned the primary groups (sometimes partly armed) into more or less effective combat units.

Russian Volunteers, Organizations and the State

In this section, I will demonstrate how the recruitment channels of volunteers from Russia worked, and how these volunteers joined the groups in the Donetsk and Luhansk Regions. I will also show how the channels through which humanitarian and military loads were sent to these regions worked, what role the Russian state played and how Russia's involvement (including governmental, non-governmental structures and ordinary citizens) affected the development of the armed groups in the Donbas.

Russian Volunteers: Recruitment, Travel Arrangements, the Role of Organizations

Russian nationals first appeared in the Donbas in spring 2014, i.e. before the start of the combat phase.[34] On the one hand, it may have been random individuals (like one of the ROA leaders) or political activists supporting the anti-Maidan protests. Some specifically went there to join one of the battalions, also thanks to the recruitment efforts made by the battalions themselves (such as Vostok). The volunteers' inflow from the Russian Federation gradually grew as the active warfare began. Personal ties played an important role in the arrangement of the Russian volunteers' arrival. The involvement of former comrades-in-arms made it easy to find the "right" people, who would help to get across the border, liaise with the training camps and individual battalions. A military background was in itself a helpful factor, it allowed to quickly put together a group of volunteers, even from strangers.

Crossing the border and interaction with a specific battalion was enabled by intermediaries—personal connections, "coordinators" whose contact details could be found in social media groups and organizations that usually first transported the volunteers to the training camps and collection points in the city of Rostov in Russia. To cross the border from Russia to Ukraine independently was the more dangerous, especially during the first months, since the

---

34   Apart from Russian nationals, nationals from other countries acted as combatants too; they were supporters of communist or nationalist (including neo-Nazi) ideologies, see https://meduza.io/feature/2018/08/03/v-italii-raskryli-delo-o-verbovke-naemnikov-na-voynu-v-donbasse-sredi-podozrevaemyh-neo fashisty-i-posledovateli-dugina.

border was still being controlled by Ukrainian border patrol. Furthermore, no one could guarantee that those who independently and clandestinely crossed the border, would meet a Russian detachment and not a Ukrainian one. If some volunteers managed to cross the border by themselves but had no connections with the battalions, they went to local collection points where they were allocated.

Apart from personal ties and information on social media, thanks to which it was possible to directly contact the coordinators who helped volunteers to cross the border and get in touch with the training camps, it was also possible to contact one of many organizations that were involved in expediting volunteers from Russia and former USSR republics. Some of these organizations were established a long time ago, for example, such nationalist movements as Other Russia, Russian National Unity or Russian Imperial Movement or those that appeared during the patriotic uplift in 2014 (Humanitarian Army, Helping Novorossiya Movement, Novorossiya Humanitarian Battalion). Among the already existing movements, Russian nationalists (imperialists, monarchists, national-Bolsheviks) were prevalent who lately had been in opposition to the Russian authorities and criticized the existing regime for its laxness. Among the new movements that sprang up during the patriotic uplift, supporters of nationalist views were also prevalent; in various ways, they mixed with the supporters of the left-wing idea in its anti-capitalist and pro-Soviet version. Both had established channels that allowed them to send volunteers to specific battalions. For instance, in the case of Other Russia, it was the Zaria battalion (LPR) and the Piatnashka battalion (DPR), in the case of the Russian Imperial Movement, it was the First Slavic Brigade. Inside these battalions, they formed separate detachments into which volunteers who had arrived through these channels were integrated.

The first volunteers, mostly nationalists, went to the Donbas as early as in spring 2014. Some members of Other Russia took part in the take-over of Crimea and later crossed the border and stayed on in the city of Slaviansk. While these were predominantly individual initiatives at the very beginning in which mostly members of existing organizations and movements were involved, later on more or less stable structures were established that ensured a regular flow of volunteers from Russia to the Donbas. For example, the Interbrigades movement was created on the basis of the Other Russia party; the main function of the movement was to deliver humanitarian aid and volunteers. These channels could be used by anyone, regardless of his or her views and political preferences. The activity of these recruitment organizations was widely advertised, including on social media; they managed the flow and quality of volunteers, depending on their assessment of the stage of the conflict. At the beginning of summer 2014, some organizations were trying to select only the most suitable candidates for warfare and rejected those without sufficient military background. Later, however, when the encirclement battles started, they became less choosy.

The organizations that provided the irregulars with material support and dealt with the traffic of volunteers performed several functions. First, they made crossing the border easier and reduced the associated risks; second, they helped volunteers to join a specific battalion; third, they provided support "on-site"; fourth, they selected volunteers rejecting some and accepting others. Sometimes, they would raise money for "reliable" members of the movement to get to and cross the border, but, normally, the volunteers would cover their travel expenses themselves. Not all organizations could offer local support and the selection of volunteers. One of the activists of the Other Russia movement recalls:

> "... Initially, it was difficult to get there in the first place. Therefore, we were helping volunteers to legally cross the border. Not going into details, we helped with it in order to prevent getting caught by the border patrol. .... Those were activities, independent from the state. Overall, it worked. It became easier when we won back the border. But most importantly, the militia was saved, since it was not integral. .... The units are very different in their quality. In supplies, ideology, in everything. Ending up in a good unit is worth a lot. Different commanders, due to their professional background or personal qualities, have a different attitude towards looking after the personnel (interview 4, male).

Interaction with Russia's Authorities

Russian organizations delivered humanitarian aid which included "dual use" goods or they provided the transport of volunteers. Some organizations raised funds, others dealt with the procurement and the delivery of the goods or organized the trip and support upon arrival. The Communist Party of the Russian Federation, for example, supported a "humanitarian" project—the Red Moscow–Patriotic Front for Helping Donbas—which collected camouflage, combat vests and radios. Some pre-existing charity foundations also supported the Donbas separatists, for example the Saint Basil the Great foundation created by the "Orthodox oligarch" Konstantin Malofeyev who had once employed both Igor Girkin (Strelkov) and Aleksandr Borodai. The St. Tikhon Foundation was created anew by Sergei Shishkin, a municipal deputy of the Moscow City Duma.[35] Mostly nationalist political movements were involved in the collection and transportation of humanitarian aid (e.g. Other Russia, E.N.O.T., Imperial Legion Russian Imperial Movement, Russian National Unity, Sputnik i Pogrom) as well as patriotic clubs and Cossack associations. Finally, in spring 2014, many different organizations sprang up that focused on the support of the "Novorossiya project," such as Igor Girkin's Novorossiya Movement, Yekaterina Gubareva's Humanitarian Foundation, the Humanitarian Battalion, the Angel Humanitarian Battalion, and the Novaya Rus Coordination Center. Some "humanitarian organizations" were involved in smuggling weapons to the Donbas.

For confidentiality reasons, I will refrain from mentioning the name of one of the organization that delivered weapons (let us refer to it as N for convenience) and the battalions it cooperated with. The interaction pattern of N was more or less typical of the summer of 2014. N's history started with a one-off event aimed at helping the activists of the separatist republics. Some of those who were later about to form N's coordinating core (that mostly consisted of famous Russian bloggers) were initially planning to go to the Donbas and join a militia themselves. However, one of its leaders (lets

---

35 http://www.rbc.ru/politics/12/08/2014/942270.shtml.

us refer to him as M) received a message from one of his "network friends" who stayed in the separatist territory which said that the situation was unclear, he also asked to send bullet-proof vests, helmets, combat boots, tactical vests, and radios for at least a few people. M had been for some time part of a nationalists and leftist political "crowd", he used his connections to raise money to purchase the material. A considerable amount was required since it was not possible to buy only a few sets. He published a message on social media; a few famous individuals in the "crowd" vouched for him. Within a week, he managed to raise a significant amount of money (around 650 thousand rubles) which he spent on the required material and sent it to Luhansk.

After his first successful attempt, M continued to supply the war material and arms to some detachments. He bought the weapons that were written off as a result of the disposal of the inventory in artillery supply depots in Russia. At the time (June–July 2014), the border between Russia and the Luhansk and Donetsk Regions was very loosely guarded by both sides, and there were no problems whatsoever as far as smuggling the goods across the border was concerned. The border patrol personnel were aware of the designation of the goods and the battalion they were being sent to. While humanitarian aid, dual-use goods, weapons, and volunteers arrived unhindered on Ukrainian territory, armed combatants crossed into Russian territory, and the Russian police did not even try to stop them. Injured combatants were admitted to and treated in Russian hospitals located first of all in the Rostov region which borders on the Luhansk and Donetsk Regions.

The organization N was in touch with several battalion commanders to whom they supplied arms and war materials. The organization also supplied medication and equipment to local hospitals and dealt with the transfer of volunteers. N's stance was to send the materials only to those who were in the "front line," i.e. directly involved in warfare. In order to establish contact with those they wanted to deliver the equipment to, N's members began to go to the ATO zone and meet the battalion commanders there from mid-summer 2014 onwards. The consignments started only after a "mediator" on the ground was sure that the battalion that had requested the support was indeed participating in the warfare.

In summer 2014, Ns weekly collected income amounted to around one million rubles. The money was all spent on purchasing equipment. The purchased goods were registered, photographed and sent to the border; after crossing the border, the materials were received by a convoy of the destination unit, and the moment of acceptance was photographed.

Various Russian government offices soon started taking an interest in M's activities and, in exchange for "keeping a blind eye on his activities," asked him to carry out some assignments, such as collecting information on the territory of the separatist republics. The information concerned Russian nationals who participated in the war on the Ukrainian side or were helping Ukrainian volunteers. The deliveries by Russian organizations, consisting of arms and equipment, food, goods and medication, enhanced the battalions' autonomy which the forming public administrations of the unrecognized republics lacked at that time. The condition for the battalion's autonomy was the lack of active government interference, both from Russia and the unrecognized republics. The separatist republics' governments were still weak and did not have sufficient resources to equip the battalions. Russian politicians, parties, official organizations, secret services and law enforcement, displayed loyalty to the Russian supportive organizations – it ranged from non-interference (border patrol personnel, police) to targeted assistance (seeing the injured at hospitals, advisers' interference in conflict situations, sending specialists to train combatants, training camps in the Rostov region (Westerlund/ Norberg 2016). Non-governmental organizations and associations, including those established in spring 2014, managed to provide equipment and volunteers for the battalions. The loosely guarded border and non-interference of the secret services in their clearly illegal activities were major prerequisites. Russia's interference did not pre-suppose direct control over what was happening on the territory of the LDPR – they were ready to support the pro-Russia forces but did not control them (Robinson 2016).

Battalions: The Combat Stage of the Conflict

According to our calculations, in summer 2014, 20 to 25 large armed groups and some small units were operating on the territory of the LDPR. It is not possible to provide an exact number of combatants; however, according to the data as of the end of June 2014, their number was around 9.000–10.000, 19.000–23.000 as of 19 August 2014, later it varied from 35.000 to 55.000 people.[36] As of summer 2014 the militias were quite disparate internally, a general hierarchical structure was lacking as well as a unified command. The militias were partly formed from already established small groups that had their leaders. Battalions often consisted of people who knew each other and who were united by a leader. Members sometimes had brought their own weapons to the battalion. Individual groups that operated under the guidance of their leader could fuse with others or left them again after the beginning of the combat phase. This affected the subornation within the battalion. One of the combatants from the Prizrak battalion described the situation as follows:

> "When Prizrak came to Alchevsk [end of June 2014], it was joined by small local units. Those were the battalions named after Nevski from Alchevsk, Brianka, and the Yermak battalion, and a few individual units. But such a structure turned out to be difficult to manage and not viable. Our unified brigade consisted of disparate units that lived lives of their own" (interview 16, male, born in 1973).

Within one and the same battalion there could have been groups fully manned with volunteers from Russia or other countries and groups that mostly consisted of locals. They could have been fully manned with people having combat experience, former law enforcement officers, members of veteran organizations or some political associations, for example, the Russitch sabotage and

---

36 https://zn.ua/UKRAINE/iz-chego-sostoit-dnr-sostavlena-shema-ierarhii-sep aratistov-147959_.html; https://vz.ru/news/2014/8/19/701132.html; https://lenta.ru/news/2017/11/28/avakov/; https://news-front.info/2016/08/03/ocenochnaya-moshh-armij-ldnr-na-1-avgusta-2016-goda-konstantin-shhemelinin/?utm_referrer=https%3a%2f%2fwww.google.ru%2f.

assault reconnaissance group.³⁷ They could also consist of ordinary people who did not have any combat or political experience. Moreover, battalion personnel often changed. Not only did individuals come and go, but also entire groups. One of the informants referred to the militia as a "feudal system," when the field commanders had their own armed detachments, and "people could move from one detachment to another" (interview 1, male, born in 1965). At times different parts of one and same battalion could occupy different areas, having a considerable degree of autonomy as regards both the battalions' internal and combat routine. Supplies, the provision of arms and munition or wages often depended directly on the commanders. There was no steady supply of weapons to the battalions. Some informants spoke of an abundance of weapons in specific units, whereas others complained about an extreme lack of weapons. Finally, in most battalions, combatants did not share the same political views. Even though units were formed on the basis of a shared ideology (Milchakov's group, detachments of Other Russia in the Zaria battalion, Volunteer Communist Battalion in the Prizrak battalion, some detachments of the Imperial Legion), members often held different political views. The unity of associations that had transformed into battalions regularly depended on the charisma and trust in their leaders. The simultaneous recruitment of individuals and groups into a battalion and separate detachments by default created an internally disparate structure with several power centers, and the commander's authority was often fictitious. The leaders of the units were usually either elected by the unit members or had been the original leaders of the group that remained under their command and authority.

---

37   The "Russitch sabotage and assault reconnaissance group" was led by Aleksey Milchakov as part of the Batman Rapid Response Group. Alexey Milchakov (born 1991 in St. Petersburg) is a Russian neo-Nazi and suspected war criminal, he has been linked to atrocities in both Syria and Ukraine. A close relationship of Russitch to the Wagner Group has been reported. Milchakov and the commander of the Wagner group, Dmitry Utkin, served in the 76th Guards Air Assault Division of the Airborne Force.

The detachment or unit commanders were responsible for organizing the training of the combatants while instructors from Russia took part in the training of the combatants. The power of the commanders relied foremost on the personal authority, which was at times easily contested as a result of internal conflicts over casualties, the lack of supplies, the change of the area of operation or disagreements with a commander's course of action.

The constant movement of individuals and groups from battalion to battalion, and the personnel turnover as a whole did not allow to form a unified "vertical of power" even at the level of specific battalions. Besides, the "vertical of power" was weakened as some groups centered around their commanders and the commanders focused on their groups. The lack of a military background of most volunteers, which inevitably led to mistakes and losses also contributed to that. This is why the group leaders often felt that they were free to disobey the battalion commanders' orders, justifying their behavior by having to take care of their own unit and the other combatants. In some cases, the conflicts were resolved with the help of Russian advisers (especially when it came to clashes between locals and volunteers from Russia with military experience). For instance, one of the respondents spoke about a "misunderstanding" with Givi, who sent them to defend Donetsk airport.[38] They became aware that he had also sent a reconnaissance group there which eventually got cut off and could not get back. They left their position to help the recon detachment get out of the cordon. Givi called the respondent a deserter. A conflict broke out between them, and Givi ordered to send the respondent down "to the dungeon." M then contacted the Rostov south-eastern brigade, and they contacted Moscow.[39] And those from Moscow sorted the conflict out straight away (interview 11, male, born around 1990). It is safe to assume that M was also helped because he had combat experience from other wars and the camp in Rostov, which he and

---

38 Givi—nom de guerre of Mikhail Tolstykh, the former Somali battalion commander.
39 The training camp in Rostov, where they were being trained before they were helped to cross the border and get to the territory of the Donetsk Region.

his group were sent to, had some connection to Russian security agencies.

The presence of the Russian advisers in the Donbas in summer 2014, different to the previous period, was only sporadic and thus, supposedly, complicated subordination within the battalions. "Punitive methods" were the main way to maintain the discipline in the battalion, but the methods of discipline enforcement varied not only from battalion to battalion but also within the battalions. Some spoke about cruel punishments for drinking alcohol while on duty and execution for looting; others, on the contrary, said that looting was encouraged by the commanders, and alcohol was not banned. Usually, the punishment for the violations (drinking alcohol, disobeying orders, "drunk shooting", looting, etc.) included correctional labor or the "pit."

Supply

In summer 2014, there was no centralized supply system for the battalions. If they did receive anything from the "center", it happened very irregularly. Therefore, the combatants very often had to procure everything, from their uniform to food, medication and equipment, themselves – this also affected their wages. When the conflict first started, many experts tried to calculate how much the Russian state spent on the militia's wages.[40] The militiamen did not receive any payments in the first months, or, if they did, only now and again, different amounts and in different currencies (in hryvnias, rubles, and dollars). The amounts of one-off payments may have varied between several thousand hryvnias and 1.000 US dollars. Here again, much depended on the leaders of the specific detachments and units. In summer 2014, the battalions were handsomely supported by the civil population. Sometimes, the civilians bought uniforms for them, but more often, they supplied the battalions with food. The combatants topped up their supplies by taking whatever they needed from abandoned shops and confiscating

---

40 http://www.rbc.ru/investigation/politics/15/06/2015/5579b4b99a7947b063440210.

vehicles or premises for "war purposes." Russia sent humanitarian aid to sustain the battalions. Part of it was distributed by the new leadership of the republics and the other part went directly to the specific battalions or units.

The battalions began to take over the tasks of the temporarily disabled government, mostly in law enforcement. They introduced curfews and precluded some violations of law. Some refer to that period as the "golden times," trying to emphasize how much better the battalions coped with governance compared to what it was like before the war. Sometimes, individual combatants and battalions also helped the locals, for example, shared the food that they were supplied with and gave local people some money. Others controlled the delivery of humanitarian aid and its local distribution. The voluntary or enforced support that combatants received from the locals was an important factor ensuring the battalions' relative autonomy from the republic's authorities.

Coordination of Battalions' Activities

The factors causing the battalions' internal disparity and complicating their coordination are repeated in the challenges faced in the coordination of the whole militia. Igor Girkin (Strelkov), who was from late April 2014 to mid-August 2014 the military chief of the separatists in the Donetsk region, explains that his attempts "in July to August to consolidate the command at least in the territory of the Donetsk Region did not succeed, since there were units that expressly refused to submit to his command and had their own financing and supply channels." Some units, such as Vostok, not only refused to submit but did not interact with "headquarters," nor did the Cossack formations. Others (Oplot, Prisrak, Batman) did submit at some point to the operational command. Girkin described his interaction with his Russian "headquarter" which was located in Krasnodon and was supposed to consolidate the republics' command: "I only sent them the operational situation every morning and evening in those front sectors where the units under my command fought."[41] The poor coordination between the battalions resulted from their relative autonomy from each other and from the republics` public administrations. The coordination between the battalions usually relied on personal interaction. Many combatants spoke about the lack of information regarding the location of other battalions, this led to accidental clashes.

During the second (combat) stage disparate groups united into battalions which were, however, still internally diverse. Often, the groups that were part of a battalion were quite autonomous from each other and the battalion commander. In a certain sense, Igor Girkin's resignation in August 2014 can be considered a landmark moment. On multiple occasions, Girkin claimed that he had been forced to leave the Donbas, otherwise the arms shipments from Russia would have been stopped. "They counted on peaceful resolution, allegedly. Because of this, my stay there was deemed counter-productive. And I will be honest, it was also done by means of certain blackmail and direct pressure, by the cessation of aid delivery from the territory of Russia."[42] The resignation of the two major characters with whom Russia's active involvement in the conflict was associated at that time (Igor Girkin leaving the military scene and Aleksandr Borodai leaving the political scene), paradoxically marked the transition from targeted interventions to institutionalized control, from disparate and rather autonomous militia detachments led by individual commanders to a centralized military structure, controlled by Russian advisers.

The Third Stage: Centralization

In September 2014, the DPR and LPR leaderships pronounced the establishment of joint armed forces and appointed Lieutenant General Korsun as Commander-in-Chief of the United Army of Novorossia, which resulted in the creation of a joint People's Militia which consisted of two corps, one deployed in the DPR and the other in the LPR. In March 2015, Igor Plotnitski, head of the self-

---

41 http://istrelkov.ru/interview/414-igor-strelkov-intervyu-izdaniyu-the-insid er.html.
42 http://svpressa.ru/war21/article/103643/?rss=1.

proclaimed Luhansk People's Republic from 14 August 2014 to 24 November 2017, signed an order according to which from April 5, 2015 onwards, all armed formations that had not joined the law enforcement structures of the republic and had not turned in their weapons by April 4, would be declared illegal. As early as on April 7, the LPR Information Centre reported that there were no illegal formations left in the republic. A similar order was signed by Alexander Zakharchenko, the head of the DPR.[43]

On the whole, the purpose of the transformation of the irregulars into the People's Militia was to destroy the autonomy of the battalions and thus dismantle the unofficial system of leadership, on which authority and discipline relied inside the battalion. Battalions were in future to receive their supplies only through government authorities. This implied the introduction of accounts and records, a centralized distribution of humanitarian aid, and the establishment of control over the battalions.

The composition of the armed forces changed, too, the irregulars turned into a regular army. The presence of Russian military advisers in the LPR and DPR became a permanent feature. They got positions in military agencies and thus institutionalized Russia's presence. The Russian advisers turned into the centre of coordination. The transformation of irregulars into a regular army began in autumn 2014, but the last battalion, Prisrak, got integrated only in January 2016. One of the first actions that led to limiting the battalions' autonomy was to establish control over the delivery of humanitarian aid. By autumn 2014, the irregulars were no longer able to rely on the resources of the territory that they controlled. Everything that could have been taken from the abandoned shops and warehouses had been taken; many locals had left, and those who stayed were themselves in need of help. In autumn 2014, the deliveries of humanitarian aid were no longer controlled by the irregulars. The units could only count on supplies that they received from the republic's authorities which increased their dependency, since if they refused to obey, they could easily been cut off from supplies.

---

43 http://svpressa.ru/politic/article/118012/.

This loosening or even break-up of close ties with local supporters changed the very nature of the armed groups and the self-perception of their members. Anti-Maidan protests, the seizure of the administration buildings, the division of the separatist territories and gaining control over them were associated not only with the disruption of order and lawlessness but also with the feeling of empowerment. The loss of this connection triggered disappointment and a feeling of senselessness for many members of the armed groups. Strange though as it may seem, the switch to "regular" salaries that began in autumn 2014 added to the demoralization of some battalions. While some battalions received payment, others did not. The arbitrariness was caused by lack of coordination in the new state structures, but not paying salaries was also a lever to influence the battalions, furthermore while corruption allowed individuals to pocket money foreseen for salaries or to fiddle with the books.

Salary payments were destined for fewer people than were actually on the payroll, which sometimes led to splits and the dissolution of some units. The formation of the People's Militia also, quite deliberately, contributed to dispelling battalions. Some battalions joined the armed forces as separate groups which allowed them to retain their staff and internal chain of command (for instance, the Batman Rapid Response Team), whereas others were created from scratch or on the basis of the disbanded units. For instance, Prisrak that was the last to be included in the regular army in January 2016, was first "asked just to disband and distribute the small groups around different battalions" (interview 16, male, born in 1973). The decision on the disbandment of Vostok which became part of the army in August 2015, resulted in the break-up of the whole battalion. The formation of the regular army coincided with the outflow of Russian volunteers. Many of them had come for several months, and it was time for them to go back home. It was made clear to the others that their services were no longer required. Some members of the Russian nationalist groups, who had also counted on establishing local branches of their movement were at some time deported outside the LDPR.[44] One of the activists and combatants from Other Russia commented:

> "What is happening there, everyone is at each other's throat. And even when we were leaving, it was already clear, that we were in the locals' way. Being there, we were in their way while they were dividing their country, stealing non-ferrous metals, robbing the abandoned houses. We are in their way, they are embarrassed to do this while we are there" (interview 2, female, born in 1980).

Ideological differences became obvious too. Initially, many combatants came hoping that it would be possible to create the real "Russian World" in Novorossiya and implement their political program without any resistance by Russia's government's law enforcement, but it became clear with time that their hopes were not meant to come true.

> "... In 2014 [in the LDPR] there were no government structures; a guerilla war was going on. As soon as the front was there and different Russian advisers turned up, as soon as Russian aid started flowing in, the LDPR slowly turned into a mini-Russian Federation. Maybe it will be good in the long term. But that was not the ideal that we had fought for. Because here, we are fighting with the [Russian] Federation, with its drawbacks, and they are creating the very same thing" (interview 4, male)

For the same reasons, some movements stopped sending humanitarian aid to the LDPR. For instance, the Novaya Rus movement curtailed its military aid program, because the "ideological principles of Novaya Rus" turned out to be diametrically opposite to the stance of the LPR leadership."[45] That said, Russia's financial presence grew. According to various sources, Russia topped up a considerable part of the LDPR budget. Finally, from autumn 2014 onwards, the outflow of the local irregulars began, some left because of "being disarmed" or disbanded, others because of conflicts with the leadership, still others did not want to obey the army discipline (interview 16, male, born in 1973).

---

44 For instance, the supporters of Other Russia: https://www.svoboda.org/a/27027191.html.
45 https://alex-anpilogov.livejournal.com/39333.html.

The creation of the regular army considerably affected the perceptions of those who had joined the militia in spring and summer 2014. Many spoke about backdated dismissals that allowed the army not to pay the promised compensations to the families of those killed in action, about the absence of help to those who were injured while in service, and about low pensions. Finally, the newly formed People's Militia consisted of young people who had not taken part in warfare but joined up when the People's Militia was created. For them, in the context of unemployment and a dramatic fall of living standards, military service looked like one of the most promising careers. With an average salary in the region of 4.000 to 8.000 rubles, the military paid much more. The privates' starting salary was 15.000 rubles; unit commanders were paid 30.000.

All these changes not limited the autonomy of the units; they also changed the very perception of military service. Effectively, despite the patriotic rhetoric, they turned military participation into just an ordinary job. The experience of spring and summer supported dispositions that dramatically differed from those necessary for service in the People's Militia, namely self-organization and initiative instead of subordination, empowerment instead of obedience, equality instead of hierarchy, opportunity to criticize the leaders instead of silence, opportunity to choose (the battalion, the leader, the behavior) instead of absence of any choice. At the initial stages of the military conflict, members of the armed groups believed that they had the authority to act on their own volition, not having to answer to anyone. They perceived the leaders of the armed groups as their equals (those who pursue the same objectives) even though they had more authority because they were trustworthy. When all of it was questioned, military service considerably lost its meaning for the members of the armed groups of the first wave.

The visits of the Russian advisers, as well as more or less regular trips to Moscow and Rostov undertaken by the LDPR officials and individual field commanders, were not a rare occasion in summer 2014. However, from autumn 2014, the presence of the advisers became permanent and their participation in the leadership of the "people's army" became institutionalized. The Russian advisers turned into commanders. The advisers were mostly high-level military men, but not necessarily with combat experience. A certain number of advisers were assigned to each unit. Their task was to turn the irregulars into an army that would have hierarchies, army discipline and relevant training.

Conclusions

The formation of armed groups in the LPR and DPR started in spring 2014 with the mobilization associated with the anti-Maidan protests. People came together on the basis of personal ties (friends and acquaintances), professional connections (former military, members of the same political groups and organizations), territorial belonging (people living in the same district or town) and ad hoc meetings with people in the rallies. Charismatic leaders united and militarized these disparate groups. The second, combat stage, was marked by the arrival of Igor Girkin's (Strelkov's) equipped and professionally trained paramilitary group in the city of Slaviansk. Armed clashes began in big cities such as Kramatorsk and Mariupol, in the aftermaths of the fire in the trade union building in Odesa on May 2, 2014. These events changed the perception of the situation on both sides and turned a conflict into a war. In summer 2014, groups and individual volunteers from Russia and other countries began to join the separatist battalions. Various movements and organizations, mostly nationalist and left-wing, set up channels which made it possible for the Russians to take part in the military conflict and get to the Donbas. The battalions were relatively autonomous from each other and the political center. The third stage — the beginning of centralization — started with the law on the creation of the LDPR armed forces in autumn 2014. The battalions became dependent on centralized resource distribution. The inflow of humanitarian aid from Russia decreased and was controlled by the new leadership of the unrecognized republics. The coercive integration of the battalions into the joint military structure, the Ministry of State Security, began. Part of the militiamen of the first wave, both locals and those from Russia, gradually abandoned the new army as they were unhappy with the changes. Finally, Russia institutionalized its presence. The Russian military advisers got permanent positions in the LDPR armed forces structures, and the budgets of the republics were mostly replenished with money from Russia. The battalions' loss of autonomy and their legalization occurred along with the strengthening of Russia's influence. Ad hoc interventions and support by pro-Russian forces were replaced by institutionalized interference and management.

References

Melnyk, O. (2014), From the "Russian Spring" to the Armed Insurrection: Russia, Ukraine and Political Communities in the Donbas and Southern Ukraine. Paper presented at the 10th Annual Danyliv Research Seminar, University of Ottawa, 29 October—1 November, https://www.youtube.com/watch?v=8anWRfBvWnc.

Westerlund, Fredrik; Johan Norberg (2016): Military Means for Non-Military Measures: The Russian Approach to the Use of Armed Force as Seen in Ukraine, in: The Journal of Slavic Military Studies 29/4, pp. 576-601.

Robinson, Paul (2016), Russia's Role in the War in Donbass, and the Threat to European Security, in: European Politics and Society, 17/4, 2016, pp. 506-521.

The Far-Right Predecessor Organizations of the Ukrainian Irregular Armed Units

Anton Shekhovtsov

Introduction

In September 2015, Dmytro Yarosh, then leader of the Right Sector political party and the irregular armed group of the same name, said in an interview to the late journalist Pavel Sheremet:

> "I feel rather comfortable being at war, because I prepared for it for 20 years. Morally and psychologically, I was ready for these things". (Sheremet 2015)

At that time, Yarosh was treated in a hospital in Dnipropetrovsk, later renamed Dnipro, for injuries he had sustained when a shell burst in a battle with pro-Russian separatists and Russian forces close to Donetsk airport earlier that year. Yarosh was one of many far-right activists who had joined the Russian-Ukrainian war on the pro-Ukrainian side, and one of many who, indeed, had prepared to fight against potential Russian aggression long before it actually started in 2014.[1] In fact, a significant part of the irregular armed groups that started to appear from 2014 onwards built upon far-right predecessor movements, groups and political parties. This chapter provides an overview of far-right parties and movements whose leaders and members formed irregular armed units after the start of the Russian-Ukrainian war in 2014. It discusses their history, ideology and activities during the 2014 revolution and the early stages of these units' formation.

By the late 1990s, all major far-right parties had already formed paramilitary subdivisions. Even though Ukraine's law "On Associations of Citizens" prohibited forming paramilitary organizations by civil associations including political parties, the far-right parties evaded this by registering paramilitary subdivisions as

---

1 Some Ukrainian far-right activists — those who were ideologically pro-Russian — joined the forces fighting against the Ukrainian army and police.

sports or youth organizations. The far-right Ukrainian National Assembly formed the paramilitary Ukrainian National Self-Defence (UNSO) in 1991; the Congress of Ukrainian Nationalists – "Stepan Bandera Trident" (Tryzub) in 1993; the "State Independence of Ukraine" (DSU) – "The Guard of the DSU" in 1993; and, finally, the Social-National Party of Ukraine – the Patriot of Ukraine in 1999. According to Ukrainian historian Eduard Andryushchenko,[2] all these paramilitary organizations had three main objectives: (1) to defend Ukraine's independence and territorial integrity in the event of foreign aggression; (2) to bring a far-right party in power in the event of a civil war or revolution; and (3) to protect a party's public activities from political opponents as well as to attack political adversaries (Andryushchenko (2011).

Table 1. Organizational origin of far-right activists who formed specific irregular armed units

Party/movement	Irregular armed unit
All-Ukrainian Union "Freedom"	Kyiv-2
	Sich'
	Carpathian Sich'
"Brotherhood"	St. Maria
Patriot of Ukraine / Social-National Assembly	Azov
Right Sector	Volunteer Ukrainian Corps Right Sector
UNA-UNSO	UNSO

The first objective was what Yarosh, a former member of the "Stepan Bandera Trident" group, had implied in the above-mentioned quote: Ukrainian far-right activists had already anticipated that Russia would act against Ukraine in the 1990s and even formed organizations that would resist such aggression. Therefore, it was only natural that – when Russia-backed separatists started an armed conflict with the Ukrainian authorities in March/April 2014 – far-right activists formed several irregular armed units (see Table 1). However, not only did they join 'established' far-right

---

2   At least until 2011, Andryushchenko was a member of the Tryzub.

units but also some units that were formed after the Maidan revolution, for example, the battalions Aidar, Tornado and Dnipro-2.

All-Ukrainian Union "Freedom"

The All-Ukrainian Union "Freedom" was registered on October 16, 1995 under the name "Social-National Party of Ukraine" (SNPU). Its registration in 1995 was an official recognition of the party that had already existed since October 13, 1991 when the SNPU's first convention took place. Yaroslav Andrushkiv was elected party chairman, while Yuriy Kryvoruchko became responsible for ideology. Oleh Tyahnybok (organization) and Andriy Parubiy (youth) also joined the SNPU. Before establishing the SNPU, its leaders led minor nationalist organizations: Andrushkiv and Kryvoruchko headed the "Guard of the Rukh", Tyahnybok — the "Student Brotherhood", and Parubiy — the Organization of the Ukrainian Youth "Legacy". For its official symbol, the SNPU chose a modified version of the so-called "wolf's hook" used by several SS divisions in the Third Reich and some European post-war fascist organizations, for example the Greek Golden Dawn.

The SNPU propagated its far-right ideology through its newspaper *Social-Nationalist* and the magazine *Reference Points* (Orientiry) as well as brochures and collections of essays it published. The ideology of the SNPU was a combination of romanticization of the Ukrainian history, White racism and anti-Russian and anti-American sentiments. For example, Parubiy, the editor of *Reference Points*, wrote that in ancient times, Ukraine had been one of the most powerful military forces in Europe and "protected the White race against the total invasion by the Asiatic hordes." (Parubiy 1998) According to another ideologue of the SNPU, "internationalist Marxism and cosmopolitan liberalism are alien to the spirit of the Ukrainian nation" considered "the root of the White race". Russia and the US, as Parubiy put it, were "two centres of globalism" that aimed at destroying the "European spirit" and "identity of European nations". Interestingly, however, the SNPU was pro-NATO, which went against the general trend among European far-right parties whose anti-Americanism was generally coupled with anti-NATO sentiments.

In the first half of the 1990s, the SNPU had already formed the paramilitary "national protection squadrons," based on the "Student Brotherhood" — but the party failed to register them officially. Their name was, most likely, a reference to the SS (*Schutzstaffel* — translated from German as "Protection Squadron"). The SNPU attempted to legalize its paramilitary wing again in the second half of the 1990s when Parubiy and another member of the party, Leontiy Martynyuk, transformed the "national protection squadrons" into the Society of Assistance to Armed Forces and Navy of Ukraine "Patriot of Ukraine". At its zenith in 1999–2001, the "Patriot of Ukraine" had 300–400 members. (Andryushchenko 2011, p. 45)

The SNPU, which was most popular in western Ukraine, especially in Lviv where it was formed, however, did not succeed in the Ukrainian national elections. It never managed to enter parliament under the proportional electoral system, and only Tyahnybok was elected to parliament in Lviv's single-member districts twice, in 1998 and 2002. He was not nominated by the SNPU but rather by two electoral alliances — the far-right "Less Words" bloc formed by the SNPU and SIA, and the national-conservative bloc "Our Ukraine".

In the early 2000s, the SNPU was in crisis, but in 2003, Tyahnybok initiated the party's re-organization process. On February 14, 2004, the party held a convention at which several important political decisions were adopted: (1) Tyahnybok replaced Andrushkiv as the leader of the party; (2) the SNPU changed its name to the less questionable All-Ukrainian Union "Freedom" (Svoboda); (3) the "Patriot of Ukraine" was disbanded; (4) the party discarded the "wolf's hook" and adopted the image of a right hand showing three fingers as its new official symbol; and (5) the political rhetoric became more moderate, while overtly racist sentiments in the party press were largely suppressed. The party leadership believed that tactical moderation would make Svoboda more respectable and, thus, more popular.

The re-organization of the party did not immediately translate into electoral success. Svoboda took part in the 2006 parliamentary elections but obtained only 0.36 percent of the vote. In the early parliamentary elections in 2007, the party doubled its vote, but it was still insignificant: 0.76 percent. Before the elections in 2007, Svoboda presented its "Programme for the protection of Ukrainians" partly integrated into the new party program in 2009. Among other things, the "protection of Ukrainians" proposed (1) introducing lustration policies that would help remove communists, former agents of the Soviet security services and adherents of former president Leonid Kuchma from Ukraine's political system; (2) introducing criminal responsibility for any manifestation of anti-Ukrainian sentiments ("Ukrainophobia"); (3) registering citizens' ethnic origin in passports; (4) withdrawing from the Russia-dominated Commonwealth of Independent States, strengthening the regional Organization for Democracy and Economic Development that included Georgia, Ukraine, Azerbaijan and Moldova (also known as GUAM) and building "the Baltic–Black Sea geopolitical axis".[3]

Svoboda achieved its first electoral breakthrough in the early regional elections in Ternopil oblast held on March 15, 2009, when it obtained 34.69 percent of the popular vote. Two major factors determined Svoboda's victory: First, the breakdown of the national-democratic political camp. It consisted of President Viktor Yushchenko's "Our Ukraine" and Prime Minister Yulia Tymoshenko's "Bloc of Yuliya Tymoshenko" (BYuT) — Yushchenko and Tymoshenko were allies during the "Orange revolution" in 2004 but had turned on each other by 2009. The conflict between the two "Orange" leaders undermined the popularity of both, while Svoboda — affiliated with the "Orange" forces but not affected by their conflicts — filled the void that Yushchenko and Tymoshenko left empty due to public disillusionment. Furthermore, Tymoshenko's bloc and another relatively popular national-democratic party "Front for Change" abstained from campaigning as they considered the early regional election in the Ternopil region illegitimate. Second, Svoboda's organizational efficacy. The party started campaigning immediately after the early elections were announced in December

---

3   Prohrama VO 'Svoboda' (chynna), 24 May (2009), Svoboda, https://web.archive.org/web/20091220221935/www.svoboda.org.ua/pro_partiyu/prohrama.

2008. Therefore, it took full advantage of the boycott of the elections by the major contenders and enjoyed its fair share of the media spotlight. Svoboda consolidated its progress in the regular regional elections in 2010, when it won seats in seven *oblast* councils transcending the boundaries of western Ukraine, i.e. Svoboda's traditional bulwark, and making its way into the central part of Ukraine, namely the Kyiv *oblast*. The year 2012 was arguably the most successful year for Svoboda in its entire history. In the 2012 parliamentary elections, which Ukraine held under a mixed electoral system, Svoboda acquired 10.44 percent of the proportional vote and won in 12 single-member districts. Thus, the party secured 36 seats in the Ukrainian parliament, while its 37th elected member, Ruslan Koshulyns'kyy, became Deputy Chairman of parliament.

Svoboda's Success

The party's success was determined by a combination of several factors. First, the assumption of power by pro-Russian oligarch Viktor Yanukovych. He became president in 2010, but the nationally oriented public expressed its indignation when his regime made a dramatic slide towards an even more corrupt, authoritarian system of governance. Many also believed that he had betrayed the national interests of Ukraine. During the first two years of Yanukovych's rule (2010–2012), popular protest against his regime became so radicalized that even pro-democratic voters were ready to support Svoboda — a party that they perceived as the most radical opposition party. Second, Yanukovych's regime, which never considered Svoboda a significant threat, instrumentalized the far-right party's ability to steal votes from the mainstream national-democratic forces (as the regional elections in Ternopil *oblast* in 2009 had shown) and helped make Svoboda more popular by increasing its media visibility and other measures aiming to consolidate Yanukovych's rule. Third, national-democratic parties opposed to Yanukovych accepted Svoboda as a legitimate ally and thus provided the far right with a window of political opportunity which it took advantage of by mobilizing its activist base and efficient campaigning. During 2013, however, the popularity of Svoboda radically declined. Public opinion polls suggested that, in November 2013, only 5.1 percent of the voters would have cast a ballot for the party. Moreover, Tyahnybok's presidential rating fell from 10.4 percent in March 2013 to 3.6 percent in November 2013.

Svoboda's determination to reclaim the popular support it had lost in 2013 was one of the major reasons why this far-right party supported the pro-European and pro-democratic protests known as Euromaidan. The latter started in November 2013 as a response to Yanukovych's decision not to sign the Association Agreement with the EU, and Svoboda used the protests as a platform for self-promotion and propaganda. The second major reason for supporting Euromaidan was Svoboda's opportunism. After the publication of sociological research following the 2012 parliamentary elections, it realized that despite originally being a Eurosceptic party it had ironically enjoyed the support of most pro-European voters among any Ukrainian party elected to parliament in 2012. Thus, to not lose its pro-European voters, Svoboda toned down its Eurosceptic rhetoric and openly supported the pro-EU agenda. The third major reason was ideological. In 2013, Ukraine faced a fateful choice: To sign the Association Agreement between Ukraine and the EU or to join the Russia-dominated Customs Union of Belarus, Kazakhstan and Russia (and, in 2015, the Russia-dominated Eurasian Economic Union). As the choice between the EU and the Customs Union was presented as a "zero-sum game", Svoboda had not much of an option but to support rapprochement with the EU as it implied a withdrawal from the Russian sphere of influence, one of the oldest ideological orientations of the party.

During the revolution, it became increasingly evident that Svoboda cooperated with a small neo-Nazi group called S14 (sometimes also spelled C14), or Sich',[4] led by Yevhen Karas. The number "14" is a reference to "Fourteen Words", a slogan coined by US white supremacist David Lane: "We must secure the existence of

---

[4] Sich' was a name of the polity of the Zaporozhian Cossacks in the 16th to 18th centuries.

our people and a future for white children". The symbol of S14 features a Celtic cross used by many White Power movements and organizations across the Europeanised world. S14 was originally formed in 2009 as an independent group but started to cooperate with Svoboda that provided a cover for their activities. Karas was a member of Svoboda and also an official representative of Andriy Illenko, one of Svoboda's parliamentary candidates in the 2012 parliamentary elections. As Ganna Grytsenko, Ukrainian researcher of the far-right, argues, "at first S14 was a kind of unofficial Svoboda side project, doing things that were useful to the party, but for which Svoboda did not want to take official responsibility". (Grytsenko 2017-18) S14 was often involved in violent protests against real estate developers in their city. (Gonta 2015) These protests were popular among residents in Kyiv who were critical of various real estate projects. And while the participation of S14 activists in these protests was beneficial for Svoboda, it could always distance itself from the actions of S14 if they went beyond the law.

On December 1, 2013, S14 helped Svoboda occupy the Kyiv city state administration building and turned it into the base of its paramilitary formation named after Sviatoslav the Brave, the ancient prince of Kyiv. C14's Sviatoslav the Brave formation was also a unit of the Maidan self-defense — a loose militant movement that defended the Euromaidan protests against the police from 2013 to 2014. While C14 did contribute to the defense of the protesters from the police, it also damaged the unity as well as the pro-democratic image of the Maidan protests as it displayed racist banners in the occupied Kyiv city state administration building, attacked journalists, volunteer medical workers and other Maidan activists. At the beginning of February 2014, police put Karas on the wanted list, but the case against him was dropped after the fall of Yanukovych's regime. In April 2014, after the start of the Russian–Ukrainian war, C14 constituted the core of the voluntary battalion Kyiv-2 that Karas had joined himself. On June 18, 2014, Svoboda's members also established the core of the Sich' battalion. However, after Ihor Gumenyuk, a Sich' fighter, threw a grenade during the violent protests near the Ukrainian parliament on August 31, 2015, killing four and wounding many more National Guard servicemen, Svoboda publicly disassociated itself from the Sich' battalion and vice versa.

In May/June 2014, Oleh Kutsyn, a former member of the paramilitary unit "State Independence of Ukraine" (DSU) who joined Svoboda after the Ministry of Justice of Ukraine had annulled the registration of the DSU, assembled a group of volunteers consisting of Svoboda's members who started collecting and delivering supplies to the Ukrainian National Guard and the army. On August 27, 2014, this volunteer group was transformed into the separate volunteer platoon "Carpathian Sich'" led by Kutsyn. In 2015, the "Carpathian Sich'" became part of the 93rd Mechanized Brigade of the Armed Forces of Ukraine. After the 93rd Brigade was pulled from the anti-terrorist operation (ATO) in early 2016, the "Carpathian Sich'" was disbanded and some of its members cancelled their contracts with the armed forces while others took up other posts in the army (Stek 2016).

Patriot of Ukraine–Social-National Assembly

When Svoboda disbanded the "Patriot of Ukraine" (PoU) in 2004, its local organizations in Zhytomyr and Kharkiv refused to disband. In Kharkiv, the PoU revived itself in 2005 under the leadership of Andriy Bilets'ky. He had been a leader of the Kharkiv branch of the far-right paramilitary Stepan Bandera Trident (Tryzub) organization. The group officially registered as a regional social organization on January 10, 2007 adopting the SNPU's "wolf's hook" as one of its symbols. In 2005 to 2007, the PoU still cooperated with Svoboda, but by the end of 2007, relations between the two organizations soured. The main reason for the break-up seemed to be ideological, as the PoU itself explained in December 2007. In particular, the PoU accused Svoboda of "the absence of the struggle with the System, suppression of the racial and immigration issues, liberalism and parliamentarianism", while boasting that the PoU was an anti-systemic, racist, authoritarian and anti-capitalist organization that fought against immigration.[5] Yet, articles of some

---

5   Zayava Organizatsii 'Patriot Ukrainy' pro rozryv stosunkiv z VO 'Svoboda', Patriot Ukrainy, 15 December 2007, https://web.archive.org/web/20071219

of the most radical members of Svoboda such as Andriy Illenko and Yuriy Mikhal'chyshyn could still be found on the PoU's website. In contrast to Svoboda that aspired to appear a respectable, if still radical right-wing populist force, the PoU, which could be described as a neo-Nazi organization, did not hide its extremism in either ideological or practical terms. According to Bilets'ky, the PoU was "a military organization that professe[d] the ideology of Ukrainian social-nationalism. [Its] task [was] to fight for the creation of a powerful Social-Nationalist movement that encompasse[d] the entire nation and gain[ed] power in the State". (Bilets'ky 2007). Bilets'ky also called for the "Racial purification of the Nation" and claimed:

> "In this pivotal century, the historical mission of our Nation is to helm and lead the White Peoples of the entire world into the last crusade for their existence. The crusade against the subhumankind headed by the Semites". (Bilets'ky 2017, p. 4)

Moreover, as the main ideologue of the PoU, Oleh Odnorozhenko, argued, Ukrainian "social-nationalists" treated "human races" as separate biological species and considered that only "the white European people" could be called "homo sapiens". (Odnorozhenko 2007, p. 51) The PoU also produced anti-immigration and racist leaflets, as well as publishing booklets promoting fascist ideas and Holocaust denial. The PoU was also active outside its publishing and Internet activities: its activists staged torch-lit marches, attacked non-Ukrainian merchants in Kharkiv, organized protests against students of Asian and African origin, and conducted paramilitary exercises in different regions of Ukraine. Various reports and witness accounts suggest that PoU members were also involved in extortion or protection rackets. Businessmen would also sometimes hire PoU members to "solve" problems with their competitors.

In 2008, the PoU initiated the creation of the Social-National Assembly (SNA) that united the PoU and some minor far-right

---

115119/http://www.patriotukr.org.ua:80/patriotukr/index.php?rub=news_w&id=260.

groups, namely the Ukrainian Alternative, National Action "Rid", and "Sich'" Association. In Kharkiv, the newly established SNA was still essentially identified as the PoU. In 2009, the organization had around 150 members,[6] while in 2010, it claimed that it had branches in 20 cities and towns across the country (Odesit 2010). Despite the propagation of neo-Nazi views and racist activities, the PoU/SNA had had few problems with the police in Kharkiv. In 2008, for instance, the police seemed to prefer not to notice any public events organized by the PoU/SNA, although it held nine that year.[7]

The PoU/SNA was less successful in avoiding police attention in Kyiv. On October 14, 2008, the PoU/SNA, as well as several other small far-right organizations such as the Ukrainian National Labour Party (that was never registered as a party) and "Brotherhood" staged a march in honor of the wartime Ukrainian Insurgent Army. The march escalated into violence, and the riot police detained 147 far-right activists, predominantly from the PoU/SNA (Bilozers'ka 2008). However, most detained activists were soon released, and only nine of them, including the PoU/SNA's Oleh Odnorozhenko, Serhiy Bevz, Vadym Troyan and Yaroslav Minervin, faced being charged with the crime of hooliganism; eventually, the charges against them were dropped.

In 2009 to 2010, the courts issued formal notices to 22 PoU/SNA members in the Kharkiv region for the breach of public order, but no further action was taken.[8] In June 2009, a leader of the minor, Kharkiv-based nationalist group "The Hope of the Nation" Oleksiy Kornyev reported to the police that he had been beaten up by PoU activists including Odnorozhenko.[9] The police opened a

---

[6] Prava lyudyny v Ukrayini – 2008. 12. Deyaki aspekty prava na zakhyst vid dyskryminatsii ta borot'by z rasizmom i ksenofobiyeyu, in: Prava Lyudyny, 24 June 2009, http://khpg.org/index.php?id=1245855623.

[7] Prava lyudyny v Ukrayini – 2008, in: Prava Lyudyny, 24 June 2009, http://khpg.org/index.php?id=1245855623.

[8] Prava lyudyny v Ukrayini 2009-2010. XII. Zakhyst vid dyskryminatsii, rasizmu ta ksenofobii, in: Prava Lyudyny, 22 February 2011, http://khpg.org/index.php?id=1298355452.

[9] Predsedatel' organizatsii 'Nadiya natsii' utverzhdaet, chto ego izbili chleny organizatsii 'Patriot Ukrayiny'. Vozbuzhdeno ugolovnoe delo (dopolneno)', in:

criminal case against Odnorozhenko, but the investigation moved nowhere for a few years.

The reason for the largesse towards the activities of the PoU/SNA might have been the backing it received from Arsen Avakov, who was the head of the Kharkiv regional state administration from 2005 to 2010. All this changed from the second half of 2011 onwards when the PoU/SNA started having problems with the police. In August that year, pro-Russian nationalist Sergey Kolesnik and PoU activists got into a fight in the PoU/SNA office in Kharkiv. Kolesnik wounded two PoU members, namely Ihor Mykhaylenko and Vitaliy Knyazhes'ky, but was himself severely beaten and stabbed (Dotsyak (2013). Mykhaylenko and Knyazhes'ky were arrested in September and charged with attempted murder. Although Bilets'ky did not take part in the fight, he was charged with robbing Kolesnik and arrested in December.

At the same time, in August 2011, several PoU/SNA activists, including Ihor Mosiychuk, Volodymyr Shpara and Serhiy Bevz, were arrested and charged with the attempt to blow up a monument to the Soviet leader Vladimir Lenin in the city of Boryspil close to Kyiv. In 2010, Mosiychuk, a former member of the UNSO and SNPU, and Shpara helped rig Vasylkiv mayoral elections in favour of Serhiy Ivashchenko who had been nominated for mayor by Yanukovych's Party of Regions (But 2010). In July 2012, Odnorozhenko was detained by the police on charges that could be traced back to 2009 when he presumably took part in the attack on the ideological opponent of the PoU/SNA (Voynyts'ky 2012). Odnorozhenko was allowed bail in November 2012, but then again arrested on December 23, 2013. Thus, Odnorozhenko was the only leading figure of the PoU/SNA who had a possibility to take part in the early stages of the 2014 Maidan revolution, and he was indeed present during the protests together with the SNA activists.

After the fall of Yanukovych's regime, on February 24, 2014, the Ukrainian parliament made a highly questionable ruling — on

---

Status Quo, 23 June 2009, http://www.sq.com.ua/rus/news/politika/23.06.20 09/predsedatel_organizacii_nadiya_naciyi_utverzhdaet_chto_ego_izbili_chle ny_organizacii_patriot/predsedatel_organizacii_nadiya_naciyi_utverzhdaet_ chto_ego_izbili_chleny_organizacii_patriot/.

the initiative of populist independent member of parliament Oleh Lyashko who led the Radical Party of Oleh Lyashko — that set free all the arrested activists of the PoU/SNA who were declared "political prisoners": Bilets'ky, Odnorozhenko, Mykhaylenko, Knyazhes'ky, Mosiychuk, Shpara and Bevz were among them.[10] The same ruling set free some other Ukrainian far-right activists, including Vladyslav Popovych who would later co-found the "OUN" armed unit together with Mykola Kohanivs'ky.[11] On February 27, 2014, the PoU/SNA's "political prisoners" were granted individual amnesty by acting President of Ukraine, Oleksandr Turchynov.

Shortly after his release, Bilets'ky returned to Kharkiv which already witnessed a heavy presence of pro-Russian separatists and Russian fighters in early March 2014. On March 14, dozens of them — including Arsen Pavlov ("Motorola") — attacked the office of the PoU/SNA with guns. In the fighting, two pro-Russian separatists were killed, and following the fighting, the police arrested around 30 people who had defended the PoU/SNA office. According to Bilets'ky, all arrested activists were later released thanks to the backing by Avakov, who at that time was acting Minister of Interior of Ukraine, following the fall of Yanukovych's regime (Butusov (2017).

According to Stepan Baida, a leader of the PoU/SNA in Donetsk, many of the group's activists went to Kyiv after the Maidan demonstrations had come to an end and gathered in the old building of the Kozats'ky hotel there.[12] During these gatherings — and against the background of the pro-Russian protests and upheavals in Ukrainian regions — the group that counted around 30 people — decided to form a self-defense unit against potential pro-Russian separatists. In April 2014, Bilets'ky, Mosiychuk, and the leader of the small far-right "Brotherhood" party Dmytro Korchyns'ky, met

---

10 Pro zvil'nennya polity'yazniv, Legislation of Ukraine, 24 February 2014, http://zakon3.rada.gov.ua/laws/show/786-18/ed20140224.
11 https://vchasnoua.com/interview/15817-zam-kombata-oun-vladislav-popov ich-ya-4-goda-vo-vremya-pravleniya-yanukovicha-sidel-v-tyur-me-za-to-chto-borolsya-s-narkobiznesom-v-svoem-gorode
12 Kak sozdavalsya polk 'Azov', UkrLife, 30 June 2015, http://www.ukrlife.tv/vi deo/suspilstvo/kak-sozdavalsia-polk-azov.

Avakov and his adviser Anton Gerashchenko in order to receive support for their self-defense unit. After approximately one month of consultations and negotiations — facilitated by Oleh Lyashko — between the Ministry of the Interior and the leadership of the PoU/SNA, they formed the Azov unit, officially named as the patrol and inspection service battalion under the command of the Donetsk Department of Internal Affairs.[13] The PoU/SNA's Volodymyr Shpara, who obtained a rank of senior lieutenant, was appointed commander of the Azov battalion while Bilets'ky retained his status of the "spiritual" leader of the movement. Korchyns'ky's "Brotherhood" started cooperating with Azov by forming the Jesus Christ Squadron within the battalion. However, given political and personal contacts between Korchyns'ky and Lyashko,[14] the Jesus Christ Squadron was integrated into the Shakhtars'k battalion under the name of the St. Maria Squadron, backed by Lyashko.

UNA-UNSO

The Ukrainian National Assembly (UNA) is one of the oldest far-right parties in Ukraine and has a long and complicated history. The UNA was founded on June 30, 1990, i.e. almost one year before the fall of the Soviet Union, as the Ukrainian Interparty Assembly (UIA) that consisted of several smaller organizations and groups. At that time, the organization opposed national-communist and national-democratic groups that dominated the pro-sovereignty movement in the Ukrainian Soviet Socialist Republic. On August 19, 1991, at the beginning of the 1991 Soviet coup d'état attempt, which aimed at strengthening the Soviet Union and removing Soviet President Mikhail Gorbachev from power, the UIA started forming paramilitary groups to confront the coup plotters. These groups were later called the Ukrainian national self-defense (UNSO). On September 8, 1991, the UIA was renamed UNA. Yuriy Shukhevych, a son of Roman Shukhevych who was one of the most

---

13 Anton Gerashchenko, "Vchera ispolnilos'...", Facebook, 6 May 2016, https://www.facebook.com/anton.gerashchenko.7/posts/1046993312054182.
14 For example, Korchyns'ky's wife, Oksana Korchyns'ka, would run for parliament in October 2014 on the list of Lyashko's Radical Party.

revered Ukrainian nationalists and a dissident in Soviet times, was elected UNA leader.

Its ideology was quite unique for Ukrainian ultranationalism, especially in the 1990s (Solchanyk (1999: 292). While the overwhelming majority of the Ukrainian far-right parties supported Ukraine's independence—i.e. in contrast to Ukrainian pro-Russian far-right parties—and focused on the Ukrainian ethnic core, the UNA insisted that Ukraine had to become the center of a pan-Slavic military-political bloc with its capital in Kyiv. In essence, this insistence implied that the UNA was ready to cooperate with like-minded, pan-Slavic parties and organizations from Belarus and even Russia. Between 1992 and 1994, members of the UNA-UNSO participated in the armed conflicts in Transnistria—fighting the Moldovan forces, in Georgia—fighting the Abkhaz separatists and in the Russian Federation (Chechen Republic)—fighting the Russian federal forces. In September 1994, Shukhevych left the UNA (he was replaced by Oleh Vitovych and Dmytro Korchyns'ky was elected deputy chair)—in protest of an allegedly increasing "pan-Slavisation" of the UNA's ideology. While the UNA successfully provoked riots and conflicts with Ukrainian law enforcement agencies, its results in the elections left much to be desired. Although it was officially registered only at the end of 1994, it nevertheless participated in the 1994 majoritarian parliamentary elections in March and won only three seats in western Ukrainian single-member districts: Oleh Vitovych, Yuriy Tyma, and Yaroslav Ilyasevych became members of parliament.

On July 18, 1995, during the funeral of the Patriarch of the Ukrainian Orthodox Church Volodymyr, UNSO members organized mass public disorders and clashed with the police. This led to the annulment of the party's registration later that year, but the UNA managed to re-register on September 29, 1997. The 1998 parliamentary elections, in which it took part under the leadership of Eduard Kovalenko, turned out to be disastrous for the party, as it failed to win any seats in the single-member constituencies and gained only 0.39 percent of the votes. During the mass protests in 2000/2001 against Ukraine's President Leonid Kuchma, known as "Ukraine without Kuchma", the UNA-UNSO was, again, involved in violent clashes with the police, and several members of the party were arrested, including one of its leaders, Andriy Shkil'. While Shkil' was in jail, a UNA faction led by Kovalenko and Mykola Karpyuk staged a coup inside the party and turned it into an organization loyal to Kuchma and the presidential administration (Lebid' 2001).[15] This was the beginning of a series of splits inside the UNA, where every splinter group claimed legitimacy as the "true" UNA. At the 2002 parliamentary elections, held under the mixed system, the UNA gained only 0.04 percent of the votes, but Shkil', who was still in jail during the elections and was removed from UNA leadership by Kovalenko and Karpyuk, still managed to win a seat in a Lviv single-member district and left jail as his election granted him immunity. As a member of parliament, Shkil' joined Yulia Tymoshenko's parliamentary group.

In 2004, in the period before the presidential election in Ukraine, which triggered the so-called "Orange Revolution", members of Kovalenko's UNA were involved in various attempts to discredit the popular national-democratic candidate Viktor Yushchenko and undermine his electoral support. Arguably the most infamous attempt to damage Yushchenko was the fascist march "in his support". It was conceived by Kuchma's presidential administration and orchestrated by the members of the UNA controlled by Kovalenko. In early summer 2004, he declared that his party would hold a march in central Kyiv in support of Yushchenko as a presidential candidate. Yushchenko's office immediately replied that they never needed that support and did their best to distance themselves from Kovalenko's provocative initiative. Yet Yushchenko's office could not stop that march, and on June 26, 2004, the march, which was supersaturated with Nazi imagery and Nazi salutes, proceeded. This was the first time the authorities granted permission to hold a mass far-right march in central Kyiv. After the march, Andriy Shkil', who led those UNA groups that opposed Kovalenko's group, expelled several members from the party, includ-

---

15 V UNA-UNSO—perevorot, Korrespondent, 19 November (2001), https://korrespondent.net/ukraine/politics/33631-v-una-unso-perevorot

ing prominent members Ihor Mazur, Roman Zaychenko and Andriy Bondarenko, for collaboration with Kovalenko, whose "fascist march" was unanimously seen as an act of "political technology" against Yushchenko. However, given the organizational chaos of the UNA in that period, it is difficult to say whether Shkil' had the legitimate right to expel anyone from the party.[16]

In 2005, the UNA had more or less stabilized. Yuriy Shukhevych, who was already more than 70 years old at that time, was elected head of the party again, while Mazur, Zaychenko and Bondarenko renewed their legitimacy in the UNA. This did not help the party in the electoral process. In the 2006 parliamentary elections, it won 0.06 percent of the votes, and it did not take part in the early 2007 parliamentary elections. At the 2012 parliamentary elections, it was supported by 0.09 percent of the voters.

In summer 2013, members of the UNA and the PoU/SNA participated in the Kyiv protests against police dereliction of duty. While the protests, which increasingly turned against the government, were still ongoing, Ukrainian investigative journalists revealed that Mazur, who was coordinating the participation of the UNA, was ready to end the protests in exchange for a financial reward from the representatives of the authorities.[17] After these revelations, Mazur officially declared that he would resign from all the leading positions in the UNA, but it is doubtful that he did resign.[18] As later developments show, Mazur was still in charge of the UNA, as Shukhevych was too old to lead the party.

---

16 Bondarenka, Mazura ta Zaychenka vyklyucheno z lav UNA-UNSO za orhanizatsiyu ta uchast' u fashysts'komu pohodi u Kyevi—Andriy Shkil, Vgolos, 24 September 2004, http://vgolos.com.ua/news/bondarenka_mazura_ta_zaychenka_vyklyucheno_z_lav_unaunso_za_organizatsiyu_ta_uchast_u_fashystskomu_pohodi_u_kyievi_8213_andriy_shkil_31283.html.
17 Glava kievskoy UNA-UNSO slozhil polnomochiya iz-za skandala s podkupom, Levy bereg, 22 July 2013, https://lb.ua/news/2013/07/22/214668_glava_kievskoy_unaunso_slozhil.html.
18 Glava politsoveta UNA podal v otstavku iz-za skandala s podkupom, in: Zerkalo nedeli, 24 July 2013, https://zn.ua/POLITICS/glava-politsoveta-una-podal-v-otstavku-iz-za-skandala-s-podkupom-126216_.html.

In early November 2014, just a few weeks before the Euro-Maidan protests, the UNA elected Oleksandr Muzychko, a convicted criminal and long-time member of the UNA-UNSO who had taken part in the First Chechen War, acting head of the political council of the party (Chimiris; Abramov 2015). During the Euromaidan protests, the UNA found itself divided. Some, like Mykola Karpyuk and Ihor Mazur, wanted to be part of the Right Sector movement, some a separate protest force. The Right Sector was largely based in the Trade Unions Building, while the UNA had its base in a tent outside of that building. Despite this division, the UNA and Right Sector often coordinated their activities during the protests.

In March 2014, after the fall of Yanukovych's regime, the UNA suffered two major blows. First, on March 17, Karpyuk was detained by Russian border guards at the Ukraine-Russia border. Apparently, Karpyuk had intended to negotiate with representatives of the Russian authorities about the non-recognition of the pre-annexation "referendum" in Crimea. Karpyuk's travelling to Russia was most likely a trap set by the Russian security services with the help of their agents in Ukraine.[19] Second, the police initiated a criminal case against Muzychko who was killed by the police on March 24 resisting his arrest.

Despite the unease of some members, the cooperation between the UNA and Right Sector during the Euro-Maidan protests led to the merging of the two at the end of March 2014 signified by the adoption of the joint name 'Right Sector'. Yarosh was elected head of the party. Original members of the UNA, namely Shukhevych, Kostyantyn Fushtey and Valeriy Voronov, joined the leadership of the Right Sector. Interestingly, the PoU's Bilets'ky and Odnorozhenko also became part of the Right Sector party's leadership, but did not stay for long.

Yet, they failed to establish an integrated and functional Right Sector party, as the UNA part of the party felt marginalized. The

---

19   Karpyuk would later be sentenced to 22.5 years of imprisonment on the apparently manufactured charges of taking part in the UNSO's Chechen campaign in the 1990s.

cooperation of the armed units failed, too. For instance, Mazur joined the "Aydar" battalion, rather than the Right Sector battalion. Because of these developments, the UNA original leadership decided to form their own battalion, UNSO, in July 2014.[20] The battalion joined the Anti-Terrorist Operation at the end of October 2014.[21] On August 20, 2015, the UNA's wing of the Right Sector party officially registered as a separate party called "UNA-UNSO" (as the one already in existence in the 1990s), with Fushtey as the head of the party; Mazur would become one of Fushtey's deputies.

The Right Sector

The Right Sector movement was spontaneously formed as a broad coalition of far-right activists at the beginning of the Euro-Maidan protests. According to Andriy Pastushenko, a participant of the protests, the name Right Sector emerged accidentally on November 24/25, 2013, when one of the opposition speakers, fearing that the police would storm the tents installed on the Maidan square in Kyiv, asked "nationalist lads" who were present there "to hold the right sector, in other words, to protect the right side" of the protest camp against the police.[22] The Right Sector movement largely consisted of activists from the Tryzub paramilitary organization, UNA-UNSO, PoU/SNA, "White Hammer" and some other smaller groups. Three major leaders of the movement, Dmytro Yarosh, Andriy Stempits'ky and Andriy Tarasenko, had previously been members of the group Tryzub.

Tryzub was formed in 1993 as a Ukraine-based paramilitary wing of the Stepan Bandera branch of the émigré Organisation of Ukrainian Nationalists (OUN(B)). The Ukraine-based political wing of the OUN(B) was the Congress of Ukrainian Nationalists

---

20 L'vovskaya UNA-UNSO otpravit v zonu ATO svoy batal'yon, Polemika, 23 July 2014, https://web.archive.org/web/20140729133848/http://polemika.com.ua/news-150429.html.
21 Batal'yon UNA-UNSO otpravilsya v zonu ATO 'vooruzhenny do zubov', Polit-Navigator, 29 October 2014, http://www.politnavigator.net/batalon-una-unso-otpravilsya-v-zonu-ato-vooruzhennyjj-do-zubov.html.
22 A. Pastushenko (Syvyy) pro pochatok Maydanu i Pravoho Sektoru, YouTube, 10 April 2014, https://www.youtube.com/watch?v=zQUTLSUIqQ4.

(KUN), a far-right party founded by Yaroslava Stets'ko, the widow of Yaroslav Stets'ko, a former member of the OUN(B) and leader of the Anti-Bolshevik Bloc of Nations.[23] Despite this legacy and the fact that the KUN nominally remained loyal to the national-revolutionary doctrine of Bandera and Yaroslav Stets'ko, the KUN was arguably the most moderate Ukrainian far-right party in the 1990s. Its deputy head was Roman Zvarych, who could be considered a national-democrat and who tried to move the party away from its ideological legacy.

Tryzub, led by Vasyl Ivanyshyn who was previously a member of the UNA-UNSO, however, differed very much from the KUN. While the original aim of Tryzub was to protect events held by the KUN against political and ideological opponents, the group was also engaged in activities, including paramilitary training starting from 1994, that went beyond this original aim of self-help. In 1996, members of Tryzub were involved in several violent incidents that endangered the legality of the entire organization. At the beginning of that year, three Tryzub members attacked one of the military bases in the Kharkiv region, disarmed the guards and seized weapons and ammunition, but were eventually detained by the police and sentenced to six and seven years of imprisonment. In Dniprodzerzhyns'k, a group of Tryzub members became involved in a conflict with an allegedly criminal group, and, during the shoot-out, one of the Tryzub members killed an opponent. In autumn 1996, around 40 Tryzub members, who provided protection services to one of the factories in Chernivtsy, engaged in a fight with special police forces. Moreover, police searched homes of many other Tryzub members and often found guns. All these incidents led to an official inquiry into the legality of Tryzub. Yet, the organization managed to avoid a ban. Still, multiple criminal cases against Tryzub resulted in a dwindling number of members (Andryushchenko 2011, pp. 48-49. The legally problematic nature of Tryzub's activities might have also been the reason why Tryzub and KUN parted their ways in 1999. Also in 1999, Yevhen Fil, one

---

23   Yaroslava Stets'ko spent 47 years outside of Ukraine and returned to the country only in 1991.

of the founders of Tryzub, replaced Ivanyshyn as the head of the organization.

Until the end of 2013, when Tryzub was part of the core of the Right Sector, the organization had kept a relatively low political profile compared to other far-right organizations. At the 2004 presidential elections, Tryzub, and some other far-right organizations and activists, were involved in various political manipulation projects aimed at undermining electoral support for President Yushchenko. At that time, apparently with the backing from the Kuchma administration, several nationalist candidates were registered for the elections (Likhachev 2005). Among them were Bohdan Boyko, leader of the People's Movement of Ukraine for Unity;[24] Yuriy Zbitnyev, the leader of the virtual far-right "New Force" party; Roman Kozak, the leader of the fringe far-right Organization of Ukrainian Nationalists in Ukraine; and Dmytro Korchyns'ky, a former leader of the UNA-UNSO and then leader of the far-right "Brotherhood" party. These candidates' objective was to steal pro-Yushchenko votes from the right-wing segment of the political spectrum and to provide the electoral fraud machine with loyal representatives controlled by Kuchma's regime. In 2004, Boyko and his allies formed a coalition named "The Movement of Ukrainian Patriots" that was joined by his own party, the UNA-UNSO group led by Yuriy Tyma, Tryzub, and a few smaller groups.

In 2010, Tryzub started cooperating with Valentyn Nalyvaychenko, head of the Security Service of Ukraine (SBU) from 2006 to 2010. In 2012, Nalyvaychenko visited one of Tryzub's training camps and gave a tak to its members. In 2013, Nalyvaychenko wrote one of the preface comments to the book "The Nation and Revolution" authored by Dmytro Yarosh, one of the leaders of Tryzub since the 1990s. In his comment, Nalyvaychenko called Tryzub "important partners [for him], a fraternal organization" and "one of the most powerful, young Ukrainian patriotic organizations" (Nalyvaychenko 2003). While Nalyvaychenko also referred

---

24 One of several parties that used the word "movement" (Rukh) to confuse the voters and steal votes from the original and respected People's Movement of Ukraine.

to his cooperation with Tryzub in the framework of social and civic activities, he did not specify his role in this cooperation. However, given the fact that Nalyvaychenko joined the centrist Ukrainian Democratic Alliance for Reform (UDAR, headed by Vitaliy Klychko in August 2012, one can assume that Tryzub members took part in the UDAR's social actions. Moreover, from April 2013 until the end of February 2014, i.e. the time of the fall of Yanukovych's regime, Yarosh was one of several assistants to Nalyvaychenko, who was a member of parliament between 2012 and 2014.

Yarosh's friendly relations with Nalyvaychenko were presumably one of the reasons why the Right Sector enjoyed logistical support from the pro-democratic forces during the Maidan revolution, namely by Andriy Parubiy, the head of the Maidan self-defense and then a member of the pro-European center-right Fatherland Party. The Right Sector was officially the 23rd *sotnia* ("hundred") of the self-defense, and its base was located in the Trade Unions Building that hosted the "Headquarters of the National Resistance"—temporary offices of the major opposition parties that supported the Euromaidan. During the revolution, the Right Sector constituted one of the units of the Maidan self-defense. It was arguably the most violent group within the Euromaidan movement, apart from individual football hooligans, or so-called "Ultras". On January 19, 2014, a few days after the pro-Yanukovych majority in parliament had voted for the harsh anti-protest laws, the Right Sector was one of the main groups that were responsible for the radicalization of the protests as it made a violent, but unsuccessful, attempt to storm parliament. As the Right Sector was generally against Ukraine's integration into any international bloc, it considered the Euromaidan purely as the vehicle of a Ukrainian national revolution and considered its pro-European sentiments of no significance.

Ideologically, organizations that constituted the Right Sector during the Maidan revolution ranged from radical national-conservatism of Tryzub to the right-wing extremism of UNA-UNSO and the neo-Nazism of the PoU/SNA and "White Hammer".[25] However, none of these ideological strands were a unifying force for Right Sector activists. The neo-Nazis — due to the lower position of the PoU/SNA and White Hammer in the hierarchy of Right Sector — were a fringe element in the movement. What united these sometimes conflicting groups at the grassroots level was a combination of vehement opposition to Yanukovych's regime, which was widely considered as anti-Ukrainian and pro-Kremlin, the desire for "national liberation" and romantic militarism. Yarosh's leadership enforced this consensus, and contrary to his demonization in the (pro-)Russian media, it was he who, at the time of the Maidan revolution, tried to present a moderate image of the Right Sector by publicly denouncing racism and anti-Semitism (Nayem; Kovalenko 2014). However, the ideological differences between different groups started to play a more significant role in the course of the revolution, and, by the end of February 2014, the most extremist faction — mostly represented by the PoU/SNA and "White Hammer" activists — largely distanced themselves from the main faction led by "Tryzub". After the police had set fire to the Trade Unions Building in Kyiv, where the Right Sector was based, "White Hammer" activists relocated to the Kyiv City State Administration building which was occupied by Svoboda and its paramilitary wing C14 (Mel'nikova 2014).

In early March 2014, after the fall of Yanukovych's regime, two members of the "White Hammer" were allegedly involved in killing three policemen. Following a statement by the General Prosecutor's Office that Euromaidan activists might have carried out the murders of the policemen, the Right Sector leadership officially expelled the "White Hammer" from the movement. The distancing of the Right Sector from the neo-Nazis might have been underpinned by Yarosh's career ambitions. At the end of February 2014, he was

---

[25] One Ukrainian journalist who had "joined" the Right Sector to write an insider report also said that the views of the Right Sector activists "ranged from romantic nationalism and 'allegiance to glorious Cossack traditions' to plain neo-fascism", see Igor Burdyga (2014): Shag vpravo, in: Vesti, No. 26, 7-13 March, http://reporter.vesti-ukr.com/art/y2014/n8/8774-shag-vpravo.html.

apparently offered the position of deputy head of the National Security and Defence Council of Ukraine (then headed by Parubiy), but he rejected the offer. He had set sights on the deputy head position of the SBU (then headed by Nalyvaychenko), which he failed to secure, however.[26]

At the end of March 2014, the Tryzub faction of the Right Sector and UNA-UNSO merged into one political organization by relinquishing the name of UNA-UNSO and changing it into Right Sector. According to Yarosh, already in April that year, Right Sector activists led by Oleh Korotash started helping the Ukrainian military in eastern Ukraine by gathering intelligence and destroying enemy checkpoints (Viter 2015).[27] In June 2014, the Right Sector decided to form their own armed unit, and Yarosh announced the formation of the Volunteer Ukrainian Corps "Right Sector" (DUK PS) under the command of another prominent Tryzub member (Andriy Stempits'ky).[28]

Conclusion

Several armed units, namely Kyiv-2, Sich', Carpathian Sich', Azov, DUK PS and UNSO that were formed shortly after the beginning of the Russia–Ukrainian war, had a long history of paramilitary or violent activity. Together with other right-wing parties and movements, they were also involved in extortion and protection rackets and engagement in political manipulations orchestrated by more influential political forces. In no small degree, the formation of these armed units was influenced by the participation of many members of these far-right organizations in the Maidan self-defense coordinated by Andriy Parubiy, who was one of the main founders

---

26 Yarosh vede peremovyny shchodo yogo pryznachennya zamglavy SBU – zhurnalist, UNIAN, 28 February 2014, https://www.unian.ua/politics/891348-yarosh-vede-peremovini-schodo-yogo-priznachennya-zamglavi-sbu-jurnalist.html.

27 Dmytro Yarosh pro Dobrovol'chy korpus 'Pravy sektor'. Slov'yans'k. 20 July 2014 roku, YouTube, 1 August (2014), https://www.youtube.com/watch?v=aSOQhNNolqc.

28 Zvernennya Providnyka 'Pravoho Sektora' Dmytra Yarosha, Banderivets, 15 July 2014, https://web.archive.org/web/20150102220916/http://banderivets.org.ua/zvernennya-providnyka-pravogo-sektora-dmytra-yarosha.html.

of the SNPU's paramilitary "Patriot of Ukraine" group in the 1990s, but who had moved on towards mainstream politics since 2004. The far-right groups' participation in the Maidan revolution radicalized them; they were involved in attacks against law enforcement and state institutions.

The majority of far-right groups had been attached to registered political parties in the 1990s to protect political events of the SNPU, UNA and KUN as well as to attack political opponents. Another original objective of right-wing paramilitary formations was to defend Ukraine's independence and territorial integrity against Russia's aggression, and this particular objective became especially relevant after the Russian occupation and annexation of Crimea in February-March 2014. Another factor was Russia's military, economic and logistical backing of pro-Russian separatists in eastern and southern Ukraine in spring that year. While some of the organizations—most notably the UNA-UNSO—that contributed to the formation of armed units in 2014 had participated in combat operations in Moldova, Georgia and Russia in the 1990s, it is unlikely that this experience substantially helped them in fighting against pro-Russian separatists and Russian volunteers and military forces. The almost 20 years gap between the wars of the 1990s and the Russian invasion in 2014 would have been too large.

Only the Azov battalion, which was re-organized into the Azov regiment in autumn 2014, can be considered a successful armed unit in terms of development and securing state support. Svoboda, which contributed to the formation of Kyiv-2, Sich' and Carpathian Sich', lost its political significance after its poor performance at the 2014 parliamentary elections and failed to promote these armed units on the state level. The DUK PS was too diverse from the very beginning. Also, due to its criminal activities and reluctance to integrate into state institutions, it lost much of its relevance, especially after Yarosh left the Right Sector in 2015. The UNSO battalion, formed and backed by the UNA-UNSO, which had never enjoyed any significant electoral support or political representation, remained in the shadow of some other armed units. At the same time, the success of Azov seems to be underpinned by the Ministry of Internal Affairs' lasting support. The then Minister of the Interior, Arsen Avakov, had cooperated with the PoU, which formed the Azov battalion, since the time when PoU's leadership and Avakov had been jointly based in Kharkiv.

References

Andryushchenko, Eduard (2011), Paramilitarni struktury ukrayins'kogo natsionalistychnogo rukhu 90-h rr. XX st., in: Naukovi pratsi istorychnoho fakul'tetu Zaporiz'koho natsional'noho universytetu, No. 30, pp. 42-51 (43).

Bilets'ky, Andriy (2007), Ukrayins'ky rasovy Sotsial-Natsionalizm — ideolohiya orhanizatsii 'Patriot Ukrayiny', in: Ukrayins'ky Sotsial'ny Natsionalizm, Kharkiv: Biblioteka orhanizatsii "Patriot Ukrayiny", pp. 3-5 (3).

Bilozers'ka, Olena (2008), Poboyishche pid chas Pravoho marshu", Livejournal, 19 October, https://bilozerska.livejournal.com/91123.html.

But, Yuriy (2010), 'Chesni ta prozory' vybory: yak tse robylos' na Kyyivshchyni, Unian, 15 November, https://web.archive.org/web/20101118030209/https://www.unian.net/ukr/news/news-406471.html.

Butusov, Yuriy (2017), 14 marta 2014 goda — dobrovol'tsy Khar'kova otrazili ataku rossiyskogo terrorista Arsena Pavlova na ulitse Rymarskoy, Cenzor, 14 March, https://censor.net.ua/resonance/431983/14_marta_2014_goda_dobrovoltsy_harkova_otrazili_ataku_rossiyiskogo_terrorista_arsena_pavlova_na_ulitse.

Chimiris, Margarita; Vlad Abramov (2015), Nasha chuzhaya voyna, Vesti. Reporter, No. 31, http://reporter.vesti-ukr.com/art/y2015/n31/19162-nasha-chuzhaya-vojna.html.

Dotsyak, Tatyana (2013), Pokazaniya menyal po prinuzhdeniyu miltsii — delo 'Patriotov Ukrainy', ATN, 17 May, https://atn.ua/obshchestvo/pokazaniya-menyal-po-prinuzhdeniyu-milicii-delo-patriotov-ukrainy.

Gonta, Boris (2015), Medvedko i C14: ot bor'by s zastroykami k ubiystvu Buziny, in: Bukvy, 18 June, https://bykvu.com/mysli/3197-medvedko-i-s14-ot-borby-s-zastrojkami-k-ubijstvu-buziny.

Grytsenko, Ganna (2017-18), BBC Report on Ukrainian Nazi Group C14 Condemned by MP John Cryer, in: Searchlight (Winter), pp. 10-11.

Lebid', Nataliya (2001), Lyal'ki i lyal'kovody. Khto pyshe p'yesy dlya novoyavlenykh reformatorov iz UNA-UNSO, Ukrains'ka pravda, 20 November, https://www.pravda.com.ua/news/2001/11/20/2985283/.

Likhachev, Vyacheslav (2005), Mezhnatsional'nye otnosheniya v Ukraine v kontekste vyborov: polittekhnologii i provokatsii, Sova Center, 22 January, http://www.sova-center.ru/racism-xenophobia/publications/2005/01/d1122.

Martynyuk, Levko (1998), Chomu na nashikh styagakh znak 'Ideya Natsii', in: Antin Radoms'ky (ed.), Pravy napryam, Lviv.

Mel'nikova, Lyubov (2014), 'Bely molot' Maydana: 'My — ne politicheskie igrushki', RIA Novosti Ukraina, 30 April, https://rian.com.ua/analytics/20140430/346505793.html.

Nalyvaychenko, Valentyn (2003), Peredmova, Banderivets, http://banderivets.org.ua/peredmova-valentyn-nalyvajchenko.html.

Nayem, Mustafa; Oksana Kovalenko (2014), Lider Pravoho sektoru Dmytro Yarosh: Koly 80% krainy ne pidtrymue vladu, hromadyans'koi viyny buty ne mozhe, in: Ukrains'ka pravda, 4 February, http://www.pravda.com.ua/articles/2014/02/4/7012683/.

Odesit, Andriy (2010), Nomery PU u tvoyemu misti, VK, 22 January, https://vk.com/note64605627_9655977.

Odnorozhenko, Oleh (2007), Sotsial-Natsionalistychny rukh ta yoho osnovni zavdannya, in: Ukrayins'ky Sotsial'ny Natsionalizm, pp. 46-54, here p. 51.

Parubiy, Andriy (1998): Nash shlyakh, in: Antin Radoms'ky (ed.), Pravy napryam, Lviv.

Parubiy, Andriy (1999), Evropa vil'nykh natsiy, in: Orientiry, No. 1, p. 22.

Sheremet, Pavel (2015), Dmytro Yarosh: Ya na viyni komfortno sebe pochuvayu, bo hotuvavsya do nei 20 rokiv, in: Ukrains'ka pravda, 22 September (2015), https://www.pravda.com.ua/articles/2015/09/22/7082096/.

Solchanyk, Roman (1999), The Radical Right in Ukraine, in: Sabrina P. Ramet (ed.), The Radical Right in Central and Eastern Europe. University Park, pp. 279-296.

Stek, Levko (2016), Stvotyyet'sya naymana armiya, yaka ne zdatna peremahaty — komandir 'Karpats'koyi Sichi', in: Radio Svoboda, 13 April, https://www.radiosvoboda.org/a/27673230.html.

Viter, Marta (2015), Pozyvny Mol'far. Pys'mennyk na viyni, in: Ukrayins'ka Pravda. Zhyttya, 6 February 2015, http://life.pravda.com.ua/society/2015/02/6/188936/.

Voynyts'ky, Andriy (2012), Odnomu z lideriv 'Patriota Ukrayiny' O. Odnorozhenku prodovzhyly aresht, Status Quo, 9 July, https://web.archive.org/web/20131004215722/http://www.sq.com.ua/ukr/news/suspilstvo/09.07.2012/odnomu_z_lideriv_patriota_ukrayini_o_odnorozhenku_prodovzhili_aresht/.

Irregular Armed Groups in Ukraine
State Savior or State-Capture?

Andreas Heinemann-Grüder

The formation of irregular armed groups in Ukraine from spring 2014 onwards was a response to Ukraine's regular security services' glaring inability of or outright unwillingness to counter the Russian-sponsored separatism and military intervention by Russia proper on the Crimean peninsula and in the Donbas. In 2014, only an estimated 6,000 out of 204,000 military men in the regular armed forces were allegedly combat ready before the military confrontation over Crimea and in the Donbas started. The army was underfinanced, underequipped, and poorly trained; the service had a bad reputation (Lavrov / Nikolsky 2015, p. 59; Lebedev 2017). A significant part of Ukraine's state security apparatus had defected to the Russian side, especially on Crimea, but in the Donbas, too. During the opening stages of the war in the Donetsk basin, the army and the police forces were largely ineffective in separatist areas, often surrendering equipment or being overwhelmed in cities by civilian crowds. Pro-Russian separatists quickly gained large swaths of the territory. The Ukrainian government also lost control of the Ukrainian–Russian border, and this allowed for the inflow of Russian Special Forces, regular troops and mercenaries as well as military supplies from Russia, often under the guise of humanitarian assistance.

The study of irregular armed groups usually focuses on conducive or enabling conditions, among them political or economic grievances, greed, access to weapons or lootable resources, opportunities such as weak statehood or on onset conditions and conflict triggers such as political murder, terror attacks, pogroms, or excessive state violence. From the perspective of micro-dynamics, one looks instead at factors that transform opportunities into action, among them incentives to join an armed group, legitimizing strategies, interaction patterns between state and non-state actors (including violence towards civilians) and among irregular groups.

The study of micro-dynamics concerns the transformation of irregular groups into political or civil society organizations as well as their contribution to or impact on state building.

In this chapter I explain the conditions of success of irregular armed groups. Success is a relative term as it could be regarded as the ability to recruit members, take action, perform as a group or as the ability to preserve group coherence. Public visibility, size, the ability to adjust to changing circumstances or to provide long-term perspectives for its leaders and members can also be treated as indicators of success. Success is relative to the level of ambition and to expectations. I assume that the combination of leadership, networks of predecessor organizations, the motivation of group members, social capital and the shared worldview of a group explain why some are more successful than others.

We identified 19 larger and persistent pro-Ukrainian groups. These are: (1) Zoloti Vorota, (2) Pravyy Sektor, (3) Dnipro-1, (4) Azov, (5) battalion imeni Dzhokhara Dudaeva, (6) Aydar, (7) Donbas, (8) Shakhtarsk / Tornado, (9) Asker, (10) Artemivsk, (11) Myrotvorets, (12) Kyiv-1, (13) Kyiv-2, (14) Sich, (15) Kulchitskyi Battalion, (16) battalion imeni Sheykha Mansura, (17) battalion "OUN", (18) Svyata Mariya, and (19) S14. Only those groups with a distinct name and group insignia, an identifiable leader, an active media presence, and a record of operation were included in our study.

Between 2015 and 2018, we had conducted several rounds of structured and semi-structured interviews with respondents in areas controlled by the Ukrainian government—altogether more than 70, among them commanders of volunteer battalions, civilians affected by the violence in the Donbas basin, members of the national parliament, representatives of Ukraine's Ministry of Defense and the Ministry of Internal Affairs, international and civil society organizations representing veterans as well as victims of human rights abuses. Furthermore, we also used secondary literature, video clips and journalistic articles for the analysis.

One can discern several types of people who joined or formed the irregular armed groups: Maidan protesters who volunteered for an irregular battalion or the territorial defense (usually without military training and only short service time); volunteers who responded to Russia's annexation of Crimea and its intervention in Donbas and who had signed a temporary service contract for a period of at least six months; people with prior professional training in the military or the police who preferred to sign up with the official "territorial defense" of the Ministry of Defense or with the regular armed forces; and members of "partisan" platoons who usually came from the area under Russia's control and who often had prior combat experience.

Overview over the Volunteer Battalions

The Ukrainian irregular armed groups belong mostly to the category of pro-government militias since they were formed as a response to the pro-Russian insurgency and the military aggression by Russia, i.e., as defenders of Ukraine's state independence (Carey / Colaresi / Mitchell 2015; Kirschke 2000; Mitchell / Carey / Butler 2014; Carey / Mitchell 2016).The Ukrainian pro-state militias differ from many pro-government militias in other parts of the world that are formed to delegate repression, to commit human rights violations or to conduct extra-legal counter-insurgency operations. Most of the Ukrainian volunteer formations were created through the active participation of the Ukrainian Ministry of the Interior or the Ministry of Defense; only few had initially been autonomous, and even these depended on procurement and maintenance by state agencies. Nonetheless, the existence of irregular armed groups always implies a certain autonomy of action and of political identity if compared to state security services that are controlled by the executive branch.

Irregular armed groups in Ukraine can be differentiated into those that existed as right wing paramilitary groups with a distinct ideology and political ambition before the Maidan, groups whose core had been formed as part of the "self-defense forces" on the Maidan since December 2013, groups that were established between March and June 2014 by orders of the then Minister of the Interior, Arsen Avakov, groups formed by the Ministry of Defense, and finally groups originally formed by private companies for security purposes or groups representing local organized crime.[1]

The term battalion is widely used with respect to the irregular armed groups, although it lacks formal precision; it usually pertains to a military group the size of which varies between 300 and 1,200 people. Armies throughout the world have been using the term differently, but a battalion consists as a rule of a couple of rotes. In the context of the Ukraine conflict, the term "volunteer battalion" pertains to a distinct military unit with a name, a commander, a headquarters and distinct location, which was mobilized for the specific purpose of resisting the Russian annexation of Crimea and the separatism in the Donbas. Groups were often summarily called battalion, regardless of their size. The term battalion has, therefore, a broad meaning. At times, battalions were relabeled into regiments or brigades. A battalion consisted, as a rule, of infantry rotes, reconnaissance, artillery, communication units, a medical unit, and logistics. A rotte is made up of up to one hundred persons, these rotes were composed in turn of platoons (Russian *взвод*). The battalions often fought together with brigades; a brigade usually consists of 1,500 to 5,000 men.

Any military is characterized by a defined and known hierarchy as well as by internalized command structures. Yet, the irregular armed groups in Ukraine were often lumped together on an ad hoc basis; the men fighting together barely knew each other. Group coherence was not a given in the irregular armed groups but had to be produced and regularly reproduced. One of the key capabilities for survival in a combat group is mutual trust, based on a shared sense of purpose, and reliable communication. In this respect, the irregular armed groups (IAGs) proved highly vulnerable at the outset.

---

1   The notion "mafia group" is a shorthand for an irregular armed group, based on personal loyalty, patronage, strict hierarchies, which is engaged in organized crime.

The Portfolio

During the high-intensity stage of the violent conflict from spring 2014 to February 2015, the IAGs performed defensive and offensive tasks, they fulfilled police functions, controlled road posts, crossed the "line of contact" for reconnaissance and subversive purposes, they defended or re-conquered municipalities held by separatists and played an essential role in the major battles of the war (Ilovaysk, Mariupol, and at the airport of Donetsk). Since the regular police were frequently absent in the zone of the "Anti-terrorist operation" (ATO), volunteer battalions under the tutelage of the Ministry of the Interior fulfilled police functions, at times against members of other battalions, too, for example in cases of theft or racketeering.[2] Some of the volunteer battalions took over tasks which the regular security services could or would not fulfill. The government appreciated the benefit of battalions, for example in reconnaissance and in special operations across the frontline. The volunteers also acted as sappers. Some groups were formed from above, others through a bottom-up process, the latter usually had an ideology of their own, and their commanders were selected autonomously from government. In most cases, however, group formation can be described as a simultaneous process — bottom-up and bottom-down processes went hand in hand.

So called partisan units — not of battalion size — were additionally formed by groups such as the Right Sector or on the basis of close family ties or preexisting friendships. The partisan units fought an "invisible" war beyond the so-called line of contact, knowing the operational area and relying on informers on the ground. These small partisan units of platoon size closely cooperated with or received orders from the Ukrainian Secret Service (SBU) and were specialized on "diversion and sabotage" operations on the territories controlled by the separatists. Partisan units collaborated with other battalions such as Azov, Dnipro-1, the Right Sector, the 25th battalion "Kyivska Rus," the 128th mountain-infantry

---

2   Interview with Aleksey Borisovich Vemidskiy from the battalion Kharkiv-1 (2017).

brigade and the Organization of Ukrainian Nationalists (OUN).[3] The SBU used these "partisans" for special operations beyond the "line of contact." To our knowledge, "partisan" units were never formally included into any government services, their legal status and the regulations, command and control structures under which they operated remain shadowy.

The Autonomy of Irregular Armed Groups

Autonomy is best perceived as a continuum, ranging from tactical autonomy on the front, underpinned by informal coordination with the regular troops as in the case of the Right Sector to a complete formal subordination with some remaining islands of autonomy in personnel policy or in the conduct of storming operations, like in the case of the Azov battalion. The volunteer battalions retained a certain degree of autonomy even after their formal incorporation into the Ministry of the Interior or the Ministry of Defense.[4] Some battalions acted autonomously in the field or resisted to subordinate to orders by the command of the ATO of the Ukrainian government. The autonomy of IAGs has therefore been relative throughout; it pertains to some freedom of action up to political insubordination.

Members of battalions with a distinct political identity were usually critical of the President as the supreme commander, they did not see themselves as mere executioners of governmental decisions. The signing of the Minsk ceasefire agreements in 2014 and 2015 or the unwillingness to launch a military attack to reconquer the Donbas were, for example, interpreted by commanders of battalions such as the Right Sector or Aydar as cowardice or as high treason.[5] As Anna Colin Lebedev observed, the combatants felt loyal to their commanders and battalions as well as to Ukraine as a country, but not necessarily to the government or the institutions of the Ukrainian state (Lebedev 2017, p. 38). Some battalions engaged

---

3   Interview with 21-year-old Konstantin Savchenko, former partisan (2017).
4   Interview Serhiy Gukov, member of the battalion Aydar (2017).
5   Interview with the then 27-year-old Anton Trebukhov, former combatant of the Azov battalion (2017).

in criminal activities or earned a record of frequent human rights violations — also a sign of autonomy from state control.[6]

The pattern of interaction between state-controlled battalions and autonomous irregular battalions was characterized by collusion rather than competition. Even relatively autonomous battalions such as Aydar operated according to commands by the general staff of the ATO.[7] The headquarters of the ATO was detached from the battleground; this left significant leeway for autonomous decision-making. Combatants repeatedly complained about the bureaucracy, inflexibility, and detachment of their respective army or National Guard headquarters. The command of the Kharkiv-1 battalion was, for example, located in the city of Kharkiv, the battalion received a command to take a city in the ATO zone, but how this was to be done was up to the battalion itself.[8]

Autonomy for long persisted in the sense of a certain freedom of action. Autonomous groups conducted, for example, reconnaissance or sabotage tours beyond the frontline. Over time, the autonomous battalions were, however, removed from the front line to control violations of the ceasefire. The commander of an irregular armed group usually received the weaponry and armament, financial and material means for his battalion from either a sub-structure of the Ministry of Defense or from the Ministry of the Interior. The commander received orders and reported back to the general staff. A frequent complaint of combatants about the interaction with the governmental apparatus relates to lengthy bureaucratic procedures and the inflexibility of government agents. Combatants often did not know rules of appropriate behavior. Policing and fighting in combat mixed.

---

6   Two battalions are most often cited in this respect, the battalions Tornado for its background in organized crime and Aydar for its human rights abuses as reported by Amnesty International, see Amnesty International (2014): Ukraine: Abuses and War Crimes by the Aidar Volunteer Battalion in the North Luhansk Region, https://www.amnesty.org/download/Documents/8000/eur5004020 14en.pdf.
7   Interview with the then 27-year-old Dmytro "Sarmat", 24th storm battalion Aydar (2017).
8   Interview with Bogdan Gen'bach, battalion Kharkiv-1 (2017).

After the signing of the Minsk II agreements on 12 February 2015, most battalions were successfully integrated into troops under the command of the Ministry of the Interior or the Ministry of Defense, but some right-wing battalions rejected the terms of integration offered by the government. Only groups with an ideology and political ambition of their own remained actually autonomous, first of all, the Right Sector, the battalion Azov or the "All-Ukrainian Brotherhood." Those deliberately unwilling to integrate were either marginalized or at least removed from the frontlines.

Predecessors: The Maidan "Self-Defense"

On the Maidan square in Kyiv, several "self-defense" units were formed from December 2013 onwards, mainly to protect demonstrators against attacks by police forces. These groups were called "hundreds" (*sotnya*) in a military fashion while the victims of police violence were named "heaven's hundred". The self-defense groups of the Maidan included people with shields, helmets, some with bulletproof vests, as well as paramedics. Most of their members had no prior military experience. Exceptions are the Afghan hundred, consisting of veterans of the Soviet war in Afghanistan (1979–89), right-wing extremist groups such as "Patriot of Ukraine" or groups that joined forces at the beginning of the Maidan in the Right Sector (*Pravyi Sektor*) as well as soccer hooligans with a previous history of violent action. The significance of the armed groups and the self-defense units of the Maidan for the later formation of volunteer battalions consists in the fact that (a) distinct groups were formed whose members knew each other, (b) a basic understanding of collective action, communication and of group discipline was gained, (c) future battalion commanders were pre-selected, and (d) peer group pressure to later join volunteer battalions was high.

There is ample video footage about the violence on the Maidan square, including riot police and protesters throwing Molotov cocktails or stones, masked men shooting with rifles, or civilians trampling on police officers. Extremist right-wing groups led much of the violence against the Yanukovich government on the Maidan square and soon demonstrated their lasting unwillingness to subdue to a state monopoly of violence.[9]

The crucial question of who was behind the shooting of police officers and the targeted killing of civilians on the Maidan square has never been adequately answered. The Estonian Foreign Minister Urmaes Paet shared in a leaked telephone conversation with EU foreign affairs chief Catherine Ashton the conspiracy theory that the snipers responsible for killing police and civilians on Kyiv's Maidan square were protest movement agent provocateurs rather than supporters of then-President Viktor Yanukovych.[10] Participants of the Maidan, who later joined volunteer battalions, usually shied away from answers when asked about the armament among "civilians" on the Maidan. Whoever the concrete actors of violence on the Maidan had been, they acted collectively.

An informal council of the diverse self-defense groups on the Maidan met regularly to discuss and assign tasks. The council was loosely coordinated by Andriy Parubiy, a co-founder of the Social-National Party of Ukraine, the predecessor of the Svoboda Party, and a former leading member of the right-wing organization "Patriot Ukrainy."[11] No formal military hierarchy with lines of command was in place on the Maidan. Maidan activists repeatedly claimed not to know Parubiy; he certainly had only a limited commanding authority. Some groups acted autonomously, for example, members of "Patriot Ukrainy," who attacked pro-government men and pro-government groups, the so-called *titushki*, even beyond the confines of the Maidan square. Video footage and eyewitnesses from the Maidan confirm that groups of men in masks, with helmets, with long sticks and in uniform acted as violent action groups on the Maidan from December 2013 onwards.[12] In the first half of December 2013, the protests on the Maidan were already

---

9   Maidan Square activists urged to fight for Ukraine in the east, The Guardian 13 May 2014, https://www.theguardian.com/world/2014/may/13/maidan-square-activists-ukraine-co-opt-kiev-protesters.
10 https://www.theguardian.com/world/2014/mar/05/ukraine-bugged-call-catherine-ashton-urmas-paet.
11 See the contribution of Anton Shekhovtsov in this volume.
12 https://www.youtube.com/watch?v=o7mOVux83p8 (on 18 February 2014); https://www.youtube.com/watch?v=uhO9CeTZ9lE;

drying up.[13] But the violence kept the protest alive and fueled its subsequent escalation. Members of the nationalist, anti-European and explicitly authoritarian Right Sector admit that they were interested in an escalation of violence on the Maidan from the very outset since they used the pro-European Maidan demonstration as a pretext for launching a regime change.[14]

Most of the victims can be ascribed to the Special Forces (Berkut) and troops of the Ministry of the Interior, who shot at people on the Maidan. The Maidan protests were de facto captured by violent right-wing groups interested in conflict escalation. Some protestors participating on the Maidan used violence against the police forces by throwing Molow cocktails and stones, shooting with huge catapults, throwing fireworks at police officers, driving a bulldozer into a police cordon, trampling on officers lying on the ground and shooting with rifles and pistols. The accounts on the timing of the occurrence of firearms among the protesters on the Maidan vary, interlocutors usually shy away from precise answers. But it is safe to assume that only those groups with prior access to weapons and respective training could have brought weapons to the Maidan.

Some right-wing paramilitary groups had exercised with firearms in the years before the Maidan. Our respondents from the "Ultras" and the Right Sector did not deny that they brought firearms to the Maidan – "sometime in January 2014" is the common claim. According to the Deputy Prosecutor General of Ukraine, Oleh Zalisko, in February 2014, 67 people were killed in Kyiv's city center, 184 sustained gunshot wounds and over 750 suffered bodily injuries.[15] Altogether, 103 protesters and 13 police officers died from gunshots in the context of the Maidan protests (not just in the city center). However, even many years after the events, the state pros-

---

13 https://www.youtube.com/watch?v=RkdOOWxhHWg (BBC News 12 Dec. 2013).
14 Interview with "Artem Skoropadskyi" (an originally Russian journalist named Artem Bychkov), press secretary of the Right Sector, 18 Jan. 2018 Kyiv.
15 https://en.wikipedia.org/wiki/List_of_people_killed_during_Euromaidan.

ecutor and the courts could not or were not willing to provide conclusive answers on who were the killers. Justice remained elusive.[16] Several film documentaries and journalistic accounts tried to answer the question "Who shot at whom on the Maidan?," but since Ukrainian courts are reluctant to investigate the Maidan shootings, conspiracy theories flourish; some Ukrainians blame Russian snipers, some Russian media speak of a CIA-inspired coup.[17]

Essential is the observation that the armed groups on the Maidan consisted both of self-defense forces and of right-wing militant groups interested in escalation. The Ukrainian sociologist Volodymyr Ishchenko found "that the far-right Svoboda party was the most active collective agent in conventional and confrontational Maidan protest events, while the Right Sector was the most active collective agent in violent protest events...the far right were not on the periphery of the Maidan protests but in the center of the events" (Ishchenko 2018).[18] The Maidan was thus not a peaceful demonstration throughout, but in part captured by actors of violence. There is no sharp dividing line between the use of violence against police forces and "*titushki*" on the Maidan square and violence during the subsequent clashes in the Donbas. The Maidan was a precursor.[19] Yet, there is a qualitative difference between urban street violence of militants and a war waged with heavy weapons and by military groups. The violence on the Maidan did not preordain the war.

---

16 https://www.ohchr.org/en/stories/2020/02/six-years-after-killings-ukraine-justice-remains-elusive.

17 https://www.youtube.com/watch?v=Ib7EkJD08e4 (BBC News 12 Feb. 2015); https://www.youtube.com/watch?v=kP9T_wGPWQw (BBC News 28 Feb. 2014).

18 Volodymyr Ishchenko (2018): Denial of the Obvious: Far Right in Maidan Protests and Their Danger Today, Vox Ukraine 3245, 16 April 2018, https://voxukraine.org/en/denial-of-the-obvious-far-right-in-maidan-protests-and-their-danger-today/

19 *Titushky* (plural; Ukrainian: тітушки, Russian: титушки; sometimes *titushkos*, *titushkas*) are mercenary agents who supported the Ukrainian police force during the administration of Viktor Yanukovych, often posing as street hooligans. "Titushki raid" is a widely used term in Ukrainian mass media to describe street beatings, carjackings and kidnappings by unidentified men in civilian clothes from behind the lines of political rallies. Titushky were employed by the Yanukovych government with a reported daily pay of 200 hryven.

Mobilization "From Above"

During the first wave of mobilization against the Russian-sponsored separatism, which was announced in March 2014, it was planned to mobilize 20,000 recruits for the regular armed forces and an equal number for the newly established National Guard. The Ukrainian president—first Acting President Turchinov, then elected President Poroshenko—issued three decrees on "partial mobilization" in 2014 (17 March, 6 May and 22 July 2014). The "partial mobilization" was heavily disputed in the national parliament (*Verkhovna Rada*), since the Communist Party and the Party of the Regions were against it, while others had asked for a declaration of a state of war. In the end, 232 deputies of the *Verkhovna Rada* voted in favor, the necessary quorum was 226 deputies—a rather miserable political support for mobilization. The Ukrainian authorities' counteroperations to the separatists were launched by the Ukrainian Security Service (SBU) in April 2014 under the acronym ATO; in January 2018, it was re-labeled into "Measures to ensure national security and defense, and repulsing and deterring the armed aggression of the Russian Federation in Donetsk and Luhansk oblasts."

18- to 25-year-old men were conscripted into the military between May-July and October-November 2014 (Home Office UK Gov 2017). The dire straits of the Ukrainian army are evidenced in its limited capability for mobilizing or incorporating reservists and volunteers. According to Anna Colin Lebedev, 35,000 Ukrainians were mobilized into the regular security forces after the first wave of mobilization was announced (Lebedev 2017, p. 34). Persons targeted for the first wave of mobilization included men with experience as paratroopers, grenade launchers, in artillery, logistical support as well as physicians, electricians, mechanics, and drivers. All in all, an estimated 105,000 men were mobilized during the three waves of mobilization in 2014, but the figures on de facto mobilization significantly differ from this targeted size.[20] In August 2015,

---

20 https://ru.wikipedia.org/wiki/Военная_мобилизация_на_Украине_(с_2014_года).

after the sixth call for mobilization, only 50 to 55 percent of the mobilized had actually shown up in their respective military commissariat, which in turn often did not know what to do with the conscripts. Approximately 30 percent of the mobilized proved inept to serve due to their physical or psychological condition (Lebedev 2017, p. 59). Furthermore, at the end of 2015, roughly 16,000 persons faced legal prosecution on the grounds of draft evasion or desertion from the ATO.

In spring 2014, the reservists and volunteers recruited for the battalions of territorial defense were often badly equipped. In May 2014, relatives of mobilized recruits even demonstrated publicly against the miserable protection of their sons.[21] Especially western regions of Ukraine are criticized for not having responded to the mobilization or for draft evasion. Whether western Ukrainians were less willing to fight than eastern Ukrainians is hard to prove, but the figures raise questions about the actual number of mobilized soldiers and underscore the significance of volunteers for the later war effort.

In 2016, 1,294 non-combat related fatalities among Ukrainian soldiers were reported by the military prosecutor of Ukraine, they have allegedly died from the inappropriate use of firearms, aggression among soldiers, from traffic accidents in the course of the ATO or suicides.[22] This high rate of fatal injuries among combatants can also be attributed to the deficit in military training. An interviewee from the Aydar battalion claimed, for example, that one-third of those who died in his battalion were killed in "friendly fire." The commemoration of "war heroes" therefore includes many who actually died from the mishandling of weapons or lack of discipline. The families often do not learn about the cause of death and do not receive any compensation. These horrendous figures may explain in part draft evasion or desertion.

---

21 https://atn.ua/obshchestvo/ekipiruyte-nashih-boycov-tak-est-ili-net-bronez hilety-u-harkovskogo-batalona.
22 "Muzhiki ne plachut": Shto delat s samoubiystvami v armii?, New Voice 21 March 2017, https://nv.ua/ukr/bbc/muzhiki-ne-plachut-chto-delat-s-samou bijstvami-v-armii-842265.html.

De facto, the mobilization of volunteers responded to the unwillingness to serve as a reservist. Additionally, between 8,000 to 10,000 people had deserted from the ATO between 2014 and 2016 after their mobilization. In the government-controlled battalions, volunteers and compulsively mobilized soldiers mixed. Recruits had at times the opportunity to choose a battalion of their own volition. A preference of volunteers for enrollment in an irregular armed group was arguably informed by the inefficient preparation of mobilized reservists and the lack of discipline in the regular armed forces. Interviewees recall how they were exposed to alcoholism in the barracks, trapped in inaction and subject to meaningless instructions while Russia was already occupying Crimea (Lebedev 2017, p. 48).

Social Background

Information on the social background of volunteer combatants is scattered. A study conducted in 2016 among war veterans, including volunteers and mobilized and contract soldiers, found that 78.6 percent had a job before they became a combatant. This indicates that among the recruits people without employment represented only a minority. A study on veterans of the ATO found that 41 percent of the volunteers had a Master's degree, eight percent a Bachelor's degree, one-third a technical education while 12 percent did not have a degree higher than secondary school and only 6.6 percent military training. Among the former combatants, 40 percent were workers or in work positions with comparatively low qualifications, 18 percent in higher qualified positions (manager, teacher, medical personnel, economist, lawyer) another 18 percent in security provision (police officers, security guards) and 11 percent heads of companies (Kharchenko / Mramornova 2016). The argument that predominantly social losers had joined the war effort is obviously wrong, the volunteers represent a cross-section of Ukrainian society instead.

Size of Battalions

It is difficult to provide an exact number of the pro-Ukrainian irregular armed groups. A reason for the trouble with the numbers rests in the informal nature of such groups. Numbers are reported through social media and become thus part of the media campaign of battalions to exaggerate the actual numbers. In September 2014, the Ukrainian news agency Hromadske claimed that roughly 50 volunteer groups had fought at that point in time for the Ukrainian side, the estimated number of volunteers was 15,000 while the battle ready regular armed forces of Ukraine were estimated at 6,000 at the time of Russia's annexation of Crimea.[23] In the very beginning, none of the volunteer battalions kept records. Only after the formal integration of almost all volunteer battalions into the regular armed forces of Ukraine or into the forces under the control of the Ministry of the Interior, the number of integrated volunteers who became rank and file were put on record. Some groups existed only for a short period of time, as subgroups or may actually never have existed as distinct groups at all. The nature of at least some of the irregular groups is fluid, several groups changed their name and form over time. No membership cards were issued, groups were merged with others, the only persistent group feature was at times the leader and his close surrounding.

According to an overview by the analytical web-portal "slovo i delo" 37 battalions took part in the ATO as of early September 2014.[24] In January 2017, Ukraine's Defense Minister Stepan Poltorak made the—admittedly dubious—statement that 40,000 "representatives of the voluntary movement" were protecting the territorial integrity of Ukraine in the ATO zone.[25] Another report specified that 40,000 "volunteer soldiers" were at that time in the Donbas to

---

23 https://medium.com/@Hromadske/ukraines-shadow-army-b04d7a683493; https://ru.bellingcat.com/novosti/ukraine/2016/11/21/ukrainian-foreign-fighters-ru/.
24 https://ru.slovoidilo.ua/articles/4543/2014-09-02/dobrovolcheskie-batalony-kotorye-prinimayut-uchastie-v-vojne-na-vostoke.html.
25 https://112.international/conflict-in-eastern-ukraine/40-thousand-volunteers-are-protecting-ukraine-today-poltorak-13495.html.

defend their motherland.[26] The rough figure of 40,000 may relate to the overall number of soldiers and police officers active in the ATO zone. Whatever the exact meaning of the Defense Minister's statement was, an overall number of 40,000 voluntary servicemen seems to be exaggerated, especially after the formal integration of the volunteer battalions into state security services.

Volunteers joined battalions individually or in groups, but did not formally register. They switched between battalions or left without formal notification. Volunteers without a contract with the Ministry of the Interior or the Ministry of Defense could leave their battalions on their own volition. According to our estimates, by August 2014 over 5,600 volunteers had joined defense battalions across Ukraine, and approximately 7,000 volunteers served by the end of September 2014. Yet, this is an estimate since the numbers were constantly in flux. People moved in and out or served only part-time. According to official statistics, altogether 329,500 Ukrainians had gained the status as a participant of the anti-terrorist operation in the Donbas by April 2018 — the figure pertains to the period from 2014 to spring 2018.[27]

Motivation of Combatants

The literature on motivations of non-state armed actors is mostly speculative, some highlight greed, others grievances, whereas the relative weight of most is likely to change over time (*Collier; Hoeffler 2002*). Motivations among the pro-Ukrainian combatants range from nationalist and patriotic sentiments, opportunities for shooting, racketeering or looting, adventurism, fleeing a miserable personal life to social pressure from peer groups. Some had joined because of their rejection of government authority, others had a record as hooligans or criminals. Still others joined battalions for per-

---

26 https://www.ukrinform.net/rubric-defense/2192869-minister-poltorak-about-40000-ukrainian-volunteer-soldiers-fighting-in-donbas.html.

27 http://gordonua.com/news/war/v-ukraine-status-uchastnika-boevyh-deystviy-poluchili-3295-tys-chelovek-gossluzhba-po-delam-veteranov-239471.html.

sonal reasons or simply sought adventure. The majority of our interviewees report patriotic reasons or a trigger event such as the violent death of a friend or attacks on family members by pro-Russian forces, which instilled an urgent sense in them to defend their own country. But few battalions had a distinct worldview of their own to attract volunteers — these were right-wing or extremist groups such as the Right Sector, Azov, UNA/UNCO or S14. A former combatant from Donetsk recalls two moments that made him decide to become a volunteer, first, the impression that roundtable meetings with protesting separatists in early March 2014 did not lead anywhere and second that known drug addicts seemed to take over his hometown (Kirtoka 2018).

For the choice of a specific battalion, its imagery and visibility on the Internet proved essential. The leaders of the later Donbas battalion, for example, announced recruitment over the Internet as early as in April 2014. Battalions with the reputation of high fighting morale, for example Donbas, Aydar, or Azov, and a competent commander were more attractive to volunteers than groups with an unknown profile. Motivations also changed in the course of the violent conflict. A person who had joined a group at an early stage of conflict escalation due to patriotic sentiments could become more interested in securing the status as a combatant and to reap in social benefits over time. In the early stage of the conflict, one group dominated among the recruits — men, whose willingness to join up was triggered by a crucial event, for example, the capture of Novoazovsk by the separatists or the imminent occupation of Mariupol. Some decided individually to join a battalion — mostly younger men without dependent family members —, others debated their decision with friends and family. Still others originated from the territory controlled by the separatists and fought because of their longing for home.

A combatant from the battalion Shakhtarsk responded that he simply liked shooting, others merely used the chaos for purposes of personal enrichment.[28] One former member of "Shakhtarsk" said

---

28 Interview with 40-year-old former member of the battalion Shakhtarsk, Serhiy "Moryak" (2017).

that he had always dreamed of a military career, but did not want to serve in the regular army.[29] Personal experiences with the separatists repeatedly played a role in joining volunteer battalions. A member of the Aydar battalion from the village Lugino recalls that he witnessed how so-called insurgents behaved like sociopaths, that he became furious and joined the Aydar battalion to stop criminals on the loose.[30] A member of the "Kharkiv I" battalion claims that he volunteered once he had witnessed how people were beaten up by separatists in an area where he had relatives and friends. The suffering from violence by people close to him as well as the inability of the regular military to recruit him beforehand — he had gone to his military district command to enroll, but nothing had happened — made him join a volunteer battalion.[31] An interviewee of the battalion Aydar reported: "We shared the Ukrainian nationalism according to the writings of Dmytro Dontsov and Mykola Mikhnovskiy, but otherwise we were apolitical, we did not have political instructions in our battalion nor did we organize political meetings."[32] The overwhelming majority of the Ukrainian battalions were not bound together by a particular ideology but shared Ukrainian patriotism or nationalism.

Leadership

Which biographical traits explain the leadership of battalion commanders? Are there common patterns that qualify them to solve collective action problems? In 2016, Andrey Shcherbak compared biographical patterns of 54 commanders from the separatist and

---

29 Interview with 28-year-old former combatant of the battalion Shakhtarsk and of Kulchitskyi Battalion, Denis Malykhin (2017).
30 Interview with 24-year-old Vitaliy "Kastro" from the battalion Aydar (2017).
31 Interview with Aleksey Borisovich Vedmidskiy, battalion Kharkiv-1 (2017)
32 Interview with 39 year old Aleksey "Rand", Ternopol, battalion Azov (2017). Dmytro Dontsov (1883–1973) was a prominent Ukrainian nationalist with social-Darwinist, anti-communist, militant, and anti-Russian convictions. Mikhnovskiy (1873–1924) was a radical proponent of Ukrainian independence before and after the breakdown of the Tsarist empire, who had agitated in favor of an armed liberation from Russia and for the ethno-nationalist slogan "Ukraine for Ukrainians". Dontsov and Mikhnovsky figure as historical embodiments of Ukrainian independence from Russia.

pro-Ukrainian battalions. Shcherbak found that on average a commander was approximately 40 years old, with only lower education, a low income and low social status before he became a commander. Just more than half, 53 percent, had a prior professional background as a military or police officer, while 47.2 percent of his sample had "experiences" with political and social activism before the Maidan protests.[33] Shcherbak holds that the commanders were mostly miserable figures, not underdogs, but lower middle class at best. He found that among the pro-Ukrainian commanders, more men had a background in the military or as police officers or bureaucrats than among the separatist commanders, where "workers" and "entrepreneurs" allegedly dominated. By focusing on "missing" qualities (for example, lower education) Shcherbak, however, failed to explain the actual leadership. The contrast between low pre-conflict status and leadership afterward requires explanation. One could claim that the violent conflict itself served as an opportunity for upward social mobility, but that would still leave open which characteristics informed leadership selection. Contrary to a regular military commander, the leader of an irregular armed group had to earn his authority. The commanders of a rotte or a battalion were often elected by their members, not nominated from above.[34] Yet, commanders were not always respected as an authority, and the enforcement of commands or regulations was not necessarily a given. Furthermore, the founders of a battalion did not always become the factual commanders — being able to recruit was not the same as to lead in combat. A difference can be made between the rather entrepreneurial logistical and "social capital" skills necessary to form a battalion and the skills of a violent specialist needed in actual combat.

---

33 Andrey Shcherbak: Analyse "Les Miserables": Biographien von "Noworos" und ukrainischen Milizkommandeuren im Vergleich. Bundeszentrale für politische Bildung, 2.7.2016, http://www.bpb.de/230419/analyse-les-miserables-biogra phien-von-noworos-und-ukrainischen-milizkommandeuren-im-vergleich.
34 Interview with 34-year-old Vadim "Sherman" in Kharkov, former member of Azov battalion (2017).

We took a closer look at the social background, education, profession, political activities, personal traits, post-conflict careers, social media activities and relevant social ties of 19 commanders from the most known pro-Ukrainian battalions.[35] The biographical information is based on personal interviews and on information available on official websites (as members of parliament, for example), from electronic news or social media. The information is incomplete, depending in part on media activism of the commanders. Furthermore, information might be distorted due to the invention, re-editing or concealment of biographical facts. The career traits of commanders are often mixed, if not seemingly messy; we, therefore, focus on dominant patterns. 15 out of these 19 commanders we looked at more closely had a military or police background, two as battle-hardened Chechen field commanders from the anti-Russian wars in Chechnya. Two had a university education in the humanities, two had a double career in the military and as businessmen, one a predominant business background while only two had a record as extreme nationalist activists. At least three had a record as serious criminal offenders.

Several conditions for leadership as a commander stand out, among them vocational training in the military or in the police and high social media activity (via Facebook, Vkontakte, Twitter, youTube), added by visibility in the public media (TV shows, frequent interviews). Apart from leaders who relied on organizational structures of pre-existing parties or movements (like the Organization of Ukrainian Nationalists, OUN, or the movement S14) the ability to recruit through social media was crucial for becoming a commander in the early stage of the formation of battalions and for

---

35 The commanders are Andriy Biletsky (Azov), Dmytro Yarosh (Pravyj Sektor), Oleksandr Pisarenko (Sich), Viktor Tolochko (Kulitskogo battalion), Nikolay Shvalia (Zoloti Vorota), Yurij Bereza (Dnipro I), Serhiy Melnichuv (Aydar), Semen Semenchenko (= Kostiantyn Hryshyn, Donbas), Andriy Teteruk (Myrotvorets), Kostiantyn Mateychenko (Artemivsk), Dmytro Linko (Svyata Mariya), Ruslan Onishenko (Shakhtarsk / Tornado), Vitaliy Satarenko (Kyiv I), Bogdan Voytsekhovsky (Kyiv II), Nikolay Kokhanivskiy (battalion OUN), Isa Munaev (Dzhokhar Dudaev battalion), Adam Osmaev (Dzhokhar Dudaev battalion), Yevhen Karas (S14), Muslim Cheberloevsk (Sheykh Mansur battalion), Lenur Islyamov (Asker and Noman battalions).

establishing a public image and prestige. Almost all pro-Ukrainian commanders quickly turned into media experts who reached out to their supporters through regular short text, audio, video or photo messages, often with several tens of thousands of followers. The command of social media was far more important for the career as a commander than conventional merits usually documented on a well-designed curriculum vitae. Communication through social media often compensated for the deficit of ideological leadership – only very few had a discernible record as ideological leaders and none as a politician before the Maidan protests. The ability to homogenize a group on programmatic grounds was seemingly only consequential for battalions with a clearly defined right-wing ideological outlook, such as "Azov" or the "Right Sector." Whereas "social capital" – the ability to network, to use social media, to perform on TV, to connect to sponsors – were critical qualities during the formation of a battalion, military leadership was essential when major battles took place. However, combatants repeatedly criticized commanders who were more active in the media in Kyiv than leading on the battleground.

We have found that contrary to studies that ascribe the success of irregular armed groups to the "legitimacy" or the provision of benefits to its members, the social capital of leaders rather than ideology informed the capacity for collective action. Social capital is understood as socially accessed resources, goods or services acquired through networks; it does not necessarily imply trust, trustworthiness or shared norms, it rather pertains to the imagery that a leader can lead his followers and that he is a patron who can deliver essentials to his clients (Pinto 2006, pp. 53-69). A patron had to be able to protect his people. Social capital is based on the hope and expectation by followers that a leader is capable of steering a course through troubled water.

An outstanding feature of the commanders of pro-Ukrainian battalions is their ability to establish relevant social networks to sponsors or patrons. Among these patronal networks, four types were essential (and often complimented each other): (1) close personal ties to the regional administration,[36] (2) recognition as leader by big business sponsors (for example, Ihor Kolomoyskiy, Serhiy Taruta, Ihor Kononenko), (3) the personal selection as commander by the Minister of the Interior (and businessman) Arsen Avakov and (4) belonging to and selection by a pre-existing societal organization such as the Congress of Ukrainian Nationalists, the Svoboda Party (Freedom Party), "Tryzub" imeni Stepana Bandery (Stepan Bandera Trident), the Korchinsky Brotherhood, the militant nationalist group "C14" or the pro Chochen movement "Svobodnyj Kavkaz" (Free Caucasus).

Semen Semenchenko, commander of the Donbas battalion, and temporarily a member of the national parliament for the Samopovich Party, may serve as an example for a multi-track career path. Born in Crimea and raised by a pro-Russian family, he took classes in four different colleges, among them a military college, which he did not finish. He was allegedly trained in finances and loans and trained as a film operator. He was "director" of an unknown company, private entrepreneur, editor of two newspapers, founder of a foundation, and organizer of a movement called "Volya Naroda" (people's will), which collected donations for environmental purposes, and he once participated in the search for a wanted offender.[37] This non-linear career path is proof of certain qualities — flexibility, self-help, learning by doing, the ability to adjust to changing circumstances, organizing groups or resources for specific purposes, tolerance of frustrations, and communication skills. To put it shortly, Semenchenko is a skipjack, he embodies elementary survival skills necessary for the adverse and unpredictable post-Soviet environment. An upper middle class, safety-oriented way of life would have disqualified him as a commander of an irregular armed group.

---

36 The relevant regional administrators were *mostly* from the Dnipropetrovsk region such as the Borys Filatov, then deputy head of Regional State Administration, deputy governor and businessman Hennadiy Korban or businessman and governor Ihor Kolomojsky.

37 https://ru.wikipedia.org/wiki/Семенченко,_Семён_Игореви.

The labeling of commanders as "miserables" (Andrey Shcherbak) is misleading; being a commander of an irregular armed group is not a white-collar job in a posh urban area. The specifics of the "business" background of some commanders are hard to verify since any had an established business record with publicly provable credentials. One can only speculate about the nature of the former business of some commanders, yet, it is striking that any flag their business credentials out. In all likelihood, most have been engaged in temporary, unstable small businesses, otherwise, they would not have skipped it in favor of becoming a commander in the trenches. Twelve out of the 19 commanders we looked at turned to politics after their brief career as battalion commanders, mostly as members of the national parliament, as party politicians or in subnational administrations. Very few remained commanders after the integration of volunteer battalions in the state security apparatus. Several ended up as criminals, one (the commander of the battalion Tornado) was convicted for crimes committed in the course of the war.

Material Support and Equipment

The battalions received their basic equipment, clothing, foodstuffs, and weapons from the Ministry of Internal Affairs or the Ministry of Defense. However, as these material resources proved to be inadequate, especially at the beginning of the war, the regular armed forces and irregular groups engaged in barter trade, trading food for arms, for example.[38] Numerous civil society or social media groups and business sponsors helped to maintain the battalions. One of these support groups was the "Self-defence of Maidan," which even had own warehouses in Melitopol, Dnipro and Kharkiv, as well as "Army SOS," an initiative of former Maidan activists. These support groups usually provided hygiene items, clothing, food, sleeping bags, night vision goggles and multi-copters (for use as drones).[39] Initially, the control of equipment was miserable, dual-use items ended up in pawn shops, items collected

---

38 Interview with 53 year old Stanislav "Stas" from Aydar battalion (2017).
39 https://en.wikipedia.org/wiki/Territorial_defence_battalions_(Ukraine).

or donated by civilians were then resold by members of battalions on the market.[40]

The equipment of autonomous combat battalions or those under command of the National Guard or the Ministry of Defense usually included rifles, machine guns, mortars, anti-tank weapons, grenade launchers, rocket-propelled grenade, rocket-propelled anti-aircraft weapons, rocket-propelled anti-tank weapons, light armored vehicles, sniper rifles, helmets and vests. While police battalions were equipped with firearms, they did not have heavy artillery or tanks. However, in early September 2014, after the deadly battle of Ilovaisk, the Ministry of the Interior decided to provide its special police and National Guard battalions with grenade launchers, mortars, machine guns, and armored vehicles. The volunteer battalions also fought with trophy weaponry caught from Russian forces.

The control over weapons is an indicator for the efficient management of a battalion. The commander or a deputy commander was in charge of the physical control over weapons and ammunition that were handed out to combatants. It is striking that very few of our interviewees from volunteer battalions reported an illicit appropriation or theft of weaponry.[41] Usually, a record of weapons' holdings was kept in a battalion, but small arms were definitely shipped outside of the ATO zone; some illegal traders were intercepted.[42] In a couple of cases, members of volunteer battalions were prosecuted for illegal possession of small arms or for marauding. Since they were in short supply during the "hot" phase of the conflict, theft of weapons would have been seen by co-combatants as treason. Existing problems with the spread of illicit small arms were caused by inadequacies of the legal system regulating the possession and use of such weapons, and the lack of a central register of firearms.[43]

---

40 Interview with Serhiy Gukov, member of Aydar battalion (2017).
41 Interview with 33 year old Yvhen Baydak, regiment Dnipro-1 (2017).
42 Interview with 25 year old Vitaly Kz'menko, former fighter of 131st battalion (2017).
43 http://www.smallarmssurvey.org/salw/building-evidence/country-level-case-studies/ukraine.html.

The material support and the financing of the irregular battalions came from diverse sources. The Ministry of the Interior or the Ministry of Defense provided equipment, weaponry, clothing, and food for those battalions formed under their tutelage. The social media networks of the battalions, veteran organizations, diaspora groups, and civilian volunteers collected money, clothing, and food for volunteer battalions. In individual cases, automobiles and small trucks were presented as gifts to battalions and after refurbishment used for combat purposes. Some entrepreneurs financially supported battalions. The then owner of the Privatbank and one of the richest Ukrainian entrepreneurs, Ihor Kolomoiskiy, offered US $10,000 for any captured separatist or pro-Russian combatant. A newspaper article of April 17, 2014 announced: "Anyone who ...arrests a Kremlin-backed saboteur and passes him to the National Resistance Headquarters in the Dnipropetrovsk region will receive US $10,000. Freeing any government building will lead to a US $200,000 reward, disarming separatists of their weapons could allow earning an additional US $1,000–2,000, Dnipropetrovsk region administration press officer Kateryna Shovkova told the Kyiv Post."[44] Kolomoyskiy supported the battalion Dnipro-1 as a kind of private militia, which also participated in the occupation of the oil company UkrTransNafta's buildings in March 2015 — an act that subsequently led to the dismissal of Kolomoiskiy as governor of Dnipropetrovsk region.

In fall 2014, the salary of a member of a Kolomoyskiy-supported battalion amounted to in-between UAH 6,000 to 10,000 per month (with an average wage in Ukraine of UAH 3,500 at that time) while the National Guard paid UAH 4,000 to its members (Lebedev (2017, p. 34). Fighting on the frontline increased the pay by UAH 4,200 per month in 2016. A member of the Donbas battalion, formally belonging to the National Guard, holds that their official monthly salary ranged between UAH 10 and 15,000 (in 2014-15), but that onlyUAH 2,400 were actually paid out — the combatant

---

44 https://www.kyivpost.com/article/content/war-against-ukraine/kolomoisky-promises-a-reward-for-fighting-against-separatists-343970.html.

was curious about who had pocketed in the difference.[45] According to Mykhailo Minakov, Kolomoyskiy supported the battalions Kryvbas, Donbas, Dnipropetrovsk, Luhansk I, Sicheslav, Kremenchuk, Kyrovohrad, and Shakhtarsk/Tornado, too (Minakov 2018). Hennadiy Korban, a businessman, politician, and patron of the Jewish community, allegedly supported the battalion Dnipro-1 as well.[46] Another supportive network was built up by Yurij Biryukov, an entrepreneur and Maidan participant, who formed the organization "Krylya Feniksa" (the wings of Phoenix) to support the under-equipped army and volunteer battalions. By July 2014, they had collected UAH 10 million, by September 2014 UAH 50 million. Those volunteers, who were integrated into government-controlled armed groups, received a regular salary, but the rank and file members complained about the low pay — at times, professionals left the state security service because of low financial incentives to stay.[47] Some battalions were definitely better equipped than others.[48]

Although some parties claimed to have their own battalions, we did not find evidence of battalions that were autonomously organized by a political party. The political party Batkivshchyna claimed, for example, to have a battalion of its own, allegedly formed and funded by the party as part of its "resistance movement." However, the 34th battalion of territorial defense called "Batkivshchyna" received financial assistance from the party as well as equipment (a Grand Cherokee Jeep, a Mercedes Sprinter, diesel generators, night vision, radio transmitters, pharmaceuticals, hygiene articles and the like).[49] The support by Batkivshchyna alone is, however, no proof that the party had a battalion of its own, it just confirms that political parties acted as sponsors.

---

45 Interview with 42-year-old Oleh Oleshko, former combatant of the Donbas battalion (2017).
46 Interview with 24-year-old Volodymyr Sheredega, former fighter of Dnipro-1 (2017).
47 Interview with Aleksey Borisovich Vedmidskiy, battalion "Kharkiv-1" (2017).
48 Interview with 38-year-old Igor' "Brodyaga" (nom de guerre) from special policy combat company "Skhidnyi korpus", city of Kharkiv (2017).
49 https://www.rbc.ua/ukr/news/-batkivshchina-peredala-boytsam-ato-voenn oe-snaryazhenie-na-24082014175000.

The provision of battalions with material goods quickly began to take on organized forms and turned into a business of its own. To supply battalions with the needed clothing or equipment, goods were sold for excessive prices; the sale itself quickly turned into a lucrative business. Rumors abound concerning the misuse of funds collected by support groups for profit-making by commanders, intermediaries or salespersons. Similarly, the distribution of humanitarian assistance to refugees or internally displaced persons evoked distrust among some Ukrainian NGOs.[50] The abundance of collected goods provided opportunities for a business in its own right, providers of goods for volunteer battalions competed among each other. Some commanders saw opportunities to advance their later political career with money made by patriotic donations (Serdyukov 2016).

Qualification and Training

The level of preparedness of volunteers in the irregular armed groups and the training itself varied tremendously among the battalions. Volunteers, who had fought in the Afghanistan war between 1979 and 1988, were already 50 years and over when they joined a battalion. They often knew each other from veteran organizations and were able to reactivate their knowledge of Soviet military training and field manuals as well as revive combat experiences.[51] The combatants usually did not undergo systematic training since professional trainers or training facilities were often missing. Those with a military or police career, with combat experience in Afghanistan or in one of the post-Soviet wars or with a background in a paramilitary organization were in a privileged position since they had at least some basic knowledge about how to handle weapons, on how to interact as a group and some tactical skills. Older volunteers aged over 45 with Soviet military training and es-

---

50 Interview with Aleksey Borisovich Vedmidsky, battalion Kharkiv-1 (2017); interview with Zvi Areli, Kyiv, 19 January 2018.
51 Interview with a group of Afghanistan veterans, who had served in the Donbas battalion, Kyiv, December 2016.

pecially veterans of the Afghanistan war were arguably best prepared for combat since they had undergone similar military training as the separatist forces commanded by Russian officers. They were thus able to anticipate combat behavior, tactical moves, and discern communication patterns of the opponent. The least prepared were youngsters without military training who out of enthusiasm at the Maidan or patriotism volunteered but were easily targeted as cannon fodder.[52] According to some volunteers, the central government and the military command demonstrated a lack of leadership at the outset of the war. According to a member of the Aydar battalion, the number of victims and the size of the territory taken by the pro-Russian forces could have been reduced.[53]

The volunteer battalions usually took everyone who was willing to join, while many regular soldiers of the Ukrainian Armed Forces did not want to fight at all in the beginning. Yet, most of the recruits for irregular armed groups were not ready for combat operations. In the special police units under the Ministry of the Interior, a more serious examination and selection, for example for physical fitness or a criminal record, took place. However, the training for police patrolling initially took only two weeks, as a member of the battalion Kharkiv-1 recalls.[54] Later, the training for police units expanded and included physical training, a shooting range, tactical preparation and legal education. Usually the training was "on the job." In the years 2014 and 2015, the training of volunteers was quite unsystematic. Young volunteers in particular often had not served in the army before. Elementary courses lasted from one week to several weeks and later up to several months. Only after the inclusion of battalions into regular structures of the armed forces or the forces of the Ministry of the Interior did serious training of battalions according to NATO standards and often assisted by trainers from the United States, the United Kingdom, and Poland take place on a regular basis.

---

52 Interview with a group of commanders of the Donbas battalion (Afghanistan veterans), Kyiv, December 2015.
53 Interview with Aydar member Serhiy Gukov (2017).
54 Interview with Bogdan Gen'bach, battalion Kharkiv I (2017).

On several occasions, foreigners took over the training of Ukrainian volunteers, among them Georgians, Polish, and Israeli military experts. Several groups such as Krym, Dnipro I and Shakhtarsk were trained by Zvi Arieli, an Israeli citizen with a background in the Israeli Special Forces, who used to live with his family in Ukraine. He had been asked by Anton Gerashchenko, an "aide" to the Ukrainian Minister of the Interior and member of parliament, to train the Donbas battalion. Arieli offered one-week-training courses in how to handle weapons and on group interaction as well as the protection of platoons for the battalion Donbas, the battalion "Poltavshchyna", for the 2nd or 3rd battalion of the 79th brigade under the Ministry of the Interior as well as for a rapid reaction group of the Special Forces from the Luhansk area (special forces that had not switched sides to Russia = Корпус Оперативно-Раптової Дії / Корпус оперативного внезапного действия). The training activities were sponsored by businessmen, although Arieli says that he did not get any remuneration for his involvement.[55] A member of the combat company "Skhidniy korpus" recalls basic training in handling weapons, by paramedics, and in police tactics on a training ground run by the National Guard.[56] However, to say that all irregulars had only received minimal training would be wrong. A former member of the Special Patrol Service of the Ministry of the Interior (the title was given to battalions after their integration into the Ministry of the Interior recalls that he underwent hard drills for three to four months, including shooting exercises and physical fitness training.[57]

Training did not just pertain to skills, internalized habits, and knowledge, but to discipline, too. According to the evidence from our interviews, it proved difficult at times to maintain discipline in the battalions. Due to the fear of informers working for the opposite side, some men were put in charge of the internal security of their

---

55 Interview with Zvi Arieli, Kyiv 19 Jan. 2018.
56 Interview with 38-year-old Igor' "Brodyaga", city of Kharkiv, police company "Skhidniy korpus" (2017).
57 Interview with 35-year-old Roman "Doktor", Kharkiv, former member of Special Police battalion of the Ministry of the Interior (2017).

battalions.[58] In some, the internal security, i.e., the punishment of actual or expected misbehavior, was harsh. Reportedly, several combatants died while internal rules including rules of silence were enforced. The code of honor placed importance on silence, non-cooperation with authorities, and non-interference in the illegal actions of group members—a likeness of omertà cannot be ruled out. Yet, inside the irregular battalions, a "liberal" or rather an anarchical atmosphere at times prevailed, in contrast to conventional military hierarchies. Combatants could take leave or could decide whether they participate in a certain operation, or they would switch to another battalion—personal decisions that would have been impossible in regular armed forces.

Foreign Fighters

Little is known about the foreigners who joined the fighting on the Ukrainian side from spring 2014 onwards. An estimate of foreign fighters on the Ukrainian side by Kacper Rękawek (2015) ranges from 109 to 268 combatants (Rękawek 2015). Foreign fighters mainly from Belarus, Georgia, and Russia (roughly 100 men from each country) had joined the pro-Ukrainian volunteer battalions. Foreign fighters from the United States, France, Germany, Norway, Sweden, Georgia, Poland, Spain, the Czech Republic, the United Kingdom, Croatia, Italy, and Canada also fought in Ukrainian volunteer battalions. Foreigners serving in a pro-Ukrainian battalion can be grouped into three different categories: First, foreigners highly critical of the political regime in Russia, for example Georgians, Chechens, or ethnic Russians; second, right-wing nationalists from abroad, among them Croats, Italians, Belarusians, Slovaks and Swedes; they had joined the Ukrainian effort because of a shared vision of extreme nationalism.[59] Third, one finds individuals from Canada or the United States (an Austrian national was mentioned

---

58 Interview with 35-year-old Borys Ovcharov, former combatant of Right Sector, Azov and OUN (2017).
59 Interview with 27 year old Anton Trebukhov, former combatant of Azov battalion (2017).

as a foreign fighter, too) with a background in the Ukrainian diaspora. Contrary to Germans fighting on the pro-Russian side, we did not come across German passport holders among the pro-Ukrainian battalions. Last, one finds men, who joined the war because of adventurism.

While adherents of right-wing groups from different European countries, as well as adventurers, mostly fought on the pro-Russian side, the Ukrainian side attracted sympathetic combatants from Eastern Europe (mainly from Georgia, the Baltic States, and Poland), Scandinavia, Western Europe and from the Ukrainian diaspora in the United States and Canada. Furthermore, some ex-patriots, whose families had emigrated to European countries, had also joined irregular battalions. Often, foreign fighters had a record of participating in other violent conflicts. An interviewee from the battalion Aydar claimed that approximately ten foreigners from the Baltic states and from Poland had fought with Aydar in 2014.[60] Another interviewee from Aydar said that "many" foreigners from Georgia, Poland, and Russia served in his battalion, but that he would not disclose the number.[61] After the formal inclusion of most volunteers into the state security services, the foreign fighters found themselves in a peculiar situation—without Ukrainian citizenship, it was impossible to award the status "participant of military acts," to them, they did not receive the respective benefits, and most quit their battalion after its legalization. However, some foreign fighters were granted Ukrainian citizenship.

Interaction with the Local Environment

A famous statement by Mao Zedong holds that "the guerrilla must move amongst the people as a fish swims in the sea." Accordingly, active support by the local environment is a key resource for the emergence and survival of irregular armed groups. Yet, "the people" are not a unified actor, some person's preferences rest with one community, others side with the opponents, and many prefer to stay clear or neutral as long as possible to not expose themselves

---

60   Interview with 27 year old Dmytro "Sarmat" from the battalion "Aydar" (2017).
61   Interview with 53 year old Stanislav "Stas", battalion Aydar, Kyiv (2017).

and to be less vulnerable. Respondents from battalions relay their mixed impression of societal support; it depended on the locality, the temporal context, and even in the same city, feelings could be very diverse. An interviewee from the Aydar battalion subjectively estimated that half of the people in the city of Shchastia were against them, 30 percent neutral and 20 percent supportive.[62] The evidence is hard to collect as "support" depends on circumstances, on shifting calculus, and it takes different forms. During the hot phase of fighting from spring 2014 to February 2015 onwards, the irregular armed groups were greeted by local people in the villages either as liberators or feared as an invading horde. Local people were scared as long as they did not know who they would have to deal with.[63] Käihkö reports about a survey conducted in July 2015 and in May-June 2016. This study showed that in 2014, 61 percent of the respondents completely or somewhat trusted the pro-Ukrainian volunteer battalions compared to 49 percent support in 2015 and 54 percent in 2016. Volunteer battalions were the second most trusted actor in Ukraine (Käikö 2018, p. 154). But the longer the war lasted, the more apathetic people became, they had one main wish — to end the war.

In 2017, we conducted semi-structured interviews with civilians of different age, sex, outlook, and professional background in the Ukrainian controlled conflict zone. All civilians interviewed had personal experience with pro-Ukrainian battalions, some were internally displaced persons (IDPs) who, before crossing the "line of contact," had also interacted with pro-Russian battalions. The overarching impression of the interviews with these civilians is a widespread sense of caution, distrust, alienation, and polarization among the populace. The experience of violent conflict interrupted communicative ties and thus demarcated groups.[64] At the time of the interview, many interviewees were quite aware of the fact that their views may identify them. The timing of an interview and its context thus influenced the views expressed. Views are not cast in

---

62 Interview with Stanislav "Stas", battalion Aydar, Kyiv (2017).
63 Interview with 28 year old "Artem", combatant of Azov battalion (2017).
64 Interview with 60-year-old IDP Volodymyr from Pervomajsk (Luhansk region), 2017.

stone and at times contradictory in nature. Civilians' views were also informed by their own socio-economic situation, the spread of social media images, hearsay and rumors (for example, irregulars as marauders) as well as personal experiences with battalions. Almost all civilian interviewees had some experiences with volunteer battalions, even if only minor ones. A male interviewee from the city of Stakhanov (under the control of the pro-Russian separatist government, renamed by the Ukrainian government into Kadiyivka in 2016) characterized the situation before the war as a fusion of government and bandits. A 22-year-old male student from Mariupol met volunteer battalion members as a protection force at a demonstration in his hometown in spring 2014, while a male interviewee from Mariupol relayed an incident where a group of drunken men shouted at volunteers that they, "Banderovtsy," had bombed their cottage. Other interviewees referred to alcohol abuse in public by volunteers.

A battalion would find it almost impossible to judge how they would be greeted by the local population. They frequently suspected that locals would collaborate with the enemy. Battalion commanders and combatants repeatedly expressed their feeling of insecurity over the behavior of locals, especially in areas heavily covered by Russian media. If the local people were more inclined to the separatist case, they would be scared when a pro-Ukrainian battalion entered their municipality. One of the first precautionary measures a battalion undertook after coming to a village or a district was to collect mobile phones from civilians to interrupt potential communication with the enemy. Since irregular armed groups had limited supplies and were constantly exhausted, they often went to local shops for water, food and energy drinks first—without necessarily paying for these items. The appearance of battalions had an impact on how they were perceived, too.[65] Trained special police battalions in uniform and with disciplined behavior made an impression different from groups which were drunk or immedi-

---

65 Interview with 38-year-old Igor' "Brodyaga", special police unit "Skhidniy korpus", Kharkiv (2017).

ately started brawls. In the cases where civilians did support battalions, they showed their support by collecting goods for volunteers, providing food, heating material, washing or repairing clothes. Medics offered hospital treatment to wounded combatants. Some civilian volunteers provided a car. A 60-year-old male pensioner from Volnovka explained his support with the feeling that the poorly equipped and filthy volunteers were defending him personally.[66] Local small or medium-sized enterprises in support of a volunteer battalion did so on a larger scale than big companies, although the hidden nature of this support makes it hard to verify respective claims.[67] But more often than not, the battalion and the local populace kept at a distance and hardly interacted at all. Combatants went in, did some shopping and moved forward, not getting to know much about the sentiments and preferences of the locals.

To our knowledge, contrary to classical warlords, the Ukrainian volunteer battalions did not "tax" local firms, multinational companies or international aid organizations nor did they forcefully extract resources from local business people. Yet, some battalions who did rob civilians and stole their possessions instilled a sense of awe and apprehension among the local populace. A member of the special patrol battalion Kharkiv I (of the police) recalls how they requested at a local bakery to provide their group of 35 men with bread on a daily basis and a farmer to deliver them with pigs.[68] Allegedly the offer was voluntary, but few probably dared to ask whether they had a choice. Except for the Tornado battalion, we found no indication of a systematic forced extraction of resources. The appropriation of houses, shops or hotels were, however, common phenomena, and stories about commanders enriching themselves by channeling off voluntary contributions by self-

---

66 Interview with 60-year-old IDP Volodymyr from Pervomajsk (Lugansk region), 2017.
67 Interview with 49 year old teacher Svetlana Nazarenko (Mariupol, 2017; Interview with 39 year old Aleksey "Rand", Ternopol, from the battalion Azov (2017).
68 Interview with Bogdan Gen'bach, battalion Khar'kiv I (2017).

help organizations abound. It is difficult to prove whether allegations of personal enrichment are part of internal group rivalries or of smear campaigns, but since the battalion commanders controlled the distribution of resources, there were ample opportunities for personal appropriation.

The boundary between civilians and combatants is not as easily drawn as may seem at first glance. The everyday life of civilians, their practices and routines are profoundly shaped by the war, the destruction of property, physical harm, death or injury of relatives and friends, displacement, loss of jobs, lawlessness, arbitrary rule, trauma affecting whole families, financial and logistical hardships; in short: A disrupted social fabric and a destroyed body politic. Civilians were able to support volunteer battalions in different ways without being an armed fighter at the frontline, for example as integrated assistants in the staff headquarters or as a civil society organization providing support and logistics to a battalion. The civilian support was motivated by their identification with Ukraine as a state, in part also by pity, since at the early stage the Ukrainian battalions were poorly fitted and equipped.[69]

The line between war and peace is fuzzy. According to many interviews, the emergence of irregular armed groups in spring 2014 seemed an extension of the absence of the rule of law before the Maidan and a result of the change of government in Kyiv. But even with hindsight, the violent separatism came as an unforeseen and unpredictable shock. A 56-year-old female engineer from the city of Mariupol recalled that she initially did not even take the separatism seriously, regardless of expressions of dissatisfaction with the national government in Kyiv.[70] Irregular armed groups infiltrated communal life, first as an exception, then as a rule to reckon with. Expectations, interpretations, and assessments changed over time. A 28-year-old male from the municipality of Stakhanov, for example, held that for him, right-wing extremist organizations, even the

---

[69] Interview with 31-year-old freelancer Alina Staylovskaya from Mariupol (2017).
[70] Interview with 56-year-old engineer Viktoriya Marchenko from Mariupol (2017). A similar recollection – cannot take the separatism seriously – provides the 34-year-old male interviewee Kirill Vishnyakov from Mariupol (2017).

"Ultras" (soccer hooligans) would have a right to exist as long as they abided by the constitution and acted in the framework of the law. He conceded that battalions that extorted property were not principally different from criminal or terrorist organizations.[71]

Civilians learned about irregular armed groups or directly interacted with them in various ways. Often, civilians had family members or acquaintances, who served in irregular armed groups and who became a source of information on battalions. Social media, the TV and radio as well as rumors contributed to passing on the image of battalions to the population. In contrast to irregular armed groups in other countries that like to stay undercover, the Ukraine conflict witnessed a tremendous self-advertisement of combatants. Video records were taken, combatants constantly took pictures with their mobile phones and uploaded them to the Internet. The deluge of video footage on irregular armed groups is mostly self-produced. A member of the Aydar battalion even claimed in an interview that some used the brand of a battalion merely for self-aggrandizement or public relation purposes.[72]

Not all civilians identified themselves in national terms as a result of the experience of violence. An internally displaced (IDP) female from the city of Donetsk had left the city after the first shoot-outs and because she was afraid of snipers. She claimed that youth unemployment and forced enrollment were key reasons for joining a battalion. Her son withstood enrollment by moving to the Russian annexed Crimea in hope to find some work there.[73] For her, the destruction in Donetsk was the main reason to move out of the war zone towards the Ukrainian-controlled areas, but not an identification with the Ukrainian state per se. Some IDPs from the separatist territories who were interviewed on the side controlled by the Ukrainians were highly cautious in their statements. An IDP from Horlivka, a city 47km north of Donetsk and since April 2014 under separatist control, gave the unlikely answer that she does not personally know people with pro-Russian positions while at the same

---

71 Interview with Il'ya Balashov from Stakhanov (nowadays Kadievka), (2017).
72 Interview with Serhiy Gukov, member of Aydar battalion (2017).
73 Interview with Lyudmila Viktorovna, internally displaced person from Donetsk (2017).

time stating that the majority of the people in Horlivka were in favor of Russia.[74]

Refugees or IDPs who fled the Russian-controlled zone towards Ukraine tend to look very critically at the change of government in the Russian-controlled areas. One female interviewee forcefully displaced from Russian-controlled Donetsk characterized pro-Ukrainian battalions as saviors. She described the lawlessness in the Russian-controlled Donetsk, the absence of power, the insecurity and life among remaining pensioners. People who stayed were scared to speak out against the Russian-controlled government, she held.[75] A female teacher from Mariupol remembers how scared she felt when the city was under the control of the "DNR" (pro-Russian People's Republic of Donetsk). Especially civilians interviewed in Mariupol, among them former supporters of President Yanukovich, claim that volunteer battalions such as Azov saved them from domination by the separatists.[76] A female interviewee welcomed the pro-Ukrainian volunteers as liberators, as courageous defenders of Ukraine and as rather disciplined units if compared to the regular army.[77] Evidently, this female interviewee perceived the volunteers as an assurance against the backdrop of prior insecurity.[78] Another interviewee from Mariupol confirmed that knowing that the highly motivated "Azov" battalion was nearby rather than poorly paid regular army fellows provided a sense of security. Especially "Azov" had allegedly enforced strict discipline in its ranks and was thus perceived as more reliable than regular security services.[79] Yet, other accounts contradict this: A 42-year-old medical doctor from Volnovakha mentioned unspecified excesses (бесчинства) and theft by "Aydar" combatants in a hotel.[80] A male 34-year-old interviewee from Mariupol mentioned alcoholism and offenses against traffic regulations as the most frequent forms of

---

[74] Interview with IDP Marina from Horliwka (2017).
[75] Interview with 69-year-old IDP Natal'ya from Donetsk (2017).
[76] Interview with 65-year-old pensioner Nikolay Muzyka from Mariupol (2017).
[77] This view was expressed a couple of times by interviewed civilians, for example interview with 57 year old medical doctor Lyudmila from Volnovakha (2017).
[78] Interview with 39-year-old Elena Zolotareva from Mariupol (2017).
[79] Interview with 28-year-old Yevhen Ovcharenko from Mariupol (2017).
[80] Interview with 42-year-old medical doctor Oksana from Volnovakha (2017).

misbehavior by volunteer battalions.[81] Battalions at times exposed their weapons; the showiness was meant to mark public dominance.

Many of the civilians interviewed in the Donbas region had initially been quite detached from the Maidan demonstrations in Kyiv—until the shooting at demonstrators in Kyiv began. In early March 2014, local communists had organized anti-Maidan protests in the Donetsk basin, but eyewitnesses recall that many participants were actually outsiders, who were transferred on buses from Russia to the Donbas.[82] The lawless behavior by the "separatists" forced many civilians to take sides; the hooliganism by the "separatists" was repugnant.[83] But public demonstrations of pro-Russian sentiments seemed to have been rather marginal in size and scope before the violent take-over of public buildings by separatists. The events formed identities, not vice versa.

An exception to the otherwise generally positive view of the volunteer battalions is the battalions "Tornado" and "Svetlana Maria" which misbehaved towards civilians.[84] An interviewee had learned about the theft of a private car and of the technical interior of a nursery school by members of the "Tornado" battalion.[85] A 49-year-old female interviewee from Volnovakha very critically referred to the battalion "Shakhtarsk" (predecessor organization of "Tornado") and an unknown battalion from Kharkov. The battalions "Azov" and "Donbas" usually are ranked better by our interviewees than "Shakhtarsk" or "Aydar".

As long as the fate of a municipality was unknown, people were gripped by paranoia. Anybody could be an informer or spy for the opposite side. A female interviewee from Mariupol added that she immediately deleted entries on her Facebook account after

---

81 Interview with 34-year-old Kirill Vishnyakov form Mariupol (2017).
82 Interview with 49-year-old bookkeeper Svetlana Yakovenko from Volnovakha (2017).
83 Interview with 28-year-old SMM-chik male from Volnovakha (2017).
84 Interview with 53-year-old female entrepreneur Anzhelina Timchenko from Mariupol (2017).
85 Interview with 49-year-old Svetlana Yanovenko, bookkeeper from Volnovakha (2017).

the city came under separatist control, she was scared that her critical leanings could become fatal to her.[86] Another interviewee from Volnovakha articulated her fear of being surrounded by neighbors spying for the Russian side. The presence of a pro-Ukrainian battalion obviously relieved civilians from an overwhelming sense of unpredictability. A female interviewee found a formula for her assessment of the pro-Russian separatists: they preferred the sausage over freedom but will end up with neither freedom nor sausage. It is likely that these expressions are biased because few interviewees living under Ukrainian control would have admitted pro-Russian leanings.

Asked about disciplinary problems among volunteer battalions, civilians from the Ukrainian-controlled side often use understanding language — in difficult times not everything is ideal, one would have to understand. At times, negative images of the volunteer battalions were spread by rumors. For respondents, it was then hard to establish whether the imagery was based on fiction rather than facts. None of the civilians we interviewed had personally experienced robbery or theft by armed volunteers but had heard from people they trusted.[87] A 49-year-old female interviewee related a story of a woman who had claimed to have been sexually abused by the battalion Dnipro I, but later admitted that she had been so drunk that she could not recall any such incident. Another interviewee related a story of a boarding house that was illegally occupied by the battalion "Donbas" in Mariupol for two years and that was left in a condition beyond further use.[88] None of our respondents seemed to fear an imminent threat to their personal integrity by battalion members.

All Ukrainian civilian interviewees were aware of pro-Russian sentiments among their neighbors, acquaintances, friends, family members, or officials, and most of them expressed some understanding for their frustrations. Interviewees in general held that

---

86 Interview with 56-year-old engineer Viktoria Marchenko from Mariupol (2017).
87 Interview with 34-year-old male (identified himself as societal activist) Kirill Vishnyakov from Mariupol (2017)
88 Interview with 53-year-old entrepreneur Anzhelina Timchenko from Mariupol (2017).

while the younger generation and the intelligentsia were rather pro-Ukrainian, older people or workers in mono-industrial cities and those watching only Russian TV were more easily attracted by pro-Russian views. None of the civilian interviewees believed that the rift between pro-Ukrainian and pro-Russian sentiments was merely a matter of Russian imposition. However, all interviewed on the Ukrainian-controlled side of the conflict shared the view that outright separatism would not have emerged without the direct military, political, and media interference from Russia proper. The interviews with civilians on the Ukrainian-controlled side unanimously evidenced that communicative ties with the outspoken pro-Russian segment of the regional populace were entirely interrupted as a result of the war experience. One female interviewee admitted that she had told the battalion "Myrotvorets" about two acquaintances with pro-Russian views.[89]

An interviewee from Volnovakha explained the difference between the "success" or failure of separatists in different cities of the Donetsk Basin with the behavior of the authorities.[90] The preferences of civilians were mostly formed by experiences in spring 2014 rather than predetermined by a Weltanschauung. The uncultured, rude, lawless behavior of the separatists, an atmosphere of vigilante justice, the imagery of hooliganism and the detrimental impact of separatism on small businesses scared off many civilians in the Donbas, regardless of their frustration with Ukrainian authorities.[91] An active civil society supporter of the pro-Ukrainian battalions was threatened by the separatist side that if they re-conquered Mariupol, he would be one of the first they would go after.[92]

All civilian interviewees were asked about their outlook onto the future. A substantial segment of those who expressed very strong pro-Ukrainian views was deeply frustrated after the initial

---

89   Interview with 32-year-old female IDP "Darya" from Donetsk (2017).
90   Interview with 42-year-old medical doctor Oksana from Volnovakha (2017). ("Все зависело от власти. Где была воля пресечь эти движения—там их пресекли").
91   Interview with 53-year-old entrepreneur Anzhelina Timchenko from Mariupol (2017).
92   Interview with 34-year-old societal activist Kirill Vishnyakov from Mariupol (2017).

post-Maidan euphoria. Several, especially the younger ones, thought about emigrating. None of them were optimistic about the future political or economic development. Most expected a frozen conflict and hoped that a resurgence of violence could be avoided. Not one single interviewee believed in conflict resolution in the foreseeable future.

Government-Controlled Groups: Territorial Defense Battalions

Ukraine had retained the Soviet tradition of territorial defense forces, formally in place since its independence from the Soviet Union in December 1991. Each regional administration had the right to form a territorial defense unit in the municipalities, based on reservists. However, these territorial defense forces existed by and large only on paper until spring 2014. The former head of the Maidan self-defense and then Secretary of the National Security and Defense Council (from February to August 2014), Andriy Parubiy, sought for a way to fuse volunteer groups with the army, and the legal regulations for the territorial defense seemed to be a way out. In March 2014, the then acting President of Ukraine, Oleksandr Turchynov, issued an order to create seven territorial defense battalions. According to the law, they were called Battalions of Territorial Defense (BTD). On 30 April 2014, Acting Chief of Staff Serhiy Pashynskiy additionally announced: "Today we have physically created seven battalions of territorial defense on the left bank, and now all governors are being instructed to create such battalions in each area."[93] On 30 April 2014, acting President Oleksandr Turchynov issued an order to create 27 territorial defense battalions altogether. Since then, all BTD have been part of the regular armed forces and under the command of the general staff. Mobilized reservists and volunteers mixed in the BTD — the overall number is estimated at 300 to 500 men in a given battalion (Lebedev 2017, p. 28.).

---

93 https://www.globalsecurity.org/military/world/ukraine/btro.htm.

From the outset, the BTD were part of the regular armed forces, governed by its general staff and subordinate to the Ministry of Defense and to the heads of administration in the respective region where they were formed. The respective regional military commission managed the recruitment, the logistical support, and the provision with weapons and equipment at the expense of regional budgets and with the additional support of regional sponsors from the business world. The control of the BTD by government implied the nomination of commanders—in contrast to volunteer battalions which were formed around a self-proclaimed or self-selected leader (commander). Governmental control extended to the hand-out, registration, and safety of weapons and ammunition. As part of the territorial defense, the regional military commissariats formed rifle battalions, and the district (city) military commissariats formed between two to five defense units of their own. An additional "defense detachment" existed for a whole region, which was charged with material support, the provision of transport means and healthcare for the territorial defense units.

The tasks of the BTD comprise the protection of public authorities, local governments, critical facilities and communications, the operation of checkpoints, fighting sabotage, the collection of intelligence on enemy forces, including illegal armed groups and criminals, the maintenance of public safety and security, the organization of resistance and the reaction to emergencies and man-made disasters in peacetime. On 10 November 2014, Stepan Poltorak, the Minister of Defense of Ukraine, ordered the territorial defense battalions to be reorganized as "motorized infantry battalions," obviously with the intention to put them under direct subordination of the Ministry of Defense and to get them out of the hold of the "territorial defense" of the regions.

Apart from the BTD, several regular units of the armed forces of Ukraine were established on the basis of volunteers, such as the 3rd airmobile battalion Phoenix or the 54th reconnaissance battalion UNSO. Apart from the BTD in a couple of regions special police battalions were created. The Ministry of Interior thus established 56 special task patrol police units, sized from company to battalion. After several reorganizations, this number shrunk to 33 units. By mid-June 2014, these special police units consisted of 3,000 men. The ministerial aide Herashchenko and Viktor Chalavan were the key contacts for organizing volunteer battalions under the auspices of the Ministry of Internal Affairs.

The legal status of the volunteer-based special police forces remained dubious:

> "While the presence of police made it possible to make arrests, the lack of a declaration of war nevertheless meant that volunteers were often left in limbo: they were using violence against their fellow citizens without any legal authority to do so. Ultimately, by Ukrainian law, our war is full of illegal things." (Käihkö 2018, p. 153).

Finally, the National Guard was created by a decree of March 13, 2014 of the Minister of Interior. While all its members were volunteers, it was integrated into the Ministry of Internal Affairs. The National Guard established several reserve battalions, among them the Donbas battalion and the General Kulchytskiy battalion formed by volunteers and former Maidan activists.

Golden Gate

On May 2, 2014, the Golden Gate police battalion was established as part of the Ministry of Interior by a decree of Minister Arsen Avakov. The Golden Gate battalion consisted mostly of volunteers who had participated in the self-defense of the Maidan. Some others joined Golden Gate because their original battalion did not receive official recognition. Men who had originally been fighting with the battalion Donbas II or the battalion Krym joined Golden Gate to get official status, including the expected benefits.[94] Even though the battalion Krym had originally been formed as part of the National Guard, it was dissolved, and its members were told to join the Golden Gate. Members were promised attractive benefits for joining this government-initiated battalion. A legal status offered several benefits: when wounded, they could claim payment of medical costs, relatives could ask for compensation in case of death, salaries would be paid, pension rights would accrue, and usually a weapon

---

94 https://www.youtube.com/watch?v=TRBVO1BqP20.

would be provided for a combatant. However, initially the conditions, such as training, were hardly better than in independently formed irregular groups.[95] The first commander of the Golden Gate was Mykola Shvalya, an officer major, who had originally fought together with Semen Semenchenko in an irregular group against Russian mercenaries.[96] In August 2014, the Golden Gate battalion participated as part of the ATO operation in the re-capture of the village Krasnyy Yar; in August 2014, the battalion experienced heavy fire from the separatists on the outskirts of Luhansk city and in the vicinity of the city of Shchastiya.

In July 2014, the Golden Gate battalion was deployed by the government for a "cleansing operation" against Azov combatants who refused to subordinate to the Ministry of Internal Affairs. However, the Golden Gate combatants rejected to use firearms against their Azov compatriots.[97] From the perspective of the Ministry of Internal Affairs, the Golden Gate battalion was a volunteer battalion "owned" by the government, or else it would not have directed Golden Gate against insubordinate members of Azov for a cleansing operation. From the government's perspective, Golden Gate had a clear advantage—it could be used for purposes the regular police would not cover.

Myrotvorets (Peacemaker)

The Myrotvorets battalion was formed by decree of the Ministry of Internal Affairs on May 9, 2014 as a "patrol service of the militia for special purposes".[98] The initial commander was Andriy Teteruk, born in 1973, who had received military training at the higher command school in Moscow between 1990 and 94 and who had then served as a contract soldier in the Russian Army for five years. One

---

95 http://gordonua.com/publications/dobrovolec-batalona-zolotye-vorota-teh-kto-ne-hochet-voevat-prizyvayut-a-nad-nami-kto-rvetsya-v-ato-izdevayutsya-uzhe-poltora-mesyaca-34433.html.
96 http://argumentua.com/stati/viktor-chalavan-obezopasit-sebya-ot-voennykh-ugroz-tolko-kontraktnoi-armiei-nerealno.
97 http://ru.warriors.wikia.com/wiki/Золотые_ворота.
98 https://mk.npu.gov.ua/uk/publish/article/158250.

of his duties during that time was the command over a reconnaissance rotte. From 1999 onwards, he served under the Ministry of Internal Affairs in Ukraine, and in the years 2006 and 2007, he was part of the peacekeeping mission in Kosovo. After that, he served as head of security for a trading center in Kyiv. The experience of a core group in peacekeeping gave the battalion its name; it consisted of 52 people in the beginning and expanded to 83 combatants.[99] On May 23, 2014, Teteruk was nominated commander of the Myrotvorets battalion, in November 2014 he became a deputy of the Verknovna Rada for the Party People's Front. Members of the Myrotvorets battalion were mostly professional military or police officers. The battalion was trained at the National Academy for Interior Affairs in the Kyiv region, allegedly according to NATO standards.[100] Myrotvorets' main task consisted of policing the hinterland, but it also participated in the battles of Ilovaysk in August 2014. Several of its members became prisoners of war of the separatists.[101] Myrotvorets represented a typical government owned battalion, formed from above, consisting of military professionals with pre-existing experience and meant to fill gaps in policing.

Autonomous Groups / Azov Battalion

Among the autonomously formed irregular armed groups with an extreme nationalist outlook, Azov is one of the most known, but it perfectly illustrates the limits of "autonomy" too. The initial core of the battalion Azov—which was formed in May 2014—was based on the "Auto-Maidan," the "Black Corp" of Ihor Mosiichuk, the paramilitary group "Patriot of Ukraine" and a group of "ultras"—football hooligans who had the tendency to use violence and who had participated in the Maidan protests.[102] In Kharkiv proper, pro-Russian and pro-Ukrainian paramilitary groups had competed—a pro-

---

99 http://i-vin.info/news/vinnytskyy-kombat-teteruk-pro-viynu-i-myr-na-front i-8396; https://petrimazepa.com/ilomainsideteteruk.html.
100 http://mykyivregion.com.ua/2017/07/14/vzyati-najkrashe-vid-svitu-i-stvori ti-svoye-vlasne-yak-trenuyutsya-bijci-mirotvorcya/.
101 https://www.youtube.com/watch?v=hF_RguYpBnU.
102 Interview with 23-year-old Maksim Shevchenko, former combatant of the Azov battalion (2017)

Russian sports club called "Oplot" (bastion) and the "Patriot of Ukraine". Oplot was formed in 2010, specialized in mixed martial arts and had participated in the anti-Maidan rallies. Together with its supporters from Rostov on Don (Russia proper) it had occupied the buildings of the regional administrations in Kharkiv in March 2014 and raised the Russian flag. Members of "Patriot of Ukraine" organized counter attacks on Oplot by occupying their headquarters in Kharkiv and by dissolving pro-Russian meetings. In the transition period from street fighters to military combatants, some members of "Patriot of Ukraine" moved over to the "Black Corp" acted as armed and masked volunteer groups in uniforms. However, the Ministry of Internal Affairs supported it with resources as early as in April 2014.[103]

The core of the Azov battalion consisted of members of the racist, neo-Nazi organization "Social-National Assembly" and of members of "Patriot of Ukraine", headed by Andrii Biletsky, fanatic football fans of the teams "Dynamo Kyiv" und "Shakhtar" (Donetsk), members of the party "Brotherhood of Dmytro Korchynsky", and activists of the OUN as well as members of a Kozak Shooting Brotherhood. Oleh Lyashko, leader of the Radical Party of Ukraine, stated that up to half of the members of Azov had been sentenced previously.[104] In January 2014, the district court of Kyiv-Svyatoshinskii had sentenced Lyashko, Serhiy Bevza, and Volodymyr Shpar, the so-called Vasylkivskiy terrorists, to six years of prison. Furthermore, the "Patriot of Ukraine" had made it their business to set enterprises of competitors on fire, to beat up critical journalists and to racketeer.[105] Some members of Azov were also adherents of the "Misanthropic Division" (MD), a right-wing group which is active in Russia and Belarus.

The decision to form the battalion Azov was allegedly taken by the deputy of the city council of Mariupol, Oleksandr Yaroshenko, the "Auto-Maidan" activist Yaroslav Honchar, the deputy of the Verkhovna Rada, Oleh Lyashko, the press-secretary of the

---

103 https://112.ua/interview/ot-pravogo-sektora-azov-otlichaetsya-bolee-sistem nym-podhodom-i-organizaciey-255219.html.
104 http://wek.ru/budni-ukrainskogo-deputata. (30.01.2015).
105 Ibid.

"Social-national Assembly", Ihor' Mosiichuk, and by Dmytro Korchynsky, the former leader of the ultra-nationalist UNA-UNSO party. The political capital of these founders and the reliance on predecessor organizations were the key resources for Azov's formation. The Azov battalion consisted at its formation in May 2014 of a group of roughly fifty men (some claim 150) — by the end of June 2014, its membership had increased to 500 people. At its peak, Azov had approximately 1,300 members. Altogether, some 5,000 people went through Azov over time.[106] A Russian webpage called "antifashist.com" published in early March 2016 a list with the names of 644 members of Azov.[107] According to the decision by the Minister of Internal Affairs, Arsen Avakov, to put volunteer battalions under the auspices of the Ministry of Interior, the Azov Battalion became a "special patrol police unit." On September 17, 2014, Azov was re-labelled into a regiment ("polk"), and in October 2014, it was incorporated into the National Guard — a move that was accompanied by the inclusion of additional specialists and the provision of artillery. Although being part of the National Guard, Azov retained its separate command, training, and area for exercises.

Azov was led by a few commanders: Its first commander was Andrey Biletsky, a former history teacher and head of the "Social-National Assembly" (SNA) who became the leader of the political party "National Corps." Before the Maidan protests, Biletsky had been pronounced guilty of extremism and attempted murder and had, therefore, served two-and-a-half years in prison. Biletsky is an adherent of a white supremacist ideology, a racist, anti-Semite and defender of "Aryan values." Oleh Odnorozhenko is one of the leaders of the SNA and also speaks in favor of a domination of the white race. Ihor' Mosiychuk, a former journalist and leading figure in the social-nationalist movement, was a deputy commander of Azov and had been sentenced to six years of prison before the Maidan for having prepared an act of terrorism. Before Azov's attack on the city of Mariupol, Mosiychuk had been accused of having attacked

---

106 https://www.svoboda.org/a/29308146.html.
107 http://antifashist.com/item/idut-po-ukraine-nacisty-polka-azov-spisok-kar atelej.html.

law enforcement officers. But the Verkhovna Rada protected his immunity as a member of parliament for the Radical Party. Maksim Zhorin was another Azov commander, a designer by training, and later on the leader of the "National Corp," with strong nationalist convictions.

The Azov commanders earned their reputation as leaders through two features—extreme nationalist convictions and a proneness to use violence in the achievement of their goals. While not all members of Azov may share a neo-Nazi ideology, a significant number of Azov combatants have neo Nazi inclinations and use national-socialist symbols. The mobilization capacity, the leadership and the coherence of Azov was based on pre-existing neo-nazi and radical right-wing groups. The symbol of Azov, the so-called Wolfsangel was also used in Nazi Germany. Yet, in 2014, the Minister of Interior, Arsen Avakov and sponsor of Azov denied any links to Nazism.[108] Violence became a source of social capital, of earning a reputation as a leader. Azov recruited its members mostly through social media like Facebook, Vkontakte and its webpage.

Vadym Troyan, a deputy commander of Azov, was the key liaison to the Ministry of Interior and thus in charge of securing a continuous flow of resources to the battalion. As part of the Ministry of Internal Affairs the Azov battalion was financed by the government, but also through social network crowdfunding and support by businesses. According to its commander Biletsky, the former governor of the Donetsk region, Serhiy Taruta, sponsored the Azov battalion as well. One of the early sponsors of Azov was the businessman Igor' Kolomoiskii, another one the deputy head of the regional administration of Dnipro and assistant of Kolomoiskii, Borys Filatov. Filatov declared in early August 2014 that he would stop financing Azov due to the fascist inclinations of one of its founders, Ihor' Mosiichuk who left Azov in August 2014 (Young 2022).

Azov included members with neo-fascist convictions from abroad as well, mostly from Georgia, France, Belarus, Canada, and

---

108 https://focus.ua/country/316552/.

Slovenia, altogether 85.[109] Foreign fighters from Russia, France, Italy, Belarus, Canada, Sweden, and Slovenia also fought in Azov. Some of the known Azov foreign fighters include Mikael Skillt, a Swedish sniper and spokesman for several neo-Nazi groups, who first trained Azov members, then participated in combat operations in Maryinka, Ilovaysk, and Shyvokone and nowadays claims that he converted from a national-socialist to a Ukrainian nationalist.[110] Another foreign fighter for Azov is Francesco Fontana, who joined Azov at the age of 53 because he allegedly enjoyed killing.[111] Gaston Besson, a at that time 47-year-old French with an anti-European, white supremacist agenda, had gained combat experience in a Croatian militia in 1991. He had trained anarchists against a G-8 meeting in France in 2001. Before joining Azov, he had shared his street-fighting experience with the Maidan protesters (Majic 2014). Among others, Azov members were trained by instructors from Georgia and the French Legion. The then Ukrainian President Poroshenko personally awarded the Ukrainian citizenship to the Belarusian Azov fighter Serhiy Korotikh (nom de guerre: Malyuta), who was one of the founders of the Russian neo-Nazi group "National-socialist society." Several other neo-Nazis from abroad joined the Azov battalion, for example, the well-known Russian neo-nazis Roman Zheleznov and Aleksandr Parinov from the gang "BORN," which is forbidden in Russia.[112]

The Azov battalion consisted of infantry, a tank division, light armored multi-purpose tractors, a battery of howitzers and a mortar battalion. While Azov's equipment was initially limited to armored vehicles, it received more heavy weapons after its inclusion into the National Guard. From May 2014 onwards, the Azov battalion participated in combat in Mariupol (May 2014) against pro-Rus-

---

109 http://www.fr.de/politik/kaempfe-in-der-ukraine-es-ist-doch-besser-wenn-es-knallt-a-517500,0#artpager-517500-1.
110 https://der-dritte-weg.info/2016/08/24/im-gespraech-mit-mikael-skillt-vom-bataillon-azov-video/; https://www.dailysignal.com/2015/08/10/meet-the-former-neo-nazi-spokesman-who-now-fights-for-freedom-in-ukraine/
111 Age pertains to the moment of joining Azov in 2014.
112 http://cyclowiki.org/wiki/Роман_Александрович_Железнов. https://zona.media/article/2014/26/12/parinov.

sian insurgents, especially against the pro-Russian Donbas battalion, as well as in Shakhtarsk, Torez, and Snizhne (May 2014), in August 2014 in the battles of Ilovaysk, Novoazovsk, and Mariupol. From September 2014 onwards, Azov was removed from frontline operations. Yet, Azov participated in the trade blockade against Russian-controlled Crimea. In February 2016, they blocked the establishment of the TV company "Inter," demanding that the channel free itself from Kremlin influence, and in May 2016 Azov launched a smoke screen around the building of the Verkhovna Rada with the aim not to allow elections in the Donbas.[113] Azov earned a record for repeated human rights violations.

A distinct feature of Azov is the formation of a political wing of its own, the political party "National Corps," headed by Biletsky. In March 2017, the "National Corps", the Right Sector, OUN, S14, KUN, and the Party "Svoboda" published a joint manifesto calling for the primacy of national interests, for a nuclear power status of Ukraine, the right to wear weapons, and for strengthening the army as well as speaking out against illegal migration. A former combatant of Azov, Serhiy Korovin (nom de guerre Horst), who served for some time as a guard to the neo-Nazi and Azov member Korotkikh, was surprisingly listed by the party "Narodnyj Front" (People's Front) party as a candidate. The "Narodny Front" was the party of the then Prime Minister Yatseniuk and Minister of Interior Avakov. Parties of diverse profiles hoped to increase their appeal by enlisting combatants. Azov also formed a so-called national brotherhood, i.e., an organization based on former combatants for maintaining public order and "protecting" small and medium-sized enterprises.[114]

Membership requirements for the "brotherhood" are physical preparedness, participation in combat and the ability to handle weapons. Azov's subgroup intends to take "public order" into its own hand, entitling itself to enforce "public order." The under-

---

113 http://112.ua/glavnye-novosti/bileckiy-v-sluchae-popytki-provesti-vybory-na-donbasse-my-vynesem-etu-radu-312729.html.
114 See their webpage: http://ndrugua.org/

standing of this "order" is arbitrary. In the city of Cherkasy, for example, the "brotherhood" entered the City Council and forced the deputies to adopt a budget to the liking of the mayor, who had hired the "brotherhood" to impress the deputies.[115] How this imposition of "order" is financed is unclear, but it is the common belief that local businessmen paid for Azov as a protection racket.

Azov's impact on Ukraine's public space is grounded in its linkage to politics, its mobilization potential, its formation of its political wing, its preparedness to take the "law" into its own hands and a certain ideological coherence. Azov could survive as a distinct group despite its formal inclusion into the National Guard. Azov became untouchable as a result of the reputation earned in the war. Azov proved able to adjust by combining different roles — the status as a state security organ, as partner of a political party, as a self-defense militia, as a protection racket, and its transformation into a militant political movement. The first commander, Biletsky, had turned politician early on, anticipating a career beyond the irregular armed group. Finally, Azov proved capable of including a broad range of nationalists, not being dogmatic in its ideology.

The OUN Battalion
(Organization of Ukrainian Nationalists)

The Organization of Ukrainian Nationalists (OUN) was initially formed at Vienna in 1929 as a right-wing organization opposed to the Soviet and Polish governments. The OUN supported the Nazi anti-semitism during World War II as it considered itself an ally of the German occupation forces. Its infamous leader was Stepan Bandera. The OUN battalion builds upon this historical basis. It had already formed a defense "hundred" named after Yevhen Konovalets during the Maidan demonstrations. Formally, the OUN joined the war effort in Ukraine as the battalion of Territorial Defense of the city of Nezhin. Since the government rejected an official registration of OUN as an independent battalion, it was first included into the Right Sector, but it dissociated itself from that in

---

115 https://www.pravda.com.ua/news/2018/01/30/7170071/

August 2014 with a commander of its own: Mykola Kokhanovskiy.[116] Kokhanovskiy (nom de guerre "Bureviy") had earned a record for hooliganism before the Maidan. The OUN recruited members through social media such as Facebook, Vkontakte and its website; most of its members came from Kyiv, the central regions, or the Donetsk region. OUN's ideology is characterized by the idea of a "Natiocracy," which should, according to its ideological founder, Mykola Stsiborskiy, encompass national solidarity, authority, hierarchy, discipline, and self-organization.[117] In March 2017, OUN, the association Svoboda, National Corps, Right Sector, S14 and the Congress of Ukrainian Nationalists (KUN) signed a manifesto to unite their political efforts.[118]

In the beginning, OUN had 30 members; it had grown to 100 people by November 2014. The OUN battalion was operating in the area of Pisky in the Donetsk region. Allegedly, the OUN and the Right Sector did not receive direct governmental support. However, its members earned state salaries through the government-sponsored Dnipro-1 battalion, which functioned as an intermediary for the governmental funding of OUN.[119] Donations and volunteers who collected money support the battalion, but whether OUN had substantial individual sponsors is not known. The donations covered food, uniforms, protective vests, and visual devices while the regular military provided OUN with weaponry, among them grenade launchers, anti-tank weapons, and anti-aircraft guns.

Following the Minsk II agreements in April 2015, the battalion was disarmed and moved away from the battle zone. OUN subsequently declared that it would not subordinate to the Armed Forces of Ukraine. Some members of Aydar and DUK joined OUN to stay independent from governmental control. Where some OUN members joined the 93rd brigade of the armed forces of Ukraine, social

---

116 https://day.kyiv.ua/ru/news/240417-dvuhletniy-put-voyny-db-oun-pokazal
i-v-foto; https://www.radiosvoboda.org/a/25475844.html.
117 http://ukrlife.org/main/evshan/natiocracy61.htm; http://oun.org.ua/ua/
home/prohrama-dobrovolchoho-rukhu-oun.
118 https://www.radiosvoboda.org/a/news/28373730.html
119 Interview with then 35-year-old Borys Ovcharov, former combatant of the Right Sector, Azov and OUN (2017).

security considerations trumped identity. OUN members became conspicuous through their criminal record. Thus, for example, in February 2018 three members of the OUN were sentenced to three to five years in prison for preparing a terrorist act along the railway near the city of Lviv; two of the sentences were suspended on probation.[120] In October 2017, supporters of the convicted threatened the presiding judge, occupied the courtroom in the city of Svyatoshinski, and partially destroyed its interior.[121] The OUN members obviously considered themselves above the law. OUN is a case of an autonomous but small battalion. Compared to Azov it lacked essential political capital; it did not broaden its portfolio to survive and was therefore not able to transform criminal activities into lucrative business.

Aydar

The battalion Aydar arose from the self-defense groups of the Maidan and members of the Right Sector, particularly a segment of the Right Sector which called itself "White Hammer". According to a member of Aydar, the battalion consisted of 117 people in May 2014 but at its prime had up to 2.000 members. How many of those were actively involved in Aydar is a secret. In 2016, the pro-Russian hacker group Cyberberkut published an excel sheet with 1570 members of the battalion Aydar, including personal data, telephone numbers, rank, the date of recruitment – the source of which was probably a computer leak.[122] Serhiy Melnichuk, a former commander of the Maidan self-defense, became the first commander of Aydar. In October 2014, he was appointed member (deputy) of the Verkhovna Rada, the national parliament, on the party list of the Radical Party, headed by Oleh Lyashko. His successor as a commander was Yevhen Ptashnyk, a lieutenant colonel of Russian origin, who had undergone training in the reconnaissance department of the higher army command school in Kyiv. Aydar was a

---

120 https://www.pravda.com.ua/rus/news/2018/02/23/7172652/
121 http://sv.ki.court.gov.ua/sud2608/pres-centr/news/388674/.
122 http://www.cyber-berkut.ru/main/20150614_00.php.

national-patriotic battalion, but without an overarching ideology, and its leadership was professional rather than ideological.

Aydar consisted of several subgroups with a certain degree of autonomy. Aydar included sniper groups, subgroups specialized in reconnaissance, a battery of howitzers, and a tank rotte.[123] People mostly originating from the Cherkasy region were in the group "Cold Ravine", another one came from Volhynia, there was a rotte consisting of veterans of the Afghan war and a "Golden Rotte".[124] In June 2014, the commander of Aydar autonomously nominated "military administrators" for the cities of Schast'o, Starobilsk, Novoaydar, Lutugino and Severodonetsk, arguing that the local police was corrupted.[125] The incident illustrates that Aydar did not confine itself to the fight with separatists, but felt entitled to take over public control. In June 2014, Aydar tried to storm the city of Luhansk without prior approval by the ATO command—another illustration of the autonomous nature of Aydar.[126] In 2015, Aydar was nonetheless included into the 10th brigade of mountain stormtroopers of Ukraine's Armed forces infantry and thus formally legalized.

Aydar was financed by a special fund (Fund for the Defense of Ukraine), which collected money through social networks. Several entrepreneurs or politicians such as Volodymyr Korban, the entrepreneur, and mayor of Dnipro, Borys Filatov, and Svyatoslav Oleynik, a comrade-in-arms of the oligarch Kolomoysky were sponsors of Aydar. Allegedly, 70 percent of the income of the "Fund for the Defense of Ukraine" was covered by Kolomoysky.[127] Some

---

123 Interview with then 53-year-old Stanislav "Stas", Kharkiv, 24th storm battalion "Aydar" (2017).
124 http://www.ukrinform.ru/rubric-lastnews/1682909-v_smele_pohoronili_ko mandira_podrazdeleniya_holodniy_yar_1647673.html; http://religions.unian. net/orthodoxy/954648-predstoyatel-upts-sovershil-otpevanie-sotnika-afgans koy-sotni-batalona-aydar-olega-mihnyuka.html; http://vz.ru/world/2015/3 /31/737393.html
125 http://www.osce.org/ru/ukraine-smm/122978.
126 http://www.unian.ua/politics/930317-minoboroni-batalyon-aydar-samostiy no-virishiv-shturmuvati-pozitsiji-boyovikiv-u-lugansku-i-potrapiv-u-zasidku. html.
127 http://obozrevatel.com/interview/81096-gennadij-korban-u-rossijskih-komp anij-myi-dolzhnyi-otnyat-vse.htm.

of Aydar's cars were taken from civilians in the separatist territories, and the Ministry of Defense supplied Aydar with weapons. Otherwise, little is known about the actual weapons holdings of Aydar. Aydar patrolled as a militia, took residential areas under its control, it engaged in reconnaissance, and some members used opportunities for marauding.[128]

Aydar commander Melnichuk befriended Vladyslav Kaskiv, former head of the National Agency for Investment and Management of National Projects. According to a former member of Aydar, Kaskiv was an intermediary for the forceful appropriation of property. Aydar allegedly received a certain percentage of the value for helping "interested" businessmen in illegal acquisitions.[129] According to a former Aydar member, a subgroup of Aydar tried to get the amber business in the regions of Rivne and Zhytomir under its control.[130] It seemed that segments of Aydar turned into a "raiding agency" for hire. Kaskiv subsequently escaped to Panama, where he asked for political asylum, but was extradited to Ukraine in 2017.[131] The political party close to Aydar was "Ukrop," which was headed by the sponsors of Aydar, i.e., the mentioned businessmen Kolomoyskiy, Korban, Filatov, and Oleynik.

Human rights violations by members of volunteer battalions reflect a deficit of regulations and rule enforcement. In the Aydar battalion, for example, a person with serious mental disorders was in charge of interrogations — he earned the nom de guerre "butcher." At times, the line between appropriate and inappropriate behavior was thin. A member of the Aydar battalion recalls that in the absence of a local militia, he detained a man who had set cottages on fire. This very detainee then filed a complaint against his illegal detention. Aydar participated in several reported human rights violations, among them kidnapping, illegal arrests, cruel

---

[128] https://forum.pravda.com.ua/index.php?topic=815799.0.00
[129] http://www.bbc.com/ukrainian/ukraine_in_russian/2015/02/150220_ru_s_dykiy_aidar_interview.9
[130] http://www.bbc.com/ukrainian/ukraine_in_russian/2015/02/150220_ru_s_dykiy_aidar_interview.
[131] https://112.ua/glavnye-novosti/pecherskiy-sud-arestoval-kaskiva-na-dva-mesyaca-s-pravom-vneseniya-zaloga-418522.html.

treatment, theft, extortion, marauding, hostage-taking, fake executions, the beating of prisoners, rape, and allegedly executions.[132] An arrested man later reported that he was tortured to admit that he was supporting separatism.[133] A so-called black rotte of the Aydar battalion was in charge of enforcing internal security in the battalion; it gained a bad reputation for using its position for the pursuit of personal interests[134]. According to the police of Severodonetsk, 38 criminal trials were opened against Aydar members.[135]

The members of Aydar had no political ambitions as a party or as a political association on its own; no distinct ideology played a role in the self-understanding of the battalion.[136] The relative autonomy of Aydar until its inclusion into the regular armed forces was based on the sponsorship by oligarchs, its mix of combat with organized crime, the political networks of its first commander Melnichuk, and a certain degree of military professionalism among its commanders. In comparison to Azov, Aydar lacked political ambition and ideological coherence; it could easily mobilize, but not autonomously survive beyond the battleground.

UNA-UNSO and the Ukrainian Volunteer Army

Die Ukrainian National Assembly-Ukrainian National Self-Defense (UNA-UNSO) was originally formed on June 30, 1990 in the western Ukrainian city of Lviv and headed by Yuriy Shukhevich, son of an officer of the Ukrainian insurgency army (UPA) against the Soviet regime. The UNA-UNSO is a Ukrainian nationalist, radical anti-Russian organization that strives for a violent change of the

---

132 https://amnesty.org.ru/sites/default/files/eur500402014ru.pdf; http://www.theinsider.ua/politics/54a9af9fa9f76/
133 Ukrainian Helsinki Human Rights Union (2017), Unlawful detentions and torture committed on the Ukrainian side in the armed conflict in eastern Ukraine, Kharkiv Human Rights Protection Group and NGO "Truth Hounds" report, Kyiv, p.18; Управление Верховного комиссара Организации Объединенных Наций по правам человека. Доклад о ситуации с правами человека в Украине16 августа – 15 ноября 2017 г., p. 11.
134 Interview with Serhiy Gukov, member of Aydar bataillon (2017).
135 https://amnesty.org.ru/sites/default/files/eur500402014ru.pdf.
136 Interview with 53-year-old Stansilav "Stas," Kharkiv, bataillon Aydar (2017).

regime, it is anti-European, against oligarchs, migrants, and homosexuals, while anti-semitism is championed at least by part of its members. UNA represents the political party, UNSO its paramilitary wing. Members of UNSO participated as combatants in several post-Soviet wars, including the Transnistria conflict (1992), in Abkhasia (1993), in Nagorny Karabakh (1992–94), in the first Chechen war (1994–96), and in the Kosovo war in 1999. The UNSO fighters usually joined groups that fought against Russian forces. In 2008, UNSO fighters fought in the war over South Ossetia on the Georgian side — a core of trained and combat-proven paramilitaries long before the Maidan. The UNA–UNSO participated at the Maidan protests in Kyiv in camouflage uniforms and sporting their flags, reminiscent of those of the Nazis with their black hooked cross on a red ground.

In 1996, the UNA–UNSO had signed a partnership treaty with the German right-wing extremist party NPD (Nationaldemokratische Partei Deutschlands). On the Maidan, the UNA–UNSO joined the Right Sector and violently attacked the police forces. The UNA–UNSO leader Oleksandr Musychko, a convicted criminal, rabid anti-communist, and anti-semite, participated in several violent acts in the Riwne region after the ousting of the Yanukovich government. In the night from March 24 to 25, 2015 he was killed by the police after he had resisted his arrest. Based on its pre-existing paramilitary organization, UNSO was established in spring 2014 as a reconnaissance battalion of the regular armed forces of Ukraine; it was named 131st special reconnaissance battalion and included Canadians and US Americans of Ukrainian origin as well as fighters from Georgia. Although the 131st battalion was formally part of the Armed Forces, its commanders were initially chosen by UNSO and only later on nominated from above. In September 2015, UNA–UNSO was registered as a political party, but a former combatant of the battalion claims that it was independent of the party — they did not see themselves as stormtroopers of a political party.[137]

---

137 Interview with 25-year-old Vitaly Kuz'menko, former fighter of the 131st reconnaissance battalion (2017).

The Ukrainian Volunteer Army (UDA or 8th UDA battalion "Aratta") allegedly consisted of 720 people and was commanded by Andriy Gergert, a former member of UNSO and participant in the Maidan protests, where he befriended Yarosh of the Right Sector. The battalion still exists with half of its former size as part of the Ukrainian Volunteer Army (UDA) under the command of Yarosh. UDA claims to be the only remaining fully independent battalion. According to Gergert, the battalion is financed by the mayor of the city of Dnipro, Borys Filatov, the governor of the Mykolaiv region, Oleksiy Savchenko, the governor of the Dnipropetrovsk region, Valentyn Reznichenko and several deputies at the national parliament, among them Volodymyr Parasyuk.[138]

Right Sector

The Ukrainian Volunteer Corps-Right Sector (DUK-PS) was formed in July 2014 as a paramilitary group based on the already existing military wing of the Right Sector to fight the pro-Russian separatism in the Donbas. The Ukrainian National Assembly, DUK and Tryzub had paramilitary organizations long before the Maidan. Founding groups of the Right Sector included "Tryzub," led by Dmytro Yarosh and Andriy Tarasenko, the Ukrainian National Assembly–Ukrainian National Self-Defense (UNA–UNSO), the Social-National Assembly and its paramilitary wing "Patriot of Ukraine," the group "White Hammer" and the "Carpathian Sich." The Right Sector was formed at an early stage of the Maidan protests by merging several groups which had existed autonomously beforehand, among them the UNA–UNSO (Ukrainian National Assembly–Ukrainian National Self-Defense) and the OUN (Organization of Ukrainian Nationalists). The leader of the Right Sector, Yarosh, initiated the formation of DUK-PS as a battalion. as early as in 1993, Yarosh had participated in founding the far-right paramilitary group "Tryzub" named after Stepan Bandera. From 2005 onwards Yarosh was supposedly the leader of "Tryzub," the military commander of DUK-PS is Andriy Stempitskiy.

---

138 Interview with 39-year-old Andriy Gergert, commander of the 8th UDA battalion "Aratta" (2017) (Aratta is a legendary highland in the Sumerian mythology).

According to its press speaker Artem Skoropadskiy, the Right Sector is against Ukraine's entry into the European Union (EU), against the "Euro"-Maidan and homosexuals. The Right Sector portrays itself as a revolutionary organization. It wants to change the existing political system, and it is especially keen to take out the oligarchs. In contrast to the Svoboda Party which wants to restrict the Russian language, the Right Sector would permit regional languages. The speaker of the Right Sector admits that his group shot at Berkut police officers on the Maidan, but he refrained from giving details about the weapons they had held on the Maidan.[139] The Right Sector had allegedly taken weapons from the Secret Service SBU, but how and when remains unclear.

The volunteers of the Right Sector / DUK consisted of a core of 60 to 80 people, and it was headed by Andriy "Cherven" Gergert. Its structure followed the blueprint of the historical Ukrainian Insurgent Army (UPA) during World War II.[140] The UPA engaged in diversionary and terror attacks and earned a reputation as an extremely cruel killer commando against Jews, Poles and pro-Soviet partisans, especially in the Volhynia region. DUK sees itself as the successor of the historical UPA, feeding thus the fascist imagery of Ukrainian volunteer battalions in Russia, but also causing deep concern in contemporary Poland. The Right Sector / DUK included several foreign fighters, among them a group of battle-hardened Chechens, Belarusians, an Austrian and an Afro-American from the United States—a former special weapons and tactics (SWAT) expert.[141] Compared to other battalions DUK-PS has a widespread network of regional reserve combatants in 18 regions of Ukraine. In July to August 2014, the volunteer battalion OUN under the command of Mykola Kokhanovsky joined the DUK-PS. After the unauthorized and failed attack on Mukachevo, many members of DUK-

---

139 Interview with Artem Skoropadskij, press secretary of the Right Sector, Kyiv 18 January 2018.
140 The UPA had fought against Soviet partisans, the Soviet Army and the NKWD as well as against the Polish underground army during World War II, especially between 1943 and 1944.
141 Interview with 43-year-old Mykhaylo Vershinin, former fighter of the DUK / Right Sector (group "Aratta") (2017).

PS moved over to the battalion Azov, one commander of DUK-PS, Ruslan Kamchaly, even advised his subordinates to switch to Azov.

In July 2014, DUK-PS participated in the battle around the city of Avdiivka, and in August 2014, they took part in the defense of the airport of Donetsk. Formally, DUK-PS was removed from the frontline in April 2015, however, the violent death of four combatants of DUK-PS in June 2016 showed that DUK-PS remained at the frontline. In August 2014, Dmytro Yarosh and Andriy Stempitskiy wrote a letter to President Poroshenko complaining about the detention or arrest of DUK-PS members and their disarmament. Both asked for the removal of the leaders in charge at the Ministry of Internal Affairs—a clear sign of the insubordination of DUK-PS against the government. In January 2015, the presidential advisor Yuriy Biryukov admitted that DUK-PS has refused to subordinate its forces to the Ministry of Defense. The government offered a legalization of the battalion, but the Right Sector rejected. Instead, Yarosh declared on February 13, 2015, that DUK-PS would retain its right to fight according to its own plans.[142] After the signing of the Minsk II agreement on February 12, 2015, DUK-PS declared it would observe the ceasefire—an indication of its willingness not to undermine the president's authority. However, in July 2015, the conflict of DUK-PS with the government escalated into a violent clash with the police in the city of Mukachevo. As some combatants of the Right Sector reportedly joined the Alpha team of the secret service SBU, the commander of DUK-PS subsequently gave the order that DUK-PS members were not allowed to join the government security services.

The Right Sector favors a revolutionary, i.e., non-democratic, regime change, but rules out a take-over of power as long as the conflict with Russia is ongoing. The speaker of the Right Sector Skoropadsky, of Russian extraction, admitted that the organization is not a democratic organization. While they advocated elections, it was only as a means of revolutionary propaganda. No left-wing party should have the right to exist. Once in power, they would immediately send the current opposition bloc to prison. A joint front

---

142 http://svpressa.ru/politic/article/149351/

of nationalist forces would be most important, but whether the Right Sector would opt for a military take-over would depend on the concrete situation. The Right Sector sees itself as a "white Christian movement" that is also against migrants. Early on, Yarosh had called for overcoming the splits between the diverse nationalist groups. He warned that any criminal business, appropriation of property, putting pressure on entrepreneurs for one's enrichment or the "roofing" of corruption schemes would be inadmissable for members of the Right Sector.[143] Formally, DUK–PS was under the command of the Anti-Terrorist Operation; it fought together with the Armed Forces and the National Guard of Ukraine, but always retained its autonomy.

The Right Sector claims to have weapons for a thousand people under its control; they could mobilize 1,500 people in three days. Even though the Right Sector rejects to join the National Guard as it wants to retain its independence from the government, it cooperates with the military command in the battle zone. The strength of the Right Sector rests on its ideological cohesion, organizational structure, and internal discipline. However, it experiences a leadership problem. Dmytro Yarosh, the founder, was not able to rally the movement around his person, in part due to his ideological inflexibility. In spring 2015, there were attempts to integrate Ukrainian Volunteer Corps into the Ukrainian Army or National Guard, but most units of the Right Sector were not among those.

Shakhtarsk

Some commanders did not rely on the social capital of pre-existing right-wing societal organizations, but on the subculture of football hooligans or extremist protection rackets (for example, Patriot Ukrainy = Ukrainian Patriot). Shadowy business, including protection rackets, extra-legal security provision or the transport of undeclared goods, have formed the original core of at least one battalion: the infamous Shakhtarsk battalion (renamed into battalion Tornado after its legalization as a police unit of the Ministry of Interior).

---

143 https://ru.wikipedia.org/wiki/Добровольческий_украинский_корпус.

Since the 1990s, the head of Shakhtarsk, Ruslan Onishchenko, had been a known Donbas racketeer in the city of Torez. Onishchenko had served seven years in prison in the 1990s and earned his income afterward in part with the transport of coal from local mines. Although the local law enforcement had tortured him in 2008 with the aim to get a share of his earnings, he became an asset for the Ukrainian authorities after the separatist takeover in the Donetsk People's Republic (DNR), because — according to a member of the battalion Shakhtarsk — he participated in a shoot-out during the DNR-referendum by the separatists on May 11, 2014. He had then left the city of Torez, at that time controlled by the separatists, together with a small group of 10 to 15 people for the Ukrainian-controlled city of Dnipro. A local mafia boss, formerly exploited by the local law enforcement for extraction purposes, had thus turned into an asset usable for sabotage against the separatists due to changing circumstances. The small group of people around Onishchenko formed the core of the battalion Shakhtarsk; it was complemented by people stemming from the Brotherhood party of Korchynskiy, some members of the Radical Party of Lyashko and members of the Organization of Ukrainian Nationalists (OUN).

Battalion Sich'-S14

S14 is a right-wing extremist, violent-prone group founded in 2010 to allegedly promote lustration, public education, and the mobilization of volunteers for paramilitary purposes. S14 uses the Celtic cross, a neo-Nazi symbol. S14 stands for the 14-word slogan "We must secure the existence of our people and a future for white children" by the US American white supremacist David Lane. The Sich battalion was formed with the participation of the Svoboda Party in June 2014; it is named after the Sich, a semi-autonomous polity of Zaporozhian Cossacks in the 16th to 18th centuries. Sich is composed of around 50 volunteers, some of whom have prior military experience.

S14 members participated in the Maidan protests and the self-defense on the Maidan square. Its members joined several battalions, among them Kyiv-2, Aydar, Myrotvorets, Svyata Mariya and the Sich battalion. The leader of S14 is Yevhen Karas' (nom de guerre "Vortex"), who ran for the city parliament in Kyiv in 2014 on the party list of Svoboda but did not succeed. S14 recruited its members among football fans of Dynamo Kyiv, Metalist Kharkiv, and Shakhtyor Donetsk. S14 saw itself as a self-proclaimed private "law enforcement," they offered their protection services to businessmen or against the "Titushki" (see above) sponsored by the Yanukovich government.[144] S14 members moved from Kyiv-2 battalion to the battalion Garpun. After the dissolution of Garpun, its combatants were mostly transferred to the battalion Myrotvorets. The battalion fought along with the Svyatyi Mykolai battalion and the Donbas battalion. The Sich battalion is formally part of the 4th company of the Kyiv Regiment, i.e., a special police battalion. On 26 August 2014, the Sich battalion started operating under the auspices of the Ministry of Internal Affairs.

Several Sich members were arrested due to allegations of having committed murder, one person killed was a member of the National Guard of Ukraine, he died during riots in Kyiv on August 31, 2015. Formally, S14-Sich registered as a societal organization on February 13, 2015; it has local branches in Dnipro, Chernihyv, Kyiv, Odesa, Vinnytsia, Kremenchuk, and in Volhynia. The leaders of Sich-S14 also formed a National Center for Legal Defense and an Education Assembly. Evidently, these societal organizations were set up to attract governmental support for seemingly innocuous activities. According to Yevhen Karas', S14-Sich received half of its earnings from individual voluntary contributions whereas one key sponsor, whose name is not known to the author, covers the rest of their expenses.[145] S14-Sich regularly cooperates with the secret service SBU in information-sharing. This cooperation pertains to other extremist organizations such as Azov and the Right Sector, too.[146]

---

144 http://news.liga.net/interview/politics/14852177-s14_kto_oni_i_pochemu_im_pozvoleno_bit_lyudey.htm.
145 http://news.liga.net/interview/politics/14852177-s14_kto_oni_i_pochemu_im_pozvoleno_bit_lyudey.htm.
146 http://news.liga.net/politics/interview/s14_kto_oni_i_pochemu_im_pozvoleno_bit_lyudey.

S14-Sich conducted its "education" activities, for example against suspected supporters of separatism, by using violence.

Initially, S14-Sich was closely related to the Svoboda Party (Freedom Party) but dissociated itself from this tutelage. Although S14-Sich members were complicit in serious crimes, the government never publicly detached itself from the battalion. The details of the cooperation with the government are not known, but even when two members of S14-Sich (Andriy Medvedko and Denis Polishchuk) were publicly charged in summer 2015 by the Minister of Interior for having committed murder, the government did not change its attitude toward the battalion as a whole—either out of fear or in exchange for the conduct of special operations by S14-Sich.[147] S14-Sich is a rather autonomous, small battalion (estimated maximum of 200 members), held together by an extremist ideology, its subsidiary organizations, the practice of violence, and at least one powerful sponsor.

Islamic Battalions

Three Islamic volunteer groups fought on the Ukrainian side. In March 2014, the "Dzhokhar Dudayev" battalion (initially named Chechen Battalion) after Chechnya's first President and insurgent leader Dzhokhar Dudayev was formed by the group Free Caucasus, an association of Chechens, who had fought against Russia in the first and second Chechen wars (1994–1996; 1999-2009), but also consisted of some Dagestanis, Ingush, Uzbeks, Azerbaijanis, and Tatars.[148] It was based in Novomoskovsk (Dnipropetrovsk region). The Chechens usually had extensive combat experience with Russian troops and offered training to Ukrainian volunteers. Some of them used to live in exile in European countries and resumed their fight against Putin's Russia after the annexation of Crimea.[149] The battalion saw the support of Ukraine as part of a broader struggle against Russia and its puppet regime under president Kadyrov in Chechnya. The battalion specialized in subversion and countering

---

147 http://rian.com.ua/analytics/20150618/369199040.html.
148 http://freecaucasus.eu/Glavnaja/press-release1.html.
149 https://www.youtube.com/watch?v=L54NTpenCkM.

subversive groups from the pro-Russian camp. Isa Munaev, a separatist fighter during the first and second Chechen wars with the rank of a brigade general and founder of the "Free Caucasus movement" was appointed commander. In the 1980s, Munaev had already served two years in Afghanistan as part of the Soviet forces. In the early 2000s, Munaev went into exile in Denmark and became a Danish citizen. He died in combat on February 1, 2015. Adam Osmaev, born in 1984 and a Chechen by origin, succeeded him. He had been suspected of trying to assassinate then-Prime Minister Vladimir Putin in 2012 and was sentenced in Ukraine for illegally keeping explosives.[150] In July 2017, a killer tried to shoot Osmaev and his wife in Kyiv, in late October 2017, there was another attack on their lives during which Osmaev's wife was killed.[151]

The battalion participated in the battles of Ilovaisk and Debaltsevo[152] but dissolved soon after the death of Munaev, since Osmaev was not able to demonstrate as much authority as his predecessor—Osmaev had no relevant combat experience. As of May 2015, the remaining members of the Dudaev battalion received a legal status by the Ukrainian Ministry of Interior. Those with Ukrainian passports were supposed to join the Golden Gate battalion, while foreign fighters were expected to join the army after having received Ukrainian citizenship.

Another Chechen battalion, named after Shah Mansur, was created by former Dzhokhar Dudayev battalion members; reportedly, it participated in defending the front line near Mariupol in 2015. Finally, a Muslim battalion formed by Crimean Tatars, the Noman

---

150 http://www.newsru.com/world/18nov2014/osmaev.html.
151 http://www.bbc.com/ukrainian/features-russian-41819158; https://www.rbc.ua/rus/news/ubiystvo-okuevoy-poyavilos-video-mesta-sobytiy-1509395562.html; https://lh.ua/news/2017/10/30/380666_aminu_okuevu_ubili_v istrelom.html.
152 The battle of Ilovaisk started on 7 August 2014, when the Armed Forces of Ukraine and pro-Ukrainian paramilitaries began a series of attempts to capture the city of Ilovaisk from pro-Russian insurgents affiliated with the self-proclaimed Donetsk People's Republic and detachments of the Russian Armed Forces. Although Ukrainian forces were able to enter the city on 18 August, they were encircled between 24-26 August 2014 by overwhelming Russian military forces that had joined the battle, https://en.wikipedia.org/wiki/Battle_of_Ilovaisk.

Çelebicihan battalion, was based in the Kherson region bordering Crimea and fought against the separatist forces, too. The Noman Çelebicihan battalion reportedly received assistance from Turkey.

Donbas Battalion

The Donbas battalion was established in April 2014 on the initiative of Kostiantyn Hryshyn (nom de guerre: Semen Semenchenko); it initially consisted of combatants who had fought against the so-called Titushiki, i.e., groups of provocateurs who were paid by the former Yanukovich government and who supported the anti-Maidan. By the end of May 2014, the Donbas battalion was divided into three segments, one became part of the National Guard, another one was fused with the 24th battalion of the territorial defense, a third segment remained autonomous and participated in defending the Dobropol'skiy, Velikonovosel'skiy, Krasnoarmeysk and Aleksandrov districts. Initially, 50 to 60 people formed the core of the Donbas battalion; it grew to up to 700 people in September 2014.[153] The recruitment took mostly place through social media, while the National Guard provided the weaponry.

The Donbas battalion consisted of reserve officers, contract soldiers, and regular soldiers, who had gone through infantry or marine training.[154] At least one rotte consisted of veterans of the Afghanistan war. In May 2014, the Donbas battalion attacked separatist roadblocks in Krasnoarmeysk. They captured 15 refugees among the local people supportive of secession and participated in the "cleansing" of Mariupol from separatists in May 2014. In August 2014, the Donbas battalion fought around the district of Artemivsk and participated in the battles around the cities of Popasnoe, Lisichansk, Pervomaysk, and Ilovaysk.[155] The Donbas battalion participated in attack operations, conducted reconnaissance operations, and guarded the "line of contact" against intruders. Since July

---

[153] http://news.liga.net/news/politics/3180498-batalon_donbass_preobrazovan_v_batalonno_takticheskuyu_gruppu.htm.

[154] https://www.youtube.com/watch?v=vZj14FXNb5w.

[155] https://www.youtube.com/watch?v=ImU2CkW5bkI&feature=youtu.be; http://censor.net.ua/b2744; https://www.ostro.org/general/politics/articles/513633/

2014, the Donbas battalion is formally under the control of the Ministry of Interior.

The Donbas battalion was funded through the "Privat Group" by the entrepreneur and head of the regional administration Igor Kolomoysky, by the Donetsk governor Serhiy Taruta, and by charitable foundations, Semenchenko, however, at one time denied having taken money from oligarchs.[156] Semenchenko and his wife established a charitable fund of their own.[157] The Donbas battalion collected money through social media, for example via Facebook accounts ("Staff for the Liberation of Ukraine" and "Blockade Staff"). The formation of the battalion was furthermore assisted by the administration of the military district of the Dnipropetrovsk region. Semenchenko claims that the Ministry of Interior did not play an active role in creating the Donbas battalion, he rather held that the Ministry of Internal Affairs tried to discredit independent battalions such as Aydar, Donbas, and Tornado to retain control. However, the Donbas battalion profited from the decision of the government to form territorial defense battalions in each region as this permitted them to procure weaponry. Its combatants allegedly earn twice as much as regular soldiers under government contract.[158]

Semen Semenchenko, born in 1974, is son to a mixed Russian-Ukrainian family and was raised on the Crimean peninsula. While his family supported the inclusion of Crimea into the Russian Federation, he became one of the best-known leaders of the volunteer battalions in Ukraine. Semenchenko's biography reflects the disillusionment about the disarray of life in post-Soviet Ukraine. He had served with the Russian army in the first Chechen war, an experience that was reportedly sobering. Maybe more decisive for his career as commander of an anti-Russian battalion was his detention

---

156 www.forbes.ru/sobytiya/obshchestvo/258279-privattank-milliarder-kolomoiskii-vedet-chastnuyu-voinu-za-edinstvo-ukra; http://news.liga.net/interview/politics/2811059-semen_semenchenko_my_pobedim_no_ne_cherez_mesyats.htm; http://news.liga.net/interview/politics/2811059-semen_semenchenko_my_pobedim_no_ne_cherez_mesyats.htm.
157 http://semenchenko-fond.com.ua/.
158 http://www.reuters.com/article/us-ukraine-crisis-oligarch-idUSBREA4M0OU20140523.

on charges of murder in 1996 (he was later released without conviction) and his participation in the Orange Revolution in 2004.

In November 2014, Semenchenko turned to politics as a deputy of the Verkhovna Rada but remained commander of a segment of the Donbas battalion, which had left the National Guard or never subordinated to it in the first place. From October 2017 onwards, this group — commanded by Semenchenko — organized a tent camp close to the Verkhovna Rada in Kyiv, which was then forcefully dissolved by police in March 2018. The uniformed campers had been demanding President Poroshenko's resignation, the creation of an anti-corruption court, a blockade of trade with the separatist territories, lifting lawmakers' immunity from prosecution and the adoption of a fairer election law.[159] Semenchenko also sharply criticized the prosecution of volunteers for criminal deeds committed in the course of the war with the separatists. He criticized the allegations against the Tornado battalion as fabricated, although he did not call for a general amnesty for participants of the war.

Conclusion

The emergence of irregular armed groups in Ukraine is a case for the "weak state–strong society" nexus since non-state actors reacted to the defunct state security apparatus or exploited it as an opportunity. The armed groups were irregular in the sense that they formally did not exist before the outbreak of violence. The volunteer battalions belong with few exceptions to the category of pro-state militia. They were crucial for stopping the spread of separatist forces and for containing the military intervention by Russia. On the backdrop of the erosion of the state monopoly of violence, all armed groups engaged in shaping the unpredictable situation on the ground. The roles of armed groups were not cast in stone, but rather time- and context-sensitive. In comparison to regular armed forces, the initially irregular battalions based on volunteers had a clear advantage — they were more flexible, not bound to a specific garrison, they were constantly on the move and far more mobile

---

159 https://www.kyivpost.com/ukraine-politics/police-remove-tent-camp-near-parliament-arrests-50-protesters.html.

than regular armed forces. Some irregular armed groups had the limited aim to compensate for the void of state defense capacities; others had domestic political ambitions going beyond the participation in military operations against the separatists, still others were merely expanding their involvement in organized crime under the guise of defending Ukraine.

Except for the right-wing paramilitary groups that already existed before the Maidan protests, the overwhelming majority of the irregular armed groups were established with the crucial support of the government; the armed groups were thus irregular, but not non-state. For solving problems of collective action in the war effort, leadership by commanders with a certain degree of autonomy was key—social networking, reaching out to sponsors, reputation, media presence, and a certain ruthlessness were essential characteristics of a successful commander. Successful commanders were those who could transform loosely connected, at best like-minded individuals into groups capable of performing acts of organized violence. After the segmentation of areas of conflict, during the transformation of battle groups into actors of governance, political and bureaucratic credentials became more relevant for assuring the survival of a group. The required leadership skills proved thus context-sensitive. Some commanders turned politicians, but the ideologues among them became rather quickly marginalized.

Two types of transformation of battalion commanders into politicians stand out. Either a political party adopted a former commander to enhance its own electoral and parliamentary standing, or a commander relied on his group and advanced his career autonomously. In the case of incorporation, the commander usually lost his position in the battalion, i.e., his core clientele. Over time, the initial benefit made the commander dependent on the party. A commander could try to steer his political career alone, but the only successful case is Andriy Biletsky, who already had a career as leader of the neo-Nazi organization Social-National Assembly.

Except for right-wing or extremist groups, the irregular battalions were more or less efficiently integrated into the regular armed forces, formalized as Special Forces of the police or as part of the

National Guard. The number of Ukrainian volunteers who quit after the legalization of their respective battalion varies but based on our assessment at least one third returned to their original civilian occupation after the Minsk II ceasefire from February 2015.

The government incorporated most of the volunteer battalions into the state security apparatus, but it can hardly afford to press for disarming or demobilizing those groups which had saved the country from dissolution. These irregular armed groups saved the Ukrainian state, but the government became a long-term hostage to actors it had relied on in its hour of need. The war experience has shaped identities: Instead of the Euro-Maidan, nationalism became dominant, not the least under the impact of vocal leaders of right-wing irregular armed groups.

References

Carey, Sabine C.; Michael P. Colaresi, Neil J. Mitchell (2015), Governments, Informal Links to Militias, and Accountability, in: Journal of Conflict Resolution, 59/5, pp. 850-876

Carey, Sabine; Neil Mitchell (2016): Pro-Government Militias, Human Rights Abuses and the Ambiguous Role of Foreign Aid. Briefing Paper 4/2016, German Development Institute, Bonn.

Collier, Paul; Anke Hoeffler (2002), Greed and Grievance in Civil War. The World Bank Policy Research Working Paper 2355, Washington, D.C.

Home Office, Government United Kingdom (2017), Country Policy and Information Note. Ukraine: Military service, London, https://assets.pu blishing.service.gov.uk/government/uploads/system/uploads/att achment_data/file/608565/Ukraine_-_Military_Service_-_CPIN_-_ v4.pdf.

Ishchenko, Volodymyr (2018), Denial of the Obvious: Far Right in Maidan Protests and Their Danger Today, Vox Ukraine 3245, 16 April, https:/ /voxukraine.org/en/denial-of-the-obvious-far-right-in-maidan-pro tests-and-their-danger-today/.

Käihkö, Ilmari (2018), A Nation-in-the-making, in Arms: Control of Force, Strategy and the Ukrainian Volunteer Battalions, in: Defence Studies 18/2, pp. 147-166.

Kharchenko, Olena I.; Olena M. Mramornova (2016), Problemy veteraniv antiteroristichnoi operacii na skhodi Ukraini. in: Visnik Kharkivskogo nacional'nogo universitetu V.N. Karazina.

Kirschke, Linda (2000): Informal Repression, Zero-sum Politics and Late Third Wave Transitions, in: Journal of Modern African Studies 38/3, pp. 383-405

Kirtoka, V. (2018): Dobrovolets, biznesmen Bogdan Chaban, Ob`jazatel`no vernus`v Donetsk. Pri odnom uslovii: tam budet ukrainiskij flag, 11 January 2018, https://censor.net.ua/resonance/3042230/dobrovole ts_biznesmen_bogdan_chaban_obyazatelno_vernus_v_donetsk_pri _odnom_uslovii_tam_budet_ukrainskiyi.

Lavrov, Anton; Aleksey Nikolsky (2015), Neglect and Rot. Degradation of Ukraine's Military in the Interim Period, in: Colby Hooward; Ruslan Pukhov (eds.): Brothers Armed. Military Aspects of the Crisis in Ukraine, Minneapolis.

Lebedev, Anna Colin (2017): Les combattants et les anciens combattant du Donbas: Profil social, poids militaire et influence politique, L'Institut de recherche stratégique de l'École militaire (IRSEM), Paris, Nov.

Majic, Danijel (2014), Kämpfe in der Ukraine „Es ist doch besser, wenn es knallt", in: Frankfurter Rundschau, 18.11., http://www.fr.de/politi k/kaempfe-in-der-ukraine-es-ist-doch-besser-wenn-es-knallt-a-5175 00.

Minakov, Mykhailo (2018), The Third Sector entering the First. Cooperation and Competition of Civil Society, State, and Oligarchs after Euromaidan, in: Raffaele Marchetti (ed.): Cooperation and Competition between Government and NGOs. Perspectives form Asia, Europe, Middle East and Africa, London.

Mitchell, Neil J.; Sabine C. Carey, Christopher K. Butler (2014): The Impact of Pro-government Militias on Human Rights Violations, in: International Interactions 40(5), pp. 812-836

Pinto, Pedro Ramos (2006), Social Capital as a Capacity for Collective Action, in: Rosalind Edwards, Jane Franklin, Janet Holland (eds.): Assessing Social Capital: Concept, Policy, Practice, Newcastle, pp. 53-69.

Rękawek, Kacper (2015), Neither "NATO's Foreign Legion" Nor the "Donbas International Brigades" Where Are All the Foreign Fighters in Ukraine?, Warsaw. PISM Policy Paper, No. 6 (108), March, https://www.pism.pl/files/?id_plik=19434.

Serdyukov, Igor (2016), Volontery: Samaya dokhodnaya professiya Ukrainy, 30.11., https://ukraina.ru/exclusive/20161130/1017922504.html.

Shcherbak, Andrey (2016), Analyse „Les Miserables". Biographien von „Noworos" und ukrainischen Milizkommandeuren im Vergleich. Bundeszentrale für politische Bildung, 2. Juli, http://www.bpb.de/2 30419/analyse-les-miserables-biographien-von-noworos-und-ukrai nischen-milizkommandeuren-im-vergleich.

Soldatova, Emma (2015), Volonterskie „zarplaty" ili kak zarabotat' na Donbase, 18 März, http://podpricelom.com.ua/analyze/as-volunteers-earn-donbas.html.

Young, Cathy (2022), Heroes of Mariupol or Neo-Nazi Menace?, The Bulwark, 25 May, https://www.thebulwark.com/heroes-of-mariupol-or-neo-nazi-menace/.

Between Frontline and Parliament
Ukrainian Political Parties and Irregular Armed Groups since 2014

Kostiantyn Fedorenko, Andreas Umland

> "It must be like the Maidan, but with military means." Arsen Avakov, former Minister of Internal Affairs, on the emerging volunteer battalions in 2014 (Hldaka et al 2016, p. 85)

This Chapter surveys the interaction between Ukraine's main political parties after the 2013–2014 Maidan uprising and the irregular armed groups (IAGs) that had emerged between spring and autumn 2014. The short life of the Ukrainian IAGs as more or less independent actors and the swift integration of most of them into Ukraine's regular forces was unusual. The relatively low political impact of the IAGs as such contrasts to the impressive political careers of some IAGs' commanders since 2014.

From Social Activism to Armed Resistance and Back

Ukraine's irregular volunteer units that, since spring 2014, had begun to form in response to Kremlin-fueled separatism in the Donets Basin (Donbas) sprang from and enjoyed the support of a variety of sources (Sergatskova 2015). These included civic groups, political parties, commercial companies and informal networks of former servicemen, protesters, experienced mercenaries, patriotic criminals, football hooligans, and minority activists. As the post-Maidan state was in shambles, the IAGs had to sustain themselves through crowdfunding, private sponsoring and political support from outside the government (Hunter 2018).

The creation of a whole number of IAGs was encouraged, triggered, supported or even organized by various government officials.[1] The Ukrainian state started—from approximately late summer 2014 onwards—to coopt, integrate, turn or disperse the new

---

1 Interview with Viktor Chavalan, Kyiv, January 13, 2017.

IAGs into regular companies, battalions, regiments and brigades subordinated to the Ministries of Defense and Interior. Some observers have claimed that former President Petro Poroshenko deliberately aimed to incorporate the volunteer groups, out of fear for his position in power (Ruzhyns'kyi 2014). Only some minor, ideologically driven IAGs kept relative independence from the state. They include the *Orhanizatsiia ukrains'kykh natsionalistiv* (Organization of the Ukrainian Nationalists, OUN) and *Dobrovol'chyi ukrains'kyi korpus* (Voluntary Ukrainian Corps, DUK). These small units are, however, exceptions to the rule that, by early 2016, the main story of the IAGs as notable non- or semi-governmental forces was essentially over. As exhilarating as the mushrooming of IAGs was throughout 2014, as astonishing was their nearly complete disappearance as a separate and widespread phenomenon during 2015.

Nevertheless, the story about Ukraine's initially irregular armed volunteer movement did not end with its almost full incorporation into the regular Ukrainian Armed Forces. A whole number of the initial IAG leaders kept in contact with, or even advanced within, those political, governmental, civil or commercial structures which had initially supported the formation of the IAGs. Some selected volunteer units—most prominently the infamous Azov battalion (later a regiment)—kept a part of their staff, identity, symbols and exclusiveness after their incorporation into the troops of the Ministries of the Interior or Defense (Bezruk/Umland 2015; Umland 2016; Gorbach/Petik 2016). A number of decommissioned commanders and privates became widely known in the development of post-Maidan Ukrainian politics, government, and society.

In the words of one of the key original organizers of the IAGs, Viktor Chavalan, who was, in 2014/2015, head of the Department for the Organization of the Activities of the Special Tasks Units within the Ministry of the Interior of Ukraine,

> "the people who formed the basis of the volunteer units in 2014 did not disappear; they are still there. Moreover, the informal ties that formed between them and were strengthened during the fights are rather strong. These are relatively powerful communities, and these people support each other in peaceful life in the solution of social and every-day-life issues. [...] That

means that, apart from the fact that this is a fighting brotherhood steeled during the war, by joint victories, by joint losses and by joint heroic deeds, there are certain problems that keep this community together." (Chavalan 2017)

The larger segment of the irregular armed groups' staff has, by 2018, returned to their pre-2014 professional lives. Some are suffering from post-traumatic syndromes, after their experience of combat, loss, injury, detention, or torture. Yet, numerous former irregular soldiers have continued to follow career-paths they started, modified or sustained within the early post-Maidan armed volunteer movement. They became soldiers, police officers, full-time politicians or political activists as well as leaders of Ukraine's vibrant civil society organizations (Burlyuk/ Shapovalova 2018).

The first volunteer troops are credited to have saved eastern Ukraine from being run over by Russia-directed hybrid and regular forces (Francis 2018). There is a widely shared perception that the *dobrobaty* — the abbreviation for *dobrovolchii batal'ony* (volunteer battalions) — saved Ukraine as a state, in mid-2014. The IAGS' role of saviors has continued to elicit since 2014 considerable popularity and political support for the initially non-state fighters as well as for all soldiers employed within Ukraine's Anti-Terrorist Operation (ATO). The majority of parties actively induced former or still active combatants to join their electoral lists for the October 2014 parliamentary and October 2015 local elections. Support from and for ATO fighters was one of the most important topics in the electoral campaigns of the parties for the 2015 local elections.

Right-Wing Parties and Their Paramilitary Branches

Although they form relatively minor Ukrainian political groupings, such parties as the Right Sector, Svoboda (Freedom) party and National Corps as well as their involvement in the fighting in the Donbas are worth considering. The organizational connection between them and some new IAGs was and, partly, still is particularly close.

The Right Sector claims to have lost about 60 to 70 members in combat,[2] Svoboda over 50 members,[3] and the Azov Battalion/Regiment 39 members.[4] One reason for considering the far right is that these Ukrainian parties as well as their armed wings are playing a disproportionately large role in the Kremlin's propaganda campaign against Ukraine. To a lesser degree, this also holds true to Western media reports.

Pravyi Sektor (Right Sector)

Although the youngest of Ukraine's three main far-right parties, the Right Sector received especially wide attention throughout 2014. It was initially a loose umbrella movement for various small right-wing groups and nationalistically inclined individuals participating in the Maidan. At its inception as an informal network of activists in late November 2013, the Right Sector consisted of several dozen people, mainly men.[5] The number of Right Sector members increased to about 300 to 500 people towards the end of the Maidan uprising (Likhachov 2018). It was only after the Maidan revolution when the number of Right Sector members and groups using this label began to grow rapidly in connection with the unfolding confrontation with Russia.

As in the case of other self-defense units on the Maidan, the Right Sector's experience and bonding during the protests from December 2013 to February 2014 regained relevance when the initially civil conflict in eastern Ukraine started, with Russian help, to gradually turn into in an armed confrontation, from approximately mid-March 2014 onwards. The first Right Sector volunteers arrived in the Anti-Terrorist Operation (ATO) area in the Donbas in April

---

2   Interview with Artem Skoropads'kyi, Kyiv, February 5, 2017.
3   Interview with Iurii Syrotiuk, Kyiv, February 7, 2017.
4   Interview with Roman Zvarych, Kyiv, January 16, 2018.
5   The later press secretary of the Right Sector stated that his group had around 70 members on December 1, 2013, mainly coming from the far right group "Trident of Stepan Bandera" led by Dmytro Yarosh. According to him, the active core of the group during the Maidan protests consisted of about 150 people. Interview with Artem Skoropadskii, Kyiv, February 5, 2017.

2014 and were largely associated with the "Dnipro-2" battalion, until the creation of a separate unit called the *Dobrovolchyi ukrains'kyi korpus "Pravyi sektor"* (Volunteer Ukrainian Corps "Right Sector," DUK), on July 17 that year (Korotash 2015). The Right Sector's Euro-Maidan leader Dmytro Yarosh became DUK's first military commander. How serious the attempts by Yarosh were to integrate DUK into the Ministry of Defense troops is disputed, as the Corps' fighters accused the government of enmity towards their unit.[6]

At the time when the DUK was formed, Yarosh also emerged as the presidential candidate of the new party Right Sector, created on March 22, 2014. However, Yarosh only received 0.7 percent in the presidential elections of May, 25 2014 while his party won 1.8 percent during the parliamentary elections on October 25, 2014. The Right Sector thus did not pass the five percent barrier and was unable to form a faction in the Verkhovna Rada (Supreme Council). Only Yarosh himself entered parliament by winning a single-mandate district in the Dnipropetrovsk region, his native region.

There were, early on, allegations of the Right Sector having ties with the infamous oligarchs Dmytro Firtash and Ihor Kolomois'kyi (Naiem 2018). At least the claim about Kolomois'kyi's initial financial support for the DUK is plausible (Yarosh 2018). Yarosh himself had acknowledged that Borys Filatov and Hennadii Korban, Kolomois'kyi's close business partners, in cooperation with the regional Right Sector activist Andrii Denysenko, "made everything possible" to enable their first military operation (Hladka et al 2016, p. 282).

While Yarosh's election was unremarkable in terms of Ukrainian domestic affairs, his successful electoral bid in Russophone Ukraine contradicted the propaganda describing Yarosh as a "fascist" (Hladka et al. 2016, p. 209). In Russia, the Right Sector is identified with Ukraine's 2013-2014 uprising and post-Maidan regime. In fact, the relations between the post-revolutionary power holders and Right Sector have been strained. On August 17, 2014, the Right Sector issued an ultimatum to Ukraine's newly elected President

---

6   Ostriv Krym, Pravyi Sektor, May 27, 2017, https://pravyysektor.info/poglyad/ostriv-krym.

Petro Poroshenko demanding the elimination of "revanchists" in the Ministry of the Interior and the liberation of detained volunteer battalion members. The Right Sector warned that:

> "[i]n the case of the non-compliance with our demands within 48 hours, we will be forced to withdraw all of our forces from the front-line, announce a general mobilization of all reserve battalions and start a march on Kyiv with the aim of conducting 'quick reforms' in the Ministry of Interior. The march columns of the 'Right Sector' will be moving in full armor."[7]

In November 2015, Yarosh stepped down as party leader, following an internal conflict with other top party officials. Subsequently, Yarosh and his followers created a new party called *Derzhavnyts'ka initsiatyva Yarosha* (Statesman Initiative of Yarosh). Yarosh also left the DUK claiming that "95 percent of the volunteers" from DUK went with him to join his newly-formed *Ukrains'ka dobrovol'cha armiia* (Ukrainian Volunteer Army, UDA). In his capacity as an MP, Yarosh started to push a bill in parliament that would legalize the UDA as a separate unit preserving its internal hierarchy. At the same time, he stressed that the UDA is "fully subjugated to the [national military] command," and that there are thus "no conflict situations" (Yarosh 2016). Whereas the remaining group calling itself Right Sector preserved its anti-systemic stance, Yarosh moved away from outrightly revolutionary rhetoric.

Andrii Stempits'kyi and Andrii Tarasenko respectively became the commanders of those parts of the DUK and Right Sector that did not leave with Yarosh. They are both largely unknown figures in the Ukrainian public. The Right Sector's website labeled the post-Maidan Ukrainian leadership an "internal occupant."[8] Artem Skoropads'kyi (alias Bychkov), the party's Russian-speaking press secretary from Sevastopol, wrote that the Right Sector consists of "professional revolutionaries" ready to become "the vanguard of

---

7   Pravyi Sektor vydvinul ul'timatum Poroshenko i ugrozhaet provedeniem 'bystrykh reform' v MVD, UNIAN, August 17, 2014, https://www.unian.net/politics/952135-pravyiy-sektor-vyidvinul-ultimatum-poroshenko-i-ugrojaet-provedeniem-byistryih-reform-v-mvd.html.

8   Druh 'Sirko' pro realii rosiis'ko-ukrains'koi viiny, Pravyi Sektor, January 18, 2017, https://pravyysektor.info/borotba/drug-sirko-pro-realiyi-rosiysko-ukrayinskoyi-viyny.

this revolution when it starts."⁹ The party appealed in 2016 to "all battalions" to protest against that year's LGBT pride parade in Kyiv.¹⁰ Otherwise, however, the Right Sector had become a minor player in Ukrainian public life already by 2018.

Vseukrains'ke ob'ednannia "Svoboda" (All-Ukrainian Union "Freedom")

The Freedom party (Svoboda) is the oldest among the more or less significant Ukrainian far-right forces. In 2004, it emerged as a result of a deliberate re-branding of the East Galician ultra-nationalist fringe group Social-National Party of Ukraine (Shekhovtsov 2011; Likhachev 2013; Rudling, 2013; Shekhovtsov 2013; Polyakova 2014; Iovenko 2015). The Freedom party came to prominence in 2012 when it entered, and formed its own faction in Ukraine's parliament after a surprise result of 10.44 percent in the proportional part of that year's parliamentary elections (Likhachev 2013). During the Maidan protests, Svoboda's chairman Oleh Tiahnybok was one of the most prominent speakers on Kyiv's Independence Square. In 2014, the Freedom Party was a coalition party of Ukraine's first post-Maidan government for several months.

In the October 2014 parliamentary elections, Svoboda won 4.71 percent in the proportional part of the voting. It thus, like the Right Sector, failed to pass the five percent threshold. While Svoboda managed to send six directly elected deputies to Ukraine's parliament, it lost not only its ministers in the government but also its faction in parliament—a disastrous result after the 10.44 percent it had received in the previous 2012 parliamentary elections (Shekhovtsov 2014).

Supporters of the Right Sector and those of the Svoboda party had taken an active part in the 2013-2014 Maidan's protests while

---

9 Skoropadskii Artem, Facenews, November 25, 2015, https://www.facenews.ua/file/2015/296174/.
10 Spiker 'Pravoho sektora' Artem Skoropads'kyi: '...A za kil'ka rokiv u nas Khreshchatykom khodytymut' holi muzhyky. Nam tse potribno chy ni? Nam tse ne potribno', Tsenzor.net, June 9, 2016, https://ua.censor.net.ua/resonance/392561/spiker_pravogo_sektora_artem_skoropadskyyi_a_za_kilka_rokiv_u_nas_hreschatykom_hodytymut_goli_mujyky.

Right Sector members and Svoboda supporters were also involved in violent clashes. In contrast to the Right Sector, Svoboda never had its 'own' volunteer battalion. Instead, Svoboda endorsed the volunteer Sich Special Troops Battalion (Tiahnybok 2015).

Viktor Chalavan referred to the example of Svoboda and its leader Oleh Tiahnybok in 2014, when reporting that "politicians and civic activists who wanted to help to create these battalions approached us," and that Sich was formed as a result of such interaction. Dnipro mayor Filatov claims to have supported Svoboda activists in their engagement with Sich, with equipment in the early phases of the conflict (Hladka et al. 2016, p. 92 and 201). However, Oleksandr Pysarenko, Sich commander, clarified: "We are called 'Svoboda's battalion' because, when we formed, Svoboda helped us a lot (…) the state did not give us [the equipment], Svoboda bought it with their own money (…). Yet saying that Svoboda equals Sich is wrong. I have never been a Svoboda member."[11] By February 2015, the party claimed that approximately 500 members were fighting in the Donbas as part of the *Karpats'ka Sich* (Carpathian Sich) company and as individuals in other units, including Aidar.[12] In late 2015, the Sich special troops battalion was re-founded as the 4th Company of the Kyiv Regiment—a special police unit subjugated to the Ministry of the Interior. *Karpats'ka Sich*, a stormtroopers platoon, was created on August 27, 2014. The party admitted that the unit consisted of "nationalists who could not get into the National Guard, Sich or other units because of criminal offences related to (…) the Maidan, the downing of the Lenin memorials and other political cases."[13] In May 2015, the Carpathian Sich "decided to get legalized" by becoming part of the 93rd Separate Mechanized Brigade of the Ukrainian Army, yet demanded to be

---

11   Komandyr batal'ionu 'Sich' Oleksandr Pysarenko: 'My zaraz budemo maty kolosal'nu problem z biitsiamy, iaki povertaiut'sia z frontu', Tsenzor, September 25, 2015, https://censor.net.ua/resonance/353520/komandir_batalyionu_sch _oleksandr_pisarenko_mi_zaraz_budemo_mati_kolosalnu_problemu_z_byits yami_yak.

12   Interview with Iurii Syrotiuk, February 7, 2017.

13   Do richnytsi stvorennia 'Karpats'koi Sichi': Shliakh vid volonterstva do shturmovoi roty, Svoboda, August 26, 2015, http://svoboda.org.ua/news/eve nts/00014998/.

kept a separate unit inside the brigade. However, in April 2016, the unit was disbanded. Its members either continued service in the regular army structure or resigned (Stek 2016).

On February 9, 2015, during a Svoboda congress, a party sub-organization called *Lehion Svobody,* with the double meaning "legion of freedom" and "legion of the Freedom party," was created. It had about 1000 members by 2017. The Legion's task is to unite party members who were or are fighting in different armed units and to support them as well as their families during and after the war. Although the Carpathian Sich was dissolved and the Sich battalion integrated into the special police forces, the Legion continues to uphold links between the Svoboda party and ultra-nationalist soldiers. The party thus retains institutionalized ties to members actively serving in Ukraine's armed forces.

Svoboda's unsuccessful 2014 list included Oleksii Myrhorods'kyi a platoon commander within the Ukrainian army's 22nd Mechanized Infantry Battalion.[14] Six party members won mandates in single-member districts—one in the Kyiv, Poltava, Rivne and Ternopil' oblasts, and two in the city of Kyiv. Out of these deputies, only one, Oleksandr Marchenko, had fought in the Donbas. In the 2015 local elections, the party was supported by 6.88 percent of the voters, thereby obtaining the fifth-largest share of votes across Ukraine.[15] Aside from Marchenko, notable Svoboda representatives and 2012-2014 members of parliament who participated in operations in the ATO included the former vice-speaker of the Verkhovna Rada, Ruslan Koshulyns'kyi; the younger brother of the party leader, Andrii Tiahnybok; the former deputy head of the Svoboda parliamentary group Oleksii Kaida; and the head of Svoboda's Lviv branch Markiian Lopachak. Another 2012-2014 Svoboda MP who fought in the Donbas within the Sich battalion was Iurii Syrotiuk. Syrotiuk was briefly arrested on September 11, 2015,

---

14 Hromadske.ua, Spysok Tiahnyboka…, *Twitter,* September 14, 2014, https://twitter.com/HromadskeUA/status/511149712939155457?ref_src=twsrc%5Etfw.

15 Na mistsevykh vyborakh pokrashchyly rezul'tat til'ky krytyky vlady," Ukrains'ka Pravda, November 9, 2015, http://www.pravda.com.ua/news/2015/11/9/7088039/; Mistsevi vybory v Ukraini 2015, https://uk.wikipedia.org/wiki/Місцеві_вибори_в_Україні_2015.

for participation in mass protests near the Ukrainian parliament that happened on August, 31 that year. Together with former Svoboda MPs Eduard Leonov, Ihor Sabii, and Ihor Shvaika, Syrotiuk was suspected of organizing this unrest (Khomenko 2016). During this event, a young Sich soldier (but allegedly not a Svoboda member), Ihor Humeniuk, threw a hand grenade at a group of police officers, wounding 141 and killing three.[16] Serhii Krainiak, a Svoboda activist, was suspected of assisting Humeniuk by setting up a smokescreen.[17] Arsen Avakov, Minister of the Interior, accused Svoboda of having planned this attack.[18]

Natsional'nyi korpus (National Corps)

The Azov Battalion was founded as a police special forces battalion on May 5, 2014, re-organized as a regiment on September 17, 2014[19] and, on November 11, 2014, integrated by order of the Minister of the Interior into the National Guard of Ukraine.[20] When asked about the Azov Regiment and the far-right activists serving in the National Guard unit, Arsen Avakov replied: "Is it better when the right radicals are out on the streets, crushing shop windows? Or when they feel responsibility and fight for it (the National Guard-the authors) for some time?" (Hladka 2016, p. 431). He and Serhiy Taruta, an oligarch who served as Donets'k oblast' governor

---

16 Hranatu kynuv 'svobodivets' iz batal'ionu 'Sich' — Avakov, Ukrains'ka Pravda, August 31, 2015, http://www.pravda.com.ua/news/2015/08/31/7079662/; Pid Radoiu pom'ianuly zahyblykh vid boiovoi hranaty rik tomu hvardiitsiv," Ukrains'ka Pravda, August 13, 2018, http://www.pravda.com.ua/news/2016/08/31/7119174/.

17 Shche odnoho kam'ianchanyna Serhiia Krainiaka pidozriuiut' v orhanizatsii biini pid Radoiu. Khlopets pid areshtom, 20 khvylyn, September 3, 2015, https://kp.20minut.ua/Podii/sche-odnogo-kamyanchanina-sergiya-kraynyaka-pidozryuyut-v-organizatsiy-10459963.html.

18 Pid Radoiu pom'ianuly zahyblykh vid boiovoi hranaty rik tomu hvardiitsiv, Ukrains'ka Pravda, August 31, 2018, http://www.pravda.com.ua/news/2016/08/31/7119174/.

19 Komandyr polku 'Azov' Andrii Bilets'kyi: Ti, khto prolyvaie krov za Ukrainu, povynni maty svii holos u vladi, UNIAN, October 11, 2014, https://www.unian.ua/politics/994779-komandir-polku-azov-andriy-biletskiy-ti-hto-prolivae-krov-za-ukrajinu-povinni-mati-sviy-golos-u-vladi.html.

20 Avakov: Poroshenko ne rozpuzkav batal'iony, *Ukrains'ka Pravda*, November 11, 2014, http://www.pravda.com.ua/news/2014/11/11/7043879/.

in 2014 and later founded the *Osnova* (Foundation) party,[21] had provided the initial funding for Azov. They claim to have provided the material support for its first and legendary military operation, the liberation of Mariupol' in summer 2014 (Hladka et al. 2018, p. 356.

Many commentators emphasize the right-wing extremist party-political background of the Azov Battalion (Gorbach/Petik 2016). MP and Azov affiliate Oleh Petrenko, once a football fan club activist from Cherkasy and short-term Right Sector member, has claimed that 50 percent of the early Azov fighters came out of the ultras movement from all over Ukraine.[22] The related *Tsyvil'nyi korpus "Azov"* (Azov Civil Corps) comprised Azov veterans and other nationalist activists, raised financial and material support for the frontlines, recruited fighters for the Azov regiment, provided, in its own words, "truthful and timely" information about developments in the Donbas, and "created a patriotic environment" via "unifying supporters around the national idea."[23]

During a meeting on October 14, 2016, the Azov Civic Corps adopted the decision to start a new, explicitly political, project: the National Corps. Rather than legally creating a new party, two already existing organizations, the *Hromadians'kyi rukh "Chesni Spravy"* (Civic Movement "Fair Action") and *"Patriot Ukrainy"* ("Patriot of Ukraine"), founded in 2005, were merged and renamed. The National Corps became the second relevant rightist party as a more or less direct result of the Donbas conflict. All right-wing parties attempt to gain political capital by referring to their affiliated military units. Its date of creation alludes both to the Orthodox holiday of Pokrova (Protection of the Mother of God), and to the date of the creation of the nationalistic Ukrainian Insurgent Army (UPA) in 1942.

Andrii Bilets'kyi, head of the Azov regiment, was also appointed leader of the National Corps. Before 2014, he had made racist statements and been known by the nickname "White Leader"

---

21 V chem osnova partii Taruty, Kommentarii.ua, 24 October 2017, https://comments.ua/politics/599224-v-osnova-partii-taruti.html.
22 Interview with Oleh Petrenko, Kyiv, January 17, 2018.
23 *Tsyvil'nyi korpus "Azov,"* http://www.volunteer.org.ua/about/.

(Umland 2016). The Azov battalion and later regiment has been using stylized, coded neo-Nazi symbols reminiscent of the Black Sun and wolfs hook, yet publicly denied that they refer to German fascism.[24] During the last years, Bilets'kyi has repeatedly denied making racist statements and even claimed that "if somebody had called me 'White Leader' face to face, [that person] would have been beaten." Bilets'kyi publicly opposes multiculturalism but admits that "to be a Ukrainian nationalist today is to believe in values, not racial prejudice," and his new party does not have an ethnic criterion to define who can and cannot be part of the Ukrainian nation (Bilets'kyi 2016). Nationalist Corps activist Stepan Baida claimed that the "Patriot of Ukraine," the Khar'kiv groupuscule out of which Azov emerged, had initially been Russian-speaking.[25]

In October 2014, Bilets'kyi became an MP from a single member district in the Obolon' district of the city of Kyiv. Initially, he had been scheduled to run as an official Popular Front candidate. However, a group of experts on the far-right sent a letter to Arsenii Yatseniuk, leader of the Popular Front, asking the then Prime-Minister not to nominate Bilets'kyi from that party.[26] As a result, Bilets'kyi ran as a formally independent candidate, with only informal support of Yatseniuk's party. His electoral success can be attributed to his fame as a military commander and representative of the pro-Maidan forces. His right-wing extremist past was not yet widely known in Ukraine in 2014 (Verner 2014). Stepan Holovko, spokesman for both the Azov regiment and Social-National Assembly, in contrast to Bilets'kyi, ran as an official Popular Front candidate in a single member district, yet he was not successful.

For a while, the formal head of the Azov Civil Corps was the well-known politician Roman Zvarych—an immigrant to Ukraine from the United States, member of the North American Ukrainian

---

24 "Pro Azov," *Azov.Press*, 8 December 2015, http://azov.press/ukr/pro-azov.
25 Interview of Andreas Heinemann-Grüder with Stepan Baida, Kyiv, January 12, 2017.
26 Eksperty prizvali Iatseniuka ne vydvigat' kombata 'Azova' kandidatom v nardepy, Obozrevatel', September 15, 2014, https://www.obozrevatel.com/politics/01652-ekspertyi-priziyivayut-yatsenyuka-ne-vyidvigat-kombata-azova-kandidatom-v-nardepyi.htm.

diaspora, one-time pupil of Yaroslav Stets'ko, activist for the Bandera-wing of the Organization of Ukrainian Nationalists (OUN), deputy of the Verkhovna Rada and two-time former Minister of Justice of Ukraine. Zvarych joined Azov in June 2014 and played, until his departure in autumn 2015, a small role in the formation and education of the Azov battalion, regiment and movement in military and political affairs. In the proportional part of the 2014 parliamentary elections, Zvarych had been candidate no. 82, for the Petro Poroshenko Bloc (BPP), but did not enter parliament as he was too low on the BPP's list. Only in April 2018, long after he had left Azov, did he become an MP replacing a BPP deputy who had been nominated to become a government member.

While he never made it to the frontline, Zvarych has claimed that he was critically involved in organizing combat training for Azov fighters led by Georgian, US American, Lithuanian and British instructors, and that he advised Azov not to use symbols and ideas that could be linked to Nazism. As Zvarych had left Azov before the National Corps party was created, Bilets'kyi denied that Zvarych played any role in the emergence of the new party. After his engagement with Azov, Zvarych started to criticize in public the political program of the National Corps.[27]

Non-Parliamentary and Emergent Parties

Politychna partiia "Hromadians'ka pozytsiia" (Political Party "Civic Position")

Civic Position describes itself as a center-right party. Its leader is former Minister of Defense (2005-2007) Anatolii Hrytsenko who took part in the 2014 parliamentary elections in an alliance with *Demokratychnyi al'ians* (Democratic Alliance). Together, they won

---

27 Interview with Roman Zvarych, Kyiv, January 16, 2018; I. Iavir, Partiia dlia 'Azovu', Politychna Krytyka, October 11, 2016, http://ukraine.politicalcritique. org/2016/10/11/partiya-dlya-azovu/; Iak sim'ia Zvarychiv peretvoryla "volonterstvo" na simeinyi biznes, Antikor, March 1, 2017, https://antikor.com.ua /articles/154573-jak_simja_zvarichiv_peretvorila_volonterstvo_na_simejnij_b iznes

3.1 percent of the vote thus missing the five percent barrier. Even though Hrytsenko is a colonel, he did not participate in the ATO, he criticized the Ukrainian government for poor decision-making and accused it of "treason."[28] The only irregular armed groups' (IAG) member on the party's electoral list was Oleksandr Kraliuk, head of Civic Position's Volyns'ka oblast section and an Aidar battalion fighter. Reportedly, Civic Position provided material support to IAGs, namely to the *"Sviata Mariia"* ("Saint Mary") and "Donbas" battalions.[29]

Ukrains'ke ob'iednannia patriotiv (Ukrainian Union of Patriots, UkrOP)

The history of the UkrOP party is closely linked to Ukraine's IAGs of 2014, as several UkrOP-related politicians, activists, and businesspeople were with the armed volunteer movement. The party was registered with Ukraine's Ministry of Justice in June 2015. Like Civic Position, it describes itself as "center-right." The party's prehistory started with the creation of the Verkhovna Rada's inter-factional UkrOP group on December 2, 2014, that included the independent MPs Borys Filatov, Dmytro Yarosh, Boryslav Bereza, Andrii Bilets'kyi, and Volodymyr Parasiuk.[30] Those four are linked to radically nationalist political organizations (Right Sector, SNA-PU, UNA-UNSO, Congress of Ukrainian Nationalists) and irregular armed groups such as DUK, Azov, and Dnipro-1.

The creation of the party with the name UkrOP is alleged to have been a brainchild of oligarch Ihor Kolomois'kyi. Initially, Borys Filatov and Hennadii Korban, former business partners of

---

28 Hrytsenko: tse niiaka ne ATO—tse derzhavna zrada!, Presa Ukrainy, April 29, 2014, http://uapress.info/uk/news/show/23146.
29 Hromadians'ka pozytsiia—L'vivs'ka oblast', Viis'kovi podiakuvaly l'vivs'kym aktyvistam 'Hromadians'koi pozytsii' za dopomohu, Facebook, July 14, 2015, https://www.facebook.com/GP.Lviv.Obl/posts/1498523790439635; Viis'kovym peredano novi topohrafichni karty vid 'Hromadians'koi pozytsii', Anatolii Hrytsenko, August 21, 2014, http://grytsenko.com.ua/news/view-viys-kovym-peredano-novi-topohrafichni-karty-vid-hromadjans-koji-pozytsiji.html.
30 Interview with Volodymyr Parasiuk, Kyiv, January 18, 2018.

Kolomois'kyi, posed as the party's leaders. However, after a conflict with Kolomois'kyi, the latter himself took over the informal leadership of the party. The party name's abbreviation *ukrop* means the herb dill—a picture of which is also in the party's coat of arms. Russian ukrainophobes had initially used the term as a derogatory term for Ukrainian soldiers in the Donbas. Yet, the term got soon adopted by Ukrainians as an expression of pride. Military chevrons with a dill symbol, authored by Andrii Ermolenko, became popular among ATO fighters.

In the October–November 2015 local and regional elections, UkrOP was the fourth most successful party and gathered 7.43 percent of the total vote country-wide. The party's nominees for these elections included a number of former IAG members or supporters. UkrOP maintained relations with the Right Sector. Jewish oligarch and UkrOP's creator Kolomois'kyi is alleged to have not only supported the creation of the Right Sector's DUK (Bukovskii 2015), he has reportedly also co-financed the creation of other originally irregular armed groups, including the Dnipro-1 and Dnipro-2 volunteer battalions, two territorial defense units, the Donbas battalion, as well as, in their early phases, the infamous Shakhtars'k and Azov battalions (Zhegulev 2014).[31] Says Volodymyr Parasiuk, a prominent Maidan activist who later served in Dnipro-1:

> "I remember who protected Ukraine in 2014. It is unpopular to praise them, but still, this was a team—Kolomois'kyi, Korban, Filatov [i.e. the later UkrOP founders] and those around them (…). All the volunteer battalions formed in Dnipropetrovsk region, there was a decent [military training] base, shooting ranges, they were the first to give out weapons." (Skorychuk 2017)

Iurii Bereza, Dnipro-1 commander, claimed that since October 2014, Filatov and his team have stopped helping the volunteer bat-

---

31 Kolomois'kyi cherez Liashka prypynyv finansuvannia batal'ioniv 'Shakhtars'k' ta 'Azov', *Rivnens'ki Novyny,* August 2, 2014, http://rivnenews.com.ua/index.php/2011-10-13-10-01-08/4579-kolomoiskyi-cherez-liashka-prypynyv-finansuvannia-batalioniv-shakhtarsk-ta-azov.

talions, and that Korban expected to use Dnipro-1 as a unit for private needs. He also claims that while Kolomois'kyi is related to the creation of Dnipro-1, "[it] never had owners."[32]

Other Non-Parliamentary Party Projects

The remaining parties of any relative significance that, like the far-right parties, failed to enter parliament in 2014—the Communist Party of Ukraine and *Syl'na Ukraina* (Strong Ukraine)—do not seem to have had any connections to the volunteer battalions worth mentioning. Neither did the minor regional parties *Vidrodzhennia* (Rebirth), *Nash Krai* (Our Land) and *Za Zhyttia* (For Life). Together with the 2014–2019 parliamentary Opposition Bloc, which also did not appear to have had any such connections, they are considered to be relatively pro-Russian in today's Ukraine. Aside from the Communist Party of Ukraine, they all originated from the Party of Regions. The agrarian party *Zastup* (Spade) which also failed to pass the threshold in 2014 does not seem to have any significant ties to IAGs either. For some time, the new *Rukh Novykh Syl Mikhaila Saakashvili* (Mikhail Saakashvili's Movement of New Forces) looked like an emerging party with some prospect. It was headed by former Odesa governor and ex-President of Georgia, Saakashvili, as well as by former deputy general prosecutors Davit Sakvarelidze and Vitalii Kas'ko. Among Saakashvili's regional teams, one ATO combatant—Serhiy Sichevs'kyi in Chernivtsi oblast—as well as some volunteers were mentioned.[33]

All-Ukrainian Union "Fatherland" (Vseukrains'ke ob'ednannia "Bat'kivshchyna")

The most prominent link between the Fatherland party headed by Yuliia Tymoshenko and the volunteer battalions was the one-time prisoner of war Nadiia Savchenko. Savchenko led *Bat'kivshchyna*'s electoral list for the October 2014 parliamentary elections, in which

---

32   https://ua.112.ua/interview/ya-khotiv-by-shchob-viina-zakinchylasia-todi-ia-povernusia-v-silske-hospodarstvo-323309.html.
33   RNS, Rukh Novykh Syl, https://old.rns.org.ua/.

the party received 5.7 percent. The party more than doubled this support to 12 percent in the 2015 local elections. Savchenko, a former volunteer for the infamous Aydar battalion, had been captured in eastern Ukraine and tried in Russia. Until her release in 2016, she was therefore treated like a hero. Savchenko's number one position was meant to demonstrate *Bat'kivshchyna*'s patriotism and exploited the female POW's then high popularity. In May 2016, Russia released Savchenko who took up her mandate in the Verkhovna Rada. Between October and December 2016, however, Savchenko left the *Bat'kivshchyna* faction. She participated in controversial unofficial negotiations with leaders of the unrecognized "people's republics" of Donetsk and Luhansk, and did so without her party's approval. She subsequently started her own party, *Hromadians'ko-politychna platforma Nadii Savchenko* (Nadiia Savchenko's Civic-Political Platform), became involved in a bizarre terrorist plot to blow up Ukraine's parliament and was arrested.

Number three on *Bat'kivshchyna*'s electoral list for the 2014 parliamentary elections, Ihor Lutsenko, a political activist, had been temporarily also an ATO fighter as a member of the Azov battalion.[34] In 2015, Volodymyr Katruk, commander of the volunteer battalion Ternopil', participated in the elections to the Ternopil' city council on the list of *Bat'kivshchyna*. Semen Salatenko, a former Dnipro-1 fighter, served, for a while as head of the Sumy Oblast Council, representing *Bat'kivshchyna*, yet resigned after a scandal and returned to the ATO zone.[35]

On April 30, 2014, Tymoshenko had called for citizens of Ukraine to participate in the "protection of the Ukrainian borders against the Russian aggressor" by way of creating and joining territorial defense battalions. In May, answering this call, two such

---

[34] Ihor Lutsenko, Pidstvol'nyky dlia Azova, Ukrains'ka Pravda Blohy, August 18, 2014, http://blogs.pravda.com.ua/authors/lutsenko/53f11d4d496c3.

[35] S. Salatenko, Esli kto-to dumaet, chto eto voina za Donbas i za Krym, to eto ne tak, — eks-glava Sumskogo oblsoveta, ushedshyi dobrovol'tsem v ATO, Semen Salatenko, Censor.net.ua, March 18, 2017, https://censor.net.ua/resonance/43 1956/esli_ktoto_dumaet_chto_eta_voyina_za_donbass_i_za_krym_to_eto_ne_ tak_eksglava_sumskogo_oblsoveta_ushedshiyi.

battalions—*Bat'kivshchyna* and *Rukh Oporu* (Resistance Movement)—were formed in Kirovohrads'ka oblast' with the support from the party. While being volunteer battalions, they were, from the start of their actions, part of the Ministry of Defense structure, and thus not classical IAGs. In November 2014, these two battalions, together with another territorial defense battalion formed in Kirovohrads'ka oblast', were merged into one unit. They have received material support from Tymoshenko's party.[36]

Radykal'na Partiia Oleha Liashka (Oleh Liashko's Radical Party)

The flamboyant nationalist and populist Oleh Liashko played a special role within the armed volunteer movement throughout 2014. He was the Ukrainian veteran politician who linked himself most demonstratively to the emerging IAGs. Presenting himself as a "people's candidate," Liashko sought, in summer 2014, to create the public impression that he was himself a frontline fighter for Ukrainian independence. However, it was soon found out that video scenes showing his participation in combat and his interrogating of prisoners of war were staged.[37] He then stopped claiming personal participation in the war. His party nevertheless won 7.4 percent in the October 2014 parliamentary elections, and 6.7 percent of the total vote across Ukraine in the 2015 local elections.[38]

In summer 2014, Liashko cooperated closely with the Azov battalion. The Azov Civic Corps site even maintains that Liashko

---

36 Batal'ion "Bat'kivshchyna" otrymav cherhovu partiiu dopomohy, https://www.tymoshenko.ua/ruh-oporu/bataljon-batkivshhyna-otrymav-chergovu-partiyu-dopomogy/.
37 Podvyhy Liashka v zoni ATO vyiavylysia dobre zrezhysovanoiu videopostanovkoiu, *TSN*, October 24, 2014, https://tsn.ua/vybory-v-rady2014/podvigi-lyashka-v-zoni-ato-viyavilysya-dobre-zrezhisovanoyu-videopostanovkoyu-384754.html.
38 Na mistsevykh vyborakh pokrashchyly rezul'tat til'ky krytyky vlady, *Ukrains'ka Pravda*, November 9, 2015, http://www.pravda.com.ua/news/2015/11/9/7088039/.

was one of the battalion's creators.[39] In an article for the Azov battalion's website, the famous right-wing journalist Olena Bilozers'ka acknowledged Liashko's role and stated

> "the Patriot of Ukraine and the Social-National Assembly are the backbone of Azov, but not all battalion fighters are nationalists. Moderates [in the battalion] do not have problems with people who have tattoos of runes or inscriptions such as '[I am a] 100% racist.' And, if someone does have such problems, he would not admit that, since in Azov, not least thanks to Oleh Liashko, it is possible to fight. Not all units are so lucky."[40]

Liashko is also alleged to have helped in the creation of the battalion *Ukraina* that was later renamed into *Shakhtars'k*.[41] However, already before the October 2014 general elections, Liashko appeared to have lost either interest in, or the support of, *Azov,* and *Shakhtars'k* was disbanded in September 2014. Still, the Radical Party made heavy use of representatives of various IAGs in its public positioning for the October 2014 parliamentary elections and also included some further activists in one way or another linked to the armed volunteers movement.

The Radical Party's list for the proportional part of the 2014 parliamentary elections included Serhii Mel'nychuk, former commander of the Aidar battalion; Artem Vitko, commander of the Luhansk-1 battalion; Ihor Mosiichuk, a former SNA-PU activist and the first press secretary of Azov, Andrii Artemenko, affiliated with the Right Sector, Oksana Korchyns'ka, wife of Dmytro Korchyns'skyy, head of the ultra-nationalist *Bratstvo* (Brotherhood) Party and St. Mary Battalion; Dmytro Lin'ko, linked to *Bratstvo* and the St. Mary Battalion, as well as, formerly, to the Azov and Shakhtars'k battalions; Ihor Kryvoruchko, a veteran of the SNA-PU and

---

39 Polk 'Azov' — polk patrul'noi sluzhby militsii osoblyvoho pryznachennia..., Tsyvil'nyi korpus 'Azov', http://webcache.googleusercontent.com/search?q=cache:F6aZOPtn-gJ:www.volunteer.org.ua/about/azov/+&cd=1&hl=en&ct=c lnk&gl=ua.
40 Tsyvil'nyi korpus "Azov, http://www.volunteer.org.ua/about/.
41 A. Filonenko, R. Onishchenko, Komandiry batal'iona 'Shakhtarsk': 95% militsii nuzhno uvolit'. Eto vragi, Obozrevatel', July 18, 2014, https://www.obozreva tel.com/interview/85209-komandiryi-batalona-shahtersk-95-militsii-nuzhno-uvolit--eto-vragi.htm.

an Azov company commander. The most prominent IAG representative on the Radical Party's list, Mel'nychuk, later left the party after a public conflict with Liashko.

Liashko alleged that he had to include Mel'nychuk in the party's 2014 ballot under financial pressure from oligarch and former head of Yanukovych's presidential administration Serhii L'ovochkin. Liashko also claimed that the armed volunteers loyal to Mel'nychuk were functioning as guards to L'ovochkin's private property. He reported that Mel'nychuk had to be expelled from the party because of an earlier protest action when Mel'nychuk, together with other Aidar fighters, tried to set the Ministry of Defense on fire. Mel'nychuk responded that Aidar had to do so to remind the government who had brought them to power and accused Liashko of political corruption (Liashko 2015).

Ob'ednannia "Samopomich" (Association "Self-Help")

This party grew out of the Maidan movement, it won 11 percent in the October 2014 elections and attracted, in particular, the vote of the middle class (Butkevych 2016). While being closely linked to many activists who went to the ATO, *Samopomich* did, unlike the ideologically close Radical Party or *Bat'kivshchyna*, not found or cofound any IAGs officially tied to the party. The party's Kharkiv branch only provided some material support to the Kharkiv-1 volunteer police battalion which participated in the ATO.[42]

In mid-2014, *Samopomich* also started to develop a special partnership with the "Donbas" battalion. This expressed itself by the fact that some of "Donbas'" representatives were on *Samopomich*'s list and became direct candidates for the 2014 parliamentary elections, they included "Donbas" commander Semen Semenchenko (real name: Kostiantyn Hryshyn) and Pavlo Kishkar, head of the battalion's "information war group".

---

42 Batal'ionu 'Kharkiv-1' vid 'Samopomochi', Samopomich Kharkiv, December 19, 2014, http://kharkiv.samopomich.ua/news/bataljonu-harkiv-1-vid-samopomochi/.

Already in 2014 "Donbas" was one of the more radical and politically engaged IAGs even though it did not have an ultra-nationalist background, unlike Azov or DUK. On November 3, 2014, a "Donbas" battalion fighter declared on air that, should Ukraine cede "even a kilometer" of its land to the DNR/LNR, Poroshenko will be overthrown.[43] Semenchenko himself was one of the most shimmering of Ukraine's new politicians coming out of the IAGs. He once served with the Soviet Black Sea Fleet in Sevastopol. According to Vitaliy Atanasov,

> "Semenchenko is accused of making risky decisions at the front, of the illegal adoption of a military rank and attempting to hide his past [...]. Moreover, [in 2015], video recordings emerged showing Semenchenko inside the Donetsk regional authority building during its occupation in March 2014." (Atanasov 2016)

Nevertheless, in late April 2014, Semenchenko was successful in summoning his Donbas volunteer battalion via a Facebook announcement that allegedly assembled around 600 potential fighters on April 25, 2014.[44] He settled in Dnipro where the Donbas battalion then established its base. Having become a politician, Semenchenko was later involved in an embarrassing episode in the young party's history in Kryvyi Rih. A popular local *Samopomich* activist, Iurii Myloboh, narrowly lost to Iurii Vilkul, the father of a prominent Opposition Bloc politician and companion of Ukraine's richest "oligarch" Rinat Akhmetov, in the second round of elections for the mayor of Kryvyi Rih, in November 2015. The party managed to push through a parliamentary decision on a rerun of this election in 2016. However, instead of Myloboh, the party now nominated Semenchenko, who predictably lost. That led to accusations of a *dogovorniak* (shady deal, fixed game) between *Samopomich* and the Opposition Bloc.[45]

---

43 Batal'on 'Donbas' vydvinul ul'timatum Poroshenko, Press Post, November 3, 2014, http://press-post.net/batalon-donbass-vydvinul-ultimatum-poroshenko.
44 Interview with Semen Semenchenko, Kyiv, January 19, 2018.
45 Partiia Sadovogo utverdila spisok kandidatov na vybory v Radu, Liga.Novosti, September 12, 2014 http://news.liga.

On January 18, 2016, Donbas members rallied near the presidential administration, demanding to investigate the lost Ilovais'k battle's circumstances and to prosecute those guilty of the defeat. On May 3, 2016, Semenchenko coordinated a popular protest against the disbanding of the infamous Tornado battalion that had been accused of marauding in Kyiv. On that day, there was a court hearing of eight representatives of Tornado who had been detained on the suspicion of having committed violent crimes, including torture.[46] Events such as these were early signs of larger developments. During 2017, Semenchenko, together with Ehor Soboliev, coordinated an unsanctioned economic blockade of the occupied territories Donbas and an anti-Poroshenko protest camp near the parliament (Vovnianko 2017).[47]

Semenchenko's actions were a marker of the growing division between the post-Maidan regime, on the one hand, and the volunteer movement, including some remaining IAGs or volunteer units that had been integrated into the regular armed forces, yet had kept their identity, on the other. In the early days, the post-revolutionary political regime and IAGs had been a largely united force. For instance, on July 4, 2014, when Poroshenko was giving a speech to parliament, the building was guarded by the "Donbas" battalion. As the then just emerging IAGs' commander Semenchenko explained that "information regarding possible terror attacks was received, [and thus] the sending of some of [the battalion's] companies to the east was temporarily halted [to protect him in Kyiv—the authors]."[48] By September 2017, however, Semenchenko's "Donbas" battalion veterans were protecting Poroshenko's rival Mikheil

---

net/news/politics/3267517-partiya_sadovogo_utverdila_spisok_kandidatov_na_vybory_v_radu.htm.

46 Sprava Tornado: Shcho slid znaty pro novyi skandal, Korrespondent.net, August 3, 2016, http://ua.korrespondent.net/ukraine/3726408-sprava-tornado-scho-slid-znaty-pro-novyi-skandal.

47 Saakashvili i Semenchenko ne zbyraiut'sia prypyniaty aktsiiu protestu, Ukrains'ka Pravda, October 19, 2017, http://www.pravda.com.ua/news/2017/10/19/7159017/.

48 Poroshenko pryishov u VR pid okhoronoiu batal'ionu 'Donbas', Ekspres, July 4, 2014, http://expres.ua/digest/2014/07/04/108900-poroshenko-pryyshov-vr-pid-ohoronoyu-batalyonu-donbas.

Saakashvili when he entered Ukraine even though he was legally not entitled to do so.[49]

Petro Poroshenko Bloc "Solidarity" (BPP)

President Poroshenko's BPP party list for the proportional part of the October 2014 elections neither included representatives of IAGs nor any other recent combatants. Poroshenko's Bloc was thus one of only two major parliamentary parties—the other being the Opposition Bloc—that did not prominently feature serving or demobilized candidates on its list (Shuklinov 2014). This may have had to do with Poroshenko's intention to position his Bloc as a catch-all party. The purpose was, perhaps, to avoid controversy over the war record of the fighters and not to alienate Russophile voters in Ukraine's east and south.

At the same time, several members of the armed and ATO-related civil volunteer movement were elected, with the help of the Poroshenko Bloc, in Single Membership Districts (SMD). Thus, Oleh Petrenko—a former football fan club member and temporary Right Sector activist in spring 2014—was elected in an SMD, in his native Cherkasy oblast. During the Maidan protests, he had been involved in street fighting. In June 2014, Petrenko joined the Azov Civil Corps. Nevertheless, he was supported by the BPP "Solidarity" party and became a member of Poroshenko Bloc's parliamentary faction, while preserving his link to the Azov Regiment and entering the National Corps.[50] Andrii Denysenko, who created the "Dnipro-1" battalion, was also elected an MP from the BPP in the Dnipropetrovsk region. He later joined the UkrOP group in parliament but left this association in 2016. Oleksandr Tret'iakov, one of the most influential MPs in the BPP faction, claims to have provided support to Azov, the Right Sector and three territorial units in 2014 (Tret'iakov 2014).

---

49 Semenchenko pro povernennia Saakashvili: U L'vovi my ochikuvaly sprob zahostrennia sytuatsii, *ZIK,* September 22, 2017, http://zik.ua/news/2017/09/22/semenchenko_pro_povernennya_saakashvili_u_lvovi_my_ochikuvaly_sprob_1172895.
50 Interview with Oleh Petrenko, Kyiv, January 17, 2018.

Despite accusations that he is "destroying" the volunteer movement in Ukraine, Poroshenko has demonstratively supported and shielded the volunteer battalions (Ruzhyns'kyi 2014). At the 2016 second anniversary of the formation of the National Guard in the Ministry of Interior, Poroshenko explicitly praised the first volunteer unit formed in 2014 in Ukraine, the Kulchyts'kyi battalion.[51] During certain scandals in connection with IAGs, Poroshenko interfered on behalf of the volunteer units, and stopped the imminent disbanding of the Aidar battalion in June 2014.[52] In other cases, such as when the Tornado battalion was accused of violent crimes, he kept silent.

Nevertheless, about two years after the victory of the Maidan, relations between the President and volunteers were becoming increasingly sour. On May 20, 2016, Poroshenko accused fighters of the Azov battalion who had burned tires and exploded petards during a march in Kyiv, that they had created "a picture [worth showing] for Russian TV." The Azov veterans' protest was targeted against possible elections in the Donbas, after Poroshenko had declared his adherence to the Minsk Agreements which prescribe such elections.[53] Since then, many volunteer units and their veteran organizations have turned against Poroshenko.

Narodnyi Front (Popular Front)

On April 7, 2014, Oleksandr Turchynov, as then Acting President of Ukraine, started the ATO, by declaring a quasi-war against pro-Russian separatists who were then capturing administrative buildings in eastern Ukraine. During the following months, Turchynov

---

51 Poroshenko pro batal'ion Kul'chyts'koho: My shanuiemo kozhnoho z zhyvykh heroiv i pam'iataiemo tykh, khto ne povernuvsia, 112.ua, March 16, 2016, http://ua.112.ua/suspilstvo/poroshenko-pro-batalion-kulchytskoho-my-sha nuiemo-kozhnoho-z-zhyvykh-heroiv-i-pamiataiemo-tykh-khto-ne-povernuvs ia-298497.html.

52 Batal'ion "Aidar" isnuvatyme i prodovzhyt' vykonannia svoikh zavdan', S'iohodni, June 24, 2014, http://ukr.segodnya.ua/regions/donetsk/batalon-aydar-budet-sushchestvovat-i-prodolzhit-vypolnenie-svoih-zadach-531197.html.

53 Poroshenko otvetil na aktsii "Azova, Korrespondent.net, May 20, 2016, http://korrespondent.net/ukraine/3685533-poroshenko-otvetyl-na-aktsyy-azov.

spoke highly of the volunteer battalions.⁵⁴ This previewed the soon-to-be-established, close connection between Turchynov's party, the Popular Front, and Ukraine's armed forces and the emerging IAGs.

Although the Popular Front became only a functioning organization in September 2014, i.e. less than two months before the parliamentary elections of October 25, 2014, it won the proportional part of these elections with 22.2 percent. The Popular Front did, however, no longer run in the 2015 local elections, as its support had plummeted by then. Since Yatseniuk, the party leader, was Ukraine's Prime-Minister during the deep crisis years of 2014-2016, the voters evidently deemed the party responsible for the socio-economic collapse of that time.

A number of prominent participants of the ATO or figures linked to the armed volunteer movement were placed on high positions of the Popular Front's party list for the proportional part of the elections. Other IAG members were elected in single-member districts with the help of the Popular Front. The most prominent list candidates among the party's top 25 positions included Andrii Parubii, former Head of the National Security and Defense Council; Andrii Teteruk, the commander of the *"Myrotvorets'"* (Peacekeeper) battalion; Arsen Avakov, Minister of Internal Affairs; Iurii Bereza, the commander of the "Dnipro-1" battalion; Anton Herashchenko, the Interior Ministry's "coordinator of the volunteer battalions."⁵⁵

Andrii Parubii, who had been the head of the National Security and Defense Council for a brief period in 2014 and then speaker of the Ukrainian parliament since April 2016, is among the most

---

54 Dobrovol'chi batal'iony zaklaly ideolohiiu rozvytku syl'noi patriotychnoi nezalezhnoi krainy",–Turchynov na prezentatsii knyhy "Dobrobaty". FOTOreportazh, Censor.net.ua, January 28, 2017, http://ua.censor.net.ua/ph oto_news/425325/dobrovolchi_batalyiony_zaklaly_ideologiyu_rozvytku_sy lnoyi_patriotychnoyi_nezalejnoyi_krayiny_turchynov.

55 Pozdnii start: Analiz predvybornogo spiska Narodnogo fronta, Liga.Novosti, September 29, 2014, http://news.liga.net/articles/politics/3429844-kokteyl_ sezona_analiz_predvybornogo_spiska_narodnogo_fronta.htm; The MP Kostiantyn Mateichenko, elected on the Popular Front list to the Verkhovna Rada in 2014, was commander of the battalion "Artemovs'k." Interview of Andreas Heinemann-Grüder with Viktor Chavalan, Kyiv, January 13, 2017.

prominent politicians linked to the IAGs. Parubii had been the commander of the Maidan's *Samooborona* (self-defense), i.e. the numerous so-called *sotni* (Hundreds) that protected the protesters. He stood thus at the origins of those IAGs that were created out of *Samoborona* Hundreds and was personally acquainted with many of the IAG commanders.

In the early 1990s, Parubii had been one of the creators of the Social-National Party of Ukraine (SNPU), the predecessor organization of Svoboda. Parubii strayed away from Svoboda in early 2005 and joined Viktor Yushchenko's moderately nationalist *"Nasha Ukraina"* (Our Ukraine) party. During the 2004 Orange Revolution, he had been the commandant of the Ukrainian House — one of the key locations in the Kyiv city center controlled by the protesters.

Against the background of his Orange Revolution experience, Parubii became the commandant of the protesting camp and came to play "one of the key functions in the organizational structure of Euromaidan" in late 2013. [56] After the protesters' victory, he was among those politicians who initiated the incorporation of the Maidan's self-defense units into the emerging National Guard. In spring 2014, Parubii ordered the Maidan's self-defense units to capture buildings of local authorities in the north of the Luhans'k oblast', to prevent them from falling into the hands of separatists.[57]

As Minister of Internal Affairs since late February 2014, Arsen Avakov played a crucial role in the formation of the volunteer battalions and later managed to merge several of them into the National Guard. Anton Herashchenko, an advisor to Avakov, was closely involved in the communication between the Interior Ministry and emerging IAGs. He supported the creation and activities of the infamous "Shakhtars'k" battalion, according to Andrii Filonenko, its commander (Karpiak 2014). Herashchenko explained

---

56 Komendant Rady: khto takyi Andrii Parubii?, BBC Ukraine, April 14, 2016, https://www.bbc.com/ukrainian/politics/2016/04/160414_parubiy_profile_upd_ms_sx.

57 Komendant Rady: khto takyi Andrii Parubii?, BBC Ukraine, April 14, 2016, https://www.bbc.com/ukrainian/politics/2016/04/160414_parubiy_profile_upd_ms_sx.

that, before the separatist combatants started to operate heavy weapons, the task of the new volunteer battalions had been merely to "bring order" to the settlements "liberated from the terrorists." They often acted "instead of the [police] that was corrupted or had defected to the enemy side" (Herashchenko 2014).

In spring 2014, the reserve colonel and former UN peacekeeper Andrii Teteruk was asked by the Ministry of the Interior to form a unit out of former Ukrainian participants in peacekeeping operations. Teteruk reported that interim President Turchinov and Avakov took a special interest in the creation of the "Myrotvorets" battalion (later, regiment) composed of military professionals.[58] Their close contact since spring 2014 apparently facilitated Teteruk's inclusion into the Popular Front's electoral list, a few months later. Teteruk emphasized that his battalion was an explicitly non-political project.

According to Viktor Chalavan, who coordinated the creation of many volunteer battalions, Kyev-1, Dnipro-1 and *Zoloti Vorota* (Golden Gate) were among the first such units. During their formation, personalities played a large role, among them Iurii Bereza and Yevhen Deidei, another Popular Front MP (Hladka et al., p. 88). Some more Popular Front MPs originated from the armed volunteer movement. Mykhailo Havryliuk, a Maidan hero with later links to the *Zoloti Vorota* battalion, won an SMD seat in the Rada in October 2014, with the support of the Popular Front (Havryliuk 2015). Andrii Biletskyi, Azov commander, ran in Kyiv with the unofficial support of the Popular Front. Mykhailo Bodnar, elected in the Lviv region in October 2014, had fought in the Kulchyts'kyi battalion.[59] Before his election, Popular Front MP Ihor Lapin had served as the commander of the 2nd Company of the Aidar battalion and received several awards for his service.

---

58 Interview with Andrii Teteruk, Kyiv, January 17, 2018.
59 "Mykhailo Bondar," *Narodnyi Front,* https://nfront.org.ua/team/member-details/mykhailo-bondar.

Conclusions

Our survey indicates various forms of interaction between parties and IAGs in post-Maidan Ukraine. Several parties, party leaders and MPs took an active part in the creation and development of IAGs in 2014. Some politicians became soldiers or commanders of IAGs. Later on, there were numerous transitions of formerly non-political IAG members into the party-political realm—either because they joined established parties or created new political organizations. By late 2014, a number of IAG commanders had become members of Ukraine's post-Maidan national parliament. Most made the jump into the Verkhovna Rada in light of and often with explicit reference to their service within an IAG. Certain IAG members tried but did not manage to enter national parliament as deputies. Still, other IAGs' representatives were elected as members of regional and local representative and executive organs.

A wave of Ukrainian IAG commanders and related activists entered Ukrainian parliamentary politics in 2014-2015, political parties began to intensify their engagement with IAGs. At times, the new people's deputies from the IAGs became involved in political infighting within or between those very parties. These developments illustrate the considerable political ambition of numerous IAG commanders and some activists who were linked to the armed volunteer movement. Between the summer and autumn of 2014, i.e. during the parliamentary election campaign, at least one significant older party and parliamentary faction, namely Liashko's Radical Party, partly reinvented itself. At least one major new party and parliamentary faction of 2014-2019, the Popular Front, claimed to represent a political force whose post-Maidan profile heavily built on their claims to represent the armed volunteer movement.

Several minor parties, like the Right Sector, UkrOP, Statesman Initiative of Yarosh, and National Corps, are closely connected to the IAGs. The National Corps represents the political arm of a more broadly organized movement that also includes the volunteer regiment Azov of the National Guard, the so-called *Natsional'nyi druzhyny* (National Militias, unarmed street guards) and the *Ekolohichnyy korpus* (Ecological Corps). The Right Sector or National Corps may be regarded as affiliated to those "few [irregular armed] organizations whose militant origins remain essential to their identities and platforms as political parties" (Acosta 2014, p. 671).

Despite the multifarious connections between the armed volunteer movement and post-Euromaidan national as well as local politics, the IAGs *as such* only played a limited or indirect role in shaping political power, actions and decisions in Kyiv. As Ilmari Käihikö observed, "[i]n the end the volunteer phenomenon only lasted for about a year, before they were turned from independent militias into state-controlled paramilitary forces. Yet years later, they continue to influence the Ukrainian nation and politics because of their proximity to the nation" (Käihikö 2018, p.148). Only concerning certain policy issues did some IAGs or their veterans exert a noticeable impact on central and local decision-making — above all with regard to Ukraine's policies vis-à-vis Crimea and the Donbas. The post-Euromaidan warnings about the dangerous future role of the IAGs and their successor organizations had not materialized.

In 2016, Malyarenko and Galbreath had concluded that "[f]or the pro-Ukrainian paramilitaries, they may prove to be both Ukraine's saving grace in the war and its greatest threat to national security in the subsequent peace" (Malyarenko; Galbreath 2016). Yet, the Ukrainian paramilitary formations had not become such threats. One of the most revolutionary inclined party — IAG alliances, the Right Sector and its DUK — split in November 2015. Its most widely known leader Yarosh left the party and its corps with a large group of his followers. Yarosh created his own party and volunteer unit whose rhetoric and political stance have been much less anti-systemic than of that of the Right Sector and DUK.

The Azov Regiment, in turn, had become a regular part of the National Guard subordinated to the Ministry of the Interior in late 2014. From 2014 to 2018, the initial Azov battalion had given birth to a politically prolific and publicly visible movement that included a party, a veteran organization and an unarmed militia. These organizations' popularity builds upon the real or perceived military victories of Azov. Yet, there has, so far, never been an indication that the (un)civil organizations that sprang out of Azov did or will resort to the use of weapons of the eponymous National Guard regiment.

Many of the armed volunteer movement's graduates demonstrated political ambitions, were politically successful and influenced Ukrainian political affairs. Yet, the IAGs or their successor volunteer units within the regular forces did not shape Kyiv's domestic policies, the Ukrainian polity and national-level politics to a notable degree, except decisions taken that concerned the conflict with Russia. One of the reasons why this did not happen may have been that the politicians that were linked to the IAGs acquired new opportunities to exert political clout. The mere existence of IAGs may have had some influence on new politicians' social standing and for the public conduct of the President, government, parliament and parties. Yet, there has never been a situation in which a direct threat of a military or para-military group to use its arms, determined a major domestic decision, the appointment of personnel or influenced the choice between alternative options not directly related to the war with Russia. In the latter, the IAGs and their regular successor units indeed exerted considerable influence.

Huseyn Aliev's assertion that the post-Maidan volunteer troops are "informal power-holders" in Ukraine is misleading. The power of certain figures once or still linked to the IAGs and their successor units in Ukraine's regular armed forces is due to the political posts that they occupy. It has little or nothing to do with their potential access to firearms and heavy weapons, or to their links to serving soldiers who could use such weaponry within the context of domestic politics (Aliyev 2018).

One of the reasons for the relatively low political salience of the Ukrainian IAGs regarding issues other than the conflict with Russia itself, as well as for the largely smooth transition of its former commanders to civilian politics is the just *putatively* civil character of the war in eastern Ukraine (Mitrokhin 2014, pp. 3-16; Freedman 2014-2015; Mitrokhin 2015; Zadorozhnii 2016). The Ukrainian IAGs emerged within the context of a proxy war between two states, Russia and Ukraine. The war in the Donbas was not primarily the result of an internal political rift within the Ukrainian state (Kudelia 2018; Umland 2014). The outbreak of the war was shaped by domestic conditions that eased the Kremlin's active meddling—as the so-called Glazyev Tapes documented (Whitmore 2016; Coynash 2016; Kudelia 2014; Katchanovski 2016; Sasse/Lackner 2018; Giuliano 2018). Yet, the war in the Donets Basin would not have broken out in 2014 without the Russian interference (Mitrokhin 2014; Shekhovtsov 2016; Wilson 2016; Umland 2018).

Most of the leaders of pro-Ukrainian IAGs found it easy to cooperate with, integrate into, and become parts of, the state—whether by transforming their groups into regular armed units or by individually transiting to electoral politics. With the partial exception of such units as the DUK and Azov, most of the groups in the Ukrainian armed volunteer movement thus fall into the category of "within-system" organizations.

Most of the Ukrainian IAGs have been successfully integrated into the troops of the Ministries of Defense and the Interior. Only some minor and the most revolutionary-inclined of the prominent pro-Ukrainian IAGs, such the Ukrainian Volunteer Corps DUK, have not become a part of the regular armed forces. The Right Sector and DUK as well as some even smaller such entities, however, are altogether exceptions rather than the rule. The Ukrainian case lends support to a previous assessment of IAGs in a cross-cultural study. Ariel Ahram asserted in 2011 that

> "...the dynamics of competition between various domestic and international forces provides an incentive for states to rely on nonstate actors instead of maximizing control over violence. State weakness and the emergence of militias do not constitute an aberration, dysfunction, or result of failure of will." (Ahram 2011, p. 135).

References

Acosta, Benjamin (2014), Bombs to Ballots: When Militant Organizations Transition to Political Parties, in: The Journal of Politics, 76/3, pp. 666-683.

Ahram, Ariel I. (2011), Proxy Warriors: The Rise and Fall of State-Sponsored Militias, Stanford.

Aliyev, Huseyn (2018), Bewaffnete Freiwilligenbataillone: Informelle Machthaber in der Ukraine, in: Ukraine-Analysen, no. 205, pp. 2-5.

Aliyev, Huseyn (2016), Strong Militias, Weak States, and Armed Violence: Towards a Theory of 'State-Parallel' Paramilitaries, in: Security Dialogue, 47/6, pp. 498-516.

Atanasov, Vitalii (2016), Kryvyi Rih needs an alternative, in: Open Democracy, February 23, www.opendemocracy.net/od-russia/vitalii-atanasov/kryvyi-rih-needs-alternative.

Bereza, Iurii (2016), Ia khotiv by, shchob viina zakinchylasia, todi ia povernusia v sils'ke hospodarstvo," 112.ua, July 7, https://ua.112.ua/interview/ya-khotiv-by-shchob-viina-zakinchylasia-todi-ia-povernusia-v-silske-hospodarstvo-323309.html.

Bezruk, Tetjana; Andreas Umland (2015), Der Fall Azov: Freiwilligenbataillone in der Ukraine, in: Osteuropa, 65/1-2, pp. 33-42.

Biletskii, Andrei (2016), Esli by kto-to nazval menia Belym vozhdem, byl by on bit, Fokus, October 4, https://focus.ua/country/358170/.

Bukovskii, D. (2015), Pochemu Kolomoiskii zakryl 'Pravyi Sektor', in: Delovaia Stolitsa, November 11, http://www.dsnews.ua/politics/pochemu-kolomoyskiy-zakryl-pravyy-sektor-11112015170000.

Burlyuk, Olga; Natalia Shapovalova (eds.) (2018), Civil Society in Post-Euromaidan Ukraine: From Revolution to Consolidation, Stuttgart.

Butkevych, Bohdan (2016), Chomu Samopomich vtrachaie pozytsii, Tyzhden', June 30, http://tyzhden.ua/Politics/168506.

Chavalan, Viktor (2017), Obezopasit' sebia ot voennyk ugroz tol'ko kontraktnoi armiei nereal'no, ArgumentUA, 4 January, http://argumentua.com/print/stati/viktor-chalavan-obezopasit-sebya-ot-voennykh-ugroz-tolko-kontraktnoi-armiei-nerealno.

Chernyshev, Roman (2014), Liudi i vily. Analiz predvybornogo spiska partii Olega Liashko, Liga.Novosti, September 26, http://news.liga.net/articles/politics/3416556-lyudi_i_vily_analiz_predvybornogo_spiska_partii_olega_lyashko.htm.

Coynash, Halya (2016), Odesa Smoking Gun Leads Directly to Moscow, Human Rights in Ukraine, September 20, khpg.org/en/index.php?id=1473972066.

Coynash, Halya (2017), Russian who defended Ukraine in Donbas driven out to face imprisonment in Russia, Human Rights in Ukraine, December 5, khpg.org/en/index.php?id=1512422913.

Davidzon, Vladislav (2014), Right-wing Ukrainian leader is (surprise) Jewish, and (real surprise) proud of it, Tablet, December 1, https://www.tabletmag.com/jewish-news-and-politics/187217/borislav-bereza.

Dorosh, S. (2015), Shcho khovaiet'sia za UKROPom, BBC Ukraina, June 24, http://www.bbc.com/ukrainian/politics/2015/06/150624_ukrop_new_party_sd.

Fedorenko, Kostyantyn; Olena Rybiy; Andreas Umland (2016), The Ukrainian Party System before and after the 2013–2014 Euromaidan, in: Europe-Asia Studies, 68/4, pp. 609-630.

Filonenko, A.; R. Onishchenko (2014) Komandiry batal'iona 'Shakhtarsk': 95% militsii nuzhno uvolit'. Eto vragi, *Obozrevatel'*, July 18, https://www.obozrevatel.com/interview/85209-komandiryi-batalona-shahtersk-95-militsii-nuzhno-uvolit--eto-vragi.htm.

Francis, Diane M. (2015), Ukraine's Volunteers Saving the Day, in: The Huffington Post, 23 July, http://www.huffingtonpost.com/diane-m-francis/ukraines-volunteers-savin_b_7832224.html.

Freedman, Lawrence (2014-15), Ukraine and the Art of Limited War, in: Survival, 56/6, pp. 7-38.

Giuliano, Elise (2018), Who Supported Separatism in Donbas? Ethnicity and Popular Opinion at the Start of the Ukraine Crisis, in: Post-Soviet Affairs, 34/2-3, pp. 158-178.

Gonta, Boris (2015), Zhyznennyi put' Igoria Krivoruchko: cherez ternii k Liashko, Bukvy, October 1, https://bykvu.com/mysli/9746-zhiznennyj-put-igorya-krivoruchko-cherez-ternii-k-lyashko.

Gorbach, Denis; Oles' Petik (2016), Azovskii shliakh: kak ul'trapravoe dvizhenie boretsia za mesto v politicheskom meinstrime Ukrainy, in: Forum noveishei vostochnoevropeiskoi istorii i kul'tury, 13/1, pp. 179-192.

Havryliuk, Mykhailo (2015), Odnym slovom, v Verkhovnii Radi—bardak. Liudy pryishly ne na robotu, a butsimto v rozvazhal'nyi tsentr," in: Antikor, 31 March, http://antikor.com.ua/articles/34664-mihajlo_gavriljuk_odnim_slovom_v_verhovnij_radi_bardak._ljudi_prijshli_ne_na_robotu_a_butsimto_v_r.

Herashchenko, Anton (2014), Iakby ne dobrovol'chi batal'iony, to liniia rozmezhuvannia s'ohodni bula b des' po Dnipru, in: Ukrains'ki Natsional'ni Novyny, 9 November, https://www.unn.com.ua/uk/news/1404737-a-geraschenko-yakbi-ne-dobrovolchi-batalyoni-to-liniya-rozmehuvannya-sogodni-bula-b-des-po-dnipru.

Herashchenko, Anton (2015), *Facebook account*, March 25, https://www.facebook.com/anton.gerashchenko.7/posts/832567173496798

Hladka, Kateryna; Dmytro, Vasilisa Hromakov; Veronika Myronova, Ol'ha Pluzhnyk, Oleh Pokal'chuk, Ihor Rudych Trofymovych, Artem Shevchenko (2016), Dobrobaty: Istoriia podvyhu batal'ioniv, shcho vriatuvaly krainu. Kharkiv: Folio.

Hunter, Montana (2018), Crowdsourced War: The Political and Military Implications of Ukraine's Volunteer Battalions 2014–2015, in: Journal of Military and Strategic Studies, 18/3, pp. 78-124.

Iarosh, Dmytro (2014), Ia by zaraz ne vidmovyvsia vid hroshei bud'-iakoho oliharkha, Glavkom, 28 July, http://glavcom.ua/publications/1257 03-dmitro-jarosh-ja-bi-zaraz-ne-vidmovivsja-vid-groshej-bud-jakogo-oligarha.html.

Iarosh, Dmytro (2016), Ia nikoly ne buv radykalom," in: Ukrains'ka Pravda, November 7, http://www.pravda.com.ua/articles/2016/11/7/7125992/.

Iavir, Irina (2016), Partiia dlia 'Azovu', in: Politychna Krytyka, October 11, http://ukraine.politicalcritique.org/2016/10/11/partiya-dlya-azovu/.

Iovenko, Artem (2015), The Ideology and Development of the Social-National Party of Ukraine, and its Transformation into the All-Ukrainian Union 'Freedom', in 1990–2004, in: Communist and Post-Communist Studies, 48/2, pp. 229-237.

Kachura, D. (2016), Pochemu Filatov ob'iavil voinu Kolomoiskomu, Depo.ua, 20 October, http://www.depo.ua/rus/politics/chomu-filatov-ogolosiv-viynu-kolomoyskomu-20102016190000.

Käihkö, Ilmari (2018), A Nation-in-the-Making, in Arms: Control of Force, Strategy and the Ukrainian Volunteer Battalions, in: Defence Studies, 18/2, pp. 147-166.

Karagiannis, Emmanuel (2016), Ukrainian Volunteer Fighters in the Eastern Front: Ideas, Political-Social Norms and Emotions as Mobilization Mechanisms, in: Southeast European and Black Sea Studies, 16/1, pp. 139-153.

Karpiak, Oleh (2014), Chy stanut' dobrovol'chi batal'iony iadrom novoi armii, BBC Ukraine, August 6, https://www.bbc.com/ukrainian/politics/2014/08/140805_volunteer_batallions_ko.

Katchanovski, Ivan (2016), The Separatist War in Donbas: A Violent Breakup of Ukraine?, in: European Politics and Society, 17/4, pp. 473-489.

Khomenko, S. (2016), Richnytsia vybukhiv 31 serpnia: shcho my znaiemo? BBC Ukraina, August 31, http://www.bbc.com/ukrainian/politics/2016/08/160831_31aug_anniversary_sx.

Konstantinovskii, V. (2014), Millioner Konstantinovskii: Mesti iz Moskvy ne boius', Obozrevatel', 28 September, https://www.obozrevatel.com/interview/96408-millioner-konstantinovskij-mesti-iz-moskvyi-ne-boyus.htm.

Korotash, O. (2015), Pozyvnyi Mol'far: Pys'mennyk na viini, in: Ukrains'ka Pravda: Zhyttia, 6 February, http://life.pravda.com.ua/society/2015/02/6/188936.

Koshulyns'kyi, Ruslan (2016), Rosiis'koiu movoiu vidrizaiut' vukha, nosy, henitalii, katuiut' tvoikh druziv. Khocha b zarady tsioho: vidiidy vid nei!, Censor.net.ua, December 19, https://ua.censor.net.ua/resonanc e/419675/ruslan_koshulynskyyi_rosiyiskoyu_movoyu_vidrizayut_ vuha_nosy_genitaliyi_katuyut_tvoyih_druziv_hocha.

Kudelia, Sergiy (2014), Domestic Sources of the Donbas Insurgency, in: PONARS Eurasia Policy Memos, no. 351, www.ponarseurasia.org/ memo/domestic-sources-donbas-insurgency.

Kudelia, Sergiy (2014), Reply to Andreas Umland: The Donbas Insurgency Began At Home," in: PONARS Eurasia, October 8, www.ponarseurasia.org/article/reply-andreas-umland-donbas-insurgency-began-home.

Kudelia, Serhiy (2016), The Donbas Rift, in: Russian Politics and Law, 54/1, pp. 5-27.

Kuzmenko, Oleksiy (2018), Ukrainian Far-Right Fighters, White Supremacists Trained by Major European Security Firm," Bellingcat, 30 August, www.bellingcat.com/news/uk-and-europe/2018/08/30/ukr ainian-far-right-fighters-white-supremacists-trained-major-europea n-security-firm/.

Liashko, Oleh (2016), Vpershe vyznaiu—pered vyboramy my domovylys' iz Liovochkinym. Inshoho vykhodu prosto ne bulo, Glavcom, September 9, http://glavcom.ua/interviews/oleg-lyashko-vpershe-viz nayu-pered-viborami-mi-domovilis-z-lovochkinim-inshogo-vihodu -prosto-ne-bulo-371621.html.

Likhachev, Viacheslav (2013), Right-Wing Extremism on the Rise in Ukraine, in: Russian Politics and Law, 51/5, pp. 59-74.

Likhachev, Viacheslav (2013), Social-Nationalists in the Ukrainian Parliament: How They got There and What We Can Expect of Them, in: Russian Politics and Law, 51/5, pp. 75-85.

Likhachev, Viacheslav (2013), Right-Wing Extremism in Ukraine: The Phenomenon of "Svoboda", Kyiv.

Likhachov, Viacheslav (2018), Chomu perebil'shennia roli ul'trapravykh v ukrains'kiy revoliutsii ne mensh nebezpechne, nizh prymenshennia, Zaborona, 3 May, https://zaborona.com/likhachov-column/.

Likhachov, V'iacheslav (2016), Vid Maidanu pravoruch: Revoliutsiia, viyna i ul'trapravi v Ukraini (2013–2016 roky) Kyiv.

Lutsenko, Ihor (2014), Pidstvol'nyky dlia Azova, in: Ukrains'ka Pravda Blohy, August 18, http://blogs.pravda.com.ua/authors/lutsenko/ 53f11d4d496c3.

Malyarenko, Tetyana; David J. Galbreath (2016), Paramilitary Motivation in Ukraine: Beyond Integration and Abolition, in: Southeast European and Black Sea Studies, 16/1, pp. 113-138.

Mamon, Marcin (2015), The Cross and the Sword: The Making of a Christian Taliban in Ukraine, The Intercept, 18 March, https://theintercept.com/2015/03/18/ukraine-part-3/.

Martsenyuk, Tamara; Ganna Grytsenko, Anna Kvit (2016), The 'Invisible Battalion': Women in ATO Military Operations in Ukraine, in: Kyiev-Mohyla Law and Politics Journal, no. 2, pp. 171-187.

Mitrokhin, Nikolai (2014), Grubye liudi: kak russkie natsionalisty sprovotsirovali grazhdanskuiu voinu v Ukraine, in: Forum noveishei vostochnoevropeiskoi istorii i kul'tury, 11/2, pp. 53-74.

Mitrokhin, Nikolai (2015), Infiltration, Instruction, Invasion: Russia's War in the Donbas, in: Journal of Soviet and Post-Soviet Politics and Society, 1/1, pp. 219-250.

Mitrokhin, Nikolai (2014), Infiltration, Instruktion, Invasion: Russlands Krieg in der Ukraine, in: Osteuropa, 64/8, pp. 3-16.

Naiem, Mustafa (2014), Za lashtunkamy Pravoho sektoru, in: Ukrains'ka Pravda, 1 April, http://www.pravda.com.ua/articles/2014/04/1/7020952/.

Polyakova, Alina (2014), From the Provinces to the Parliament: How the Ukrainian Radical Right Mobilized in Galicia, in: Communist and Post-Communist Studies, 47/2, pp. 211-225.

Polyakova, Alina (2015), Parties and Subcultures in the Process of Mobilization: The Internal Dynamics of the Radical Right in Ukraine, in: Michael Minkenberg (ed.): Transforming the Transformation? The East European Radical Right in the Political Process, Extremism and Democracy, London, pp. 319-347.

Puglisi, Rosaria (2015), A People's Army: Civil Society as a Security Actor in Post-Maidan Ukraine, in: IAI Working Papers, 15/23.

Puglisi, Rosaria (2015), General Zhukov and the Cyborgs: A Clash of Civilisation within the Ukrainian Armed Forces, in: IAI Working Papers, 1517.

Puglisi, Rosaria (2015), Heroes or Villains? Volunteer Battalions in Post-Maidan Ukraine, in: IAI Working Papers, 15/8.

Rinhis, A (2016), Hats'ko ta ioho komanda: DemAl'ians 2.0, in: Ukrains'ka Pravda, 26 July, http://www.pravda.com.ua/articles/2016/07/26/7115976/.

Rudling, Per A. (2013), The Return of the Ukrainian Far Right: The Case of VO Svoboda, in: Ruth Wodak, J.E. Richardson (eds.): Analyzing Fascist Discourse: European Fascism in Talk and Text, London 2013, pp. 228-255.

Ruzhyns'kyi, S. (2014), Navishcho Petro Poroshenko znyshchuie dobrovol'chi batal'iony?, *iPress.ua*, 21 August, http://ipress.ua/articles/navishcho_petro_poroshenko_znyshchuie_dobrovolchi_batalyony_81076.html.

Salatenko, S. (2017), Esli kto-to dumaet, chto eto voina za Donbas i za Krym, to eto ne tak, — eks-glava Sumskogo oblsoveta, ushedshyi dobrovol'tsem v ATO, Semen Salatenko, Censor.net.ua, *18* March, https://censor.net.ua/resonance/431956/esli_ktoto_dumaet_chto_eta_voyina_za_donbassdon-bass_i_za_krym_to_eto_ne_tak_eksglava_sumsk ogo_oblsoveta_ushedshiyi.

Sasse, Gwendolyn; Alice Lackner (2018), War and Identity: The Case of the Donbas in Ukraine, in: Post-Soviet Affairs, 34/2-3, pp. 139-157.

Semenchenko, Semen (2016), Ia dlia 90% rodstvennikov — predatel', eto stalo prichinoi smeny familii, 112.ua, *12* May, https://112.ua/interv iew/ya-dlya-90-rodstvennikov--predatel-eto-stalo-odnoy-iz-prichin-smeny-familii-310896.html.

Sergackova, Ekaterina (2015), Freiwillig: Kleines Who's Who ukrainischer Bataillonskommandeure, in: Osteuropa, 65/1-2, pp. 23-32.

Sergatskova, Ekaterina (2015), Looting, Torture, and Big Business: A Look at Volunteer Groups Fighting the Separatists in Ukraine," *Meduza*, 1 July, meduza.io/en/feature/2015/07/01/looting-torture-and-big-b usiness.

Shekhovtsov, Anton (2014), From Electoral Success to Revolutionary Failure: The Ukrainian Svoboda Party," in: Eurozine, 5 March, http://www.eurozine.com/articles/2014-03-05-shekhovtsov-en.html/.

Shekhovtsov, Anton (2013), From Para-Militarism to Radical Right-Wing Populism: The Rise of the Ukrainian Far-Right Party Svoboda, in: Ruth Wodak, Brigitte Mral, Majid KhosraviNik (eds.), Right Wing Populism in Europe: Politics and Discourse, London, pp. 249-263.

Shekhovtsov, Anton (2016), How Alexander Dugin's Neo-Eurasianists Geared up for the Russian-Ukrainian War in 2005-2013, in: Euromaidan Press, January 26, euromaidanpress.com/2016/01/26/how-alexander-dugins-neo-eurasianists-geared-up-for-the-russian-ukrai nian-war-in-2005-2013/.

Shekhovtsov, Anton (2011), The Creeping Resurgence of the Ukrainian Radical Right? The Case of the Freedom Party, in: Europe-Asia Studies, 63/2, pp. 203-228.

Shekhovtsov, Anton; Andreas Umland (2014), Ukraine's Radical Right, in: Journal of Democracy, 25/3, pp. 58-63.

Shuklinov, Petr (2014), Assorti ot Poroshenko: kto est' kto v spiske prezidentskogo bloka, Liga.Novosti, October 23, http://news.liga.net/articles/politics/3740506-komanda_poroshenko_kto_est_kto_v_spiske_prezidentskogo_bloka.htm.

Shurkhalo, Dmytro (2014), Dobrovol'chi batal'iony — mizh viinoiu ta politykoiu, in: Radio Svoboda, 15 August, https://www.radiosvoboda.org/a/26531775.html.

Skocpol, Theda (1979), States and Social Revolutions: A Comparative Analysis of France, Russia and China, Cambridge.

Skorychuk, Nataliia (2017), Molodi ta zukhvali. Parasiuk ta ioho pryntsypy, Glavcom, April 8, http://glavcom.ua/interviews/molodi-ta-zuhvali-parasyuk-ta-yogo-principi-407859.html.

Stek, L. (2016), Stvoriuiet'sia naimana armiia, iaka ne zdatna peremahaty — komandyr "Karpats'koi Sichi, in: Radio Svoboda, April 13, http://www.radiosvoboda.org/a/27673230.html.

Teteruk, Andrii (2017), Onyshchenko vytratyv 30 mil'ioniv dolariv, shchob znyshchyty Iatseniuka, in: Narodna Pravda, 13 September, https://narodna-pravda.ua/2017/09/13/andrij-teteruk-onyshhenko-vytratyv-30-miljoniv-dolariv-shhob-znyshhyty-yatsenyuka/.

Tiahnybok, Oleh (2015), Svoboda i Chest'! "Sich" — rik u viini za Ukrainu, in: Svoboda, 12 June, http://svoboda.org.ua/news/articles/00014078/.

Tret'iakov, Oleksandr (2014), Pry Iushchenkovi buv bezlad, za Ianukovycha — svavillia. S'ohodni treba rozbudovuvaty krainu, pryvodyty ii v poriadok, Gazeta.ua, 26 November, http://gazeta.ua/articles/opinions-journal/_pri-uschenkovi-buv-bezlad-za-anukovicha-svavillya-sogodni-treba-rozbudovuvati-krayinu-privoditi-yiyi-v-poryadok/585362.

Umland, Andreas (2013), A Typical Variety of European Right-Wing Radicalism?, in: Russian Politics and Law, 51/5, pp. 86-95.

Umland, Andreas (2016), Dobrovol'cheskie vooruzhennye formirovaniia i radikal'nyi natsionalizm v poslemaidannoi Ukraine: nekotorye osobennosti vozniknoveniia polka 'Azov', in: Forum noveishei vostochnoevropeiskoi istorii i kul'tury, 13/1, pp. 141-178.

Umland, Andreas (2016), Dobrovolcheskie vooruzhennye formirovaniia v postmaidannoi Ukraine, in: Politychna Krytyka, March 15, http://ukraine.politicalcritique.org/2016/03/dobrovolcheskie-vooruzhyonnye-formirovaniya-i-radikalnyj-natsionalizm-v-poslemajdannoj-ukraine/ (accessed February 9, 2018).

Umland, Andreas (2014), In Defense of Conspirology: A Rejoinder to Serhiy Kudelia's Anti-Political Analysis of the Hybrid War in Eastern Ukraine, in: PONARS Eurasia, September 30, www.ponarseurasia.org/article/defense-conspirology-rejoinder-serhiy-kudelias-anti-political-analysis-hybrid-war-eastern.

Umland, Andreas (2018), The Glazyev Tapes, Origins of the Donbas Conflict, and Minsk Agreements, Foreign Policy Association, September 13, foreignpolicyblogs.com/2018/09/13/the-glazyev-tapes-origins-of-the-donbas-conflict-and-minsk-agreements/.

Umland, Andreas; Anton Shekhovtsov (2013), Ultraright Party Politics in Post-Soviet Ukraine and the Puzzle of the Electoral Marginalism of Ukrainian Ultranationalists in 1994-2009, in: Russian Politics and Law, 51/5, pp. 33-58.

Vasylchenko, Iu. (2014), Liashko zalyshyvsia bez batal'ioniv, in: Delovaia Stolitsa, September 12, http://www.dsnews.ua/politics/lyashko-zalishivsya-bez-batalyoniv-12092014143500.

Verner, N. (2014), Komandir 'Azova' idet v narodnye deputaty, LB.ua, 23 September, http://lb.ua/society/2014/09/23/280282_kombat_azova_podal_dokumenti.html.

Vovnianko, Dmytro (2017), Siomki' vid 'Samopomochi', Tverezo.info, September 10, http://tverezo.info/post/22815.

Whitmore, Brian (2016), How to Manufacture a War, in: The Power Vertical, 26 August, www.rferl.org/a/how-to-manufacture-a-war/27947359.html.

Wilson, Andrew (2016), The Donbas in 2014: Explaining Civil Conflict Perhaps, but not Civil War, in: Europe-Asia Studies, 68/4, pp. 631-652.

Zadorozhnii, Oleksandr (2016), Hybrid War or Civil War? The Interplay of Some Methods of Russian Foreign Policy Propaganda with International Law, in: Mohyla Law and Politics Journal, no. 2, pp. 117-128.

Zhegulev, I. (2014), Privattank: milliarder Kolomoiskii vedet chastnuiu voinu za iedinstvo Ukrainy, in: Forbes, May 27, http://www.forbes.ru/sobytiya/obshchestvo/258279-privattank-milliarder-kolomoiski i-vedet-chastnuyu-voinu-za-edinstvo-ukra.

Zhyrokhov, M. (2016), Kirovohrads'kyi batal'ion "Rukh oporu, CHELine, December 20, http://cheline.com.ua/news/mens-club/kirovogradskij-bataljon-ruh-oporu-47885.

Ukrainian Volunteer Groups
Oversight by the Government

Leonid Poliakov

The occupation of the Autonomous Republic of Crimea (ARC) in spring 2014 and the subsequent military intervention of the Russian Federation in Ukrainian Donbas, as well as the Armed Forces of Ukraine's and other security structures' initial inadequate preparation for confronting this aggression, triggered the emergence of Ukrainian volunteer units in spring and summer of 2014.[1] Their emergence bridged this situation and allowed time to mobilize regular Armed Forces, thus minimizing the territorial, industrial, and human losses in Ukraine. Volunteer battalions were organized "from the top", namely upon the initiative of the country's leadership, and "from below". that is by Euro-Maidan participants in Kyiv, Kharkiv, Vinnytsia, Lviv and other Ukrainian cities, or were sponsored by Ukrainian patriotic movements, political parties and individual rich businessmen.

Prerequisites for the Creation of Volunteer Battalion

The Russian military's occupation of public buildings in the Autonomous Republic of Crimea (ARC), including that of the Supreme Council of the ARC, signalled the beginning of the Russian Federation's military aggression against Ukraine. The new Ukrainian leadership had to take urgent action. On February 28, 2014,[2] the Security

---

[1] The author would like to thank his interview partners, among them Yuri Syrotiuk, a Deputy of the Verkhovna Rada of Ukraine (2012-2014), acting Minister of Defense of Ukraine (2014), Ihor Teniukh, Director of the Department of the Special Task Police Units of the Ministry of Internal Affairs of Ukraine (2014-2015), Viktor Chalavan, a company commander of the Aidar 24th territorial defense battalion (2014), Yevhen Diki, and a member of the Right Sector (2014-2016) who asked not to be named.

[2] The full text of the short-hand report of the Security and „efense Council of Ukraine of February 28, 2014 *CENSOR.NET*, February 23, 2016, http://censor.net.ua/resonance/375717/polnyyi_tekst_stenogrammy_zasedaniya_snbo_ot_28_fevralya_2014_goda.

and Defense Council of Ukraine debated in accordance with Art. 4 of the law of Ukraine "On the defense of Ukraine", the introduction of martial law as a response to the military aggression. However, several vocal members of the Council argued against announcing martial law and an impulsive military reaction to the Russian invasion. Valentin Nalivaychenko, leader of the Security Service of Ukraine (SBU) at that time, warned:

> "Throwing an inefficient army, police and the SBU, the Crimean department of which almost fully defected to the enemys side, into warfare means getting into Putin's entrapment, opening the way for a full-scale intrusion into Ukraine for him, including capturing Kyiv. And that means losing the state — and thousands, thousands of deaths".[3]

As a result, only one person voted for martial law — Oleksandr Turchynov, Chair of the Verkhovna Rada and acting President of Ukraine. The other members of the Security and Defense Council of Ukraine opted for tapping the potential of volunteer battalions. Stepan Kubiv, head of the National Bank of Ukraine at that time and member of the Security and Defense Council, suggested:

> "We need to revive the army. Instead of kids and 'migrant workers', we need serious guys with military experience: Afghan veterans and others. They should be recruited to the armed forces, to the Ministry of Internal Affairs, to the SBU. The patriots who have been through Maidan should be recruited". Lieutenant-General Viktor Gvozd, leader of the Foreign Intelligence Service of Ukraine, echoed him and said: "...we need an efficient army, professional intelligence and secret services. We need time to create all these. We have many patriotically driven guys who will serve, but they have to be uniformed, given weapons and taught how to fight."[4]

March-April 2014

In early March 2014, Lieutenant-General Andrei Taranov, Deputy Head of the Presidential Administration of Ukraine, bluntly acknowledged the dire straits of the military:

---

3 Nalivaychenko: Putin planned a blitzkrieg, by March 8, 2014, the troops of the Russian Federation should have reached Kyiv, *GORDON*, February 22, 2016, http://gordonua.com/news/politics/nalivaychenko-v-planah-putina-byl-blickrig-do-8-marta-121121.html.
4 Ibid.

„We had certain [military] forces in the east of Ukraine till 2010. And then they ceased to exist. During Yanukovych's rule, the defense system of the country was totally destroyed. His ministers were consistently destroying the sphere of national security."[5]

In 2012, then-President Yanukovych had approved a program to reform the Armed Forces of Ukraine, which foresaw a cut of the existing personnel of 192,000, including 144,000 military and 48,000 civilians, to 100,000 (85,000 of the military and 15,000 civilians) by 2014 and to 70,000 military personnel by 2017. The program was adopted, and its implementation turned the armed forces into a small symbolic and weak defense agency, which would be helpless once confronted with military aggression. Such a depressing result was not only due to the sabotage of the pro-Russian bureaucrats in Ukraine. The constant lack of funding and understanding of the role the Armed Forces of Ukraine were to play in the system of state policy resulted in the failure of all attempts to reform it. "Reforms" seemed to boil down to permanent personnel cuts between 1991 (780,000) and 2013 (130,000). When the necessity arose to use the army for its intended purpose, i.e. for the defense of independence and territorial integrity, the Armed Forces of Ukraine were not adequately prepared.

Oleksandr Turchynov recollects the beginning of the war:

"Army resources were not enough to defend the country, and I promoted the creation of the National Guard, which we formed with internal troops as its base and reinforced, first of all, by the volunteers. And the most important thing was that I addressed our citizens, asking them to become volunteers and defend the country. Because even with mobilization, it was impossible to reverse the momentum without the volunteers' readiness to fight for their country. This is how the reinforcement of the National Guard with volunteers and the creation of the special battalions of the Ministry of Internal Affairs began..."[6]

---

5   Taranov: Every murderer will be found and punished, even after the war, Liga.net, May 04, 2015, http://news.liga.net/interview/politics/5671123-taranov_kazhdyy_ubiytsa_budet_nayden_i_nakazan_dazhe_posle_voyny.htm.

6   This is how the war started: An interview with Oleksandr Turchynov, *CENSOR.NET*, October 24, 2014, http://censor.net.ua/resonance/308694/tak_nachinalas_voyina_intervyu_s_aleksandrom_turchinovym.

The legal framework, which regulated the use of the Armed Forces, did not foresee the military situation in spring 2014. At the beginning of the anti-terrorist operation (ATO) the Ukrainian law "On combating terrorism", which at the time was under revision, stated that the use of the Armed Forces of Ukraine was only allowed "in the event of a terrorist act in the air space, in the territorial waters of Ukraine", whereas on the onshore territories of the country "the Armed Forces of Ukraine participate in anti-terrorist operations in the military facilities".[7] There was also a vague possibility of them interfering "in the event of an emergence of terrorist threats to national security from outside of Ukraine." Some experts admitted the possibility of Russian aggression against Ukraine, but all versions of a potential response by the Armed Forces of Ukraine were based on that law. Until February 2017, the possibility of using the Armed Forces of Ukraine on its national territory within the framework of the law "On combating terrorism" was not legally foreseen.

According to the legislature of that time, the SBU Anti-Terrorist Centre (ATC) was mainly in charge of organizing and carrying out anti-terrorist operations and coordinating the activities of those who combat terrorism or are involved in specific anti-terrorist operations. As early as at the beginning of April 2014, it became clear that administrative buildings and military units were seized and Ukrainian citizens killed not by just "rebels" or "miners and tractor drivers", but by special units of Russia's security agencies, trained to effectively use various types of weaponry to set up ambushes or shoot helicopters; activities that clearly had a military character. In particular, Igor Strelkov, an agent of the Federal Security Service of the Russian Federation, and Igor Bezler, an agent of the Main Intelligence Directorate of the General Staff of the Armed Forces of the Russian Federation, led the operations to seize administrative buildings in the cities of Slaviansk and Horlivka. The puppet governments of the so-called Donetsk People's Republic (DPR) and the Luhansk People's Republic (LPR) were headed by Alexandr Boro-

---

7   https://online.zakon.kz/Document/?doc_id=30589467.

dai, founder of the Russian nationalist TV station Den-TV, and Marat Bashirov, a member of Russia's anti-monopoly agency. Both early leaders of the so-called separatist republics were political spin doctors associated with Russia's secret services.

In early May 2014, the character of the separatists' activities had reached such a scale that only properly trained and equipped military units of the Armed Forces of Ukraine were able to confront them. Russia, however, kept denying its participation in the military confrontation. The leadership of Ukraine had to initiate adequate resistance and to legitimize it quickly. These initial measures included the approval of the law of Ukraine "On the National Guard of Ukraine" and the amendment of the laws "On mobilization training and mobilization", "On the police" (pertaining to the creation of the special tasks patrol police) and "On the defense of Ukraine" (pertaining to the formation of the territorial defense units).8 Only at the beginning of June 2014, the legal and regulatory basis for extensive use of the Armed Forces of Ukraine against illegal armed formations as part of the ATO framework was established. However, until the end of 2014, the efficiency of the Armed Forces of Ukraine did not match the threat emanating from the Russian-separatist formations. During the whole of 2014, the volunteer battalions thus remained essential for countering the separatists.

The Formation of Volunteer Battalions

The formation of the future volunteer units in Ukraine began in the first days of March 2014, immediately after the start of Russia's aggression in Crimea and the mobilization of the separatist movements in the east (Kharkiv) and in the south-east of Ukraine (Donetsk, Luhansk, Mariupol, Zaporizhzhia, Mykolaiv, Odesa). The formation of these units proceeded mostly in three ways. For one from the "top", i.e., by the acting President of Ukraine, Oleksandr Turchynov, the Minister of Internal Affairs Arsen Avakov, the Sec-

---

8 Security Sector Legislation of Ukraine. DCAF and CACDS, 2017, https://www.dcaf.ch/sites/default/files/publications/documents/Security%20Sector%20Legislation%20Ukraine%202017_eng.pdf.

retary of the Security and Defense Council of Ukraine Andriy Parubiy. Two, from the "bottom", i.e., by self-formation of patriotic and nationalist organizations and groups and, three, sponsored by wealthy patriots, such as the Dnipro businessman Ihor Kolomoisky and (to a lesser degree) some other well-off citizens, political and social organizations as well as communities of Ukraine. Among the armed groups that came into being through sponsors are the Right Sector Dnipro-1 battalion, the Karpatska Sich' battalion and the 131st separate reconnaissance battalion.

The motivation, self organization and self-sacrifice of Maidan self-defense groups in Kyiv and other Ukrainian cities played an essential role in recruiting members for armed volunteer groups. The former commander of the Maidan self-defense, Andriy Parubiy, continued to issue orders to these groups even way after the end of the Maidan protests in February 2014. In these orders, Andriy Parubiy called upon the self-defense volunteers to actively defend the Ukrainian state from Russia's aggression and urged them to form units in various security agencies within the shortest time possible and to equip them with patriots who will defend the territorial integrity and independence of Ukraine. They were to enforce order in the rear territories, to form a reserve and provide technical assistance to the regular battalions.[9]

The Formation of Volunteer Battalions from the "Top"

Discussions about the possibilities of recruiting volunteers continued after the above-mentioned meeting of the Security and Defense Council of Ukraine on February 28, 2014. On March 14-15, 2014, after the approval of the law of Ukraine "On the National Guard of Ukraine", more than 500 Maidan activists voluntarily joined the National Guard of Ukraine (NGU) reserve and departed to the base of special operations units in Novy Petrivtsi on the outskirts of Kyiv.[10] This law provided that the NGU shall resist the military aggression against Ukraine and respond to the military conflict

---

9   Parubiy's decrees of May 5, 2014 and July 03, 2014.
10 The law of Ukraine "On the National Guard of Ukraine". Art. 1, Para 2. In accordance with the law on the interaction with the Armed Forces of Ukraine, the

through military (combat) actions and by participating in the territorial defense. Andriy Parubiy, who was appointed leader of the Security and Defense Council of Ukraine after the Maidan, played a key role in the transition of Maidan volunteers to National Guard recruits. Parubiy's authority rested on his charisma and leadership of Maidan`s self-defense.

Pursuant to Major General Stepan Poltorak's order, the NGU commander at that time, a separate battalion within the 27th brigade of the NGU's North Operational-Territorial Command was formed on March 16, 2014. About 80 percent of the battalion's personnel were initially activists of the Maidan self-defense, whereas the other 20 percent were former special operations soldiers of the Ministry of Internal Affairs. Initial frictions between special forces and volunteers were soon brought under control, and after three weeks of preparation, on April 5, 300 people swore their oath as military personnel of the 1st National Guard reserve battalion. Major General Serhiy Kulchitsky, the head of the National Guard Department for Combat and Special Training oversaw the drill (Zhirokhov 2016). Immediately after having sworn their oath, the National Guard battalion, consisting of 350 combatants, departed to the east of Ukraine, first to Pavlohrad in the Dnipropetrovsk region, and afterwards, from April 15, 2014 onwards, to combat duty in the area of Izium–Slaviansk (Svidrov 2014).

On May 3, 2014, Andriy Parubiy, appealed on his *Facebook* page again to patriotic citizens, urging them to join the National Guard of Ukraine 2nd volunteer battalion:

> "The first battalion of the NGU which was formed from participants of the Maidan self-defense is taking part in the anti-terrorist operation in Slaviansk and Kramatorsk. We need backup. The call-up for another National Guard reserve battalion has been announced—on a reservist contract or on a permanent basis. You have to be 18 to 50 years of age, should neither have a

---

National Guard of Ukraine shall participate in resisting a military aggression against Ukraine and response to the military conflict by means of military (combat) actions and by performing missions of the territorial defense, https://www.rbc.ua/rus/news/rada-sozdala-natsionalnuyu-gvardiyu-ukrainy-13032014 114500.

criminal record nor have been in prison, and you need to have medical clearance".[11]

On April 24, 2014, the National Guard 2nd reserve special operations battalion was created. On May 16, 270 volunteer combatants completed their training and swore their oath, and on May 29, 2014, the battalion departed to the ATO zone in the area of Sloviansk and Kramatorsk to serve at checkpoints.[12] On the same day, Major General Serhiy Kulchitsky and nine combatants of the NGU 1st battalion died in a MI-8 helicopter which was shot down by the separatists not far from the Karachun mountain. Later, in July-August 2014, a special operations battalion named after General S. P. Kulchitsky was created from the personnel of the 1st (155 combatants) and 2nd (170 combatants) reserve battalions. Combat theatres of the Kulchitsky battalion included Krasnyi Lyman, Sloviansk, Artemivsk (Bakhmut), Debaltseve, Myronovske, Stanytsia Luhanska, Vuhlehirsk and Ilovaisk. During the war in 2014, 25 combatants of this battalion were killed, and another 82 were wounded.[13]

Special Operations Units of the Ministry of Internal Affairs

In an interview with the author, Viktor Chavlan, Director of the Department of the Special Operations Police Units (2014-2015), recalled the formation of "special operations units" of the Ministry of the Interior:

> "On April 4, 2014, a meeting took place at the Ministry of Internal Affairs, which was held by Arsen Avakov. Initially, the plan was to create the units

---

11   NSDC calls up for additional recruitment to the National Guard, *iPress*, May 04, 2014, http://ipress.ua/news/rnbo_ogoloshuie_dodatkovyy_nabir_u_natsionalnu_gvardiyu_62782.html.
12   First volunteers: What do we know about Kulchitsky's battalion, TV channel 112a, March 14, 2107 https://ua.112.ua/ato/pershi-dobrovoltsi-shcho-my-znaiemo-pro-batalion-kulchytskoho-298430.html, and 'They were the first: Kulchitsky's battalion', website Cheline, September 04, 2016, http://cheline.com.ua/news/mens-club/voni-buli-pershimi-bataljon-imeni-kulichitskogo-25242.
13   Ibid.

> within the National Guard, but there were debates... At that time, most generals were not ready to change their post-Soviet psychology and make tough, unconventional decisions. This is why, first, only one battalion was formed, which was later named after Kulchitsky. In the end, only two battalions were created in the National Guard, the second one being the Donbas battalion. "...In accordance with the law 'On the police', it is possible to create special operations patrol guard police units... We started to create these units as special operations police units within the Chief Directorate of the Ministry of Internal Affairs of Ukraine...Such police units were created on the basis of twenty-one regional directorates....We simplified the enrolment procedure; the volunteers were selected according to a fast-track process. The candidates were going through medical check-ups, special inspections were carried out—we could not take on people who had been charged with especially grave crimes or offences against persons. Those who had expunged or removed convictions were accepted to these units. Statistically, we only had four percent of people who had had problems with the law in the past.[14]

According to Chavalan, it was the merit of acting President Turchynov and the Minister of the Interior Avakov to realize that the police might be much quicker in absorbing and transforming volunteer battalions than the military. The formation of special operations police units (police volunteer battalions) began in the second half of April 2014, after the leadership of the Ministry of Interior (Avakov in particular) realized that the police in the eastern parts of Ukraine were demoralized, defected en masse to the enemy or did not fulfil their responsibilities—they simply did not turn up for work, left or handed over everything to the separatists. Similarly, the internal troops abandoned warehouses, left weaponry and ammunition behind or handed over weapons, turned in people and in some instances went to serve the Russians in the self-proclaimed Luhansk and Donetsk People's Republics.

The Azov battalion was the first special police formation created by order of the Minister of Internal Affairs. It participated in

---

14 Interview with Viktor Chavalan, December 2016. The law „On the national police" (July 2, 2015) provided that the Ministry of Internal Affairs, with the permission of the Cabinet of Ministers of Ukraine, are able to create special police units to enforce order in the facilities and territories of utmost economic importance or those affected by natural disasters, environmental pollution, or catastrophes, https://cis-legislation.com/document.fwx?rgn=78349.

the liberation of Mariupol in May-June 2014. "Kyiv-1" was the second, and Zoloti Vorota, also formed in Kyiv, was the third battalion. By the Minister's order, the commanders of these units were appointed, and the weaponry and logistics were provided by the Directorates of Internal Affairs (in the regions). The Ministry of Internal Affairs also established contact with those groups of Ukrainian patriots that already existed in the Luhansk and Donetsk regions, who had taken up weapons and had fought against the separatists, particularly Semen Semenchenko's and Mykola Shvaliy's group, which later on turned into the Donbas and Zoloti Vorota battalions. It was important for the Ministry of the Interior to make sure that those were not bandit groups or had a mission to infiltrate Ukrainian troops on behalf of the Russian enemy.

Viktor Chavalan set up the Department of the Special Operations Police to coordinate the battalions. All in all, 37 battalions were subsequently created and provided with funding. Three of them only existed on paper, since in the autumn of 2014, then-President Poroshenko terminated the formation of such battalions. By the end of the battle of Debaltseve (January / February 2015), the number of personnel of the special operations police battalions had reached 6,500 combatants. This figure does not include the Donbas battalion, which was part of the National Guard, and the Azov battalion, which was transferred to the National Guard by the end of 2014. Azov was already armed with heavy weaponry, for example tanks and mortars and could thus not be part of the police units.

The Dnipro-1 unit was formed in Dnipro, supported by the businessmen-politicians Ihor Kolomoyskyy and Hennadiy Korban who covered their material needs. This unit was formed between the end of May – mid-June 2014. In Dnipro, apart from the Dnipro-1 battalion, the infamous Shakhtarsk battalion was also formed (later disbanded) as well as the Sicheslav battalion. The Dnipro-1 combatants originally did not want to transform into police units. They knew many members of the National Guard unit named after Kulchitsky. They had already been a well-organized group beforehand and had seized weaponry from the Russians. Minister Arsen Avalov, the Minister's adviser Anton Gerashchenko and Viktor Chavalan invited them to the Ministry of Internal Affairs. The

Dnipro-1 battalion was thus put under the formal tutelage of the National Guard.

The formation, integration and participation of self-organized combatants in warfare necessitated training in military skills. Initially, the self-organized groups were armed with hunting and captured weapons. The Zoloti Vorota battalion, for example, had seized two Rapira 100 mm anti-tank cannons, a BMD-1 airborne assault vehicle, a BMP-2 infantry fighting vehicle, all of which were manufactured in Russia, within two weeks (from August 26 until September 5, 2014). The seized weaponry was handed over to the military, while the BMP and BMD combat vehicles were handed over to the Luhansk-1 police unit. Captured small arms such as machine guns, guns and mortars were first reported to the Chief Directorate of Internal Affairs, then a special expert commission checked whether they had been listed in criminal proceedings or whether these arms were registered as stolen from the Ukrainian authorities or officials. If not, then these weapons were registered and entered the storage of the special operations police units.

The law of Ukraine "On the police", permitted the quick formation of "special police units" armed with small arms and legally staffed by volunteers and their use for "enforcing order" or "cleansing" territories occupied by the separatists. Thus, the police structures' flexibility played a positive role in the quick and legal formation of the volunteer battalions as compared to the National Guard and, even more so, the Armed Forces, which were bound by strict formal limitations. As a result, from April 14, 2014 onwards, i.e., effectively since the beginning of the ATO, 56 units of special operations patrol service were created on the territory of the Donetsk and Luhansk regions with a total number of 6, 700 personnel.

Territorial Defense Battalions of the Ministry of Defense

Art. 18 of the law "On the defense of Ukraine" provided for the creation of territorial defense battalions (TerDB). Accordingly, the General Staff developed a mobilization plan and a plan for the territorial defense. Even though, on March 17, 2014, the Verkhovna

Rada approved limited mobilization,[15] it was not possible to form these battalions right away since the law foresaw that they were to be formed via the military registration and enlistment offices. But, in the previous year, during President Viktor Yanukovych reign, the numbers of the military registration and enlistment offices had been considerably cut. In 2013, conscription was abolished.[16] It took virtually the whole second half of March and half of April 2014 to restore the mobilization capacities of the military registration and enlistment offices.[17]

In April 2014, the formation of the territorial defense battalions began in the Ministry of Defense of Ukraine; the battalions recruited both volunteers and mobilized personnel. Some battalions consisted of volunteers only, such as the Kyiv Rus 11th TerDB from the Kyiv region, the 20th TerDB from the Dnipropetrovsk region, and the Aidar 24th TerDB from the Luhansk region, which consisted of volunteers from central and western Ukraine, but was formed in the Luhansk region. As of September 2014, the formation of 44 of these battalions was reported.[18] Despite their designation as territorial defense battalions with local missions, the dire situation forced the leadership of the Armed Forces to send some of the battalions to the ATO zone by mid-summer 2014. However, the situation in Donbas changed dramatically—after the regular troops of the Armed Forces of the Russian Federation had crossed the Ukrainian border and joined the fighting, the territorial defense battalions, which were only armed with small arms and equipped with cars, could not effectively resist the armored vehicles and artillery of the Russian regular troops.

---

15 http://zakon2.rada.gov.ua/laws/show/1126-18/paran2#n2.
16 Chaotic mobilisation: military registration and enlistment offices lose data bases and corruption thrives, *News TV channel "24"*, August 05, 2014, https://24tv.ua/ru/haoticheskaya_mobilizatsiya_voenkomati_teryayut_bazi_dannih_i_protsvetaet_korruptsiya_n471538
17 Ministry of Defense: Territorial defence battalions are created in the regions. Ministry of Defense press-office, April 30, 2014, http://www.kmu.gov.ua/control/uk/publish/article?art_id=247260349&cat_id=244277212.
18 37 battalions participate in the ATO: infographic. LIGA Biznesinform Information agency, September 03, 2014, http://news.liga.net/news/politics/3155678-37_batalonov_uchastvuyut_v_ato_infografika.htm.

The Formation of Volunteer Battalions from Below

The majority of the self-organized groups such as Azov (later under the Ministry of Internal Affairs), Donbas (later part of the National Guard of Ukraine) or Aidar (later under Ministry of Defence) began to look for ways of legalization after having formed their organizational core. Andriy Biletsky, the future Azov commander, and some participants of the Euromaidan in Kyiv who had returned to Kharkiv, initiated the formation of the Azov battalion (later regiment) in early March 2014. Andriy Biletsky was a historian who headed the radical nationalist organization "Patriot of Ukraine" in Kharkiv. His group organized an armed response to the Kharkiv separatists and Russian agents provocateurs, among whom was the notorious "Motorola" (Arseni Pavlov, 1983-2016), a militant from Russia who later headed the pro-Russian battalion Sparta. On March 14, 2014, the first battle of Ukrainian volunteers against the pro-Russia separatists took place, in which the separatists suffered losses and retreated (Butusov 2014).333333 The original core of the Azov unit consisted of members of the "Social National Assembly" and "Patriot of Ukraine", activists of the "Automaidan" and various groups of the Maidan self-defense.[19] Later, hooligans of the Dynamo Kyiv football club, members of Dmytro Korchynsky's "Brethren Party", activists of the Organization of Ukrainian Nationalists and members of the Cossack Shooters Brotherhood joined Azov. The deputy battalion commander, Yaroslav Honchar, added that the battalion's core consisted of people who had gone out to the Maidan as early as November 21, 2013. Members of the "Misanthropic Division" (MD), an internationally operating radical right-wing organization, were also represented in Azov. Volunteers with neo-fascist views from Sweden, Italy, Russia, France, Belarus, Canada, and Slovenia were also part of the regiment.[20]

---

19 Automaidan (Ukrainian: Автомайдан) was a pro-European movement involving the use of cars and trucks as means of protest that first began in late 2013 in Kyiv within the advent of Euromaidan.
20 Regiment of white people. What do we know about Azov, Correspondent.net, May 05, 2016, http://korrespondent.net/ukraine/3678807-polk-belykh-luidei-chto-my-znaem-ob-azove

Having rallied around himself about 200 people at the early stage, Andriy Biletsky, however unsuccessfully, tried for about a month to receive weaponry and the official status of a military formation. His group managed to obtain its legal status only in April 2014, after the Ministry of Internal Affairs began to form volunteer special police units. After the successful military operations around Mariupol, the whole detachment of Andriy Biletsky received the status of "Azov battalion of the Ministry of Internal Affairs." In late 2014, the Azov battalion obtained the status of a regiment and was transferred to the National Guard of Ukraine.

Not all self-organized groups wanted to obtain legal status, especially the Right Sector. This organization had obtained its name during the Maidan protests as a result of its location on the square. The Right Sector consisted of several patriotic organizations, among them "Tryzub", Ukrainian National Assembly – Ukrainian People's Self-Defense (UNSA-UNSO), some radical right-wing organizations that left the Right Sector after Maidan, and football fans who joined in; in total, around 300 people.[21] According to Dmytro Yarosh, the leader of the Right Sector, the paramilitary organization "Stepan Bandera Tryzub" was the basis for the creation of the group (Shramovitch 2015).

For ideological reasons and due to its distrust in the Ministry of Internal Affairs (in particular, because of the death of Right Sector activist Olexandr Muzychko during his detention), the leadership of the Right Sector refused to cooperate with the Ministry of Internal Affairs. The Ministry of Defense, in turn, rejected the Right Sector's demand to grant the battalion a certain autonomy.[22]

After the unsuccessful negotiations over gaining official status, the Right Sector's leadership decided to act independently. Even though the Constitution banned "the creation and functioning of any armed formations not provided by law" (Article 17), it granted the right of the Ukrainian people to "directly exercise power" (Article 5) and stated that "the defense of the Motherland,

---

21 The Right Sector is Thinking of Becoming a Party and Take Part in the Election, Ukrainskaya Pravda, February 03, 2014, http://www.pravda.com.ua/rus/news/2014/02/3/7012417/.
22 Ibid.

the independence and territorial integrity of Ukraine ... is the obligation of the citizens of Ukraine" (Article 65). On April 20, 2014, the Right Sector volunteers carried out their first operation. Led by Dmytro Yarosh and authorized by the ATO operational headquarters, they assaulted a separatist checkpoint close to Slaviansk. Twenty volunteers equipped with hunting weapons tried to break through the checkpoint and disable the television tower transformer on the Karachun mountain in Slaviansk to impede Russian TV propaganda (Komarovski 2016). The operation resulted from the group's ardent desire to join the battlefield. At that time, the main part of the Right Sector was undergoing operational training at the Desna training centre of the Armed Forces of Ukraine. After basic combat training and organizational build-up, several units of the Right Sector Volunteer Ukrainian Corps (RS VUC) were formed with several hundred personnel. In July 2014, the RS VUC, in coordination with the brigades of the Armed Forces of Ukraine, engaged in warfare in the Donetsk area. It liberated Krasnogorovka, Avdiivka and resisted the separatists at Donetsk airport (Shuklinov 2014).

Similar to the Right Sector, the OUN battalion (Organization of Ukrainian Nationalists) rejected formal subordination. In July 2014, the OUN battalion had originally been formed as the "Nezhin territorial defense battalion". Its commander was Mykola Kokhanivski from the Maidan self-defense (OUN First Kyiv Sotnia). After the official registration of the battalion failed, its leadership decided that the battalion should join the RS VUC. Its name was subsequently changed from "Nezhin battalion" to "OUN battalion". It took part in the fighting in the Donetsk region (Saur Mogila, Peski).

The Formation of Volunteer Battalions by Sponsors

According to a widely held opinion in Ukraine, the governorship of the oligarch and billionaire Ihor Kolomoyskyy in the Dnipropetrovsk region and his generous help in the formation of several volunteer battalions were very important, if not decisive, in that the south-west of the Donetsk region, the Dnipropetrovsk and Zaporizhzhia regions did not fall prey to the separatists and Russian propaganda. After having become Governor, Ihor Kolomoyskyy, aided by his business partners Hennadiy Korban, Svyatoslav Oleynik and Borys Filatov, set up a multi-million Foundation for the support of "National military Formations" as well as the community advisory headquarters. Kolomoyskyy decisively replaced the old and unreliable officials in the region and established successful communications with various interest groups. A pool of 1,700 paramilitary personnel was created to defend the region. The Dnipro-1 battalion and other volunteer units later emerged from this pool.[23] According to Viktor Chalavan, Kolomoyskyy and Korban

> "...did much for the units of the Dnipropetrovsk formation, but they did not directly steer them. They were controlled by the Chief Directorate of the Internal Affairs in the Dnipropetrovsk region".[24]

Many other well-off Ukrainian citizens followed Ihor Kolomoyskyy's example, among them Vitaliy Klychko, a famous boxer and mayor of Kyiv, who contributed 3.2 million hryvnias (~ $ 12.000 in May 2014) to the needs of the Kyiv-1 battalion.[25] However, in 2014, no one else had such political influence on volunteer battalions formed in the Dnipropetrovsk region as Kolomoyskyy did. Companies associated with the former president of Ukraine, Petro Poroshenko, supported the volunteers with 500 million hryvnias (~ $ 43.200.000 in May 2014).[26] Support of the volunteers also came from prominent businessmen, personal donations, and regional foundations. There are no summary data available on the

---

23 Maksim Butchenko: Kolomoyskyy Region, Novoye Vremia, No.2, May 23, 2014, p. 21.
24 Interview with the author, December 2016.
25 Klichko Brothers to Finance Manning the Kyiv Battalion in the ATO Zone, 7 Days. Ukraine, June 29, 2014, http://7days-ua.com/news/braty-klychky-profinansuyut-ukomplektuvannya-bataljonu-kyjiv-u-zoni-ato/
26 Poroshenko spent more than half a billion hryvnias to help the Ukrainian Army, Media. Gordon.UA, August 31, 2017, http://gordonua.com/news/war/poroshenko-potratil-na-pomoshch-ukrainskoy-armii-bolee-polumilliarda-griven-smi-205064.html

various forms of aid for volunteer battalions. It was quite usual for voluntary donations to be transferred to a foundation supporting the Armed Forces of Ukraine or a foundation supporting some volunteer battalions. Many sponsors did not want to go public. It is safe to assume that voluntary financial aid to the volunteer battalions and the Armed Forces of Ukraine in 2014-2015 was quite significant.

The support by certain political parties and non-governmental organizations can also be considered as "sponsorship" of volunteer battalions. One of the most well-known examples is the formation of the "Karpatska Sich'" volunteer battalion as part of the 93^d mechanized brigade; the battalion was formed by members of the All-Ukrainian Union Svoboda political party. Another example is the formation of the 131st independent reconnaissance battalion of the southern operational command by members of the Ukrainian National Assembly—Ukrainian People's Self-Defense (UNA-UNSO), which became a political party in April 2015. In both cases, the volunteers were first and foremost Maidan activists. According to Ihor Teniukh, acting Minister of Defense in February-March 2014, who had coordinated the Svoboda detachments on the Maidan (16 Svoboda members were killed there):

> "The All-Ukrainian Union Svoboda that delegated people to the Maidan self-defense structure also had their 'own' independent detachments. Upon the decision of the Svoboda political leadership, I was responsible for those detachments on the Maidan. The number of personnel in the detachments varied, but it was on average around 4,000 people".

Ihor Teniukh insisted that the members of Svoboda should seek strictly legal ways of recruitment for their members through military registration and enlistment offices.[27] As for the UNA-UNSO representatives, they cooperated with the Right Sector on the Maidan and in the first months of the military conflict. However, in July 2014, the UNA-UNSO leadership preferred to coordinate their actions with the Ministry of Defense of Ukraine. On the

---

27 Ours in the ATO Yuri Bachal, Codename Sapsan, 131 Separate Reserve Battalion (Kuren UNSO), UNA-UNSO site, March 05, 2016, http://unso.in.ua/uk/new/nashi-v-ato-yuriy-bachal-pozyvnyy-sapsan-131-orb-kurin-unso.

basis of the former command post of the Armed Forces of Ukraine, near the village of Gushchintsi of the Kalinovsk District in the Vinnytsia region, the UNA-UNSO training center began then to operate. In August 2014, its representatives joined the 54th independent reconnaissance battalion and the 81st separate air mobile brigade. And in early 2014, the 131st independent reconnaissance battalion which was later joined by UNA-UNSO volunteers was created out of the 54th independent reconnaissance battalion and part of the 139th independent reconnaissance battalion.[28]

Transformation and Integration of Volunteer Battalions

During the violent summer of 2014 in the Donetsk region, many volunteer battalions participated in the fighting against illegal armed separatists groups as well as against regular troops of the Russian Federation. Despite their strong motivation, the volunteer battalions were not prepared for this kind of enemy. The unpreparedness of the volunteer battalions, which were created in a rush and were hardly properly armed, was, in effect, quite common. Reinforcing the territorial defense battalions with anti-aircraft platoons and mortar batteries did not significantly improve their efficiency. During the summer and autumn of 2014, they suffered heavy losses and had to retreat together with the regular troops of the Armed Forces of Ukraine and the volunteer battalions of the Ministry of Internal Affairs. The military coordination of these volunteer battalions and the units of the Armed Forces as well as the provision of fire support was deficient. In August 2014, upon demand of the military command, one of the Deputy Ministers of Internal Affairs was sent to the ATO zone to coordinate the actions of these volunteer battalions. The poor coordination with the Armed Forces during the clashes with the Russian regular troops was one of the reasons why volunteer battalions suffered heavy losses, in particular near Ilovaisk, where, together with the units of the Armed Forces

---

28   Ours in the ATO Yuri Bachal, Codename Sapsan, 131 Separate Reserve Battalion (Kuren UNSO), UNA-UNSO site, March 05, 2016, http://unso.in.ua/uk/new/nashi-v-ato-yuriy-bachal-pozyvnyy-sapsan-131-orb-kurin-unso.

of Ukraine, the Dnipro-1. Myrotvorets, Svitiaz, Kherson, Ivano-Frankivsk and Donbas battalions were defeated.[29]

Some volunteer battalions (Aidar, Shakhter) had significant problems with discipline. But while the Aidar battalion demonstrated lax discipline and yet high combat efficiency—thanks to a considerable number of motivated Maidan veterans (around 300 people)—the Shakhter battalion, which consisted of shady commercial circles of Donbas, was accused of looting. It was thus disbanded and transformed into the Tornado battalion of the Ministry of Internal Affairs. Yevhen Diki from Aidar said in an interview:

> "...we were covering our artillery, carried out reconnaissance, dealt with the fortification of our camp which moved from Polovinkino to Schastye. From time to time, we carried out assault operations in coordination with the paratroopers of the 80th air mobile brigade. Together, we liberated Trekhisbenka and Georgiyevka. Heavy battles were fought for Vergulevka, Khryashchevatoye, Novosvitlivka. It was then that...that we appreciated the importance of bulletproof vests. ...in the battles for Vergulevka near Luhansk, we captured quite a few personal documents of the enemy. It turned out that many Russian nationals were fighting against us. In early August 2014, there were two Russians per one local. This was how we fought near Luhansk till the end of August, until the Russian regular tank and mechanized troops began to act against us."[30]

In September 2014, the formation of the new special battalions of the Ministry of Internal Affairs and the territorial defense battalions of the Ministry of Defense of Ukraine was discontinued. The decision was taken to include the territory defense battalions into the brigades of the Armed Forces of Ukraine as mechanized infantry battalions. In October 2014, the Deputy Chief of General Staff, General-Major Viktor Nazarov (acting ATO Chief of Staff in the midst of the war in the summer of 2014), said:

> "The faults in the coordination of the volunteer detachments with the units of the Armed Forces of Ukraine provided grounds for the commencement of their integration process into the Armed Forces, the National Guard or

---

29 Interview with Anatoli Matios: No one Put a Full Stop in the Ilovaisk Investigation, *CENSOR.NET*, August 21, 2017, https://censor.net.ua/resonance/452450/anatolyi_matos_nhto_krapku_u_rozslduvann_spravi_po_lovayisku_ne_staviv.
30 Interview with the author, January 2017.

turning them into special battalions of the Ministry of Internal Affairs of Ukraine. Now, this process has been largely completed."[31]

At the end of 2014, the Azov battalion, which at that time had already been armed with heavy weaponry, was transformed into a regiment and transferred to the National Guard under the command of the Ministry of Internal Affairs. In February 2015, thanks to its increased combat potential, the Azov regiment managed to drive the enemy back as far as 15 km from Mariupol and gained a foothold in the settlement of Shyrokyne. During that period, the Dnipro-1 battalion of the Ministry of Internal Affairs defended the northern side of Mariupol. Part of this battalion also won glory defending Donetsk airport together with the Right Sector and the 93[d] mechanized brigade of the Armed Forces of Ukraine that, in part, consisted of the "Karpatska Sich" volunteer battalion from the Svoboda party. After having retreated from Luhansk together with the 80th independent air mobile brigade of the Armed Forces of Ukraine, the Aidar battalion held the positions northwards of Luhansk, close to the locality of Stanitsa Luganskaya. The Donbas volunteer battalion (National Guard of Ukraine) in coordination with the 128th mountain infantry brigade and other units of the Armed Forces defended Debaltsevo. During the defense of Debaltsevo, the territorial defense battalions were already fighting as parts of the brigades of the Armed Forces, namely as mechanized infantry battalions. As for the Right Sector, its units were never integrated. Its leadership had originally refused to cooperate with the Ministry of Internal Affairs in forming and arming the Dnipr-2 battalion. The Ministry of Defense rejected the Right Sector's proposals to retain its structure and to grant a certain autonomy.

After the end of the active combat phase in Donbas in February 2015—around Donetsk airport, Mariupol (Shyrokyne) and Debaltsevo—the "contact line" of the opposing forces mostly stabilized. In Minsk, the peace agreements were signed, which opened opportunities for a political regulation of the conflict, allowing the

---

31 Analysis of the Warfare near Ilovaisk after the Intrusion of the Russian Troops on August 24-29, 2014', website of the Ministry of Defense of Ukraine, October 19, 2015, http://www.mil.gov.ua/news/2015/10/19/analiz-illovausk--14354.

Ukrainian government to focus on bringing the volunteer battalions under its control and minimizing the informal influence of commercial and political sponsors. The government's more decisive actions to limit the "sponsors'" impact were triggered by the attempt of armed individuals, which were disguised as National Guards personnel, to oppose the changeover of the CEO of the Ukrnafta state company, who was close to Ihor Kolomoyskyy (Siniak 2015).

The integration of the volunteer battalions into government agencies was protracted. The reassignment of more than 50 territorial defense battalions of various degrees of combat readiness to the Armed Forces of Ukraine was completed in May-June 2015. In particular, the Aidar 24th assault battalion (the former 24th TerDB) joined the new 10th independent mountain assault brigade of the land forces of the Armed Forces, the Krivbass 40th TerDB was already fighting as part of the 17th tank brigade, the Patriot 43d TerDB (Dnipropetrovsk region) joined the 53d mechanized brigade, and the Kyiv Rus 11th TerDB and the Cherkasy 20th TerDB joined the 72nd mechanized brigade. The "Karpatska Sich" company (from the Svoboda party) fought as part of the 93d mechanized brigade — it was disbanded in 2016 due to the leadership's personal disagreement with the personnel policy of the Armed Forces of Ukraine command. The Prykarpatia 5th TerDB was disbanded after the unauthorized abandonment of its position by the majority of the battalion in August 2014.

In 2015, the National Guard, included four volunteer units i.e., the Azov regiment, the battalion named after Kulchitsky, the Donbas battalion, and the Kruk 4th battalion. Part of the volunteers of the Donbas National Guard's 2nd special battalion were registered as the Donbas-Ukraine 46th separate battalion of the Armed Forces within the new 10th independent mountain assault brigade of the land forces. The rest of the National Guard Donbas battalion joined the National Guard's 18th regiment in Severodonetsk.

As for the Ministry of Internal Affairs, the turning event for the transformation and integration of the volunteer battalions into ministry troops occurred in August 2015 when the police volunteer battalions were moved away from the so-called red line. The Myrotvorets battalion, deployed in Kyiv, formed the basis for the Mirotvrorets regiment of the Ministry of Internal Affairs, which was merged with the Kyivshchina and Garpun battalions. The Tornado special task patrol police was disbanded for grave crimes committed by its personnel. The order was signed on June 18, 2015 by Arsen Avakov, the Minister of Internal Affairs. Except for the convicted and fired individuals, the rest of the personnel joined the Myrotvorets regiment.[32]

Some units of the Right Sector, after the retreat from the embattled Donetsk airport, continued to remain at the front line. In April 2015, an attempt was made to pressure these Right Sector battalions into disbanding, but the attempt failed. A military clash was avoided, and Dmytro Yarosh, the leader of the Right Sector, agreed to become an adviser to the Chief of the General Staff of the Armed Forces. Still, the pressure on the Right Sector persisted, since the organization acted not only at the front but also far behind the lines. In particular, on July 11, 2015, armed skirmishes between members of the Right Sector and the police took place in the city of Mukachevo, Zakarpattia region, which led to several casualties and the destruction of vehicles.[33] The exchange of fire in Mukachevo between the Right Sector local division and the police exposed a problem that spread in 2015, after the end of active warfare. Volunteer battalions' veterans got involved in commercial disputes deep in the heartland of Ukraine. Private security agencies and individuals unrelated to the volunteer battalions acted under the guise of being volunteers. The integration of the volunteer battalions into governmental security agencies became urgent.

In November 2015, the Right Sector split over disagreements between Dmytro Yarosh, the then leader of the Right Sector, and his close associates regarding cooperation with the government.

---

32 Part of the Combatants of the Tornado Company joined the Mirotvirets Regiment, *Zerkalo nedeli*, July 29, 2015, https://zn.ua/UKRAINE/chast-boycovroty-tornado-popolnila-ryady-polka-mirotvorec-183989_.html.

33 The Details of the Conflict in Mukachevo Become Known". *FAKTY*, July 11, 2015, http://fakty.ua/202687-stali-izvestny-prichina-konflikta-v-mukachevofoto.

Dmytro Yarosh, elected as deputy of the Verkhovna Rada of Ukraine in 2014, announced his disaffiliation from the Right Sector's "National Liberation Movement". Together with Dmytro Yarosh, the most combat effective 5th and 8th Right Sector Volunteer Corps battalions and the "Hospitalieri" medical battalion left. The so-called Ukrainian Volunteer Army (UVA) was created based on these former Right Sector units. In December 2015, Yarosh announced the formation of a new social and political movement named DIYA (State Initiative of Dmytro Yarosh), which resulted in the UVA becoming an armed group under the aegis of this party. The UVA formations mostly joined the Armed Forces of Ukraine, and those who did not gathered in small groups, sometimes coming out to the front line and working in coordination with the Armed Forces.

Some estimates put the number of personnel that remained with the Right Sector at around 600 people—an armed formation under the aegis of the Right Sector party. Unlike the UVA units that mostly retreated from the front line, the Right Sector combatants remained at the front line until June 2016, when four combatants died. After that, many of its combatants joined the Armed Forces or the Security Service of Ukraine (SBU). Volodymyr Solovyan notes:

> "...even though the RS VUC and UVA did not officially join the governmental structures, at the level of the ATO territorial headquarters, reliable communication was set in place with these units. According to the UVA Chief of Staff Serhiy Ilnytskiy, the UVA 5th and 8th battalions are holding positions on the outskirts of Avdeyevka and at Shyrokyne (the total strength of the units is up to 600 personnel), and the UVA Hospitalieri UVA medical unit operates along the whole front line."[34]

Many combatants of the Right Sector signed contracts with the Ministry of Defense, joining the 54th separate mechanized brigade. Part of the Right Sector had also signed contracts with the SBU Alpha special operations center.

During 2016 and 2017, most volunteer units formed in 2014 were integrated further into governmental structures. The Ministry

---

34 Vladimir Solovyan: Integration of volunteer battalions into security structures: Will the Israeli experience be useful?, CACDS, June 29, 2017, http://cacds.org.ua/ru/comments/1123.

of Defense, where the former territorial defense battalions were mostly transformed into regular mechanized infantry battalions, achieved their integration earlier. Former volunteer battalions such as the Aidar 24th assault battalion (former 24th TerDB) and the Donbas-Ukraine 46th special designation battalion, which acted mostly between Donetsk and Mariupol, managed to retain their identity to a considerable degree.[35]

In 2016, the transformation processes were still going on. The Kyiv-1, Kyiv-2, Zoloti Vorota special operations police battalions, the Saint Mary battalion until October 2014 part of the Shakhtarsk battalion — were transformed into one unit — the Kyiv regiment. The Kharkiv-1 and Slobozhanshchina battalions were also transformed into one unit — the Kharkiv battalion. The Dnipro-1 battalion (served in the area of Slaviansk-Bakhmut) and the Myrotvorets battalion (its main deployment site was in Severodonetsk) were reformed into the Dnipro-1 and Myrotvorets regiments.[36]

After the transformation, 22 special operations patrol police units operated within the National Police in the regions and in Kyiv, among them three regiments (Dnipro-1, Myrotvorets and Kyiv), nine battalions (Vinnytsia, Skif, Ivano-Frankivsk, Kirovograd, Luhansk-1, Lviv, Storm, Poltava and Kharkiv) and ten companies (Svitiaz, Sicheslav, Krivbass, Mykolaiv, Sumy, Ternopil, Vostochny Korpus, Khersonm, Bogdan and Chernihiv). In early 2017, the personnel of the above-listed units amounted to 4,898 formal positions, of which 3,996 were actually filled.[37]

Close ties still exist between some integrated volunteer battalions, volunteer veteran organizations and paramilitary groups of patriotic and nationalist parties and organizations. Some of them had existed before Russia's aggression (Svoboda, UNA-UNSO, Tryzub, Patriot of Ukraine), and the others were formed in the

---

35 Interview with Viacheslav Vlasenko, Donbas-Ukraine Battalion Commander: Liliya Ragutskaya. The Legendary Battalion Commander Shared Atrocious Details of the Battles against Russia's Military in Donbas, *Apostrophe*, November 08, 2017, .
36 Annex 2. Report Volunteer battalions 2nd edition, (in Ukrainian) Kharkiv, Folio, 2017, p. 305.
37 Ibid.

course of withstanding the aggression (the Right Sector, DIYA, Azov National Corps, the Youth branch of the Azov regiment). The "Lehion Svobody" operates under the aegis of the All-Ukrainian Union Svoboda, as a combatant union of all the Svoboda members within the Armed Forces of Ukraine, National Guard, special purpose units of the Ministry of Internal Affairs and volunteer battalions, which took part in the Russia-Ukraine war. "Lehion Svobody" consists of more than 1,000 Svoboda members.[38]

Conclusion

When Ukraine was first confronted in 2014 with the Russian Federation's aggression, tens of thousands of Ukrainian citizens rose to defend the country in the initial stage of the conflict in spring to autumn of 2014. Many were immediately integrated into the existing governmental structures, such as the Armed Forces of Ukraine, the Ministry of Internal Affairs and the National Guard, but their mobilization was imperfect and rather protracted. Thousands of volunteers began to organize into volunteer formations and arm themselves with the state's help, with the aid of political and commercial sponsors and on their own. The ability of a considerable part of the active Ukrainian citizens, men and women, to self-organize allowed the state to gain some time to mobilize human and material resources as well as to receive aid from overseas partners and thus to minimize the territorial losses which would likely have resulted from the aggression of the Russian Federation. When the Ukrainian security agencies got considerably stronger, all volunteer formations were either integrated or practically brought under state control. At the same time, many veterans volunteers and political parties of the patriotic and nationalist wing — did not fully trust the state. Therefore, a considerable volunteer mobilization potential remained under the aegis of political parties. These volunteers were ready to respond quickly to a future military aggression as paramilitary and veteran patriotic associations.

---

38 Lehion Svobody Fighting for Ukraine, Press-office of the All-Ukrainian Union Svoboda, October 17, 2016, http://svoboda.org.ua/media/videos/00111052/.

The volunteers' authority and experience was at times used by fringe politicians and dishonest businessmen who pursued their own political or commercial interests. But such semi-criminal activity has not spread on a large scale and has been gradually restrained by the state. On the whole, the creation and functioning of volunteer battalions has demonstrated the readiness of the Ukrainian citizens to fight for their nation-state. The mobilization of volunteers demonstrated that the Ukrainian leadership needs to maintain the efficiency of the state security sector, to limit the scope of activity of non-integrated paramilitary formations and to maintain proper interaction with patriotic organizations.

References

Butusov, Yuri (2017), March 14, 2014 – the Kharkiv Volunteers Repelled the Attack of the Russian Terrorist Arsen Pavlov in Rymarskaya Street, Censor.net, March 14, http://censor.net.ua/resonance/431983/14_marta_2014_goda_dobrovoltsy_harkova_otrazili_ataku_rossiyiskogo_terrorista_arsena_pavlova_na_ulitse.

Komarovski, Alexandr (2016), Opinion: Evolution of the Volunteer Movement in Ukraine, Glavnoye, October 24, https://glavnoe.ua/news/n287478.

Shramovitch, Viacheslav (2015), Dmytro Yarosh: We still Have to Get Crimea Back (in Ukrainian), BBC Ukraine, February 11, http://www.bbc.com/ukrainian/politics/2015/02/150211_yarosh_interview_vs.

Shuklinov, Piotr (2014), Yarosh: Under no circumstances, shall we overthrow the state, LigaNovosti, October 24, http://news.liga.net/interview/politics/3791246-dmitriy_yarosh_lyudey_kremlya_iz_rady_vynesem_vpered_nogami.htm.

Siniak, Dmitri (2015), Soldiers of the Invisible Front. How many Pocket Armies are there in Ukraine?, Focus, April 21, https://focus.ua/country/327967.

Svidrov, Aleksei (2014), National Guard reservists rise to defend the territorial integrity of Ukraine. Ministry of Internal Affairs. Novoctimira.ua, April 13, http://www.novostimira.com.ua/novyny_102938.html.

Zhirokhov. Mikhail (2016), They were the first: Battalion named after Kulchitsky, September 04, http://cheline.com.ua/news/mens-club/voni-buli-pershimi-bataljon-imeni-kulichitskogo-25242.

The Long Shadow of the War
Return and Reintegration of War Veterans

Julia Friedrich, Theresa Lütkefend

The Stakes of Veteran Reintegration

The violent conflict in eastern Ukraine (2014-2022) has caused massive human suffering and altered the fabric of Ukrainian society. Along with 1.5 million internally displaced persons (IDPs)[1] and a death toll of approximately 13,000 people (OHCR 2020), the nearly 400,000 Ukrainian veterans[2] who did return from the frontline by the end of 2020 were among the most visible representations of the war's consequences. War veterans are often traumatized, suffer from post-traumatic stress disorder, are prone to aggressive or depressive episodes, may demand privileged treatment due to their prior exposure to violence and often vocally advance political claims based on their "moral capital" as war participants. As history demonstrates, war veterans are often recruited by extremist or paramilitary groups that do not acknowledge the state monopoly of violence. Risking to marginalize ex-combatants could increase the appeal of radical groups. Veterans frequently compete with other vulnerable groups over access to scarce resources. The following chapter addresses the adjustment and coping practices of Ukraine's government and society towards war veterans. It is based on a total of 36 interviews with key stakeholders and three focus group interviews with veterans. Key stakeholders included returned veterans who fought on the Ukrainian side in Donbas, ministry officials, international organizations active in Ukraine, veteran unions, and civil society actors.[3] The responsibility for successful

---

1 Internally Displaced Persons (IDPs), UNHCR Ukraine, https://www.unhcr.org/ua/en/internally-displaced-persons.
2 Interview with senior Ministry of Veteran Affairs official, September 15, 2020, Berlin/Kyiv.
3 Between August and October 2020, we conducted in-depth interviews with 17 women and 19 men from 10 different cities in western, southern and eastern

reintegration does not lie solely with the government—it is both a societal and individual process. In the following chapter, we will examine the difficulties in organizing support for veterans, identify bureaucratic, political and social obstacles, and we propose ways to mitigate these obstacles.

Ukrainian veterans are a heterogeneous group. Many were civilians before taking up arms, while others were trained military professionals. They come from an array of socio-economic backgrounds, and they range in age from their early twenties to early retirement. Veterans also had a variety of motivations for joining the fight in Donbas. Some were political activists during the Maidan protest movement, some saw it as their patriotic duty to defend their country. For others, the war represented a chance to earn money or was part of their duty as military professionals. Some had worked as guns-for-hire before the war. Still others considered the conflict part of a far-right ideological war. Most Donbas veterans joined the fight for a mix of reasons. Some had joined volunteer battalions, others participated as regular soldiers. Each veteran, therefore, has different preconditions for reintegration. We use the term "veteran" for the approximately 400,000 people who have participated in combat on the Ukrainian side between 2014 and 2022, during either the Anti-terrorist Operation (ATO) or the Joint Forces Operation (JFO). Some of these veterans are still active service members, working for the Ministry of Defense (MoD), the Ministry of Internal Affairs (MoIA) or the National Guard in various capacities. Some have returned to the conflict zone after their initial demobilization and are either continuing their military service or engaging in public and volunteer activities related to the conflict.[4] Others have returned to their previous jobs or taken up a new civilian life. In 2015, following the adoption of the Minsk II Agreement, the frontline had become increasingly static. Combatants faced "long

---

Ukraine, as well as in and around Kyiv. The Razumkov Center conducted focus groups sessions with ex-combatants from western Ukraine (in and around Lviv), eastern Ukraine (in and around Kharkiv), and in and around Kyiv in October 2020. The Ministry of Defense declined various requests for interviews.

4   Results of focus groups interviews, conducted October 3-12, 2020, by the Razumkov Center, Kyiv.

periods of boredom and repetition followed by ferocious attacks," (Sanders 2017, p. 40) which has been mentally draining for many and led to an increase in the number of accidents, imprudent uses of weapons, suicides, and murders (Zajaczkowski 2019). It is important to differentiate whether a veteran served between 2014 and 2015 (when very intense fighting occurred in places such as Ilovaysk and Debaltsevo, and at Donetsk airport) or after 2015 — or after 2022). In 2018, the Ukrainian government converted the ATO into the Joint Forces Operation, a combat operation formally under the command of the Ukrainian Armed Forces General Staff.

Reintegration: Practices and Shortcomings

Combatants returning from the Donbas combat zone have changed the societal image of a veteran. The number of veterans of the violent conflict with Russia continued to grow up to roughly 400,000 veterans before the start of Russia's full-fledged war in February 2022. The total number of veterans in Ukraine was estimated to be even over one million[5] if one includes veterans of the Second World War, the Soviet–Afghan war, and United Nations Peace Operations, to which Ukraine has contributed in the past.[6]

Ex-combatants returning from Donbas have not only changed the societal view of veterans; they have also brought about significant changes in legislation and practice regarding the provision of social services for veterans. This is largely the result of a strong lobbying effort that ultimately led to the creation of the Ukrainian Ministry of Veterans Affairs (MoVA) in 2018. However, despite improvements to veterans' access to information concerning their rights and benefits, reintegration measures remain insufficient. Support for veterans is organized as a system of benefits for which veterans must apply individually. However, these benefits are not

---

5   Legal100, Shcho zrobyla Verkhovna Rada dlia veteraniv ta viiskovykh za pershe pivrichchia 2020 roku" 2020b, https://legal100.org.ua/wp-content/uploads/2020/07/2020_analitichnii--_zvit.pdf.
6   Ukraine's Participation in the UN Peacekeeping Activities," Permanent Mission of Ukraine to the United Nations, 2016, https://ukraineun.org/en/ukraine-and-un/peacekeeping-activities/.

set up to address reintegration needs adequately. Mental and physical health constitute two particularly underserved areas. Veterans, civil society organizations, ministry officials, and international actors have criticized this benefit-centered approach to reintegration as outdated and inefficient and have proposed new reforms. At the same time, these actors are involved in the reintegration process at different levels and do not always cooperate with one another.

Ukraine has been pursuing reforms of its mode of governance since 2014, battling the influence of oligarchs and corruption. While Russian efforts to destabilize the country fueled resistance to these reforms, the persistence of established Ukrainian elites who continued to hamper reform has been an internal problem in its own right. Ongoing reform efforts impact many of the government institutions responsible for veteran reintegration. The socio-economic situation in Ukraine exacerbates veterans' difficulties. A tough economic climate, rendered even more onerous by the COVID-19 pandemic, decreased the chances of finding a job.[7] In addition, generally weak social services and healthcare provision negatively impact veterans' ability to receive these services.[8] The social stigma associated with mental health, particularly directed at men, increases veterans' reluctance to seek help (Bertouille 2019).

State Actors Are Unequally Involved in Reintegration

The MoVA was created to signal that veterans' well-being was a political priority, but this has neither been reflected in its structures nor its budget. Under pressure from a civil society campaign, the Ukrainian government under Prime Minister Volodymyr Hroisman created the MoVA in 2018. It was merged with the Ministry for Reintegration of the Temporarily Occupied Territories in Prime Minister Oleksiy Honcharuk's cabinet in 2019, only to be re-established as an independent ministry under Prime Minister Denys

---

7   UN Study Documents Devastating Impact of COVID-19 in Ukraine," UNDP, September 28, 2020, https://www.undp.org/content/undp/en/home/news-centre/news/2020/UN_study_documents_impact_COVID19_in_Ukraine.html.
8   UNICEF Ukraine, Social Policy Programme, September 17, 2020, https://www.unicef.org/ukraine/en/social-policy-programme.

Shmyhal in 2020; its structures remain in flux. Its funding is limited: Ukraine's budget for 2021 allocated roughly 11.32 million Euros (374 million hryvnia) to the MoVA, slightly less than the 2020 budget did.[9] The ministry has a limited mandate and is therefore substantially smaller and has considerably fewer resources than other ministries involved in veteran affairs.

Creating the MoVA was an attempt to simplify the reintegration process by designating a responsible entity at the state level.[10] Although this led to a certain degree of streamlining concerning the organization of veteran issues, the process remains complex. Since veteran affairs are a cross-cutting issue, a variety of state actors have been involved in designing and implementing reintegration measures. Ten different institutions are involved in various aspects of veteran reintegration, and competencies remain scattered.[11] The MoD and the MoIA each have their "own" set of Donbas veterans. The MoD is responsible for veterans who are military professionals (as opposed to volunteers or recruits who only participated in the ATO/JFO). These professionals usually have better access to benefits and programs.[12] The MoIA is responsible for members of the National Police and the Ukrainian National Guard who participated in combat operations, including former volunteer battalions.[13]

The lack of harmonized standards makes reintegration inconsistent and subject to regional differences. In many ways, local authorities are the 'first responders' when it comes to veteran reintegration. Usually, when a soldier demobilizes, the responsible unit—either in the MoD or the MoIA—gives them their documents, and the veteran goes home. It is then up to local authorities to follow up. Local branches of the Ministry of Social Policy (MSP) are in charge of handing out veteran benefits and thus play a particularly

---

9   Legal100, Derzhavnyyi biudzhet na 2021 rik dlia veteraniv, https://legal100.or g.ua/wpcontent/uploads/2020/09/info_derzhbyudzhet_2021.png
10 Interview with civil society representative, August 20, 2020, Berlin/Kyiv.
11 Interview with MoVA official, September 9, 2020, Berlin/Kyiv.
12 Interview with international organization, September 21, 2020, Berlin/Kyiv.
13 Interview with MoIA official, October 16, 2020, Berlin/Kyiv.

crucial role as they are also tasked with communicating with veterans about their right to benefits. Whether and to what extent this obligation is fulfilled depends on the individual local offices. After this initial consultation, there is no follow-up mechanism.[14] The decentralization reform that strengthens local authorities also influences this process because actors such as the MoVA are less aware of how their policies are implemented and whether these actions are adequate in the different regional contexts. The MoVA has been establishing branches in various regions to serve as intermediaries between veterans and the MSP. However, it is often civil society organizations and veteran associations that engage most with veterans and serve as advocates for their rights.

Finally, the Verkhovna Rada, Ukraine's parliament, is an important actor in veteran affairs in its capacities as legislator and watchdog. It has repeatedly changed and amended the 1993 Law on Veterans. Some members of parliament (MPs) are themselves veterans and have advocated for veteran rights jointly with other MPs—for instance, by creating a Special Commission on the Status of Veterans.[15] The former parliamentary committee on veterans was merged with the committee on social policy to form the Social Policy and Veteran Affairs Committee at the beginning of the new legislative period in 2019. Various MPs criticized this decision as deprioritizing veteran affairs, similarly to the temporary merger of the MoVA and the Ministry for Reintegration of the Temporarily Occupied Territories.[16]

Civil Society and Community-Based Actors Fill the Gaps

In addition to the structures and institutions provided by the state, a myriad of civil society organizations (CSOs) advocate for veterans, including ATO/JFO unions. Different types of CSOs are unevenly spread throughout Ukraine, with clusters in Kyiv and regional centers. Given the low barriers for NGO registration, many

---

14 Interview with civil society representative, August 25, 2020, Berlin/Kyiv.
15 Interview with member of parliament, October 12, 2020, Berlin/Kyiv.
16 Interview with member of parliament, October 12, 2020, Berlin/Kyiv.

civil society and veteran organizations exist on paper but are inactive. Particularly in the case of veteran unions, outsiders cannot always discern which associations are trustworthy. Political orientation, especially far-right sentiments, further complicates this situation. Some international donors are at times reluctant to provide financial support to veteran associations or projects related to veterans in general. Still, some associations have successfully organized funds from international donors, such as an ATO veteran union in southeast Ukraine that received funds from the European Bank for Reconstruction and Development to create a community space for veterans and IDPs. Some CSOs and veteran associations apply for state grants for concrete projects, while others operate on a purely volunteer basis. There are rare cases of shell organizations designed to launder money.[17]

Veteran associations can be very important providers of peer-to-peer support for ex-combatants and often assist veterans in accessing their rights and benefits. In contrast to other CSOs, these organizations consist only of veterans. However, not all veterans want to join veteran associations, and in some rural areas, such associations do not exist.[18] There are some promising initiatives involved in creating a single ATO veteran union to cover several villages in certain areas. ATO unions often serve as mediators and lobbyists for veterans dealing with local authorities and act as their primary information source. However, political interest groups sometimes exploit veteran associations. Some of these associations are driven or influenced by far-right actors. Traditional gender roles can place practical constraints on women's opportunities to join ATO unions. Thus, women often have greater difficulty accessing these unions since they are expected to take care of their households, and there may be limited childcare options on union premises.[19]

---

17 Interview with civilian volunteer for ATO veterans, October 5, 2020, Berlin/Kyiv.
18 Interview with veteran, male, Tornado battalion, September 11, 2020, Berlin/Kostiantynivka.
19 Interview with international organization, September 18, 2020, Berlin/Kramatorsk.

Some veteran associations have successfully influenced state policy concerning veterans. Twenty-two veteran association representatives — one from each region — consult with the MoVA through a "Veteran Council." This council was initiated in 2019 by then-minister Oksana Koliada to engage veteran representatives and heads of veteran associations from all parts of the country.[20] Two other councils consult with the MoVA: a council of mothers and families of the deceased, and a "Public Council" with members elected by the public. While in theory, any Ukrainian can vote for the members of this council, in practice, members are elected by interested parties. These councils do not formally cooperate with one another, and their influence varies. The MoVA has been criticized for allowing known members of far-right organizations to join the Public Council.[21]

In contrast to veteran associations, regular CSOs are usually made up of combat veterans and civilian volunteers. Many of these civilians actively supported the war effort, and some have been pushing for veteran rights since the first waves of demobilization in 2015. These organizations often serve as a gateway for international actors. Foreign stakeholders are more open to financing CSOs than veteran unions because there is less uncertainty about their political leanings. However, funding is not always easy to come by, and grant cycles are often short. Given the multitude of CSOs, work is often duplicated. Since benefit and support structures are quite fragmented, the most successful models seem to be so-called "veteran spaces," such as the "Veteran Hub" in Kyiv, where veterans can come for consultations and activities.

Benefit Packages

In Ukraine, the most encompassing reintegration measures are a range of Soviet-era benefits to which officially registered veterans

---

20 Interview with former senior MoVA official, October 13, 2020, Berlin/Kyiv.
21 Ukraine's Ministry of Veterans Affairs Embraced the Far Right — With Consequences to the U.S., Bellingcat, November 11, 2019, https://www.bellingcat.com/news/uk-and-europe/2019/11/11/ukraines-ministry-of-veterans-affairs-embraced-the-far-right-with-consequences-to-the-u-s/

are entitled. The 1993 law "On the Status of War Veterans: Guarantees of Their Social Protection" designates close to 50 benefits, including a monthly pension as well as an annual payment, free transportation, several medical benefits, free access to state sanatoria, housing benefits, additional annual leave, and free tuition for veterans and their children, as well as other targeted educational support.[22] This law is under constant scrutiny and has been amended numerous times since 2015 when the number of veterans in Ukraine increased sharply.

To be eligible for these benefits and services, veterans must receive a "participant in combat activity" status (*uchasnyk boyovykh diy* = UBD). For some veterans, the administrative hurdles to receive this status can be high. As a consequence, the number of veteran statuses awarded does not necessarily match the number of people who fought in Donbas, and there is no national registry of all ATO/JFO veterans in Ukraine to date. Veterans receive UBD status from the authority they reported to during their active service, i.e., the MoD or the MoIA. However, veterans who were volunteers did not register with either authority and consequently did not automatically receive their paperwork after demobilization, unless they joined a formal structure (Armed Forces, the National Guard, or a branch of the police) after the battalions were integrated into state security services. In 2019, the Verkhovna Rada passed a bill to address this, attempting to ease the registration process for former battalion members. While veterans welcomed this measure, some still do not have UBD status.

One source of discontent for many veterans is that while some struggle to receive UBD status, others simply buy or request it even though they did not participate in combat (e.g., if they worked in the MoD offices in the Donetsk or Luhansk regions).[23] There is also a gender dimension to this problem: Because women were not legally allowed to participate in combat activity until 2018 (Hrytsenko 2020), many women have a harder time receiving their

---

22 Verkhovna Rada, Pro Status Veteraniv Viyny, Harantiyi Yikh Socialnoho Zakhystu, https://zakon.rada.gov.ua/laws/show/355112/print1453801044135460#Text.
23 Interview with former senior MoH official, September 3, 2020, Berlin/Kyiv.

UBD status (Martsenyuk 2020). Female veterans who do receive a UBD certificate are often officially listed as having served as seamstresses, cooks or in other supporting roles, when in fact they were snipers or frontline troops. While they can still receive benefits, this misrepresentation impedes their eligibility for the treatment of physical injuries sustained in combat.[24]

Even when veterans receive their UBD status, gaining access to benefits may still be challenging. Often, their peers are their primary source of information—which means that isolated individuals in rural areas find it more difficult to learn about their benefits and how to access them. Some benefits, such as the monthly stipend and free transport, are rather easy to receive, whereas others can be more challenging. For instance, employment remains a crucial area of reintegration. Veterans are often offered unskilled labor positions for which they are overqualified, and some jobs are especially unsuitable for women. Retraining efforts are all the more important. However, training programs are not easily accessible: Even if tuition is free, veterans are rarely given preferential treatment when applying for loans that would allow them to study as opposed to work.[25]

Health Needs

Veterans are confronted with the intricacies of healthcare provisions. Some hospitals specialize in veteran care but fail to sufficiently meet their needs. Many argue that, instead of creating specialized facilities, it would be more sensible to strengthen the entire system and provide a special "veteran package" for them to access at local facilities. While this might be a more sustainable solution, it would be protracted and costly to implement. However, the overwhelming majority of veterans have to deal with some physical handicaps as a result of their service. Women often face very specific health issues, e.g., back pain and reproductive problems. Veterans with disabilities are classified into three different groups (I,

---

24 Interview with veteran, female, representative of the Women Veteran Movement, September 4, 2020, Berlin/Kyiv.
25 Interview with member of parliament, October 12, 2020, Berlin/Kyiv.

II, or III), which translate into different monetary benefits. This classification system is widely criticized as unfair and prone to corruption. Additionally, some veterans report having to appear before a medical commission to provide proof of their disability once a year, which is draining and makes little sense for veterans with permanent disabilities, such as amputations.

With regard to psychological trauma, there is no uniform policy on psycho-social support.[26] Mental healthcare provision is currently organized via stays in state-run sanatoria, typically for two weeks. However, these efforts do not provide the necessary support. State practitioners are badly paid and not trained to treat war-related mental health conditions. While some volunteers provide such services, they do not operate in all regions and are often insufficiently qualified, as it is fairly easy to get certified online. Recent efforts to improve mental health services for veterans have focused primarily on post-traumatic stress disorder (PTSD). The social stigma surrounding mental health often leads to situations in which veterans recommend that others seek psychological aid but do not do so themselves (Bertouille 2019). Gender dynamics add to this: Women are expected to express and address their feelings about the war, whereas men feel they have to stay strong and refrain from showing any emotion. If psychological ills remain untreated, veterans may resort to alcoholism or aggression. Veterans' families are most affected but insufficiently supported. There are no programs in place to combat domestic violence.[27] The fact that domestic violence is generally prevalent but happens behind closed doors in Ukrainian society exacerbates this problem (Busol 2020). Peer-to-peer support seems to help break this stigma: Veterans are more inclined to seek psycho-social support from other veterans who are psychologists, and peers who seek psychological support have a positive influence on other veterans. Social stigma affects the reintegration of minorities, such as LGBT+ veterans who face severe discrimination both within and outside the veteran community.

---

26 Interview with MoVA official, September 9, 2020, Berlin/Kyiv.
27 Interview with local MoVA official, September 14, 2020, Berlin/Mykolaiv.

Some veterans actively support the LGBT+ community, while others openly attack gay veterans both verbally and physically, questioning their participation in heavy combat. Homophobia often goes unpunished in Ukraine (Vikhrov 2020). Other politically underrepresented groups, such as women, have also actively campaigned for their rights. A successful example of breaking social stigma against female soldiers and veterans is the "Invisible Battalion" information and advocacy campaign led by Maria Berlinska and her colleagues in the Ukrainian Women Veteran Movement. Having faced severe institutional and societal obstacles, they succeeded in making previously inaccessible military combat positions open to women and are now a strong voice in the veteran community.[28] Women still face higher hurdles to reintegration,[29] from more severe prejudice on the part of the general public to significant obstacles in receiving benefits and services (Martsenyuk 2019).

Benefits Do Not Encourage Reintegration

Veterans and reintegration agents hold that the benefit-centered system must be reformed and changed into a service-oriented system. "Give us the fishing rod, not the fish" has become a sort of slogan among veterans, civil society representatives, veteran associations, and the MoVA. One MoVA official made it clear that the state does not have the capacity to provide benefits to every veteran for the rest of their life.[30] Civil society actors argue that the law on veterans does not create opportunities for reintegration.[31] For instance, the provision that veterans should be "first in line" to receive land does not provide any sustainable tools for reintegration. Yet, in practice, they still encounter difficulties obtaining land. And among those veterans who obtained a plot, many end up giving it up to the highest bidder for cash. Interested businessmen can obtain

---

28 Interview with civil society representative, August 21, 2020, Berlin/Kyiv.
29 Interview with international organization, September 28, 2020, Berlin/Washington, DC/Kyiv.
30 Interview with MoVA official, September 9, 2020, Berlin/Kyiv.
31 Interview with civil society representative, August 20, 2020, Berlin/Kyiv.

adjacent plots of land from different veterans for little money, thus assembling a larger, more valuable plot of land.

Many civil society actors advocate for a more individualized veteran support system. For instance, young veterans have a greater need for educational and training opportunities or parenting classes than their older peers, who may require treatment for physical conditions. In addition, while some veterans may want to jump right back into civilian life, others may prefer to take some time to recuperate. An e-registry for veterans will inform veterans about their rights and benefits and also provide data to the MoVA.

Obstacles to Reintegration

We identified three major obstacles—administrative, political and social—to veteran reintegration. One obstacle to reintegration is the lack of a coherent policy on veteran reintegration at the ministerial level. State actors generally support veteran reintegration, however, ongoing institutional reforms and ministries' general tendency to work in silos impede reintegration. There is also a lack of institutional capacity: The MoVA does not have the political buy-in, funding or staff required. Consequently, it also lacks authority vis-à-vis the local and regional administrations that provide veteran benefits. Finally, all ministerial actors are well aware that veteran affairs are a politically sensitive issue that will not easily generate political gain.

The MoVA's mandate and capacities do not match: Despite its mission to coordinate veteran policy, a lack of political support means its funding and institutional capacity are insufficient (van Metre / Boerstler 2020). The ministry remains underfunded, which in turn leads to a dearth of personnel. As a result, the MoVA lacks expertise and is unable to hire the experts and practitioners required to generate it.[32] The MoVA does not have the necessary administrative reach in the various regions to ensure the implementation of a coherent veteran policy. While the ministry can try to influence local authorities, it does not have any formal authority over

---

32 Interview with MoVA official, September 9, 2020, Berlin/Kyiv.

them.³³ The MoVA opened offices in different regions to serve as mediators between veterans and local authorities.³⁴

The implementation of veteran policy by local and regional administrations does not necessarily correspond to the decisions made in Kyiv—but this is not always clear to veterans.

There is no empirical evidence suggesting that local administrations systematically underserve veterans for political reasons. Even if individual Ministry of Social Policy (MSP) caseworkers may be prejudiced against veterans, the prevalent opinion is that these personal views do not result in deliberate disservice to veterans. Rather, the considerable regional and local variance in service provision is due to a lack of administrative capacity. However, cooperation between different administrative bodies can be complicated by political differences. As one MoVA official put it when referring to the government-controlled areas of Donetsk and Luhansk, cooperation becomes difficult when local administrations think "veterans want to kill every person who speaks Russian."³⁵

Given that the MoVA was created as the result of a civil society campaign, it traditionally enjoys good relations with civil society actors, although their respective roles remain ill-defined. On the one hand, ties between veteran associations or other civil society actors and the MoVA are strong—for instance, through the various advisory councils. Ministries are well aware that civil society cooperation is a necessity since successfully implementing any policy requires buy-in from the veteran community. On the other hand, there are many instances in which the MoVA could put civil society expertise to better use. Both within and outside the ministry, the prevailing opinion is that the MoVA's role should be to formulate,

---

33 Interview with senior MoVA official, September 15, 2020, Berlin/Kyiv.
34 Metodychnyi Posibnyk. Rekomendatsii dlia pratsivnykiv terytorialnykh orhaniv Ministerstva u Spravakh Veteraniv Ukrainy, Legal100, https://legal100.org.ua/wp-content/uploads/2020/09/rekomendatsii-dlya-terorganiv-minveteraniv.pdf.
35 Interview with MoVA official, September 9, 2020, Berlin/Kyiv.

finance and coordinate policies while civil society actors with the necessary expertise and contacts should implement them.[36]

Inter-Ministerial Relations Impede Reintegration

By creating the MoVA in 2018, the Ukrainian government made one ministry responsible for veteran affairs. While this clear designation of competencies and responsibilities is important, it gives all the other actors previously involved in reintegration an excuse to evade their role in the process. For the MoD, for instance, the ongoing war takes priority over veteran reintegration, which it considers the MoVA's concern. The MoVA does not have the standing to demand or incentivize cooperation from other ministries. Instead, it finds itself sandwiched between two very large, powerful players: the MoD and the MoIA, which each have their "own" ATO/JFO veterans under their care. The distribution of responsibilities shared between the MoVA and other ministries is quite arbitrary. To give an example: While the MoVA is supposed to formulate policy, the MSP provides all veteran benefits. Generally, inter-ministerial cooperation is not sufficiently institutionalized.[73] Knowing people is crucial, cooperation thus often depends on personal connections.

Administrative hurdles to inter-ministerial cooperation are exacerbated by the fact that the Ukrainian security sector lacks parliamentary oversight (Akimenko 2018). Even though the Verkhovna Rada Committee on National Security and the Committee on Law Enforcement have formal responsibility for overseeing the armed forces and the police respectively, both the MoD and the MoIA are large, opaque structures. Therefore, introducing parliamentary controls and hiring more civilians to work at the MoD would be crucial to increasing accountability.[76] This could in turn help to strengthen inter-ministerial cooperation and to increase awareness of reintegration measures.

---

36   Interview with civil society representative, August 25, 2020, Berlin/Kyiv; interview with MoVA official, September 9, 2020, Berlin/Kyiv; interview with former senior MoH official, September 3, 2020, Berlin/Kyiv.

More Data Needed for Coherent Policies

A significant lack of data greatly hinders the formulation of a coherent government policy on veteran reintegration. No one knows the exact number of veterans or how they are distributed across Ukraine, and there is no comprehensive data on the rate of employment, suicide or domestic abuse. Ministerial officials' misguided sense of the need to protect veterans (or their own ministry) feeds into this phenomenon. For instance, the MoIA does not include "veterans" as a separate category when registering suicides, as they fear that this could be perceived as discriminatory. The MoD maintains a registry of military personnel who presumably committed suicide during their service, but not all suicides are registered because the families of the deceased would no longer be eligible for benefits. In this way, the lack of data may be the result of good intentions, but it ultimately hampers the understanding of the extent to which veterans commit suicide and reinforces the trauma that families experience. It also makes designing policies to counter veteran suicides more difficult.

The ministries have an even stronger disincentive to record and report politically sensitive issues because they fear feeding into negative stereotypes about veterans. For example, the number of veterans who join far-right extremist movements remains unknown. Similarly, there is a genuine lack of knowledge regarding whether and to what extent veterans are recruited to join illegal private security groups. This indicates a reluctance to discuss issues that Russian disinformation campaigns have heavily exploited in the past. While it is understandable that officials do not want to create any bad publicity for veterans, these efforts may be counterproductive. If the extent to which veterans are radicalized or become involved in criminal activities remains unknown, this gives credence to the stereotype that a majority of veterans are far-right radicals or take part in such activities.

Political Polarization

The lack of comprehensive reintegration policies and the limited employment opportunities for veterans combine with a highly polarized environment in which weapons are readily available. Many veterans are civically engaged and care deeply about the future of their country. Some veterans have joined radical right-wing groups that pose a threat to reintegration: Their narratives aim to polarize and divide Ukrainians, alienating them from civilians and non-radical veterans. Far-right groups are also prone to use violent tactics. Since these groups have the loudest voices, the public tends to perceive them as representative of all veterans. In effect, this drowns out the voices and opinions of the majority of veterans.[37] Political actors can fuel radicalization by manipulating veterans or using them for publicity, thus increasing veterans' mistrust of politics and politicians. Political, social and economic marginalization increases the appeal of far-right groups. Some veterans are hired by private businessmen for their security services. Veterans as political stakeholders

For many veterans, particularly volunteer fighters, their political engagement during the Maidan protests and their combat experiences in Donbas represent a continuous struggle against Soviet-style bad governance and Russian domination. Upon their return, weak governance is the next battle in the same struggle, and thus some veterans associate bad governance with pro-Russian attitudes. This mindset creates societal and political fault lines between those who support an "independent Ukraine" and those who do not. As a consequence, veterans consider issues such as unsuccessful health reform, economic decline and corruption to be part of the same larger struggle as the ongoing conflict in Donbas. Many veterans believe that they must stand up against injustice and violations of law and order. While some experience despair and apathy as a result of this constant struggle and wonder why they fought in the first place, others turn these feelings into action. This action can

---

37 Interview with civil society representative, August 25, 2020, Berlin/Kyiv.

take the form of social or political activism, such as working to secure female or LGBT+ veterans' rights.[38] However, for veterans who either have strong ideological convictions or few other options, this feeling of a constant futile struggle can lead to radicalization.

The line between criticism and radical action is not always clear-cut. Veteran's criticism of President Zelensky's attempts to end the conflict in Donbas is a good example of this blurred line between democratic political engagement and far-right movements. In October 2019, thousands of veterans and others attended a "march against capitulation" in Kyiv organized by the far-right Azov movement and veteran associations, among other sponsors (Roth 2020). The fact that nationalists have captured this debate discredits the necessary discussion about Zelensky's policies and the trade-offs that Ukrainian society is willing to make to achieve peace in Donbas.

The line is equally blurred when it comes to veterans' readiness to return to the frontline. Many veterans are prepared to return to combat, independent of their other ideological convictions. They often feel personally responsible for the outcome of the war with Russia. Moreover, they do not want to pass on the task of resolving the war to their children. Each individual veteran may thus have a different incentive to return to the frontline in Donbas, but radical actors can use this personal choice as part of a larger power struggle.

Far-Right Organizations Spoil Social Peace

The danger posed by far-right veteran movements and the extent to which nationalist ideology has infiltrated Ukrainian policymaking should not be downplayed, but it should also not be the sole focus of international attention on veterans. Nationalist movements and the threat they pose to Ukrainian democracy have received a disproportionate amount of coverage in the international media. At

---

38 Interview with veteran, male, Donbas battalion, August 20, 2020, Berlin/Kyiv

the same time, these movements impede veterans' social and political reintegration by rendering more moderate veterans virtually invisible, thus further alienating them from the rest of society.

Veterans hold a broad spectrum of views on nationalism, and only a minority of ex-combatants hold radical views or join nationalist movements. On one end of the spectrum, nationalism is considered patriotism. Many joined the armed forces or volunteer battalions based on similar convictions. On the other end of the spectrum, several well-known far-right movements, including Azov with associated organizations such as Centuria or National Militia, and the Right Sector advocate a nationalist ideology. The number of members of the Azov movement in its various forms before the start of the war on February 24, 2022 is uncertain but was claimed to be around 10,000 (Colborne 2019). The distinction between different structures associated with Azov, the former battalion and the movement is not always clear-cut. There is no reliable data on the number of people who support these nationalist movements but given that they emerged from former battalions (or vice versa), one may assume that veterans are prominently associated with them (Shekhovtsov 2019).

The degree of societal influence generated by the nationalist activity of extreme-right groups varies greatly. The Azov movement and the corresponding National Corps party (*Nazional'ny Korpus*) are the most well-known of these actors and have succeeded in creating an international brand. While the Azov battalion was formally reintegrated into the Ukrainian National Guard in 2015, the movement exercises different functions today and may serve as an "organ of state security, a political party, a societal organization, and a protection provider for businesses" (Heinemann-Grüder 2019). Its activities in a large community space outside Kyiv include children training at a shooting range.[39] *Freikorps* is an example of a much smaller movement with less than 20 core members, including veterans, seeking combat experience. While substantially less influ-

---

39 Interview with a male veteran, Azov battalion, September 5, 2020, Berlin/Kyiv.

ential, its members are known for their attacks against LGBT+ persons and have started an initiative to lobby for the legalization of weapons for private use ("self-defense").[40]

At the ballot box, far-right groups in Ukraine have very little political influence, but they have succeeded in infiltrating the mainstream discourse to a disproportionate degree (Likhachev 2020). Radical right-wing actors, although small in number, are the most influential political actors in organizing veterans. Veterans do not always need to actively join such groups—in fact, they rarely become formal members. Rather, these groups infiltrate veteran unions and offer funding or (more or less legal) side jobs. This can be attractive to those struggling in the formal job market. These groups can also offer something many others cannot: a narrative and an ideological underpinning for why fighting in the war made sense.

Other political actors have an interest in veterans as well: In the past, political parties of all stripes have approached veterans for the sake of publicity. As focus-group interviewees expressed, political parties sometimes use veterans to manipulate or put pressure on their opponents. This can further a sense of political marginalization among veterans and undermine their trust in the government. While many veterans work for legal private security companies, for instance, as security guards, a minority of veterans who lack other options constitute an attractive pool of potential recruits for powerful individuals who have underlying economic interests in pursuing criminal activities (Nagai 2019). Very little is known about oligarch-sponsored private security groups and the types of services they provide.-The role ideology plays in this should not be overstated. Some of these paramilitary or criminal groups existed before the Maidan protests, and some members who are now veterans were already part of these groups before they fought in the war. These organizations operate on a local level and usually protect the infrastructure of a single business person or are contracted to "solve" business disputes. It would be unfair to consider those

---

40   Truth Hounds, "Fraikor': Borotba Za Chystotu Ukrainskoi Rodyny, Hel-Laky i 'Yakis-Tam Protystoiannia'2020, https://truth-hounds.org/frajkor-borotba-za-chystotu-ukrayinskoyi-rodyny-gel-laky-i-yakis-tam-protystoyannya/;   interview with veteran, male, Freikorps, October 5, 2020, Berlin/Kharkiv.

who engage in criminal activities—whether against the backdrop of an extremist ideology or for pragmatic reasons—as representative of all veterans. At the same time, it would be unwise to ignore the risk of more veterans joining far-right movements or private business people's illicit security services resulting from the Ukrainian government's insufficient prioritization of reintegration efforts.

Divisions between Veterans and Civilians

Reintegration is not only the joint responsibility of veterans and the state: It is also a task for society as a whole. And it is indeed a challenging one. Ukrainian society has undergone profound changes since 2014. The ongoing violence has changed the social fabric of many communities in which civilians, veterans and internally displaced people (IDPs) now live side by side. Ukrainian society is finding ways for veterans and the larger population to coexist without significant societal friction. These tensions are nonetheless growing, as we found in our focus groups. Veterans often feel misunderstood or disappointed by a perceived disinterest among civilians. Civilians are inexperienced at interacting with returnees who are often mentally or physically strained, be they strangers or close relatives. This clash of different realities manifests itself in various forms of misunderstanding and estrangement; through an increase in stereotypes enforced through skewed media representations; and in subsequent stigmatization of and discrimination against veterans, at least until the beginning of the war in February 2022.

After their formative combat experience, veterans often search for a new place in society. The experience of combat influences how a person positions themselves within its surroundings. Veterans generally agree that participating in the war changed them as people—in terms of their personality, behavior, values, and perception of the world around them. These changes may manifest in heightened engagement in society and politics, but they can also result in intolerance, frustration or a propensity toward radical action. Veterans also differ in the extent to which they consider themselves members of a distinct group within society. For some, this identity is clearly important. Combat experience united many of them—for instance, in a shared understanding of patriotism and mutual trust. At the same time, they do not necessarily believe that the rest of society shares these traits.[41] The war experience created a difference between those who served and those who did not. However, not everyone shares such a strong sense of identification. Some regard their status as a veteran as just one part of their larger identity and do not see a difference between their needs and values and those of other social groups.

The ongoing war has a significant impact on veterans' search for a place in society. Many veterans expressed a readiness to return to fighting, and they felt that the uncertainty about the future impeded their ability to plan ahead. Their constant psychological connection to the violent conflict prevents them from switching from "soldier" to "veteran." The ongoing conflict keeps many veterans in limbo, preventing them from letting go and wholeheartedly building a new life.

The Undefined Role of Veterans

Before Russia's resumption of full-scale violence in 2022, the uncertainty of veterans was linked to the lack of societal debate about the conflict. As the conflict in Donbas was so closely tied to their past sacrifices and plans for the future, veterans believed it necessary to discuss the future of non-government-controlled areas and Ukraine as a whole. Many veterans believed that the majority of Ukrainians did not share their concern for the Russian controlled Donbas. Veterans struggled to recognize that many civilians had moved on with their lives and returned to their everyday problems. It was frustrating for them to see the people they had risked their lives to protect had lost interest in the conflict.

Most veterans, according to our focus group interviews, do not expect to be treated as heroes, but they still believe in the cause. At the same time, civilians — especially those with no close ties to people directly involved in the conflict — wanted to return to a certain level of normality. Veterans who are also internally displaced

---

41   Focus group result.

persons (IDPs) often feel that a discussion on the non-government-controlled areas' future is not taking place.[42] Veterans are part of a larger group of people affected by the war who are all striving to find a place in society. However, many veterans do not like to consider themselves part of the same group as IDPs, as illustrated by the vehement protests against merging the Ministry for Reintegration of the Temporarily Occupied Territories (which is responsible for IDPs) with the MoVA in 2019. This attitude reflects veterans' strong sense of group identity as well as a belief that their standing as defenders of Ukraine must be valued. IDPs have different needs and problems, which require their own political solutions (International Crisis Group 2020). However, like veterans, IDPs' needs are also barely met — perhaps even more so, because they lack the strong lobby that has pushed veteran affairs into the spotlight in Ukrainian politics.

Relations between veterans and their families and close friends are often characterized by a lack of communication and mutual understanding. Some veterans struggle to obtain support from their families, largely because their partners, parents and siblings are overwhelmed, inexperienced and do not know how to best approach a person who has experienced the trauma of war. Consequently, families and friends sometimes avoid the topic entirely — to the detriment of veterans, who would often like to express themselves but do not find or dare to claim the space to do so in their most intimate environments.[43] Others lose their support systems because family members or friends disapprove of their combat activity: Either they are confronted with disapproving remarks (e.g., "we did not send you there"), or lose their friendships entirely. In light of this inexperience in communicating with them, or avoiding unpleasant comments and the pressure to justify their actions, veterans sometimes consciously avoid mentioning their background in conversations with civilian friends and acquaintances.

---

42   Interview with veteran, male, representative of a veteran business in Kyiv, September 18, 2020, Berlin/Kyiv.
43   Interview with mother of a veteran/former PoW, September 5, 2020, Berlin/Dnipro.

Thus, veterans' alienation from society and their resulting orientation toward peer groups proceeds similarly at the individual level as it does in wider society. Many veterans' social environments have changed dramatically since they returned home: While their pre-conflict circles of friends have shrunk, they have formed new friendships among their comrades-in-arms. Many veterans only feel truly understood within this group, where they are sure to receive physical, financial and moral support, and where they feel they can trust those whose reliability and loyalty have been tested in extreme, life-threatening situations. While veteran associations function as an essential support system, they also reinforce the tendency of many veterans' to keep to themselves.

Veterans Face Stereotypes in Society

Stereotypes reinforce the developing gap between veterans and civilians and have become more prevalent in recent years. In 2014 and 2015, a wave of patriotism and close attention to the events in Donbas went hand in hand with a positive attitude toward and "heroization" of ATO fighters. The army remains one of the most trusted institutions among the general population in Ukraine (International Republican Institute 2020). However, veterans agree that societal attitudes toward the conflict, and veterans in particular, had changed for the worse in the years up to Russia's renewal of war in February 2022: The image of the patriot who defends their homeland, raises conscientious children, starts their own business, and works for the benefit of the country has been replaced by a view of veterans as people who have mental health problems, substance abuse problems, issues with aggression, and who will not shy away from using a weapon. It is difficult to counteract this particular stereotype, as these issues are in fact prevalent phenomena among veterans. Another common accusation is that veterans joined the ATO to gain privileges and benefits. The latter criticism is often directed at female veterans, who are confronted with a combination of stereotypes of both veterans and women. For instance, people question whether they really participated in combat, assume they forged or bought their UBD certificate, or believe they only went to the frontline to find a husband. Men who did not participate in combat are particularly likely to discriminate against women who did (Van Metre, Boerstler 2020).

> "I had this awful situation. I was seven months pregnant and traveling home from work on the shuttle bus. I showed my UBD card to the driver, but he laughed and said, 'What body part did you use to earn it?'" Veteran, female, FGD East

The media plays a central role in creating and maintaining these stereotypes of veterans. Russian propaganda has pushed the narrative of the dangerous veteran, particularly with regard to volunteer fighters. Therefore, many veterans associate high consumption of pro-Russian state television with a pronounced anti-veteran bias. Political attitudes toward Russia and Russian attempts to influence narratives and destabilize Ukrainian society vary across different regions. A regional MoVA official who works in southern Ukraine described the difficulty of promoting reintegration in an area where

> "a large share of the population thinks of veterans as criminals and fascists [...] and is waiting for either the return of the Soviet Union or [...] the liberating Russian army."[44]

Ukrainian media also reinforce existing stereotypes. Whereas news reports covered public mourning for "fallen heroes" in the early years of the violent conflict, reports on veterans later on primarily focused on violent behavior. A politicized Ukrainian media landscape in which media outlets are mostly owned by oligarchs drives polarizing views—by reinforcing highly divisive issues (e.g. regarding the Ukrainian language) or amplifying Russian narratives (Albrecht 2019; Hedenskog; Hjelm 2020). As with all stereotypes, views on veterans in Ukraine are often based on anecdotal evidence. Veterans stress that a small number of comrades behave in ways that are unacceptable, and they are not surprised that such people are condemned and disrespected. This grain of truth is par-

---

44 Interview with local MoVA official, September 14, 2020, Berlin/Mykolaiv.

ticularly detrimental when stereotypes fall on fertile ground: Insecurity about how to interact with veterans prevails among civilians, and those who do not have personal ties to a veteran are often unable to get the reality check they need to challenge their biases. At the same time, as long as psycho-social support for veterans remains sporadic, war-induced trauma can lead to violent behavior, and in rare cases, individual veterans may pose a threat to the general public. Many of these generalizing narratives could be more easily refuted if there were reliable statistics on the extent to which veterans actually engage in violent or criminal behavior.

These stereotypes can translate into stigmatization of and discrimination against veterans. For example, bus drivers are reported to deny veterans free public transport even though they are entitled to this benefit, while other veterans experience discrimination online. Many are also discriminated against when they try to return to their old jobs or start a new career. Employers are often reluctant to hire veterans because they fear they may not be suited for the workplace (World Bank 2017). This helps to explain why many veterans prefer to work with other veterans or start their own businesses.

Discrimination in the workplace is particularly damaging as regular work helps veterans to adapt to a new way of life. The impact of stereotypes on international actors' decision-making on projects must not be underestimated, too. Many international stakeholders fear of indirectly funding far-right extremist groups. They may also see veterans as resisting efforts to settle the conflict in Donbas (van Metre / Boerstler 2020). To mitigate negative stereotypes, the MoVA is making an effort to promote a positive image of veterans. This campaign is designed to present veteran success stories to the public, yet it cannot substitute a societal discussion on what role Ukrainians expect veterans to play within their society.

Lessons to be Learned

To combat the divide between civilians and veterans in Ukraine, state, local and international actors should assist with the reintegration of veterans into their families and communities. Ukraine needs a screening process to vet and classify veteran associations and civil society organizations to address international donors' reluctance to fund veteran affairs organizations. Civil society actors and veteran unions need to enable female veterans to join and contribute. These organizations should be safe spaces where female veterans can openly discuss issues such as sexual harassment experienced on the frontline. Training on sexual harassment for male veterans could also help achieve this goal. Almost all reintegration stakeholders advocate that a needs-based system should replace the current benefit-centered one in the long term. The MoVA, the Cabinet of Ministers and the Ministry of Social Policy (MSP) should implement the planned e-registry as soon as possible. An independent oversight body should evaluate or take charge of land allocation to avoid corruption. Given that many veterans would prefer cash loans, parliament and the relevant ministries could consider ending the policy of land allocation altogether. Existing education and training programs should be made more accessible to all veterans. If proper oversight can be guaranteed, a micro-credits program could be an option to improve economic reintegration. Civil society and international actors could organize joint events and training for businesses and veterans to foster mutual understanding. Trade unions and employers' associations can play a crucial role in this regard. Furthermore, overall access to psycho-social support should be improved and expanded to include veterans' family members. Rather than investing in specialized veteran hospitals, it makes sense to give veterans easier access to specialized services (a "veteran package") in the standard healthcare system.

Political engagement with veterans is crucial in order to disincentivize them from joining far-right, neo-fascist movements. These groups should be monitored and their role in the veteran community closely watched. A screening and vetting process can help to distinguish trusted organizations from radicalized groups. A societal debate on the reintegration of the non-government-controlled areas will be crucial to the future of Ukraine, and engaging with veterans on this issue should not be left to those who aim to exploit them for ideological reasons and political or financial gain.

References

Akimenko, Valeriy (2018), Ukraine's Toughest Fight: The Challenge of Military Reform. Carnegie Endowment for International Peace, February 22, https://carnegieendowment.org/2018/02/22/ukraine-s-toughest-fight-challenge-of-military-reform-pub-75609.

Albrecht, Erik (2019), In Ukraine's Vibrant Online Media Landscape, Viability Remains a Challenge. In: Deutsche Welle, July 1, https://www.dw.com/en/in-ukraines-vibrant-online-media-landscapeviability-remains-a-challenge/a-49062846.

Bertouille, Flavie (2019), What's Next for Veterans in Ukraine? Policy Brief, International Alert, March, https://www.international-alert.org/sites/default/files/Ukraine_Whatsnextforveterans_%20EN_2019.pdf.

Busol, Kateryna (2020), Domestic Violence in Ukraine: Lessons from COVID-19, Chatham House, July 23, https://www.chathamhouse.org/2020/07/domestic-violence-ukraine-lessons-covid-19.

Colborne, Michael (2019), There's One Far-Right Movement That Hates the Kremlin, in: Foreign Policy, April 17, https://foreignpolicy.com/2019/04/17/theres-one-far-right-movement-that-hates-the-kremlin-azov-ukraine-biletsky-nouvelle-droite-venner/

Hedenskog, Jakob; Mattias Hjelm (2020), Propaganda by Proxy – Ukrainian Oligarchs, TV and Russia's Influence. The Swedish Defence Research Agency, 2020, https://www.foi.se/rapportsammanfattning?reportNo=FOI%20Memo%207312.

Heinemann-Grüder, Andreas (2019), Geiselnehmer oder Retter des Staates? Irreguläre Bataillone in der Ukraine, *Osteuropa*. Vol. 3–4, pp. 51-80.

Hrytsenko, Hanna (2020), Women in Ukraine's Military: An Opportunity for Change, PeaceLab Blog, April 28, 2020, https://peacelab.blog/2020/04/women-in-ukraines-military-an-opportunity-for-change.

International Crisis Group (2018), Nobody Wants Us': The Alienated Civilians of Eastern Ukraine, Report no. 252, October 1, https://www.crisisgroup.org/europe-central-asia/eastern-europe/ukraine/252-nobody-wants-us-alienated-civilians-eastern-ukraine.

International Organization for Migration (2020), Life after Conflict: Survey on the Sociodemographic and Socioeconomic Characteristics of Veterans of the Conflict in Eastern Ukraine and Their Families, Jan., http://ukraine.iom.int/sites/default/files/veteransreintegration_survey_2020_eng.pdf.

International Republican Institute (2020), Sixth Annual Ukrainian Municipal Survey, 2020, https://www.iri.org/sites/default/files/ukraine_feb_2020_poll.pdf.

Kirillov, Dmitriy (2019), Ekskursiya v 'Azov'. Odin Den' s Ukrainskim Polkom Spetsnazncheniya, Radio Liberty/Radio Free Europe, June 21, 2018, https://www.svoboda.org/a/29308146.html.

Martsenyuk, Tamara (et al.) (2019), Invisible Battalion 2.0: Women Veterans Returning to Peaceful Life, UN Women, November, https://www2.unwomen.org/media/field%20ofice%20eca/attachments/publications/2019/11/invisible%20battalion%2020eng.pdf?la=en&vs=3417.

Nagai, Marina (2019), Situational Analysis Case Study Kherson Region, International Alert, https://www.international-alert.org/sites/default/files/Ukraine_Kherson%20Case%20Study_EN_2019.pdf.

OHCHR (2020), Report on the human rights situation in Ukraine, 16 November 2019 to 15 February 2020, March 12, https://www.ohchr.org/Documents/Countries/UA/29thReportUkraine_EN.pdf.

Roth, Andrew (2019), Thousands March in Kyiv to Oppose East Ukraine Peace Plan, in: The Guardian, October 14, 2019, https://www.theguardian.com/world/2019/oct/14/thousands-march-kyiv-oppose east-ukraine-peace-plan.

Sanders, Deborah (2017), The War we want, the war that we get: Ukraine's Military Reform and the Conflict in the East, in: The Journal of Slavic Military Studies 30, Issue 1, pp. 30–49.

Shekhovzov, Anton (2019): Radikale Parteien, irreguläre Verbände. Ukrainische Milizen aus dem rechtsextremistischen Milieu, *Osteuropa*, Vol. 3–4, pp. 149-162.

Van Metre, Lauren; John Boerstler (2020), The Trip from Donbas: Ukraine's Pressing Need to Defend its Veterans, Atlantic Council, September 21, https://www.atlanticcouncil.org/in-depth-research-reports/issue-brief/ukraines-veterans/.

Vikhrov, Natalie (2020), Ukraine's LGBT+ war veterans boost battle for equality, Equal Eyes, 18 Feb., https://equal-eyes.org/database/2020/2/18/ukraines-lgbt-war-veterans-boost-battle-for-equality.

World Bank Group (2017), Socio-Economic Impacts of Internal Displacement and Veteran Return: Summary Report. May, http://documents1.worldbank.org/curated/en/571011497962214803/pdf/116489-REVISED-Updated-Report-Socioeconomic-Impacts-Internal-Displacement-Veteran-Ret.pdf

Zajaczkowski, Johann (2019), Homogenität und Fragmentierung. Ukrainische Freiwilligenbataillone im Wandel, *Osteuropa*. Vol. 3–4, pp. 81-101.

Between Two Worlds
Internally Displaced Persons

Vyacheslav Likhachev

The armed conflict in eastern Ukraine since 2014 has caused the worst forced migration and displacement in Europe since World War II. The fighting that began in April 2014 has been posing a constant threat to the lives and health of those living in Ukraine's Luhansk and Donetsk regions and to those residents of Crimea who did not succumb to their annexation by Russia. More than 14,000 civilians had died in the armed conflict before Russia launched its full-fledged war against Ukraine on 24 February 2022. On 6 December 2022, the UN High Commissioner for Refugees recorded 7,832,493 refugees from Ukraine across Europe due to Russia's aggression.[1] In late autumn 2022, nearly seven million people were forcibly displaced within the country. The numbers constantly change as a result of Russia's attacks against Ukraine's infrastructure. According to figures provided by the Russian government, 971,417 refugees had gone to Russia by 26 May 2022. In April 2022, Ukrainian officials believed the number of Ukrainian children forced to leave for Russia and involuntarily entering the Russian adoption system totaled around 150,000.[2] According to official Ukrainian sources, on 21 April 2022, more than 915.000 people were forced to leave for Russia under the impact of the war.[3]

The following chapter focuses on the survival and adjustment strategies of persons displaced since 2014. It is based on press articles, analyses and interviews conducted by the author, mostly be-

---

1   https://data.unhcr.org/en/situations/ukraine.
2   Ombudsmen Mariya Lvova-Belova: Ostavshikhsya bez roditelei detei iz LNR i DNR vazhno ostroit v rossiiskie semi, https://info24.ru/news/ombudsmen-mariya-lvova-belova-ostavshihsya-bez-roditelej-detej-iz-lnr-i-dnr-vazhno-ustroit-v-rossijskie-semi.html.
3   https://www.ukrinform.ru/rubric-ato/3470134-denisova-rossmi-soobsili-cto-v-rf-iz-ukrainy-vyvezli-bolse-milliona-ludej.html.

tween 2017 and 2019, as part of his work at the Vostok-SOS Charitable Foundation. The interviewees were IDPs who had left the war zone in the early months of the armed conflict and those who had crossed the so-called contact line dividing the Russian- from the Ukrainian-controlled part of Donbas. Most expert reports and sociological studies have focused on internally displaced persons in Ukraine, mainly on the integration of IDPs into society and the observance of their rights. These reports and studies are addressed primarily to the Ukrainian authorities and international organizations. Even though their target group is practitioners rather than researchers, many are written at a high academic level and contain credible information (Zacharov 2014; Balakireva 2016; Donbas SOS et al. 2017; Platformi 2017). In addition to the UN High Commissioner for Refugees (UNHCR) mission in Ukraine, Ukrainian non-governmental organizations have also documented violations of international humanitarian law in the context of the armed conflict in eastern Ukraine (Denisenko et al. 2017; Gritsenko/Odegov 2018; Vovk et al. 2018; Likhachev 2018).

The majority of casualties of the war in 2014/2015, including civilians, occurred during the most active hostilities, especially during the battles of Ilovaisk (August 2014) and Debaltseve (February 2015).[4] The number of civilian deaths had been decreasing since then but remained still significant, according to the UN High Commissioner for Human Rights (OHCHR).[5] The shelling of civilian objects and settlements in the front-line area, which resulted in the suffering of many civilians, continued even after the relative stabilization of the so-called contact line in the spring of 2015. In addition, mines and other explosive remnants of war have posed a significant risk.

The changing front lines and the seizure of new territories by both sides were accompanied by massive, indiscriminate shelling

---

4 https://www.ausa.org/publications/siege-ilovaisk-manufactured-insurgencies-and-decision-war.

5 Doklad o situatsii s pravami cheloveka v Ukraine 16 avgusta—15 noyabrya 2019 goda. UVKPCh OON, dekabr 2019. https://www.ohchr.org/Documents/Countries/UA/28thReportUkraine_RU.pdf.

of populated areas. More than 50,000 houses were destroyed or severely damaged in the fighting between 2014 and 2020.[6] Both sides systematically violated international humanitarian law. As a result of the shelling, objects that were protected under international humanitarian law — schools, medical institutions and elements of infrastructure necessary for the livelihood of the civilian population — suffered substantially. The inhabitants of the areas where the fighting took place sought to leave it en masse. A significant proportion left via the eastern border to Russia. The border has not been under the control of the Kyiv government since the start of the violent conflict. Determining the number of refugees from the war zone in Donetsk and Luhansk oblasts to Russia is, therefore, not easy. According to the Russian Federal Migration Service, 820,000 Ukrainians entered and did not leave Russia between 1 April and the end of the summer of 2014, but only 130,000 of them applied for asylum or refugee status.[7] It seems that some of the refugees who only stayed temporarily did not go to the state authorities, limiting themselves to the assistance of relatives or seeking temporary unofficial earnings. As of 2015, some 150,000 Ukrainians had applied for temporary asylum in Russia.[8] By 2018, more than 100,000 Ukrainian citizens had been granted temporary asylum in Russia, and another 300,000 had been granted Russian citizenship.[9] According to Human Rights Watch Ukrainian civilians were being for-

---

6   https://www.ohchr.org/Documents/Countries/UA/28thReportUkraine_RU.pdf.
7   More than 800,000 Ukrainian refugees have left for Russia — Russian Migration Service// BBC News Ukraine. 30 August 2014, https://www.bbc.com/ukrainian/rolling_news_russian/2014/08/140830_ru_n_fms_ukraine_refugees.
8   Komitet "Grazhdanskoe sodeistvie". Bezhentsy iz Ukrainy v Rossiiskoi federatsii, 2015, https://www.refworld.org.ru/docid/57a45f854.html.
9   Nam vernuli ukrainskie pasporta. Bezhentsy iz Donbasa zhaluyutsa na otkazy v prodlenii vremennogo ubezhishcha, Kommersant 27 October 2018, https://www.kommersant.ru/doc/3784569.

cibly transferred to Russia since the beginning of the war in February 2022.[10] The U.S. Department of State estimated that at least 900,000 Ukrainian citizens had been forcibly relocated to Russia.[11]

Since 2014, there has been a surge in Ukrainian emigration to other countries, especially of persons and groups who were able to obtain a legal migration status. For example, emigration from Ukraine to Israel and Germany increased significantly. In 2019, the Russian Ministry of Internal Affairs spoke of 77,000 Ukrainian citizens who had been granted refugee status or temporary asylum.[12] However, even official sources differ widely. The State Duma claimed that approximately 350,000 Ukrainians had been granted temporary asylum after 2014.[13] Russian officials also voiced quite unrealistic numbers. For example, Federation Council deputy chairman Yuriy Vorobyov claimed at a roundtable in the upper house of parliament that Russia had received two and a half million Ukrainian refugees.[14] But most of those forced to leave their homes moved into Ukrainian government-controlled territory, becoming internally displaced persons (IDPs).

Various Causes of Displacement

The first wave of displacement in April/May 2014 consisted of relatively few activists from pro-Ukrainian political groups and social movements, primarily participants in the Euro-Maidan protest campaign from Donetsk and Luhansk. Attacks on their peaceful assemblies, which were already accompanied in March 2014 by brutal beatings and killings of protesters, meant that there was a direct threat to their lives and health. In April 2014, following the seizure

---

10 https://www.ohchr.org/en/statements/2022/09/human-rights-concerns-related-forced-displacement-ukraine.
11 https://www.politico.com/news/2022/09/08/ukraine-forced-russia-deport-united-nations-00055394.
12 V MVD podschitali imeyushchikh vremennoe ubezhish, https://www.politico.com/news/2022/09/08/ukraine-forced-russia-deport-united-nations-00055 39che v Rossii ukraintsev, RBC 16 April 2019. https://www.rbc.ru/rbcfreenews/5cb565a19a79477e04c7bb4e.
13 Gosudarstvennaya Duma Federalnogo Sobraniya Rossiiskoi Federatsii, 7 May 2019. http://duma.gov.ru/news/44830/.
14 RIA Novosti 7 March 2017, https://ria.ru/society/20170307/1489451543.html.

of public buildings by pro-Russian groups and Russian saboteurs and the mass distribution of weapons to their supporters, pro-Ukrainian activists became targets of systematic harassment by the Russian irregular armed groups that by then de facto controlled the main population centres of Donetsk and Luhansk regions. Hundreds of people were illegally detained, beaten and tortured, or killed. Thousands travelled deep into Ukrainian territory, to Kharkiv, Dnipropetrovsk (now Dnipro), Kyiv and Lviv, driven by well-founded fears for personal safety. Some of them had personally encountered violence at the hands of representatives of irredentist armed groups and learned first-hand what it meant to "get in the basement", i.e. torture cells. Upon reaching the first checkpoint manned by Ukrainians, they felt they had literally escaped from hell.

Due to the rapidity of events, the unprecedented nature of the situation and a certain power vacuum caused by the transition period after the Euro-Maidan protests, the first IDPs did not receive any official status and assistance from the state, relying mainly on personal ties and informal infrastructural connections. As these were primarily political and civic activists, many could rely on personal support networks. Some had travelled to Kyiv periodically to participate in the Euro-Maidan protest campaign from the early winter of 2013/2014 onwards. Many had joined the Ukrainian volunteer armed units, which were then beginning to form. They were motivated both by patriotism and an interest in returning home. Others started to create a public infrastructure to assist the next, much larger wave of displaced persons, which did not take long to arrive.

The intensification of hostilities and the offensive of the Ukrainian armed forces from June to August 2014 caused a real exodus of the population from the region. First and foremost, people left the combat zone itself. And yet, there were hardly any settlements in Donetsk or Luhansk oblasts during this period where residents would have felt safe. Many towns and villages were shelled, including those perceived as relatively distant from the highly fluctuating front line. In many cases, people left bombed out houses and flats in which it was physically impossible to stay—mortally frightened but happy to be alive. In their own way, they were also returning to life from a hellish nightmare. At that time, not only citizens loyal to the Ukrainian government but also a large part of the hitherto politically indifferent population became increasingly aware that uncontrolled pro-Russian armed groups had seized control of a large territory. Laws had ceased to be in force, state institutions were no longer functioning, and nothing could guarantee the physical safety of the population. In any event, the fugitives were driven from their homes by a well-founded fear for their lives and the lives of their loved ones. Families with children and young people, who were more mobile than the older generation, were the most likely to flee during this period.

People left their homes in a hurry, often unable to pack even the most basic necessities. At the same time, however, most of them were morally encouraged by the hope generated by the progressive advance of the Ukrainian armed forces and volunteers, albeit not as rapid as initially expected. Even those who did not support the start of the anti-terrorist operation (ATO) and did not trust the new government in Kyiv were also hopeful that the fighting would end soon. According to interviews conducted by the author, press accounts and respondents' recollections in the summer of 2014, almost no one expected to be gone for long. Many IDPs with children said they were worried at the time whether they would be able to return to their liberated cities in time for their normal lives before the start of the new school year. As the Ukrainian Army advanced after the fighting ended, some did get the opportunity to return home after the Ukrainian government retook control of their hometowns and villages. But most who had left "for a couple of weeks" (this is how many put their expectations at the time) found themselves cut off from home for years.

As of late autumn 2014, some IDPs started to return to territories controlled by Russian forces. They had left because they had primarily feared for their lives due to the hostilities but had no clear political or ideological preferences. However, decisions to cross the so-called line of contact could result in unexpected outcomes. For example, Volodymyr Fomichev, a young native of Makiyivka (Donetsk region) and participant in the Euro-Maidan, who had moved to Kyiv in 2014, returned to the Russian-controlled part of Donbas on New Year's Day 2016 primarily to visit his parents. He mistakenly thought it was safe. Soon, however, he was arrested by the so-called Ministry of State Security of the Donetsk People's Republic and, after two months of torture, was "sentenced" to a long prison term. Two years later, he returned to Ukrainian government-controlled territory as part of an exchange.

As hostilities decreased, more IDPs began to return to their homes — or what was left of them. The main reason was the primary economic difficulty of settling in a new place. Assistance from relatives and NGOs could not last forever, and IDP benefits from the state were only symbolic in nature. Affordable housing became the main problem. According to a report by the National Monitoring System on the Socio-Economic Characteristics of Internally Displaced Persons, those who had a flat or house in areas not controlled by the Ukrainian government were the first to return. The next most important reason for return was family reunification, i.e. with relatives who could not or did not want to leave.[15] According to another survey, the majority of respondents cited 'high rental prices'" as the reason for their return.[16]

While it is possible to find inexpensive housing in rural areas and small villages, depression and unemployment prevail in such settlements. In early 2020, according to the study "National Monitoring System for Internally Displaced Persons in Ukraine" by the International Organization for Migration, 53 per cent of able-bodied IDPs were unemployed. According to UNHCR, 60 per cent of IDPs 'can barely make ends meet.'[17] In large cities, where jobs were even scarcer, food, public transport and rents, in particular, were

---

15 Pereselentsii povertayutsya na nepidkontrolnu teritoriyu cherez privatnu vlastnist i vidsutdnist neobkhidnosti platiti za orendu, Interfax-Україна, 9 April 2019, https://ua.interfax.com.ua/news/general/579396.html.
16 Peretin linii zitknennya cherez kontrolni punkt v izdu-viizdu. BF „Pravo na zachist", Agenstvo OON s spravakh bizhintsev, Cherven-lipend 2017 roku, http://vpl.com.ua/uk/materials/3752/.
17 V Ukraine 53 % pereselentsev do sikh por ostayutsja bez raboty, Informator 25 February 2020, https://informator.media/archives/324260; Missiya UVKPCH OON v Ukraine, 20 April 2018, https://twitter.com/UnitedNationsRU/status/987421889944530944.

more expensive. Having already spent their savings and earning only low wages in the unskilled labour market, many were simply unable to continue living as internally displaced persons.

In addition to socio-economic hardships, some IDPs were confronted with prejudices and even faced discrimination because of their region of origin. Such situations, although not decisive, also affected the integration of migrants.[18] Another frequently cited reason for return was that older relatives who had remained at home needed care or guardianship. But overall, significantly more people continued to leave territories under Russia's control even after the hostilities had diminished. The armed conflict, then officially called the anti-terrorist operation (ATO), lasted much longer than most Ukrainians had anticipated back in early summer of 2014. Despite a general decline in the intensity of hostilities after the September 2014 Minsk ceasefire agreement and a general reduction in the intensity of fighting as well as the relative stabilization of the contact line, the ceasefire agreement was not respected by either side. The complete withdrawal of heavy weapons from the front line, as envisaged by the Minsk agreements (September 2014 and February 2015), did not take place. Guns continued to be fired, and people continued to die. As the offensive by pro-Russian armed groups and the Russian Army at Donetsk airport and Debaltseve in the winter of 2015 demonstrated, a further escalation of violence could not be ruled out.

The situation stabilized following the signing of the Minsk agreements in February 2015 and less intense fighting by spring 2015. Fighting continued but primarily affected populated areas in the immediate vicinity of the "line of contact". The increasing professionalism of the combatants, the set-up of permanent positions that became the prime object of shelling, and the absence of large-scale offensive operations led to a fall in civilian casualties compared to the first year of the war. Despite spikes in fighting in late 2017 and the spring and summer of 2018, the situation did not fundamentally change until 24 February 2022.

---

18   According to an opinion poll, 13 percent of the IDPs faced discrimination, Donetskie novosti 5 May 2018, https://dnews.dn.ua/news/675238.

The flow of IDPs from Russian-controlled areas, the self-proclaimed "People's Republics" decreased after 2015, but not dried up. In 2017/2018, the author spoke at entry and exit checkpoints with families leaving these areas. The main reasons forcing people to leave their homes and seek survival opportunities were not the hostilities themselves but their consequences, such as their economic situation. The destruction of infrastructure and the breakdown of customary social ties, unemployment and a sharp decline in living standards have forced people to seek a more stable life in the territory controlled by the Ukrainian government. Another reason is the lack of minimal security and safety. Despite efforts by the pro-Russian de facto regimes to reduce the criminal and political "mayhem" of the first year of the war, the redistribution of property continued, and the level of violence, either purely criminal or initiated by irregular armed groups for propaganda reasons, remained high. Finally, even many rank-and-file supporters of the irredentist pro-Russian movement were disappointed with the results. A direct annexation to Russia following the model of the annexation of Crimea the separatists had hoped for did not occur until February 2022.

The severing of infrastructural ties with Ukraine and the unfulfilled expectation of full integration with Russia caused a host of economic and bureaucratic problems for the population. It was difficult to take "independence" seriously with the self-declared "People's Republics" not being recognized by any other country. Caught in a big black hole in the middle of Europe, many people became seriously worried about their children`s future. What prospects would they have in the separatist regions, even if they stayed in their hometown or their own flat? The prospects were bleak without a job and no documents recognized anywhere outside the ephemeral "republics". Where would children go with a secondary education certificate issued by the "Ministry of Education" of the "Donetsk (or Luhansk) People's Republic"? Concern for children's prospects remained a serious factor for relocation even after the relative stabilization beginning in spring 2015.

The continuation of hostilities and the challenging socio-economic situation encouraged mobile youth and families with children to also leave the government-controlled areas adjacent to the contact line. However, even though their circumstances were similar to those of IDPs from Russian-controlled areas (except for people from a few legally defined localities close to the contact line), they did not qualify as IDPs (as did people who moved to Kharkiv or Kyiv from Donetsk or Luhansk before the spring of 2014). This is why, in reality, the number of people displaced from the war zone and Russian-controlled areas was much higher than the formal statistics showed, not to mention the fact that not everyone who had been entitled to an IDP status actually applied for it at the local social protection departments.

From 2015 to 2016, the number of officially registered IDPs had reached 1.7 to 1.8 million people. Since 2017, the number of IDPs had started to decrease. In early 2020, according to the official data of the Ministry of Social Policy of Ukraine, 1,442,000 internally displaced persons were registered in the country.[19] A significant part of the former residents of Russian-controlled areas who were registered as IDPs had not moved anywhere since 2016 due to the Ukrainian government's policy of paying pensions. The formal government statistics do thus not fully correspond to the real state of affairs.

As making payments to Russian-controlled areas was impossible, the Ukrainian government devised a procedure for paying pensions only to resettlers. This is controversial, if not blatantly illegal and has provoked a mass fictitious "resettlement" of the elderly. The closer retired IDPs were to the "contact line", the higher their numbers. Having obtained IDP status in a village near the checkpoint (or where relatives were, but the closer to their actual home, the better), pensioners could regularly cross the "contact line" and return. For example, in the front-line town of Popasna in the Luhansk region, about 4,800 IDPs were officially registered, but only about 4,001 of them lived in the locality, according to Popasna

---

19 https://www.msp.gov.ua/news/18321.html.

city head Yuriy Onishchenko. The former head of the Donetsk regional civil-military administration, Heorhiy Tuka, then Deputy Minister for Temporarily Occupied Territories and Internally Displaced Persons of Ukraine, estimated the number of "real" internally displaced persons at 600,000 to 800,000. Most of those who had left had also left the hell of war. However, they faced social, economic, administrative, bureaucratic and psychological difficulties adapting to their new residence. For many, this "purgatory" proved to be a daunting challenge.

Civil Society Self-Help

Those fleeing the war zone were under no illusion that the Ukrainian state or any international organizations would take over full responsibility for their future lives. Displaced persons relied primarily on support from relatives and friends. The choice of a region for relocation was primarily conditioned by the presence of relatives (Sasse 2017). However, the need for external assistance remained great (Ukrainskii ofis 2017). The state was unable to provide the IDPs with security and the possibility to continue a normal life at those places from where they had been forced to flee from, but it was also ineffective in providing social support and assistance for the displaced. Ukrainian civil society structures, including those established by the IDPs themselves, and international humanitarian organizations did far more to assist IDPs than the government did. In the early months of the war this was perhaps unsurprising. The "provisional government" formed by parliament after President Yanukovich had fled to Russia was made up of people, albeit experienced, who at the time had come into office literally "from the street", i.e. the Maidan square. The political leaders were primarily concerned with legitimising the new government by holding elections as soon as possible. State structures were utterly helpless and confused. The scale of the challenges they faced, meanwhile, was unprecedented.

A significant part of Ukrainian society proved capable of providing support to internally displaced persons. The recollections of the Vostok-SOS Charity Fund's founders describe the situation in the first months of the violent conflict quite well. As internally displaced persons from Crimea and Luhansk, many had been activists in various public initiatives and human rights organizations before the war. During the Maidan protest campaign, they organized public actions in their towns and occasionally travelled to Kyiv. They were forced to leave even before the outbreak of organized violence (in March 2014 from Crimea and April/May 2014 from Luhansk). The informal Vostok-SOS initiative initially focused on supporting IDPs, later, it shifted its efforts to providing humanitarian aid to people living on the front lines and establishing community life in liberated cities. Tens of thousands shared warm clothes, children's clothing and medicines and helped with housing and job searches. Entrepreneurs approached the Foundation with offers of employment, including housing, as a priority for the displaced. All in all, some 230,000 people have received some kind of assistance from the initiative, ranging from one-off legal advice by telephone to targeted fundraising for medical treatment. With the help of the Foundation, some 20,000 people are resettled in houses and flats of Ukrainians who have expressed their willingness to shelter internally displaced people who lost their own homes (Vostok SOS 2016).

Vostok-SOS is not a unique, but a typical example. There have been many similar initiatives. Activists of the "Crimea-SOS" initiative, which provided assistance not only to people from the Russian-occupied peninsula but also to former residents of the country's eastern regions, found accommodation for more than 1,000 IDP families, and 170,000 IDPs received various types of support and assistance.[20] In the summer and autumn of 2014, one of the most important centers for assistance to internally displaced persons in Kyiv was the Frolovska 9/11 Volunteer Centre (established by the Svoi Foundation), which quickly turned into a huge warehouse of clothing, medicines and other humanitarian aid brought in by Kyiv residents. In its first year of operation, 15,000 IDPs con-

---

20   https://krymsos.com/ru/about/krym-sos/.

tacted the centre, and 45,000 received various items of humanitarian aid collected by project volunteers and provided by donors.[21] Similar community centres for internally displaced persons were established in Kharkiv, Dnipro, Lviv and other cities.

In addition to assisting with material needs, Ukrainian NGOs—alone or with the help of international donors—have created an entire system for the social adaptation and psychological rehabilitation of IDPs. The portfolio included supportive therapy for those who have post-traumatic stress disorder or lost loved ones, workshops to increase competitiveness and employability in various professional areas, computer and foreign language courses and a wide range of activities for children—from preparation for the independent external evaluation (IEE) to robotics classes.

These examples illustrate the tremendous synergy between civil society organizations and ordinary Ukrainians willing to help the displaced. Since the summer of 2014, the media have often focused on scandalous stories related to conflicts between IDPs and the local population. Real or fictitious cases of disrespect for Ukrainian state symbols or examples of socially condemned or deviant behavior received particular attention in the media. Often, these reports were highly exaggerated, distorted or simply false. However, such stories easily spread on social media. A favorable context for disseminating negative emotions was established years earlier when the socio-political confrontation recorded a tendency to stigmatize residents of Donbas as carriers of the Soviet anti-Ukrainian and semi-criminal mentality. In the context of the armed conflict, the demand for negative information about the "Donbasians", who allegedly welcomed Russian aggression en masse, was somewhat understandable. Partly due to such information campaigns, IDPs have faced discrimination, particularly in the rental housing market or when seeking employment. At the same time, however, a significant part of Ukrainian society has been able to empathize and show solidarity with those from the conflict region. When the war broke out, there was a certain "competition" between

---

21 Kak pomoch 15-ti tysyachami. Opyt volonterov tsentra "Frolovskya 9/11", UP Zhizn 17 Juli 2015, https://life.pravda.com.ua/volunteers/55a8a6e1b3ca4/.

different areas of urgently needed social activities. Despite the high mobilization of Ukrainian civil society, the scale of the problems was not commensurate with the capacities on the ground. Activists were literally torn between the need to help the army and the front line, to serve in public service, support reforms and defend Ukraine's interests in the international arena, in particular by advocating for the release of Ukrainian political prisoners in Russia ("Kremlin hostages"). Resources were extremely stretched. It was a challenge to find support for charitable initiatives in the early months of the war when major international donors had not yet had realized the magnitude of what was going on while activists almost exclusively had to rely on societal support. However, the volume of local crowdfunding and humanitarian aid raised for the IDPs was staggering.

Over the course of the years since 2014, the situation has changed. Whereas in 2014, IDP assistance initiatives operated primarily as volunteer activists supported by crowdfunding, by 2016, informal initiatives had become charitable foundations and registered NGOs, working primarily on grants from international donors. The influx of funds from abroad has largely alleviated the disastrous humanitarian situation for IDPs and civilians near the front line. However, by 2018/2019, the volume of international aid began to decline. Many organizations had to abandon direct humanitarian assistance. Access to much-needed legal assistance for displaced persons has decreased. Support did not suffice to meet even the basic needs of the hundreds of thousands of internally displaced persons. The lack of conditions for settling in a new place, especially limited material resources, forced many to return to territory outside of Ukrainian government control. When asked 'What would you have done differently based on today's experience' (2014-2015), Alexandra Dvoretskaya, former director of the Vostok-SOS Foundation, told the author that more effort should have been made to put pressure on the authorities. The authorities, in her view, practically ignored the government's obligations to ensure effective implementation of IDP rights. The government should have developed and implemented a system of institutional integration of IDPs. While at the beginning of the armed conflict the lack of state efficiency in protecting and assisting IDPs can be explained, later on observers increasingly characterized the authorities' actions as 'sabotage', 'discrimination' and 'violation of rights'.

The Government

In 2017, the Ministry of Social Policy launched a board game called 'Wanderings of a Displaced Person', which was designed to address a serious issue in a humorous way. Its aim was to provide the player with an overview of the difficulties faced by IDPs in obtaining official status. It was a simple, traditional board game. The initiative provoked mixed reactions,[22] many IDPs found the play a cynical exploitation of their tragedy. 'I wonder why there is still no "genocide" or "bury a relative" game,' a resettler from Donetsk bitterly commented. Some state representatives also expressed dissatisfaction, believing that the game's authors were exaggerating. Meanwhile, the rules of the game echoed the unpalatable reality. When a player hit field number 89 with their token (already quite close to the finish line) they were told that they had to return to the uncontrolled territory to care for a sick relative. 'Because you have been looking after a relative for more than 90 days, your status as an internally displaced person has been revoked,' the rules informed further. 'Start the game all over again.'[23]

The time-consuming bureaucratic procedures were a constant source of stress for many IDPs. At the same time, many lamented that the long queues to obtain a migrant certificate and humiliating checks confirming actual residence at their temporary accommodation did not provide any additional benefits or preferences. Those from Russian-controlled areas need only to go through these procedures to receive the same access to administrative services, medical care and educational facilities as all "normal" residents of Ukraine. On numerous occasions, we heard statements like, "I

---

22 V Ukraini rozgorivsya skandal cherez gru pro pereselentsiv, Apostrof 27 September 2017, https://apostrophe.ua/ua/news/society/accidents/2017-09-27/v-ukraine-razgorelsya-skandal-iz-za-igryi-o-pereselentsah-video/108432.
23 The game might be viewed here: https://gordonua.com/ukr/photo/events/-po-dorozi-sprobujte-ne-zaginuti-minsotspolitiki-vipustilo-nastilnu-gru-pro-bl ukanni-pereselentsiv-fotogalereja-208588.html.

would not have done this certificate at all, but you cannot go anywhere without it, neither to a clinic nor to the tax office."

In November 2017, the government adopted an IDP Integration Strategy, which lasted until 2020 and was fragmented, lacked a strategic vision and ignored the most acute problems, such as pension payments and housing provision.[24] In addition, the Action Plan for the Implementation of the Strategy, adopted only one year later, in November 2018, did not include additional funding for IDP-oriented programs. It was supposed to be implemented within the current budgetary funding of the ministries.

However, it would be unfair to claim that the state did nothing at all for IDPs. First, they received a monthly allowance of 442 hryvnias per person of working age and 1,000 hryvnias per child (€16 and €37, respectively). And while many say that this is not the kind of money for which it makes sense to go through all the red tape, for others, it was a tangible help. Considering that we are talking about more than one million people, this was a serious burden on the budget. Second, the government declared its desire to help the displaced with housing. Housing had become the most severe problem for many IDPs, if not the majority.

In the second half of 2014, facing the onset of winter, finding a roof over the heads of those who had fled from the war zone by settling them in dormitories and non-residential premises was key. While rent was significantly lower than market rates, IDPs often had little choice about where they were settled. State authorities and municipal councils helped around 20,000 to 30,000 people with housing, i.e. about the same number of resettlers as non-governmental organizations. Since it was the local governments that handled the resettlement, there are no complete consolidated national statistics.

However, the authorities did not expect to shelter people from the conflict zone for years, and not just for a few months. Such assistance was primarily important for the most disadvantaged migrants. Over time, they found it most difficult to pay rent (if they

---

24 https://org.zmina.info/content/uploads/sites/2/2020/02/al%CA%B9terna tyvnyy_zvit-_hromads%CA%B9kykh_orhanizatsiy.pdf.

had to pay it) and to pay for utilities. The economic recession and the demands of the International Monetary Fund forced the government to substantially increase tariffs for heating, gas and electricity. As a result, many resettlers in municipal housing began to accumulate debts. Between 2016 and 2019, this led to a series of scandals involving the eviction of hundreds of IDP families from dormitories and modular camps.[25]

At the same time, government programs targeting the economically active and affluent part of IDPs were initiated. For instance, the "Affordable Housing" program envisaged state support for purchasing flats worth up to 50 per cent of their value. In other words, the government was only able to help the few who already had money, who had been lucky enough to sell their properties in the Russian-controlled areas (which of course had fallen significantly in value since the conflict began) or to save a substantial sum before the war. At least dozens of IDPs benefited from this program.[26]

The housing problem has been and remains a major concern for IDPs. The government has openly argued that it cannot be resolved for financial reasons. 'We don't have that much money', said Yuriy Hrimchak, former Deputy Minister for the Temporarily Occupied Territories and Internally Displaced Persons.[27] Finally, government programs for specific target groups of IDPs have been most successful. Security sector personnel – police, security and border guard officers – settled in parts of the Donetsk and Luhansk

---

[25] Bezhentsam s Donbasa dali schitannye dni na vyselenie iz Kyivskogo obchshezhitiya, Ukrinform 4 January 2016, https://www.ukrinform.ru/rubric-socie ty/1940800-bejentsam-s-donbassa-dali-schitannyie-dni-na-vyselenie-iz-kievs kogo-obschejitiya.html; Za dolgi na kommunalke: Pereselentsam, prozhivayuchshim v modulnom gorodke grozit vyselenie, Donetskie novosti 28 March 2019, https://dnews.dn.ua/news/710353; Gorodskie vlasti prosyat pereselentsev pokinut modulnyi gorodok v Kharkove, Sait goroda Kharkova 12 July 2019, https://www.057.ua/news/2451305/gorodskie-vlasti-prosat-pe reselencev-pokinut-modulnyj-gorodok-v-harkove-foto.

[26] Dostupnoe zhilye dlya pereseletsev, SvoiCity, 11 October 2018, https://svoi.ci ty/read/pravila/7969/dostupnoe-zhile-dlya-pereselencev-obyasnyaem-kak-k upit-kvartiru-po-gosprogramme.

[27] Zhilye dlya pereselentsev: Led tronulsya?, Pereselentsy 12 November 2019, http://vpl.in.ua/zhile-dlya-pereselentsev-led-tronulsya/.

oblasts controlled by the government were offered rental assistance or provided with flats.

The possibility for IDPs to enter universities on a preferential basis was part of the resettlement package, too. As part of its efforts to develop small and medium-sized enterprises, the government also offered preferential loan terms for IDPs and veterans of the ATO. Various international programs provide IDP businesses with initial financial support, often on better terms than the Ukrainian state. Such assistance was crucial for the most active and potentially successful part of the displaced from the conflict zone. In addition, in many cities, with donor support from foreign partners, vocational retraining courses for internally displaced persons were opened at state employment centers. Courses for accountants, administrators or hairdressers, which do not require lengthy studies or a vocational diploma for successful further employment, are popular among IDPs.

This kind of vocation-oriented, targeted support seems to be the best form of support for IDPs to enable them to adapt to a new life. In contrast, cash benefits do not seem to help IDPs much. It might make sense to pay a substantial lump sum to resettle after having fled rather than making a monthly payment of an insignificant amount. Unfortunately, government bureaucracy, an unwillingness to accept political responsibility and the sluggish state machine have made it difficult for IDPs to access administrative services and have restricted their rights.

IDPs and Voting Rights

One of the most contentious issues of IDP politics was the restriction of voting rights. The only election IDPs could meaningfully participate in was the 2019 presidential election. Even though registration to vote at the place of actual residence required going through a certain procedure and entailed long queues at the polling stations just before closing time, in principle, all IDPs who made a minimum effort were able to exercise their right to vote in the presidential election. In May 2014, on the contrary, the first fugitives from Donetsk and Luhansk did not have a chance to formalize their residency in their new places of residence. In the 2014 parliamentary elections, as in 2019, IDPs only voted for parliamentary candidates in the nationwide constituency of political parties without being included on the ballot for candidates in majoritarian territorial single-mandate constituencies. In addition, IDPs could not participate in the election of local self-government bodies in 2015. Neither Donetsk nor Luhansk regional councils were elected in 2015. In practical terms, in the rest of the country, despite their large cumulative numbers, IDPs were unlikely to have had any real influence on the outcome of the elections. However, many IDPs were painfully aware of the lack of effective participation in the formation of local governments in the oblasts, districts and localities where they lived, worked and paid taxes. On a symbolic level, many felt that larger Ukraine refused to accept them as full citizens or suspected them of being disloyal. In reality, it was more a question of technical difficulties and the sluggishness of the bureaucratic system.

Ukraine has an archaic system of residence registration, a kind of vestige of Soviet registration (*propiska*). Millions of citizens who do not have permanent residence registration do not participate in the formation of local self-government. Mobile citizens, active taxpayers, are thus often not registered as voters. This situation artificially increases the role of pensioners residing at the place of official registration, which creates the opportunity for vote-buying and manipulation of election results by interested stakeholders. This issue, however, can be fully resolved only by reforming the institution of residence registration (Lunova/Nastina 2019; Lunova et al. 2020). But, in late 2019, a new Electoral Code was approved, and amendments to the Law on the State Voter Register were adopted, allowing for a relatively easy change of a citizen's voting address, whatever their permanent registered address of residence may be. The issue of the displaced persons effective political participation had finally been partially resolved by law. However, the government still had not addressed the most acute and painful issue of full pension provision. In February 2020, the *Verkhovna Rada* did not have enough votes to pass amendments to Ukrainian legislation on the right to a pension that would have allowed residents of Russian controlled areas to receive their legal entitlements without having to register as IDPs. The amendments were rejected at the request of the government. Deputy Finance Minister Yuriy Dzhygir asked MPs to withdraw the bill as implementing its provisions would involve significant additional spending from the state budget.[28] The government thus almost blatantly admitted that the only reason for not paying earned pensions to certain categories of Ukrainian citizens (residents of the occupied territories) was to save budget funds.

Receiving pensions is the most acute problem for internally displaced persons. Human rights activists describe the situation as discriminatory. In addition to the fact that residents from NGCA can only receive pensions after registering as IDPs, a Cabinet of Ministers' decree introduced additional checks and restrictions in 2016. Courts of all kinds, including the Grand Chamber of the Supreme Court, have repeatedly ruled that decisions based on this regulation are illegal, but the decree remains in force.[29]

Pensioners who have registered as IDPs are required to undergo identification in person at the state-owned Oshchadbank. There are specific procedures to verify a pensioner's actual residence at the place of temporary registration in Ukrainian government-controlled territory as an IDP. If this verification fails, payments can be suspended. They can also be suspended for other reasons, for example, based on information from the secret service SBU that a citizen resides in the occupied territory. The Pension Fund has also "lost" pensioners by mistake, for example, during the installation of new software, condemning tens of thousands of people to an unscheduled verification procedure and several months of waiting for legally due payments.

In 2018, the number of IDP pensioners was 700,000, but the number of IDPs who received pensions was 555,003 — not all could

---

28 Rada provalila golosovanie za pensii dlya zhiteley okkupirovannogo Donbasa, Bukvy 5 February 2020, https://bykvu.com/ru/bukvy/rada-provalila-golosovanie-za-pensii-dlja-zhitelej-okkupirovannogo-donbassa/.

29 Verkhovnyy sud priznal nezakonnym prekrashchenie vyplaty pensii zhitelyam okkupirovannogo Donbasa, depo.Donbas, 5 September 2018, https://dn.depo.ua/rus/dn/verhovniy-sud-viznav-nezakonnim-pripinennya-viplati-pensiy-zhitelyam-okupovanogo-donbasu-20180905832591.

prove that they met all the required conditions or initially managed to do so but subsequently dropped out of the list of pension recipients. There was a wide public outcry in 2018 over the pension deprivation of Igor Kozlovsky, a well-known scientist from Donetsk, who had previously spent two years in illegal detention in the Russian-controlled territory and was only released after an "exchange" in December 2017. As Kozlovskiy had travelled to Europe (he had met with Czech President Miloš Zeman and had testified before the European Parliament about human rights violations in Russian-controlled territories), the Pension Fund ruled that he was not living at his temporary registration as an IDP and suspended his pension payments.[30] Only after the media brought this scandal to light did payments to the scientist resume. For tens of thousands of less public pensioners, it has been much more challenging to get their legitimate money, which is the only source of livelihood for many. The fact that the Ukrainian state refused to pay pensions to residents of Russian-controlled territories and created a discriminatory regime for payments to resettled pensioners, violates national legislation and Ukraine's obligations under international treaties.

However, the pension system has been widely misused too. The vast majority of people who crossed checkpoints before 24 February 2022, were actually IDPs living on Russian-controlled territory who collected pensions on Ukrainian-controlled territory. They travelled to the nearest government-controlled locality to collect money, bought food and medicines and confirmed their status. Many Ukrainian officials and public figures have repeatedly criticized the very fact that pensions were paid to fictitious IDPs, who were widely referred to as 'pension tourists'.

Meanwhile, the conditions at the border crossing points often proved to be a cruel ordeal for the 'pension tourists'. Old age, illness, the need to queue for hours in all kinds of weather under the open sky or symbolic canopies led to frequent deaths at checkpoints. In 2019, 40 people died crossing the contact line. The cause

---

30   Uchenyy Kozlovsky, provedya dva goda v plenu boevikov, lishilsya pensii v Ukraine, Novoe vremya 22 June 2018, https://nv.ua/ukraine/events/uchenyj-kozlovskij-provedja-dva-hoda-v-plenu-boevikov-lishilsja-pensii-v-ukraine-2478057.html.

of death for 32 of them, according to human rights activist Levon Azizian's statistics, was a medical condition (another six died in a road accident, two were killed by a landmine). Thirty-five of the dead were over the age of 60.

IDPs as a Resource

Ukrainian officials and large parts of society tend to perceive IDPs as a problem that is difficult to solve as any solution seems "unaffordable". Yet, it seems justifiable to consider them as a source of human capital. The towns in Ukrainian-controlled areas of the Donetsk and Luhansk oblasts are a case in point. Most IDPs were active, visible and influential in socio-economic life. Except for Mariupol, a large and developed centre even before the war, other towns in the Ukrainian-controlled part of Donetsk and Luhansk oblasts, such as Sloviansk, Kramatorsk, Severodonetsk, Lysychansk or Rubizhne barely had 100,000 inhabitants. Compared to them, not only Donetsk, a city of millions but also Luhansk, Makiivka or Horlivka seemed like big cities. For many professionally qualified specialists and people in business, the big cities, i.e., Kyiv, Kharkiv or Dnipro, were obvious destinations when they left the Russian-controlled territory. But some had personal and professional connections in smaller towns in their home region, which came in handy during the initial period of adaptation after the move, while others did not want to move far from relatives or their homes left in Russian-controlled areas. Entrepreneurs, teachers, journalists, lawyers, doctors or sports coaches who moved from Luhansk to Severodonetsk or from Donetsk to Sloviansk brought very different social experiences and intellectual potential to these urbanized small towns. Thanks to savings or targeted aid from international organizations, settler business people started their own small businesses, trainers started sports sections, editors started new local websites. Before the war, Donetsk and Luhansk were not only industrial centres but also major cultural and educational centres. The relocation of higher education institutions was of great importance for the development of the Ukrainian-controlled areas of Donetsk and Luhansk oblasts. The Volodymyr Dahl East Ukrainian National University moved from Luhansk to Severodonetsk and the Horlivka Institute of Foreign Languages to Bakhmut. Luhansk and Donetsk law, medical, construction and agricultural universities moved to Sloviansk, Kostyantynivka, Krasny Liman, Starobelsk, Kramatorsk and Rubizhne. In addition to the influx of budget funds and quality teaching staff, the relocated universities kept many young people from moving to distant large cities.

Many IDPs who had moved from the Russian-controlled areas to the Ukrainian-controlled part of Donetsk and Luhansk were patriotic. "Pro-Ukrainian" views were often more intrinsic to them than to the average local residents. They knew the threats to their well-being and security posed by the pro-Russian separatist movement and were prepared to counter it in the public sphere. In this sense, for the Kyiv authorities, IDPs represented strong political support in the region.

IDPs, whom the authorities perceive as a burden, thus potentially represent a significant resource for the state, society and economy. The necessary costs of assisting IDPs should be seen as an investment. If Ukraine had approached the integration of IDPs in the same way as Israel assists Jewish immigrants, i.e. with reasonable initial settlement assistance, opportunities for professional retraining and favourable conditions for business development, it would certainly more than compensate the initial investment over time. Given the demographic trends in Ukraine, the Kyiv government needs to encourage young families with children to relocate to the territory under its control. Unfortunately, the lack of adequate analysis and strategic planning in the Ukrainian administrative apparatus has inhibited a sensible approach to integrating resettlers.

References

Balakireva, O. (ed.) Vimusheni pereselentsi gromadi: uroki dlya для efektivnoi suspilnoi adaptatsii I integratsii, Kyiv 2016, http://ief.org.ua/docs/sr/295.pdf.

Denisenko, D.; V. Novikov; A. Korinevich: Zaboronena mishen: medichni zakladi pid myd obstrilami, Lugasnkii pravozashchitnyi tsentr „Alternativa", Kiyiv 2017, https://jfp.org.ua/system/reports/files/106/uk/Target2_Alternative_MF_Web.pdf.

Gritsenko, N.; O. Odegov: Zochini bez pokarannya. Porushcheniya prav lyudini pid chas zbroinogo konfliktu na skhodi Ukraini, Kiyiv: Skhidnoukrainskii tsentr gromadskikh initsiativ, 2018, https://jfp.org.ua/system/reports/files/123/uk/Crimes_UKR_compressed.pdf.

Likhachev, Vyacheslav: Ucheba na linii ognya, Vostok SOS, Kyiv 2018, https://issuu.com/vostok-sos/docs/ucheba-na-linii-ognya-rus.

Lunova, A.; A. Filishina; A. Babko; A. Bondarenko; A. Koryachenko; V. Timoshuk; V. Musatenko; E. Shkolnyi; O. Borys; O. Chorna; S. Tyutyunik: Zelena kniga sistemi reestratsii mistsiya pozhivaniya dlya uryadu Urainy, Tsentr prav lyudini ZMINA, 2020, https://org.zmina.info/content/uploads/sites/2/2019/12/ZMINA-Green-Paper-UKR-for-web.pdf.

Lunova, A; O. Nastina: Reestratsiya mistsya prozhivaniya buti chi ne buti, Tsentr prav lyudini ZMINA 2019, https://org.zmina.info/content/uploads/sites/2/2019/09/ZMINA-ta-MPR-broshura-pro-SRMP-Buty-chy-ne-buty-for-web.pdf.

Sasse, Gwendolyn: The Voices of the Displaced in Ukraine and Russia. Carnegie Europe. 13 February 2017, https://carnegieeurope.eu/strategiceurope/67979.

Ukrainskiy ofis Mizhnarodnogo doslidnitskogo agenstva IFAK Institut. Okremi rezultati sotsiologichnogo doslidzheniya "Osoblivosti sotsialnoi adaptatsii ta integratsii vnutrishnyu peremishschennykh osib (VPO)) do mistsevikh gromad teritorii ikh teperishogo prohivaniya, Kyiv 2017, https://drive.google.com/file/d/1vkzeSKVr6A4k_wk NoetnbSid-eaBHeDM/view.

Vostok -SOS: «My pselili bolshe chem 20 tysyach chelovek v chastnoe zhilyo, Gromadskoe radio 6 May2016, https://hromadske.radio/ru/news/2016/05/06/vostok-sos-my-poselili-bolshe-chem-20-tysyach-chelovek-v-chastnoe-zhile.

Vovk, M.; V. Glushchenko; Yu. Gukov; A. Egorova; E. Sakharov, B. Knirov; G. Obdienko; N. Okhotnikova; O. Richko; Ya. Smelyanskaya; I. Sosonskii; G. Tokarev; P. Shab; G. Shcherbak: Nasilnitsy zlochniki, skoeni v khodi zbroinogo konfliktu na skhodi Ukraini 2014-2018rr., Kharkiv 2018, http://library.khpg.org/files/docs/1552985409.pdf.

Zakharov, B.: Zabezpechennya prav vnutrishnyo peremishnyo osib, in E. Zakharov, O. Martinenko (ed.) Prava lyudini v Ukraini – 2014.

Media Policy of Armed Groups in Ukraine

Kostiantyn Fedorenko

Since 2014, the media have played a significant role in the formation of public opinion about the political protests in Ukraine in November and December 2013 and in the spring of 2014, i.e. the Euromaidan and the anti-Maidan counter-mobilization, as well as the violent conflict and subsequent war in the east and south of Ukraine. We analyze the media channels used by the armed groups for recruitment, we scrutinize the legitimization of their actions, and communication with their followers. We also analyze the armed groups' views on the parties to the conflict and on key topics such as Russia's involvement, the Minsk Agreements, and Ukraine's prospects. We will focus on the content and style of these media messages rather than their perception.

The Role of the Media in Armed Conflicts

The 20th century has shown that the media have a considerable impact on armed conflicts. The media, especially radio, played a crucial role in the rise of Nazism and mass indoctrination.[1] In the USSR, the role of the radio in World War II propaganda was so critical that the Nazi government allegedly promised a reward for the head of the charismatic broadcaster Yuri Levitan.[2] A more recent and well-known example is the role of the "Free Radio and Television of the Thousand Hills" in Rwanda, which called for the genocide of the Tutsi people. During the proceedings of the International Criminal Tribunal for Rwanda, the radio's editor-in-chief was found guilty and sentenced to life imprisonment.[3]

---

1   https://www.princeton.edu/csdp/events/Petrova04042013/Petrova04042013.pdf.
2   http://kops.uni-konstanz.de/bitstream/handle/123456789/34895/Zakharine_0-348618.pdf?sequence=3&isAllowed=y.
3   http://www.haguejusticeportal.net/index.php?id=8415; https://unictr.irmct.org/.

As recent studies of media outlets have shown, the Western Balkans still actively use emotional and hateful language to talk about their former adversaries,[4] thus holding on to the rhetoric that characterized their media during the armed conflicts of the 1990s.[5] More recently, social media have played a special role in the staging of protests and in military conflicts. Social media have played an important role in the mobilization of the population and creation of the networks for the so-called Arab Spring in 2008, although they played an even more important role in communicating the crucial events during the protests to the outside world.[6] Countries such as China, Russia and Turkey, seeking to retain their autocratic regimes and internal stability, actively restrict the use of certain social media.[7] The ubiquity of social media and the trust that large groups of citizens place in them make so-called information warfare, i.e. the use of public information for military purposes, especially important. Information warfare is based on the dissemination of propaganda messages that can significantly affect the parties' world views and the course of a violent conflict.[8] Social media allow for the rapid spread of news about the course of a conflict but make it difficult to verify and contextualize information.[9] Projects such as StopFake expose fake messages used in information warfare; they show how seriously parties to modern conflicts take communication, and how much false or manipulative information is disseminated.[10]

---

4   http://www.institutemedia.org/Documents/PDF/Raporting%20neigbours%2030-06-2015.pdf.
5   http://www.sferapoliticii.ro/sfera/188/pdf/188.05.Scekic.pdf.
6   http://www.journalism.org/2012/11/28/role-social-media-arab-uprisings/.
7   http://time.com/4101870/these-4-states-and-one-terror-group-rule-social-media/; http://www.wired.co.uk/article/russia-google-telegram-ban-blocks-ip-address.
8   https://www.independent.co.uk/news/long_reads/war-twitter-social-media-ukraine-isis-change-information-facebook-syria-videos-images-share-a8202141.html
9   http://www.journals.uio.no/index.php/TJMI/article/view/898
10 https://www.stopfake.org/en/news/.

Euro-Maidan, Its Aftermath and the Role of the Media

In the winter of 2013/14, many Euromaidan activists and their political leaders legitimized their protests, claiming social support by referring to "the people".[11] On November 29, 2013, the joint resolution of the political activists and leaders of the opposition parties condemned President Yanukovych for the "betrayal of the Ukrainian people" when he refused to sign the European Union–Ukraine Association Agreement.[12] This narrative became widespread after a special operations unit attacked the protesters.[13]

The protesters were part of the media loop. The pro-European intelligentsia and students were active on social media and in the comment sections of news sites. Those who did not participate in the protests—especially those living outside Kyiv—received their information mostly through the conventional or social media. Since the Ukrainian media covered the protests extensively, it was difficult to remain unaware of the ongoing events. The information that media consumers received influenced their willingness to participate in or oppose the protests. It clearly mattered how the facts were framed and how they fit with personal prejudices.

From the point of view of the opponents of Euro-integration, the claim that President Yanukovych "betrayed the Ukrainian people" (by not signing the Association Agreement) and the subsequent attempts by Euromaidan supporters to speak on behalf of the "people" were illegitimate. While some did not originally oppose the protests, the influence of the exclusively negative coverage of the protests they received made them think otherwise. United by feelings of resentment, they then used social media to share their views; the number of participants in the Russian-dominated VK groups (*Vkontakte*) who opposed Euromaidan grew very quickly. The VK network was probably the most popular means of such

---

11 http://glavred.info/politika/evromaydan-podgotovil-novogodnee-obraschenie-naroda-k-prezidentu-ukrainy-opublikovano-video-267335.html.
12 http://www.theinsider.ua/history-euromaidan/
13 Ibid.

communication. The media thus played an active part in further dividing the population, which subsequently had a significant impact on the conflict in eastern Ukraine.

It is safe to assume that some of those who supported the anti-Maidan agenda later supported Russia's annexation of Crimea and sided with the separatists in the Donbas conflict. The anti-Maidan groups regularly published news items in which they referred to the region as Novorossiya (New Russia—a regional government from Tsarist times). Traditional regional divisions resurfaced during the Euro-Maidan and in the communication among its opponents. This communication, often transmitted through social and traditional media, provided significant support for the separatist movement. Serhiy Kudelia, who looked at the Ukrainian roots of the protest mobilization of the local population in Donbas, noted that the use of violence by Euro-Maidan activists gradually led to the government's loss of power and that "now any civil protest included some violence potential" (Kudelia 2016, p. 8f.).

In response to the militarization of the Euromaidan, paramilitary units were created in eastern Ukraine under the pretext of protecting the local population from nationalists, i.e. from a threat which did not actually exist for the locals at the time but which was perceived as a probability of future bloodshed. These paramilitary units portrayed themselves as protecting against nationalists, especially the Right Sector, which, in April 2014, parts of the Donbas population perceived as "a threat to the citizens and integrity of the country" (Kudelia 2016). In fact, the presence of Right Sector activists during Euromaidan was considerably exaggerated—their number did not exceed 300.[14] The difference between the perception of the Right Sector in Donbas and the reality may be explained by the relative popularity of the Russian media in eastern Ukraine.[15] In April 2014, the Russian media mentioned the Right Sector as often as the ruling United Russia party.[16] This myth about the strong and

---

14 http://hadashot.kiev.ua/content/vyacheslav-lihachev-kto-tam-shagaet-prav oy.
15 http://www.old.dif.org.ua/ua/events/telebacnih-novin.htmhe.
16 https://censor.net.ua/news/284076/v_rossii_pravyyi_sektor_dognal_edinuy u_rossiyu_po_kolichestvu_upominaniyi.

numerous Right Sector from which the Donbas allegedly needed to be "protected", as from the other nationalists, co-created by the media, became a source of mobilization for the people in Donbas. Many of them "traditionally supported the union of Ukraine and Russia" and "deplored the split of the Soviet Union", as Kudelia notes. After the annexation of Crimea, nearly two-thirds of the region's population had a positive attitude toward Vladimir Putin, while in the other regions, no more than 20 percent supported him (Kudelia 2016, p. 11). Kudelia states that "resentment toward the Ukrainian nationalists" strengthened the "effect of the messages on the 'fascist junta in Kyiv' coming from the Russian channels" (Kudelia 2016, p.12). The mobilization of irregular armed groups on both sides was aided by appeals to prejudices, values, and world views, as well as by partisan media coverage of the unfolding events.

Media as a Method of Recruitment

One of the primary tasks of any armed group is the recruitment of new members. This is especially true in the context of a full-scale conflict that has resulted in a large number of casualties. The media played a significant role in the mobilization of both parties to the violent conflict. The irregular armed groups used the media to recruit for their units and to raise material support and later, when the war reached its peak (in 2014–2015), to lobby for their replacement.

What media resources could these groups count on? One type is media directly produced by the armed group, in other words, controlled by its participants. These are social media sites and propaganda leaflets. From 2014 onwards, the Azov battalion had issued an irregular frontline newspaper, The Black Sun.[17] External advertising is also one of the directly controlled resources, since it is ordered by the combat group, regardless of who finances the order. Advertising targets those who, if not yet 'initiated', have at least

---

17 http://azov.press/page/search?search=%D1%87%D0%BE%D1%80%D0%BD %D0%B5+%D1%81%D0%BE%D0%BD%D1%86%D0%B5.

heard of the respective armed group and want to know more. These media outlets communicate with supporters.

A second type, with much more varied resources, is the media which are not under the control of an armed group but are willing to publish favorable content. The armed groups cannot directly influence the coverage, but as they act as sources of information and newsmakers, they indirectly influence the agenda of these media. Media such as TV channels or news stations covering general politics are crucial to the armed groups as they deliver messages that may present them as heroes, or convoy the ideology of a particular group. The media not directly controlled by the armed groups thus at least contributed to their legitimization.

Funding

Besides mobilizing for participation in combat, the media encouraged their audiences to contribute to it financially or in-kind. Armed groups often published information about the goods they needed, calling for the collection of needed items or funds as a whole.[18] Sometimes, fraudsters abused the trust of citizens in volunteers, for instance, by collecting donations for a non-existent Izium battalion.[19] One form of fundraising was to organize events, the proceeds of which were used for the needs of armed groups.[20] Some combat groups published their bank account numbers to which money could be transferred or addresses where needed goods could be collected.[21] Occasionally, they published reports on how these funds were spent.[22] Some social media groups were fully dedicated to providing financial support to the armed groups.[23]

---

18 https://www.facebook.com/BN.Kyiv2/photos/a.1526752284204551.1073741828.1524438831102563/1564490700430709/; https://www.facebook.com/svoboda.ua/posts/909290215788205; https://www.facebook.com/events/424177854649382/.
19 https://portal.lviv.ua/news/2014/06/13/175740.
20 https://vk.com/wall-72444174_61608.
21 https://vk.com/batalion.azov?w=page-72444174_49694095, https://vk.com/polk.dnipro1?z=photo19823890_337972161%2F780ee32db1195b648f.
22 https://vk.com/wall-57424472_180280
23 https://vk.com/spasidonbass; https://www.facebook.com/centrdopomogy/.

It is known that supporters of the Ukrainian Army often claim that volunteers played a crucial role in ensuring its activities[24][25]. In some cases, the mobilization of volunteer assistance was based on personal contacts. Calls for help were disseminated through the media, especially digital media. The news about the volunteers' activities was aimed at potential new participants.[26] Survey data of the Democratic Initiative and the Kyiv International Institute for Psychology collected in 2014 shows that 32.5 percent of Ukrainians transferred funds for the needs of the Army; 23 percent transferred money, donated in-kind or food through charity funds or voluntary organizations.[27]

It is impossible to estimate the exact number of volunteers recruited through the media or the amount of money raised thanks to the media, but raising money and providing other material support was one of the main goals of the armed groups' media policy. Even after the majority of the Ukrainian irregular armed groups were integrated into government structures, some continued to attract stable sources of external support (Azov and Dnipro-1 are examples) through fund-raising.

The Ukrainian diaspora independently raised funds for aid, joined in to help the Army and put pressure on their governments to assist Ukraine,[28] although the influence of the media on the diaspor''s activities is also hard to assess'. The Ukrainian volunteer project Army SOS had an English-language version of its website.[29] But also in Russia, several events were dedicated to raising funds to support "the people's republics".[30] 'The majority of the diaspora

---

[24] https://tsn.ua/ukrayina/v-ukrayini-privitali-volonteriv-bez-yakih-ne-vistoyali-b-maydan-i-ukrayinska-armiya-395891.html; https://www.ukrinform.ua/rubric-society/2324579-ukrainske-volonterstvo-avise-unikalne-jomu-zavdacuemo-suverenitetom.html..

[25] https://www.ukrinform.ua/rubric-society/2324579-ukrainske-volonterstvo-avise-unikalne-jomu-zavdacuemo-suverenitetom.html.

[26] https://censor.net.ua/news/347942/v_kieve_otkryty_dve_novye_gruppy_po_sozdaniyu_maskirovochnyh_setok_dlya_armii.

[27] https://life.pravda.com.ua/society/2014/10/22/182504/.

[28] https://www.theglobeandmail.com/news/world/ukraine-canadas-unofficial-war/article23208129/

[29] http://armysos.com.ua/en/.

[30] https://vk.com/page-29534144_47770406.

groups wished to help 'their' party to the conflict and wanted to learn about the war through their respective media. This is what the media operating in areas controlled by Ukraine and the media of the Russian-controlled 'people's republics' did by mainly delivering information favoring their respective party.

External Advertising

The Ukrainian irregular armed groups rarely used external advertising. In November 2015, 24 city lights appeared in Mariupol depicting pictures of killed Azov fighters.[31] The city council had put up the city lights as social advertising. On Ukraine's Independence Day (August 24, 2015), the party Svoboda gave an example of the transformation of 'social capital' into 'political capital', showing large numbers of pictures of fighters supporting Svoboda on billboards in Kyiv, including the pictures of fighters from the Karpatska Sich battalion, formed by Svoboda. This political advertisement also used the combat unit's name "Lehion Svobody" to unite the party members who fought against Russian forces in the Anti-Terrorist Operation. The pictures showed the following slogan: "The heroes congratulate you".[32] Similar advertisements also appeared in other cities[33]. The pictures of famous uniformed party members who had fought in the war were part of electoral campaigns.

In the Luhansk and Donetsk "people republics" (LDPR), no specific armed group was actively promoted. While most of the billboards calling on people to join the separatist armed forces did not mention the names of combat groups and appeared to have been put up by the administration authorities, in Ukraine, the advertising media calling to join the armed forces of Ukraine was quite widespread. Such advertisement legitimized the activities of the volunteer battalions and facilitated the recruitment of new fighters.

---

31 https://vk.com/batalion.azov?w=wall-72444174_39920.
32 http://prportal.com.ua/Peredovitsa/tyagnibok-ta-piar-pid-chas-viyni.
33 http://infomist.ck.ua/u-dobrovolchij-choti-vilnyj-grafik-rotatsiyi-novovyyavlenyj-boyets-deputat/; http://zz.te.ua/kajda-zodyahnuv-kamuflyazh-i-stav-bihbordnym-herojem/.

Aesthetically, advertisements in the Luhansk and Donetsk "peoples republics" were directly related to Soviet propaganda placards,[34] thus serving the discourse of 'fighting fascism'. City lights in the Luhansk and Donetsk "people republics" in memory of the pro-Russian commanders "Givi" and "Motorola" were the most widespread dedicated to pro-Russian irregular armed groups.[35] Billboards were also found referring to the social media network "VK" group "Center for Military Training" and People's Militia in Donbas (Pavel Gubarev).[36]

Social Media Webpages

Social media were the main means of communication between the armed groups and their followers. Most of the pro-Ukrainian armed groups had their own websites—for a long time, they were hosted by the Russian platform VK. The pro-Russian armed groups posted almost exclusively on VK. However, pursuant to the decree of former President Poroshenko, based on the decision of the National Security and Defense Council of Ukraine (NSDC) on sanctions against large Russian media groups, in particular, Yandex and Mail.ru, access to the latter's VK was blocked in Ukraine.[37] Although this decree officially aimed to introduce economic sanctions, Poroshenko himself explained the restriction of access to large Russian services with security reasons.[38] Oleksandr Turchynov, the head of the NSDC until May 2019, claimed at that time that Russia's special services use their media outlets as an "agent recruitment network and for propaganda".[39] However, the largest official VK

---

34 http://www.yaplakal.com/forum2/topic844178.html; http://news.dn.ua/articles/31-vysshii-gradus-patriotizma-iii-nasledie-sovetskoi-propagandy-v-dnr.html.
35 http://novosti.dn.ua/news/266614-centr-donecka-uveshan-bylbordamy-s-gyvy.
36 http://s00.yaplakal.com/pics/pics_original/8/9/6/3464698.jpg.
37 https://www.unian.ua/politics/1926399-v-ukrajini-nabuv-chinnosti-ukaz-pro-blokuvannya-vkontakte-i-odnoklassnikov.html.
38 https://www.unian.ua/politics/1925164-poroshenko-prokomentuvav-zaboronu-rosiyskih-saytiv-v-ukrajini-u-pidsanktsiyniy-sotsmereji.html.
39 https://www.ukrinform.ua/rubric-polytics/2229259-rosijski-socmerezi-blokuut-cerez-verbuvanna-ta-spigunstvo-turcinov.html.

pages of the Ukrainian combat groups—Azov and the Right Sector—were still regularly updated.[40] Obviously, the administrators were aware that many Ukrainians bypassed the blocking of Russian social media and continued to actively use them.

On the whole, the pages of irregular armed groups can be divided into two large and fundamentally different types. The first type includes small, often restricted-access pages for internal purposes of those who serve or have served in a particular group; their main purpose is communication among comrades within the unit, usually after demobilization. Open pages of this type may publish news, but rarely, and as a rule, have few subscribers. Among Ukrainian groups, this type of content is typical of regional battalions, such as Ternopol[41] or Cherkasy.[42] The second type aims to address an external audience so that groups can communicate with supporters. They contain news associated with the activities of a particular group or news full of ideological bias. Some of these pages are no longer updated, although the armed groups represented on them remain active, whereas others are on a regular basis. They usually contain contact details for those who wish to join the unit, and in some cases, to arouse readers' interest in recruitment. Comments are either hidden or strictly moderated.

It is interesting to note that despite the considerable popularity of Givi and Motorola (one of their pages had 11,839 subscribers[43] and the other 7,728[44]), the Sparta battalion page had only 64 subscribers.[45] The 'Somali' battalion had several social media groups, which together did not exceed 180 subscribers. No single pro-Russian armed group was particularly popular on the Internet. The largest VK page associated with separatists was "Oplot", with 29,279 subscribers at one point time.[46] The most popular pro-Russian armed group pages on social media were "Anti-Maidan"

---

40 https://vk.com/batalion.azov; https://vk.com/ps_ukraine.
41 https://vk.com/btro_cherkassy.
42 https://vk.com/btro_cherkassy.
43 https://vk.com/givi777motorola555.
44 https://vk.com/givi_rip.
45 https://vk.com/b.sparta.
46 https://vk.com/fightclub_oplot

(486,777 subscribers),[47] "Novorossiya militia news" (448,057 subscribers) and the "Donetsk | Luhansk | Novorossiya" sites (335,957 subscribers)[48].

Some pages were not directly controlled by the irregular armed groups but covered the violent conflict from an ideological perspective or reported mainly on military clashes. Among the pro-Ukrainian armed groups, the most illustrative examples of such pages were "We are patriots of Ukraine" (407,548 subscribers)[49] and "Ukraine Live — News/ATO" (625,543 subscribers).[50] The spread of far-right rhetoric and the support of nationalist parties was one of the dangers associated with Ukrainian groups on social media.

The composition of the subscribers varies dramatically depending on their place of residence. For example, 70.5 percent of the subscribers to the "We are patriots of Ukraine" site indicated that they live in Ukraine. 71.9 percent of the "Ukraine Live— New/ATO" subscribers indicated the same. At the same time, 29.9 percent of the Anti-Maidan, 30 percent of the "Novorossiya militia news" and 32.2 percent of the "Donetsk | Luhansk | Novorossiya" page subscribers said that they lived in Ukraine. In contrast, 45.7 percent of the Anti-Maidan, 46.4 percent of the "Novorossiya militia news" and 41.5 percent of the "Donetsk | Luhansk | Novorossiya" site subscribers claimed Russia as their country of residence.

The armed groups used Facebook to a much lesser extent. This is especially true for the groups that fought on the pro-Russian side. Only the "Russian Orthodox Army", the "People's Militia of the Luhansk People's Republic," and the "Vsevelikoe vojsko Donskoe" (Almighty Don Army)" had Facebook pages, but with less than 100 subscribers each. In contrast, 48.112 people followed the page of the Right Sector, 81,413 people followed the page of the "National Corpus", which also published news from the Azov battalion. The number of followers of these pages has been growing since May

---

47   https://vk.com/antimaydan
48   https://vk.com/soutukraine
49   Here and below, the groups statistics as of 28 December 2017 are provided.
50   https://vk.com/live_ukr

2017, taking into account the ban on Russian social media.⁵¹ A significant part of the open social media groups dedicated to irregular armed groups were neglected and used only as sources of archived information. In contrast, the pages of the Right Sector, Azov, or Karpatska Sich were updated regularly – the generally very high motivation of the nationalists and their links to parties may be an explanation for this.

Social activists and politicians selected Facebook as the main means of communication. In contrast, the Russian "Odnoklassniki" social network was more popular among older users. In 2017, for example, the top 100 Russian-language Facebook pages (in terms of the number of subscribers) were those of the then Minister of Internal Affairs of Ukraine, Arsen Avakov and his advisor Anton Gerashchenko who had the oversight of the Ukrainian volunteer battalions, as well as Dmytro Tymchuk and Yuri Butusov, journalists who actively covered the Donbas conflict from a pro-Ukrainian perspective. Among those writing from a pro-Russian point of view, only Zakhar Prilepin, the Russian writer who went to Donbas as a volunteer, was among the top 100 Russian-language pages.⁵² Obviously, the separatists did not consider Facebook an important platform; in Russia, Facebook is mostly used to maintain business contacts. The most popular pro-separatist pages were thus on VK and LiveJournal.⁵³

Some bloggers used LiveJournal to support one party to the violent conflict or the other, covering it from an ideological perspective, sometimes announcing calls for donations. One Ukrainian blogger, Igor Bigdan (ibigdan), the former director of LiveJournal in Ukraine, stopped posting after the occupation of Crimea because of the pressure put on him by the Russian company SUP, which de facto owned LiveJournal.⁵⁴ The blog LiveJournal Gorky Look (Sviatoslav Nosov) published satirical texts with a decidedly pro-

---

51 http://watcher.com.ua/2017/06/19/na-facebook-vzhe-9-mln-ukrayintsiv/.
52 https://www.svoboda.org/a/28307364.html.
53 https://www.shopolog.ru/metodichka/analytics/social-nye-seti-v-rossii-zima-2015-2016-cifry-trendy-prognozy/.
54 https://www.svoboda.org/a/27316228.html

Ukrainian perspective.[55] From 2014 to 2015, readers of Ukrainian Internet sites actively disseminated his texts. Nosov, in particular, openly referred to his activities as *"Kriegspropaganda"* (war propaganda), stating that for him "the facts are not important: take any gibberish, publish it and let them [Russians] explain themselves".[56] Conversely, as of 2016, the Live Journal's top 100 included six blogs whose authors not only took a clear pro-Russian position supporting the LDPR or criticizing Ukraine but also wrote more or less regularly about the course of the violent conflict and the armed groups involved in it. Among them was Eduard Limonov (1943–2020), a former Russian writer and National-Bolshevik politician who had actively covered the Donbas conflict between 2014 and 2015. The other top Russian bloggers were Lev Vershinin (putnik1), a science fiction writer who was an enthusiast of the so-called Russian Spring and actively supported the LDPR and the idea of Novorossiya.[57] After the temporary de-escalation of the violence, he criticized the Russian authorities for not being tough enough against Ukraine, the West, and the internal opposition. The blog of Oleg Makarenko (fritzmorgen), who founded the national socio-political journal "PolitRussia," had the highest rating among the supporters of Putin's regime and the LDPR. According to data from hackers in 2012, it was funded by the Kremlin.[58] Other authors who actively wrote about the armed groups in the Donbas conflict and openly supported the LDPR were the founders of the Gubernatory.ru "analytical expert network",[59] Sergei Nikitski (nikitskij), a military–political journalist who referred to himself in his LiveJournal banner as a "loudspeaker of totalitarian propaganda", as well as Boris Rozhin (colonelcassad) and Oleg Matveychev (matveychev-oleg). Pro-LDPR bloggers such as "el-murid", "zergulio" or "yurasumy"

---

55 http://gorky-look.livejournal.com/
56 https://gorky-look.livejournal.com/191634.html; https://censor.net.ua/resonance/451900/gorkiyi_luk_vse_chto_govorit_vata_mne_absolyutno_pofig_esli_ih_zlit_to_chto_ya_pishu_porusski_eto_prekrasno.
57 https://putnik1.livejournal.com/2807610.html.
58 http://politrussia.com/o-proekte/; http://politsovet.ru/36674-v-zhivom-zhurnale-poyavilsya-poimennyy-spisok-kremlevskih-blogerov.html.
59 https://ljpromo.livejournal.com/683729.html.

rose to the top 100 Cyrillic sites.⁶⁰ Some other bloggers, such as "awas1952", "andreyvadjra", "asaratov", "chipstone", "kungurov", "manzal", or "drugoi" did not cover specific activities of the armed groups but conveyed their ideology.

Traditional Media and Digital News Portals

Social media pages, as well as popular pages of supporters, served as an important means of communication for and about the armed groups in Donbas. However, the reach of even the largest of them was limited compared to traditional media. Social media sites often target those who already support a particular ideology or party to the conflict as well as those who are motivated to receive information on the development of the conflict. Once a large segment of the population consumes an armed group's media, it may gain additional legitimacy. A specific case is the websites created by the LDPR authorities, such as "Russian Spring" (rusvesna.su) and "Novorossiya News" (novorus.info). They resemble ordinary digital news portals and cover a wide range of topics, but they have a distinctly ideological bias.

The most popular Ukrainian news portals, such as 24tv.ua, segodnya.ua, tsn.ua, were founded before the violent conflict, but their language clearly supports the Ukrainian side. Even the homepage of the newspaper "Segodnia" (segodnya.ua) owned by the oligarch Rinat Akhmetov, who had financed the pro-Russian Party of the Regions before the violent conflict, presented views supportive of the Ukrainian military. As one observer noted, the Ukrainian media's coverage of the "Anti-Terrorist Operation" made "excessive use of their own assessment of the situation and emotions" and "actively violated the principle of credibility".⁶¹ All in all, the Ukrainian media did not present information about the war critically but tended to glorify the armed forces of Ukraine and demonize the other party. A Ukrainian expert assessment in 2015 stated: "On the one hand, we have 'heroes', 'defenders', 'our boys',

---

60 https://www.livejournal.com/ratings/users?country=cyr.
61 http://osvita.mediasapiens.ua/monitoring/daily_news/mizh_svoimi_y_ch uzhimi/.

with whom the journalist associates himself, and on the other hand, 'invaders', 'terrorists', 'pro-Russian militants" — thus reinforcing the dichotomy between friend and foe.[62] Many in Ukrainian society found such reporting appropriate. In 2014, Anna Sventakh published an overview of Ukrainian print media on the UAInfo platform, criticizing them for being too neutral in their language; she specifically criticized the newspaper Segodnia for refusing to call the LDPR military terrorists.[63] This state of affairs is not unique to the Ukrainian side. The Donetsk Institute for Information (DII) rightly claimed that "the Ukrainian regional and DPR media environments are just parallel, they often present the views and assessments of only one party to the conflict." The DII experts found that "almost 20 percent of evening news stories in the DPR TV channels use hate speech". The picture was the same in the print media. The DPR media deliberately distorted Ukrainian words and used extremely hostile rhetoric. Pejorative terms such as 'heroi', 'svidomiye' or 'kastriulegoloviye' were often used, as was Soviet World War II vocabulary to describe Nazis.

LDPR media (rusvesna.su, novorus.info, or "Russian Spring") regularly used the words "ukropy" (literally dill—a Russian-language slur for Ukrainians), fascists or "banderists". In terms of style, the LDPR media are more colloquial or resemble party newspapers than normal media.

The Ukrainian media, in turn, used the term "rushists" (Russian fascists).[64] Ukrainian media were also highly emotional and biased. The Ukrainian sites "tie 24tv.ua" and "tsn.ua" frequently mentioned the term "rushist". Both sides used ethnic pejoratives: While Russians used "khokhly" for Ukrainians, Ukrainians used "katsapy", "moskali", or "rusnia" for ethnic Russians. The use of

---

62 https://ua.ejo-online.eu/2715/etyka-ta-yakist/%D1%83%D0%BA%D1%80%D0%B0%D1%97%D0%BD%D1%81%D1%8C%D0%BA%D1%96-%D0%BC%D0%B5%D0%B4%D1%96%D0%B0-%D0%B2%D0%B8%D1%81%D0%B2%D1%96%D1%82%D0%BB%D1%8E%D1%8E%D1%82%D1%8C-%D0%B2%D1%96%D0%B9%D0%BD%D1%83-%D0%B5.

63 http://uainfo.org/blognews/343396-ato-v-meda-montoring-drukovanih-zm-za-perod-z-pochatku-chervnya.html.

64 http://dii.dn.ua/analytics/128-mova-z-oznakamy-vorozhnechi-v-drukovanykh-media-donbasu-ta-na-tb-monitoring.

hate speech in the media against the enemy served to legitimize military action.

Key Media Messages of Combat Groups

On the Ukrainian and the LDPR side, the combat groups legitimized themselves through their combat experience and heroism on the front lines. The Ukrainian media portrayed the battalion Azov and the Right Sector as efficient, highly motivated units that could recruit not only ideologically driven nationalists but also other volunteers.[65] However, the Ukrainian irregular armed groups tried to appear moderate in public so as not to alienate various segments of the population. Viacheslav Likhachov claimed that on the declarative level, the policy of the Azov leader Andriy Biletsky and former head of the far-right organization "Patriot of Ukraine" had changed, but in reality "the radicals have just learned to keep up appearances in the decent society, never changing their views".[66] Similarly, the Right Sector tried to create a moderate public image.[67] And yet, they resorted to the rhetoric of fighting an "internal occupation".[68]

It appears that the LDPR groups had no need for moderation in their messages. Unlike the Right Sector and the National Corps, which were involved in politics and planned to participate in elections, these combat groups did not need any democratic support in the opaque electoral procedures of the pro-Russian "people's republics". The rhetoric in the media environment of both Ukraine and the Russian-controlled areas of Ukraine is consistently harsh, with the media drawing a clear friend vs. foe scenario. The LDPR media actively used the Soviet code system, referring to the enemies as fascists and "banderists", i.e. collaborators with the Nazi

---

65 http://www.pravda.com.ua/rus/articles/2015/04/16/7064867/; http://www.pravda.com.ua/columns/2015/04/19/7065157/; http://texty.org.ua/pg/article/editorial/read/54936/Dobrovolci_i_soldaty_Chym_vidriznajutsa_pidrozdily_ATO.
66 http://www.wwbrary-vn.eajc.org/page18/news53778.html.
67 https://pravyysektor.info/.
68 https://pravyysektor.info/prosvitnyctvo/oriyentyry/vnutrishnya-okupaciya-ukrayiny-i-yiyi-rezhym.

occupation during World War II. The perennial enemy is given a new guise, while on one's own side, there are only eternal heroes. The collocation "Victory Day", crucial to the Soviet narrative and associated with World War II, was frequently used on the "Novorossiya News" and the "Russian Spring" site. Usually, these texts either focus directly on the expected victory over the Ukrainians or draw parallels between the Great Patriotic War (the name traditionally used in the Soviet narrative for the USSR's fight against Germany from 1941 to 45) and the current conflict. Advertisements in the LDPR calling for the defense of the "people's republics" often used the aesthetics of Soviet wartime placards and the banners of the "Russian Spring", and "Novorossiya News" sites used the St. George ribbon, a Russian military symbol.

On the Ukrainian side, analogies were drawn between the current conflict and the history of the country, equating the criminal character of the Soviet and current Russian regimes. The websites of the Azov and Right Sector battalions invoked the Cossack tradition, and Andriy Biletsky stated: "We must remember each [brother who died] and honor their memory. They are now close to Sviatoslav's kinsmen, Khmelnitski's Cossacks, Shukhevitch's rebels and among millions of other unknown defenders; they have now become our immortal army".[69] The Right Sector echoed: "Our friend Berest urged us not to be afraid and feel the spirit of the warrior, kinsman, Cossack, rebel and to bravely stand up for the defense of Ukraine".[70] In the narrative of the right-wing groups, there is a clear connection between the contemporary warriors fighting against Russia in the east and south and the history of Ukraine.

Both sides considered the 2014 and 2015 Minsk Agreements on a ceasefire between Ukraine and the separatists ineffective. A phrase used in the Ukrainian TCH program in September 2016 summed up the disappointment: "...the word 'Minsk' has almost become a synonym for broken promises and unfulfilled hopes".[71] The "Russian Spring" website, in turn, regularly blamed the

---

69 https://vk.com/wall-72444174_62304.
70 https://vk.com/wall-75895219_14900.
71 https://tsn.ua/ukrayina/cherez-2-roki-pislya-peremir-ya-visnazhena-ukrayina-vse-sche-v-stani-viyni-the-washington-post-743792.html.

Ukrainian armed forces for the failure of the Minsk Agreements,[72] while Ukrainian news outlets blamed the separatists for the very same.[73] The Right Sector blamed some unspecified "liberals" who would "not acknowledge the war as a way of preserving the existence and longevity of the nation and its state" and were therefore willing to agree to the Minsk Agreements in the first place.[74] Andriy Biletsky stated that the Minsk Agreements were "a piece of paper bearing no legal obligation" and that "their full implementation means the federalization and disintegration of the country".[75] On the other hand, one of the pro-Russian authors of the "Novorossiya News" website referred to them as "a treacherous Minsk collusion", as "sacrificing one's own people for the alien fascist state".[76]

In the LDPR discourse, Ukraine was a poor and corrupt country, deprived of freedom, a kind of "liberal fascism" that imposed "homosexuality and propaganda of perversions".[77] In the separatist media, almost every article about the socio-economic situation in Ukraine was written from a derogatory perspective. In mainstream LDPR discourse, Russian-speaking Ukrainians were perceived as potential allies.[78] The prospect of a visa-free regime for Ukrainians in the Schengen area was first described as unrealistic and later as useless because of the poverty of Ukrainians—the appeal of visa-

---

72 http://rusvesna.su/news/1450458166.; http://rusvesna.su/recent_opinions/1468609193.
73 https://tsn.ua/video/video-novini/dlya-zrivu-peremir-ya-teroristi-navmisno-obstrilyuyut-pidkontrolni-yim-naseleni-punkti.html; https://tsn.ua/politika/zriv-peremir-ya-bezpeka-ta-postachannya-vodi-pro-scho-govorili-pid-chas-peregovoriv-u-minsku-863993.html.
74 https://vk.com/wall-75895219_10245.
75 https://vk.com/wall-72444174_67669.
76 http://novorus.info/news/analytics/47541-plotnickiy-i-zaharchenko-suschestvuyut-do-teh-por-poka-suschestvuyut-minskie-soglasheniya.html.
77 http://novorus.info/news/analytics/47541-plotnickiy-i-zaharchenko-suschestvuyut-do-teh-por-poka-suschestvuyut-minskie-soglasheniya.html; http://novorus.info/news/economy/49634-ukraina-i-itogi-2016-eto-uzhe-evropa-ili-budet-esche-huzhe.html; http://novorus.info/news/analytics/50639-politicheskiy-blickrig-kolonizacii-ukrainy.html; http://novorus.info/news/policy/35328-ukraina-gotova-k-diktature-liberalnogo-fashizma.html; http://rusvesna.su/tags/gomoseksualizm-i-propaganda-izvrashcheniy.
78 http://rusvesna.su/news/1488568175; http://rusvesna.su/news/1509658570; http://rusvesna.su/news/1472718488.

free travel for Ukrainians had to be countered.⁷⁹ Ukraine was portrayed as a near-totalitarian state in which the Russian-speaking "brothers" were oppressed, or as a fascist state. At the same time, Ukraine was portrayed as a weak and unsuccessful state.

In contrast, LDPR media portrayed Russia, just like the USSR, as the state that was fighting fascism. Moreover, in the event of a confrontation with NATO, Russia would surely win.⁸⁰ While the Russian government long denied its military involvement in Donbas (except for a few volunteers), the LDPR media openly wrote about Russia's involvement. On the "Novorossiya News" site and on the "Russian Spring" site, the phrase "northern wind" was often used — a reference to the involvement of the Russian military in Donbas.⁸¹ The image of a formidable force "on our side" was meant to maintain the morale of the fighters and to legitimize the military actions against Ukraine as necessary to defend Russia's interests. However, the LDPR discourse on Russia was split: While some authors remained loyal, others wrote: "Shame upon all of us — from the president and the 'elite' to the 'ordinary citizens' since we allow the Kyiv Nazi junta to occupy Novorossiya and to terrorize its people".⁸² They called for a more active involvement of Russia: "Only the betrayal of its vital interests in Novorossiya, Malorossiya, Syria and other regions where these interests are under threat may lead to Russia's defeat", i.e. if Russia does not betray its interests, "absolutely no one and nothing" would stand in its way.⁸³ Some authors who regularly covered the conflict, "putnik1" and "el-murid", for example, spoke about Russia's "betrayal", i.e. of its national interests, of Donbas and the idea of the "Russian Spring".⁸⁴ Igor Girkin

---

79　http://rusvesna.su/news/1497700904.
80　http://novorus.info/news/vmire/25008-rossiya-nato-komu-kogo-boyatsya.html; http://novorus.info/news/analytics/41650-rossiya-unichtozhit-armiyu-ssha-i-nato-za-3-nedeli.html.
81　http://rusvesna.su/recent_opinions/1441985190.
82　http://novorus.info/news/analytics/47694-rossiya-dolzhna-vernut-dolg-novorossii.html.
83　http://novorus.info/news/analytics/50164-sokrushit-rossiyu-mozhet-tolko-sama-rossiya.html.
84　https://el-murid.livejournal.com/3445834.html; https://putnik1.livejournal.com/6094560.html; http://putnik1.livejournal.com/5874772.html.

(Strelkov), who played a leading role in organizing and commanding the pro-Russian military forces in Donbas, claimed that "twisty politicians" and "traitors" were in power in Russia by supporting the Minsk Agreements.[85] Russia was allegedly acting indecisively; it should have defeated Ukraine by force, the sooner the better.[86] The violent solution was presented as the only possible outcome.

Many Ukrainians had perceived Russia as the enemy of the country's integrity and as an accomplice of the separatists long before the war broke out.[87] The Russian statement "we are not there [nas tam niet]" about the alleged absence of Russian troops (before February 2022) was often quoted and mocked with the ironical phrase "they-are-not-there [ikhtamniety]".[88] The presence of Russian troops legitimized, in turn, the fight against the separatists as accomplices of the Russian invaders. The media and the Ukrainian Ministry of Defense used the term "Russian terrorist troops" or "Russian occupational troops".[89] Some predicted an inevitable or at least probable disintegration of the Russian Federation or the collapse of the Russian economy.[90] The image of a weak enemy was intended to boost morale and downplay the asymmetry in the economic and military potential of the Russian Federation and Ukraine.

---

85 https://vk.com/wall347260249_228763.
86 https://putnik1.livejournal.com/5834597.html.
87 https://tsn.ua/politika/rosiya-v-centri-kiyeva-oformlyuye-dokumenti-z-ord lo-i-zaperechuye-teritorialnu-cilisnist-ukrayini-1054045.html.
88 http://sprotyv.info/ru/tags/ihtamnety.
89 http://www.mil.gov.ua/news/2017/12/11/rosijsko-teroristichni-vijska-vipu stili-tri-reaktivni-snaryadi-rszv-grad-po-m-avdiivka-shtab-ato/; https://radio.vesti-ukr.com/lenta/44289-minuloyi-dobi-rosijsko-teroristichni-vijska-22-razi-porushili-rezhim-tishi.html.
90 http://fakty.ictv.ua/ua/svit/rosiya/20170701-rozpad-rf-nemynuchyj-dvi-prychyny/; https://www.ukrinform.ua/rubric-society/2346389-sim-scenariiv-rozpadu-rosii.html; https://tsn.ua/groshi/ekonomika-rosiyi-zrostaye-povilnishe-nizh-za-chasiv-zastoyu-v-srsr-eks-ministr-finansiv-rf-862270.html; https://tsn.ua/groshi/minuliy-rik-z-yiv-bilshe-30-mlrd-rezerviv-rosiyi-570787.html.

Conclusions

The media played a mobilizing role during the Euromaidan and the violent Donbas conflict. The bias with which information was presented (beginning with the Euromaidan) shaped personal attitudes and confirmed existing prejudices. The mobilization of the Donbas population started as a response to the change of power in Kyiv and the perceived threat emanating from Ukrainian nationalists. The Russian media had deliberately exaggerated the salience of Ukrainian nationalists.

To recruit members of irregular armed groups and to ensure their legitimacy and material support, these groups had to turn to the media. The media can be divided into two groups: those controlled by the irregular armed groups themselves (primarily social media, leaflets and advertising) and general news portals or traditional media. While the former targeted those already interested in a given armed group and often shared its ideology, the latter had a much wider public. The media that were not controlled by the armed groups were used to reach out to that wider public. Military achievements and ideological narratives justified their actions and led to an increase in their membership.

The main platform for the representation of the armed groups was the social medium VK. Even though it was blocked in Ukraine in May 2017, some VK pages of the Ukrainian armed groups continued to be updated. The social media pages of the armed groups can be divided into those aimed at comrades-in-arms and those aimed at a larger external audience. The latter often covered current political news from an ideologized perspective and provided contact information for potential volunteers. The LDPR armed groups were more visible in their recruitment messages, while the Ukrainian groups came to be controlled by the government over time and were largely filled through mobilization.

The media, which reached large audiences with clearly biased perspectives and provided extensive media representation, were essential for both parties to the conflict. Compared to Russian-controlled areas, the Ukrainian armed groups had a lower presence on Facebook. On Facebook and LiveJournal, popular bloggers covered the activities of the irregular armed groups. For a while, the most popular Russian-speaking Facebook users were actually more likely to support the Ukrainian armed groups—the lingua franca of the pro-Ukrainian armed groups had been Russian for a long time.

Both Ukrainian and LDPR media presented biased, emotionally charged information, using a clear friend–foe dichotomy, labeling the opponent with words such as fascist or terrorist. Hate speech was more common in the LDPR media; the Ukrainian media still tried to adhere to professional standards, although they also actively used the antagonism of the friend–foe divide. The armed groups were supposedly fighting for a greater "we" community.

Azov, the Volunteer Ukrainian Army, the Right Sector, "Karpatska Sich", and right-wing Ukrainian armed groups updated their social media pages very regularly. In their public messages, they tried to present themselves as moderate nationalist forces in their bid to attract non-right-wing volunteers and ensure the political support of the parties associated with them. The image of efficient and motivated armed units served this political purpose. Right-wing groups in Ukraine often referred to historical parallels with the Cossacks and to warriors of the Ukrainian Insurgence Army during World War II. On the part of the LDPR, the historical parallels with World War II, USSR symbolism, and the labeling of the enemies as fascists were constantly observed. Their armed groups did not try to appear moderate—they obviously did not need any electoral support. Both parties to the conflict were critical of the Minsk Agreements, believing that these were not in line with the national (Ukraine's and Russia's) interests. They accused their leaders of being too compromising. The parties also blamed each other for constant violations of the ceasefire.

In the LDPR discourse, Ukraine was a poor, corrupt country deprived of freedom, where Russian speakers were oppressed. The latter were often portrayed as Russia's potential allies. In this discourse, Ukraine was a fascist state, intolerant of dissent and unsuccessful at the same time. Russia, on the other hand, was perceived as an ally fighting fascism. LDPR supporters spoke openly about Russia's military involvement in the Donbas conflict. For the Ukrainian media, Russia was and is an accomplice of terrorists: its troops have been de facto present in Donbas since spring 2014. In the official reports of the Ukrainian Ministry of Defense, the terms Russian terrorist or Russian occupational troops were frequently used, which the media picked up in their reporting.

It is difficult to assess whether these images of the enemy which the media had fed to its audiences can be overcome. It is most likely that the images of the enemy will be reinforced as long as the military conflict is going on, and even after the violent conflict is over, the antagonistic images of the adversary will remain for years. Ukraine has demonstrated the extreme importance of the media as a key component of any contemporary military conflict. It allows the mobilization of the supporters, the presentation of the conflict to the external audiences and the manipulation of facts and figures.

Reference

Kudelia, Serhiy (2016) The Donbas Rift, in: Russian Politics & Law, 54:1, pp. 5-27.

Russia's Corporate Warriors

Andreas Heinemann-Grüder

Hardly any war has ever been fought exclusively with regular soldiers. Notwithstanding this truism, the increasing prominence of state-sponsored armed and mercenary groups has notably expanded the repertoire of contemporary warfare. Over the past decade such groups have been deployed both in support of regular armed forces and as shadow armies in conflict theatres from Ukraine to Mozambique. Apart from their flexibility and relative cost efficiency, the prime benefits of these groups derive from the fact that they provide plausible deniability for state actions, exercise an unconstrained license to kill, and escape the restrictions of the *jus ad bellum* and *jus in bello* under international law. Even in the case of serious violations of humanitarian and human rights law, they can rarely be held accountable. This chapter explores the sphere in which Russia's state-controlled irregular armed groups operate and the scope of their activities, focusing in particular on the notorious Wagner Group, and their impact on violent conflicts.[1]

The role of state-sponsored irregular armed groups in Russia's strategy to extend its influence abroad has been increasing since the annexation of Crimea and the Donbas war against Ukraine in 2014/2015. These militias act in coordination with the Russian Ministry of Defense, the secret service (FSB), the foreign intelligence service, and the presidential administration. Russia's corporate warriors embody the fusion of business interests and military power in Russia's political regime. At the same time, they are war profiteers and serve as task forces to carry out high-risk and secretive missions—and they practice extermination warfare.

---

1 The overarching term used here is "state-controlled irregular armed groups" Private security companies and private military companies are treated as a subcategory. State-controlled irregular armed groups also include irregular (so-called volunteer) battalions. In contexts where such groups pursue commercial interests, the term "corporate warriors" can be used as a shorthand.

Siloarchy: The Fusion of Oligarchic and Military Interests

Russia's irregular military companies have become the regime's agents of influence, war profiteers, and an auxiliary force for state security agencies. Wagner's combatants provide agile ground forces for reconnaissance, sabotage operations, and indiscriminate killing. Part of Wagner's *modus operandi* is 'disciplining' disobedient or recalcitrant elements among its own ranks through torture and killing.

Russia's military companies are an instrument of Russia's expansionist foreign policy. They can be deployed flexibly and covertly, as well as swiftly, and they cannot be held accountable for crimes, or only to a limited extent. Within their missions, business interests and military objectives are intertwined. Russia's military companies serve to destabilize pro-Western and shore up anti-Western governments. Deaths and injuries among irregular combatants are officially invisible. The exploitation of lucrative gold, diamond, oil or gas deposits in the countries where these forces are active reflects the fusion of oligarchic and military interests.

The Wagner Group is a state-terrorist group. It can be compared to the *Einsatzgruppen* of the SS Security Service and the Security Police, to the Waffen SS or to death squads that terrorized populations in the era of Latin American dictatorships. In many ways, the Wagner Group, with its capacity for arbitrary violence, represents the abolition of legal and civil standards of conflict behavior. It embodies the coexistence of legal security apparatuses and commercial entrepreneurs of violence in Russia's political regime. Providing Moscow with a cover of plausible deniability for Kremlin-backed operations in various parts of the world, Wagner's troops penetrate regions of limited or fragile statehood and liquidate opponents there. Wagner is emblematic of the so-called siloarchy in Russia, that is, the fusion of the power ministries (*siloviki*) with oligarchic interests.

Violence as Business

Violent conflicts always provide ample opportunities for enrichment, exploitation, and the exercise of covert influence. In these contexts, mercenary and irregular armed groups are frequently deployed either on behalf of states or with their tacit permission (Singer 2001/2002; Avant 2005; Chesterman; Lehnardt 2009; Eckert 2016; Mandel 2002; Jones et al July 2021). Thus, while states outsource the organization and conduct of violence, they remain the main contractors of such groups, rendering the designation of "private military company" (PMC) something of a misnomer. Moreover, while PMCs often pursue commercial interests, their missions, resources and protection from prosecution usually derive from states—meaning that their operation is contingent on the logistics of state armed forces—effectively rendering them an add-on to conventional security and military operations.

Commercial companies seldom have the personnel and equipment to provide security beyond property protection. To an important extent, the key component of the PMC business model is the capability to undertake offensive combat operations. PMCs with combat units commit assault and homicide and often use weapons of war. None of this can be directly attributed to the contractor. PMCs recruit former intelligence officers, special forces, former police officers, pilots, or security guards; some are highly specialised, while others offer a broad portfolio of skills. While PMCs' activities encompass a wide range of sectors, the most significant field of activity is undoubtedly the provision of combatants or security forces as well as armaments.

Russia's Irregular Armed Groups

While there are numerous publications on Western private military and security companies, until recently Russia's irregular armed groups have garnered comparatively little scholarly attention (Marten 2019). This is at odds with the fact that the importance of state-controlled irregular armed groups has been increasing for the Kremlin since it began its war against Ukraine in 2014/15 and its military intervention in Syria in 2015, followed by its increasingly assertive involvement in armed conflicts in African and Asian countries. Currently, Russian-sponsored irregular armed groups operate in Africa, the Middle East, Asia and Latin America, and include military-equipped units in Ukraine, the Central African Republic, Libya, Mali, Sudan, Syria and Venezuela. A defining feature of such paramilitary groups is that they operate with the threat or use of physical force. While some of these groups operate below the threshold of overt combat operations, they share the common characteristic of having military force at their disposal.

Combatants in state-sponsored irregular armed groups, particularly PMCs, are often referred to as mercenaries. Article 47 of the 1977 First Additional Protocol to the Geneva Conventions stipulates six criteria for mercenaries: A mercenary is any person who: '(a) is specially recruited locally or abroad in order to fight in an armed conflict; (b) does, in fact, take a direct part in the hostilities; (c) is motivated to take part in the hostilities essentially by the desire for private gain and, in fact, is promised, by or on behalf of a Party to the conflict, material compensation substantially in excess of that promised or paid to combatants of similar ranks and functions in the armed forces of that Party; (d) is neither a national of a Party to the conflict nor a resident of territory controlled by a Party to the conflict; (e) is not a member of the armed forces of a Party to the conflict; and (f) has not been sent by a State which is not a Party to the conflict on official duty as a member of its armed forces'.[2]

This definition criminalizes mercenaries. However, it is hardly applicable in practice, because at least one criterion is usually missing. International humanitarian law distinguishes between combatants, i.e. persons authorized to participate directly in hostilities, and non-combatants in international armed conflicts.[3] Combatants are

---

2 International Committee of the Red Cross, 'Protocol Additional to the Geneva Conventions of 12 August 1949, and relating to the Protection of Victims of International Armed Conflicts (Protocol I), 8 June 1977', International Humanitarian Law Databases, https://ihl-databases.icrc.org/en/ihl-treaties/api-1977/article-47/commentary/1987?activeTab=undefined.

3 International Committee of the Red Cross, 'The principle of distinction between civilians and combatants', International Humanitarian Law Databases, https://ihl-databases.icrc.org/en/customary-ihl/v1/rule1; Médecins Sans Frontières,

considered to be members of armed forces and must be identifiable as such; they are authorized to engage in acts of violence, but only to the extent that they have been authorized to do so by a party to the conflict (Liu 2010; Cameron 2006). Combatants cannot be punished *per se* for their participation in acts of violence, while non-combatants face criminal prosecution. Legally, employees of commercial security and military companies become combatants under the Geneva Conventions only if they are under the command of regular armed forces.

Russian-sponsored irregular armed groups consist of *de facto* combatants, even though their *de jure* status may be disputed. Against the backdrop of the war against Ukraine, recent legal amendments adopted the term "volunteer" to designate irregular combatants, equating combatants from the infamous Wagner Group, for example, with volunteers that formed the pro-Russian separatist battalions in 2014/15 in Ukraine. "Volunteers" are thus portrayed as part of an overall military-patriotic effort, but their legal status remains vague.[4] On 20 April 2023, Russia's State Duma finally granted Wagner combatants the status of veterans of armed conflicts.[5]

Under international law, combatants are treated as a party to a conflict. However, combatant status applies only to an interstate armed conflict—meaning that the legal status cannot be assigned in the context of civil or interstate wars. Employees of PMCs can be granted combatant status even if they are not members of regular armed forces: they would then also be legitimate military targets, they could be treated as prisoners of war, and they could also be prosecuted. However, it is often impossible to determine whether

---

'Private Military Companies: Overview of the phenomenon' https://guide-humanitarian-law.org/content/article/3/private-military-companies/.

[4] Putin signs legislation banning "discrediting" and "fakes" about volunteers and mercenaries, Meduza, 18 March 2023, https://meduza.io/en/news/2023/03/18/putin-signs-order-banning-discrediting-and-fakes-about-volunteers-and-mercenaries.

[5] Gosduma dala naemnikam ChVK Vagner pravo na status "veteranov boevykh deystvii", (Russia's State Duma grants Wagner mercenaries right to status of 'combat veterans'), in: Ukrainskaya Pravda, 20 April 2023 https://www.pravda.com.ua/rus/news/2023/04/20/7398772/.

private security or military companies are integrated into the command structures of regular armed forces. It is precisely the ambiguity of their status and the at times fuzzy distinction between legal private security companies and illegal private military companies that allows state actors to deploy them arbitrarily.

As legal entities, PMCs cannot be prosecuted in either national or international courts for violations of the law. At best, the employees of PMCs can be prosecuted on the basis of individual criminal responsibility for war crimes, crimes against humanity, or genocide—crimes that are notoriously difficult to prosecute. The effort to hold PMCs to account is further complicated by the fact that these groups usually enter into immunity agreements with the contracting states.

A number of conventions on mercenaries are generally applicable to PMCs, including the International Convention against the Recruitment, Use, Financing, and Training of Mercenaries (ICRUFTM), Protocol (I) Addition to the Geneva Conventions, and the Organization of African Unity's Convention on the Elimination of Mercenarism in Africa (Riordan 1989; OAU Convention 1977). One attempt to subject private security and military companies to a code of conduct is the Montreux Document, adopted in September 2008 and signed by 58 states by 2021, but not by Russia, Israel and Turkey (ICRC 2020). However, as is the case the majority of such documents, it is not binding under international law. As "armed formations" are illegal under the Constitution and the Criminal Code in Russia, PMCs have been seeking legal regulation of their status since 2017 (Khodarenok 2017). Russian commercial security companies have an interest in distinguishing themselves from mercenaries or terrorists.

Russia's Corporate Warriors

Although the Wagner Group received the most media attention, there are almost a dozen other Russian private security or military companies on the market.6 The RSB Group, MAR, Shchit (Щит =

---

6 The following overview does not claim to be exhaustive, but serves to illustrate the scope of services offered.

'shield'), Moran Security Group, Patriot, Redut-Antiterror (Center R) and Antiterror-Orel are among the most well-known of these. The RSB Group (Russkaya Slushba Bezopasnosti, the Russian Security Service) offers protection from 'military-terrorist operations'[7]. It advertises its services as respecting relevant UN Security Council resolutions and the UN Charter and adhering to the international 'Code of Conduct for Private Security Companies'. RSB specializes in protection against Somali pirates, hostage rescue and espionage.

Several Russian military companies are active in Syria. One of them is Shchit, which was established in 2018 and is based in Kubinka near Moscow — very close to a unit of the Special Airborne Forces (Spetsnaz). Its task in Syria was to guard facilities and infrastructure belonging to Stroytransgaz a company owned by an acquaintance of Vladimir Putin, the oligarch Gennady Timchenko. Stroytransgaz has interests in the Al Sharqiya phosphate mines near Palmyra, two gas processing plants, and a gas pipeline. Shchit was also apparently involved in combat operations, with the deaths of three Shchit employees reported in July 2019.[8] Apparently, Shchit transmogrified into the PMC Redut after 2019.

According to Igor Girkin, an ex-officer of the GRU military intelligence agency who rose to prominence during the 2014 annexation of Crimea and the Russian-fueled war in the Donbas, the Redut company is also operating in Syria to protect Gennady Timchenko's subsidiaries.[9] The Patriot company operates in Syria as well, allegedly under the direct control of Russian Defense Minister Shoigu. The military company Antiterror-Orel is one of the oldest such companies in Russia. It was founded by reservists and veterans of

---

7   See the front page of RSB's website: https://rsb-group.org/about.
8   Chastnaya armiya „Shhit". V Rossii razoblachena eshhe odna ChVK, naemniki kotoriy gibnut v Sirii (Private army 'shield' another PMC exposed in Russia, whose mercenaries are dying in Syria), TSN, 29 July 2019 https://tsn.ua/ru/s vit/chastnaya-armiya-schit-v-rossii-razoblachena-esche-odna-chvk-naemniki-kotoroy-gibnut-v-sirii-1386135.html.
9   "Patriot" i "Redut" Pomimo "Vagnera" v Sirii deystvuyut eshche 2 ChVK iz Rossii' (Patriot' and 'Redoubt' in addition to 'Wagner' in Syria, there are 2 more PMCs from Russia), TRT na russkom, 1 June 2021 https://www.trtrussian.com /novosti-rossiya/patriot-i-redut-pomimo-vagnera-v-sirii-dejstvuyut-eshe-2-c hvk-iz-rossii-5624845.

the GRU and the Navy, as well as by members of the FSB's Vympel Department.[10] Since 1998 it has been engaged in protection of industrial sites and provides military training. The Moran Security Group, originally an offshoot of Orel, advertises on its website that it has been providing security services since 1999.[11] These examples demonstrate the diverse range of services offered by Russian PMCs, the blurred lines between military and mere security services, the formal registration of these companies in Russia and abroad, the frequent provision of security in exchange for the right to exploit natural resources and the pattern of recruitment among former special forces and military veterans.

The Wagner Group

The rise of the Wagner Group exemplified the collaboration between Russia's autocratic regime and organized crime elements, as well as demonstrating Moscow's willingness to sacrifice large numbers of its own combatants on the battlefield. The Wagner Group was the most prominent of Russian state-controlled irregular armed groups, spearheading Russia's aggressive all-out war against Western spheres of influence and its goal of the resurrection of a Russian empire.

The Wagner Group was founded in the spring of 2014 by former Lieutenant-Colonel Dmitry Utkin. Utkin had already worked for the Moran Security Group and had previously been a member of the 2nd Special Reconnaissance Brigade of the Russian military intelligence service GRU and served as a commander of the Slavonic Corps PMC in Syria. (Marten 2019; Hauer 2018; Heinemann-Grüder 2022). As it evolved, the Wagner Group recruited into its ranks former members of the Slavonic Corps, the GRU, the Russian Airborne Forces (VDV), various Spetsnaz units, and former Ministry of Defense staff. This force was initially assembled to provide

---

10 "V for „Vympel": FSB's Secretive Department "V" behind assassination of Georgian asylum seeker in Germany', Bellingcat, 17 February 2020 https://www.bellingcat.com/news/uk-and-europe/2020/02/17/v-like-vympel-fsbs-secretive-department-v-behind-assassination-of-zelimkhan-khangoshvili/.
11 See the MSG website: http://moran-group.org/en/about/index.

military support to the separatists in Ukraine's Donbas region and later on for ensuring strict vertical subordination of separatist field commanders under the military command of Moscow, extending to the punishment and killing of commanders deemed defiant or disobedient.

The Wagner Group has been active in Ukraine, Syria, Sudan, South Sudan, Libya, the Central African Republic, Madagascar and Mozambique, Botswana, Burundi, Chad, DR Congo, Congo-Brazzaville, Guinea, Guinea-Bissau, Nigeria, Zimbabwe, and the Comoros Islands. Wagner operated under the aegis of the GRU, which equipped, trained, and commanded it—despite Wagner's regular rows with the Ministry of Defense (MoD) over the provision of heavy weapons, ammunition, and logistical support. Frictions with the MoD existed over tactics too, but the Wagner Group offered two crucial benefits for the Kremlin—its casualties were domestically invisible, and it compensated for the deficits of the regular army. In early 2016, the Wagner Group numbered about 1 000 operatives. In August 2017, this number had reportedly grown to 5 000, and in December 2017 it had risen to about 6 000[12]. In January 2023, a Ukrainian news agency, referring to British sources, estimated the number of Wagner combatants in Ukraine at 50 000 men.[13] The exact numbers were difficult to assess however, as mercenaries signed temporary contracts and rotated after deployments. Furthermore, a substantial number of Wagner combatants have been killed or severely wounded during the war against Ukraine. Fighters enlisted in the Wagner Group included convicts, mostly murderers and violent offenders, who since the summer of 2022 have been recruited directly from penal colonies for deployment to the frontline in

---

12　Glava apparata SBU Igor Guslıkov: kto nam "slivaet" informatsiyu o boevikakh "Vagnera"? Ya ne mogu raskryvat nashi istochniki v FSB (The head of the SBU apparatus. Igor Guskov: who is 'leaking' information about Wagner militants to us? I can't reveal our sources in the FSB), in: Ukrajins'ki Novini, 8 October 2018, https://ukranews.com/interview/2063-ygor-guskov-kto-nam-slyvaet-ynformacyyu-o-boevykakh-vagnera-ya-ne-mogu-raskryvat-nashy-ystochny ky-v.

13　https://www.unian.net/war/britanskaya-razvedka-podschitala-chislo-boev ikov-chvk-vagner-v-ukraine-12115905.html.

Ukraine, in exchange for promised pardons and amnesties. Estimates of the number of recruited convicts range from 20 000 to 50 000.[14] These convicts, with few exceptions, were used as cannon fodder.

Wagner in Ukraine

In early May 2014, the Wagner Group helped separatist forces overcome Ukrainian security forces, take control of local municipal administrations and towns, seize ammunition depots and conduct reconnaissance. Wagner mercenaries also meted out retribution in the "Luhansk People's Republic" against wayward pro-Russian battalions.[15] In Ukraine, the Wagner Group practiced what it had learnt in Syria and Africa: ruthless, indiscriminate murder. The Wagner Group was involved in the shooting down of a Ukrainian military aircraft in June 2014, the storming of both Luhansk airport and Debaltseve, as well as, in 2022, the massacre committed in the town of Bucha. From August 2022 onwards, the siege and capture of the cities of Soledar and Bakhmut in Donbas was conducted by Wagner troops. The Wagner Group suffered severe losses. Ukrainian estimates claim the loss of up to 40 000 Wagner combatants, figures that cannot be independently confirmed.[16]

Wagner in Syria

After Wagner proved its worth in Donbas, the Group joined Russia's military intervention in Syria in September 2015 (Gabidullin 2022; Al-Atrush / Pitel 2022; Syrian Center for Media 2022; Gibbons-Neff 2018). In Syria Yevgeniy Prigozhin, who controlled the

---

14 Kevin Liptak, US believes Wagner mercenary group is expanding influence and took delivery of North Korean arms, CNN, 22 December 2022, https://edition.cnn.com/europe/live-news/russia-ukraine-war-news-12-22-22/h_436bd7e67edbcf6307b6432165f9bffa.

15 ChVK Vagnera razoruzhaet brigadu Odesa (PMC Wagner disarms the Odesa brigade), Agentstvo Voenkor.Info, 10 January 2015, https://web.archive.org/web/20160915101646/http://voenkor.info/content/5570.

16 Wagner Group loses about two-thirds of its personnel in battles for Bakhmut and Soledar, Ukrinform, 18 January 2023 (https://www.ukrinform.net/rubric-ato/3655038-wagner-group-loses-about-twothirds-of-its-personnel-in-battles-for-bakhmut-and-soledar-expert.html.

oil company Evro Polis, was involved in recapturing occupied oil and gas fields on behalf of the Syrian Energy Ministry. 25 percent of the profits from the oil and gas fields went to Evro Polis after their liberation from Islamic State (IS) control. The Wagner Group fought with over 1.000 fighters in Syria where it still operates. Equipped and armed by the Russian Ministry of Defense and supported from the air by Russian fighter aircraft, the Wagner mercenaries did the 'dirty work' against the Islamic State and Syrian opposition groups on the ground. The Wagner Group deployed its forces as shock and awe troops. Wagner also trained and recruited local combatants and commanded anti-insurgency operations. In countries such as Syria, Libya, Mali or the Central African Republic, the Wagner Group has been maintaining autocratic regimes in power or assists putschists to gain power.

Wagner in Libya

In 2020, Wagner fighters, financed in part by the United Arab Emirates (UAE), supported General Khalif Haftar's forces in Libya. According to information provided by the chairman of the Libyan "High Council of State", Khalid al-Mishri, in December 2021, at times as many as 7.000 Wagner fighters have been deployed in Libya, with 30 combat aircraft at their disposal.[17] However, these figures should be treated with caution. A UN investigative report covering the period from March 2021 to April 2022 proved that the Wagner Group violated international law in supporting Khalif Haftar. By the spring of 2022, approximately 900 of the previously 2.200 Wagner combatants were believed to remain in Libya—the rest having been withdrawn to fight in Ukraine (Erteima 2022).

Wagner in Sub-Saharan Africa

PMCs are part of a broader strategy to reclaim Russian influence in Africa (Haidara 2022). Wagner mercenaries had been deployed to

---

17 Over 7.000 Russian mercenaries still in Libya: Al-Mishri', in: Daily Sabah, 12 December 2021, https://www.dailysabah.com/world/africa/over-7000-russian-mercenaries-still-in-libya-al-mishri.

Sudan, the Central African Republic (CAR), Madagascar, Libya, Mali, and Mozambique as of 2017. By the end of 2019, the Wagner Group already had an office in 20 African countries. In September 2019, Wagner sent between 160 and 200 of its personnel to Mozambique to subdue the insurgency of the so-called Central African Province of the Islamic State (IS-CAP) on behalf of the incumbent government. However, the inability of the Wagner force to combat the IS-CAP insurgency led to a humiliating withdrawal in December 2019.

After a 2017 meeting between President Putin and Omar al-Bashir, then president of Sudan, in Sochi, security cooperation between Russia and Sudan picked up steam. In late July, 500 Wagner fighters appeared on the border between Sudan and the CAR. The 2021 military coup in Sudan that had replaced the interim civilian government was supported by the Russian government, with Wagner mercenaries quashing anti-government protests.[18] According to Samuel Ramani, author of a book on Wagner in Africa, the Wagner Group later on switched sides and supported the insurgent General al-Burhan. Since April 2023, Wagner allegedly sides with the Rapid Support Forces (RSF) that fight against the troops of General al-Burhan, who is now the country's *de facto* leader (Ramani 2023). Meanwhile, Prigozhin had denied that Wagner troops had been present in Sudan after 2021 (Khorton, Mvai, Atanesyan 2023). In Sudan, one of Prigozhin's companies was allowed to export gold from a Sudanese mine.

In April 2023, the Kremlin said that 170 "civilian advisors" had arrived in the Central African Republic (CAR) to train government forces. Back in 2017, the UN Security Council had suspended an arms embargo on the CAR and approved the deployment of 175 Russian trainers for the local military. With the exception of five soldiers, all were Wagner mercenaries. In the CAR, the Wagner Group provided security protection services for President Faustin-

---

18 Russia's Wagner Group helps put down Sudan's anti-government protests', Warsaw Institute, 18 January 2019, https://warsawinstitute.org/russias-wagner-group-helps-put-sudans-anti-government-protests/.

Archange Touadéra. Since December 2020, an additional 300 soldiers from the Russian army have reportedly supported the president against opposition rebels. Russian Special Forces, Wagner mercenaries, and the CAR's pro-government military protected President Touadéra during his presidential election campaign in December 2020 and undertook joint military operations in the Bangui area against insurgent groups. A UN working group on human rights violations by mercenaries accused the Russian mercenaries in the CAR of committing serious human rights abuses along with the pro-government army, including rape, summary executions and targeted killings, torture, enforced disappearances, and murders (Amin 2022).

The presence of the Wagner Group made it considerably more difficult for the UN mission MINUSCA to operate in the CAR, because they restrict the mission's freedom of movement. Since the capture of Boda, the Russian-controlled timber company Bois Rouge has been exporting precious woods from the CAR to Russia on a large scale. The importer in Russia, Broker Expert, is based in St. Petersburg and was a trading partner of Prigozhin's empire. Since at least 2019 companies from Russia have been granted long-term mining licences by the CAR government, particularly for gold and diamond mines in Bambouri, Bornou, and Adji (Olivier 2022).

Wagner in Mali

Russia's intervention in Mali marks the beginning of its military power projection in West Africa. Russia was quick to step in and fill the security vacuum left by President Macron's political defeat in Mali and the subsequent withdrawal of French troops from the country (Haidara 2022). The Wagner mission in the CAR can be interpreted as a blueprint for its operations in Mali. While French units and UN missions have been unable to demonstrate success against Islamist groups for years, Wagner mercenaries claim to resolve conflicts with insurgents within a matter of weeks. Approximately 1.000 Wagner Group fighters have been operating in Mali since the autumn of 2021. Wagner was only able to make inroads in the country due to the failure of the EU training mission in Mali.

During the EU mission, the security situation in Mali deteriorated progressively.

Initially the Wagner Group enjoyed a comparatively good reputation among Malian soldiers—a group of military officers had seized power in Mali in August 2020—because Wagner provided material and food, and its personnel accompanied Malian troops on combat missions. Wagner mercenaries were unperturbed by human rights abuses committed by Malian soldiers. Over time, however, Malian troops have become increasingly disillusioned with the Wagner Group as it has come to dominate joint operations. Moreover, one consequence of the Wagner forces' indiscriminate killing operations was that relatives of villagers who had been arbitrarily killed began to join jihadist groups, thus adding to their numbers. At the end of March 2022, a massacre in Moura, a Malian village with inhabitants from the Peul and Fulani ethnic groups, resulted in the deaths of between 200 and 400 people, and showed that the army and Wagner do not seek to distinguish between jihadists and civilians. On the ground, Wagner is dependent on logistics, enemy reconnaissance by the Malian military, and the Malian military's knowledge of the local language and culture, which makes its forces quite vulnerable. The Wagner Group's approach in Mali is similar to that which it has employed in Ukraine and Syria: it acts as a ruthless killing machine.

The Wagner Group after Prigozhin's Mutiny

On the backdrop of unfulfilled promises of Russia's so called "special operation" against Ukraine and the ensuing heavy military losses, the Wagner Group revolted against the Russian Defense Minister Sergei Shoigu and Chief of General Staff Valery Gerasimov on June 23-24, 2023. Yevgeny Prigozhin, then head of the Wagner Group, occupied with his men military facilities in Rostov-on-Don and advanced with a military convoy on Moscow, meeting almost no resistance from Russia's security forces. Prigozhin had accused the Russian Defense Ministry of launching an attack on the Wagner forces and killing a very large number of its people. He furthermore claimed that Russia was not at all threatened by

Ukraine before the war. He accused the military leadership of deceiving the Russian president and the public and stated that the reports about Russian armed forces' successes were "complete, total nonsense" (Aris 2023; Heinemann-Grüder 2023).

The mutiny of the Wagner group and the killing of its leaders Yevgeniy Prigozhin and Dmitri Utkin on August 23, 2023, shed some sharp light on the modus operandi of Russia's regime and its use of irregular armed groups. The conflict over the conduct of war against Ukraine and the tensions between competing security agencies culminated in the mutiny. Prigozhin had vocally voiced the frustration over military mismanagement, unachievable goals, the disregard for the survival of Russia's soldiers, and the constant spread of lies. He exposed the propaganda about Ukrainians allegedly wanting to be liberated by Russian forces from fascism.

Originally, the Wagner Group had benefitted the Russian regime by the deniability of its operations, its provision of reliable killer troops, its flexibility and the public invisibility of its losses. The Wagner Group was paraded in Russia's political system as a licensed critic of the Ministry of Defense and the General Staff. In this respect, Wagner was an instrument for the Kremlin. Prigozhin could not have criticized the Defense Minister Shoigu without acquiescence from the Kremlin. Under the leadership of Yevgeniy Prigozhin the Wagner Group was primarily interested in commercial gains and the exploitation of natural resources in countries of operation, but its relative autonomy had turned into a liability. The Defense Minister and the Chief of General Staff were keen to stop Prigozhin's spearhead pointed at them. Ultimately, the Defense Minister and the Chief of General Staff provoked Prigozhin to act and Putin to make a choice.

The mutiny and the killing of Wagner's leadership evidence not just the culmination of tensions, but the end of a mode of governance that was characterized by competition between different security agents, the partial outsourcing of the war to mercenaries, the coexistence of regular and irregular armed groups and the commercialization of military services. The Wagner mutiny highlighted the fractures within Russia's security establishment and the partial loss of political control. Putin had preferred to play the security agencies off against each other in order not to be dependent on one agency alone. Wagner's mutiny exposed the risks of this pattern.

The mutiny evidenced a "wag the dog" phenomenon and a deep crisis of legitimacy. While insubordination of the military is quite common in fragile, corrupt and highly polarized countries of the "Global South", the political control over the military had usually been very strong in the Soviet era as well as in post-Soviet Russia. The only exception had been the August putsch in 1991 against the tattered Soviet president Mikhail Gorbachev. Vladimir Putin was thus struck by surprise. He had lost, at least temporarily, control over his own creation—the regular use of irregular armed groups for conducting undeclared wars. The state monopoly of violence visibly crumbled domestically and in face of the outside world. For a short moment the prospect of Putin losing his iron power grip emerged.

Regaining Control

What lessons did the Russian regime draw from the Wagner mutiny and what are the prospects of the Wagner Group and related state-controlled military companies? Putin condemned the insurgency as a betrayal of Russia and had to quickly regain the semblance of still being the only one in command. Observers expected a harsh reprisal. Surprisingly, a deal was initially struck with the Wagner Group after mediation by Belarusian President Alyaksandr Lukashenka. The insurgents had been promised freedom from punishment if they would move to Belarus or subordinate to the command of the Ministry of Defense. Prigozhin would go into exile in Belarus. However, Prigozhin as well as the military leader of the Wagner Group Dmitri Utkin and other Wagner people, died two months later in a plane crash—presumably a targeted killing in order to remove the leadership of the Wagner Group and to regain control over its combatants. The violent removal of Wagner's leadership and the follow-up had first to be professionally prepared, in difference to the messed-up attempted murder of the ex-spy Skripal in Great Britain and the poisoning of Navalny.

Shortly after the mutiny, Andrey Troshev, also known by his call sign "Sedoi", was mentioned in Russian media as the real commander of the Wagner Group,[19] but the official contact point for providing Russia's services in Africa is definitely no longer the leadership of the Wagner Group, but the Russian state. One of the crucial tasks after the killing of Prigozhin was to demonstrate continuity and reliability of Russia's service provision. The Kremlin wants to show that there is a clearly identifiable political direction, and that Russia's mercenaries will continue to exist, yet with less autonomy. The further operation of Russian miliary companies is namely part of Russia's ambitious Africa strategy—it enables the Russian government to assist military putschists, to keep anti-Western governments in power, to seed anti-Western sentiments, to offer arms sales and to exploit natural resources. The Wagner Group thus remains a vital instrument of Russia's power projection in unstable, fractured and anti-Western Asian and African countries. State-controlled military companies such as the Wagner Group train and equip military putschists especially in Africa, conduct indiscriminate killing operations against insurgents, offer media campaigns, provide weapons and ammunition, replace UN-mandated international stabilization missions and function as door-opener for Russian arms sales and investment.

On 16 September Yunus-Bek Evkurov, one of the Russian Deputy Defense Ministers, and Andrey Averianov, an infamous general of the GRU (Russian military intelligence), were to meet political leaders from Mali, Burkina Faso and Niger. The duo had visited Libya, one of the African bases for Wagner's mercenaries, already a day before the plane crash in which Wagner's boss had been killed. Evkurov and Andrei Averianov have one quality in common that sets them apart from Yevgeny Prigozhin—they are loyal and less boastful personalities than the former Wagner boss. Both are taking part in reorganization of Russian operations in Africa.

Evkurov and Averianov held talks with representatives of the countries which the late Prigozhin had last visited. The two Russian

---

19 https://www.reuters.com/world/europe/putin-met-top-wagner-commander-troshev-kremlin-2023-09-29/.

officials indicated to the local authorities that Moscow remains committed to their governments. Evkurov, who had led the violence-ridden republic of Ingushetia in the North Caucasus from 2008 to 2019, is the new face of relations between the Kremlin and African regimes. Averianov in turn is known as head of the GRU's notorious 29155 unit, which specializes in sabotage and assassination. His spies poisoned the ex-double agent Sergei Skripal in 2018, blew up an ammunition depot in the Czech Republic in 2014 and attempted to stage a pro-Serb coup in Montenegro in 2016. Before taking charge of the GRU Uni 29155, Averianov had carried out special operations in Afghanistan, Chechnya and on the Crimea, too.

Take-over of Wagner's Portfolio by Loyal Companies

The Wagner Group has been part of a network of military companies servicing the Russian state. Russian military companies sign contracts with foreign governments. Governments in the Central African Republic, in Sudan, Mali, Burkina Faso or Niger solicit the services of Russian military companies in order to protect their autocratic regimes and to kill insurgents. Russia's military companies train special forces, supply combatants, organize disinformation campaigns and exploit natural resources. The network of businessmen who benefit from Russia's state-sponsored military companies and their web of shell companies is still in existence. There are vested interests in keeping the system in place. The portfolio of the Wagner Group Wagner is taken over, at least in part, by competitors such as Gazprom's private military company or the military company Redut.

Redut has a long history of operating for Russia abroad, it had been created by former employees of the Russian Ministry of Defense, Foreign Intelligence Service and the Russian Special Forces. Redut partially took over the military operations of the Wagner Group in Ukraine and in Syria and Africa. The oligarch. former KGB officer and boss of Redut, Gennady Timchenko, has been recruiting fighters from Wagner. Putin still needs the services originally offered by Wagner.

While the Wagner Group operated in the past as a semi-clandestine action group, Russia is more and more openly demonstrating its support for the autocratic regimes in place. The presence of deputy defense minister Evkurov and GRU general Averianov in African countries embody this evolution. Reducing the former autonomy of the Wagner Group requires some reorganization. Wagner's flexibility and the offer of a broad range of services remain valid. Irregular armed groups will remain useful for the Russian regime. The Russian military establishment will probably even broaden its reliance on irregular forces.

One lesson from Wagner's mutiny is that it is advantageous to have several military companies at ones disposal. Even before the mutiny, the Kremlin therefore strengthened its cooperation with Redut in order to make itself less dependent on Wagner. Russia's state-owned Gazprom set up a private military company, too. The military companies can only be deployed locally, they cannot replace an entire army across the board. In the Ukraine war, they are thus a supplement, but no replacement to the regular armed forces.

Policy Implications

Russia's irregular military companies have become the regime's agents of influence, war profiteers, and an auxiliary force for state security agencies. Russia's military companies are an instrument of Russia's expansionist foreign policy. Its military companies serve to destabilize pro-Western and shore up anti-Western governments. European policymakers should be concerned about the destabilizing impact of Russia's miliary companies, because their presence in conflict-affected regions deepens societal divides, contributes to the recruitment of Islamist militants and undermines efforts to improve governance and security sector reforms.

In order to curb the spread of Russian-sponsored irregular armed groups, the EU might consider offering training courses for policymakers in relevant countries, as well as for the security establishment and the media, on legal standards for private security and military companies. The EU could also consider enhancing intelligence fusion capabilities among its Member States. Moreover it could trace the financial transactions of Russia's corporate warriors and take steps to block such transactions where possible. It could also sponsor fact-finding missions in order to document human rights violations. It could go even further and on the basis of such findings declare the Wagner Group and its successors terrorist organizations. Finally, the EU should consider offering leniency and exemption from prosecution to Wagner ex-combatants who are willing to cooperate in judicial investigations into war crimes.

References

Al-Atrush Samer; Laura Pitel (2022), Russia reduces number of Syrian and Wagner troops in Libya, in: Financial Times 28 April 2022, https://www.ft.com/content/88ab3d20-8a10-4ae2-a4c5-122acd6a8067.

Amin, Mohammed (2022), Syrian fighters participated in Wagner Group massacres in Central African Republic', in: Middle East Eye, 9 June 2022, https://www.middleeasteye.net/news/syria-fighters-wagner-group-attacks-central-african-republic.

Aris, Stephen (2023), The Post-Mutiny Context of Wagner and Private Military Forces in Russia, in: Russian Analytical Digest, No 303, 18 October 2023, pp. 2-3.

Avant, Deborah D. (2005), The Market for Force: The Consequences of Privatizing Security, Cambridge.

Cameron, Lindsay (2006), Private Military Companies: Their status under International Humanitarian Law and its impact on their regulation, in: International Review of the Red Cross, 88/ 863, pp. 573–611.

Chesterman, Simon; Chia Lehnardt (eds.) (2009), From Mercenaries to Market: The rise and regulation of private military companies, Oxford.

Eckert, Amy E. (2016), Outsourcing War: The just war tradition in the age of military privatization, Ithaca, New York.

Erteima, Mohammad (2022), 1,300 Wagner mercenaries sent from Libya to help Russian forces in Ukraine, Anadolu Agency 26 March 2022, https://www.aa.com.tr/en/russia-ukraine-war/1-300-wagner-mercenaries-sent-from-libya-to-help-russian-forces-in-ukraine/2545629.

Gabidullin, Marat (2022), Wagner—Putins geheime Armee: Ein Insiderbericht, Berlin.

Gibbons-Neff, Thomas (2018), How a 4-hour battle between Russian mercenaries and U.S. commandos unfolded in Syria', *New York Times* 24 May 2018 https://www.nytimes.com/2018/05/24/world/middleeast/american-commandos-russian-mercenaries-syria.html.

Haidara, Boubacar (2022), Analyse: Pourquoi Wagner prospère, in: New African, 17 February 2022, https://magazinedelafrique.com/politique/analyse-pourquoi-wagner-prospere/.

Haidara, Boubacar (2022), The private military company Wagner, the instrument of a proxy war by Russia against France in its African 'pre-square'?, in: M. Korinman (ed.), Le nouveau rideau de fer, Paris, pp. 393–416.

Hauer, Neil (2018), Russia's Favorite Mercenaries, in: The Atlantic, 27 August 2018, https://www.theatlantic.com/international/archive/2018/08/russian-mercenaries-wagner-africa/568435/.

Heinemann-Grüder, Andreas (2022), Russlands irreguläre Armeen. Das Beispiel "Wagner", in: Osteuropa, 72/11, pp. 127-155.

Heinemann-Grüder, Andreas (2023), Dogs of War. Russia's corporate warriors in armed conflicts, European Union Institute for Security Studies, Brief 10, June 2023, https://www.iss.europa.eu/sites/default/files/EUISSFiles/Brief_10_Private%20military%20companies%20%281%29.pdf.

Heinemann-Grüder, Andreas (2023), The Wagner Group after Prigozhin, in: Russian Analytical Digest, No 303, 18 October 2023, pp. 4-6.

International Committee of the Red Cross (ICRC) (2020), The Montreux Document on Private Military and Security Companies, 11 June 2020, https://www.icrc.org/en/publication/0996-montreux-document-private-military-and-security-companies.

Jones, Seth G.; catrina Doxsee; Brian Katz (2021), Russia's Corporate Soldiers: The Global Expansion of Russia's Private Military Companies, Center for Strategic & International Studies, July 2021, https://www.csis.org/analysis/russias-corporate-soldiers-global-expansion-russias-private-military-companies.

Khodarenok, M., Chastnye armii zhelayut uzakonitsja. Na kakikh osnovanijakh rabotayut rossijskie ChVK (Private armies wish to become legalised. The basis of the work of Russian PMCs), 26 July 2017 www.gazeta.ru/army/2017/06/26/10736969.shtml.

Khorton, Dzheyk, Piter Mvai, Grigor Atanesyan (2023), Chem ChVK "Vagner" zanimaetsya v Sudane' (What PMC 'Wagner' does in Sudan), BBC News, 24 April 2023 https://www.bbc.com/russian/features-65371266.

Liu, Hin-Yan (2010), Leashing the Corporate Dogs of War: The Legal Implications of the Modern Private Military Company, in: Journal of Conflict and Security Law, 15/1, pp. 141–168.

Mandel, Robert (2022), Armies without States: The Privatization of Security, Boulder.

Marten, Kimberly (2019), Russia's Use of Semi-state Security Forces: The Case of the Wagner Group, in: Post-Soviet Affairs, 35/3, pp. 181–204.

Médecins Sans Frontières, Private Military Companies: Overview of the phenomenon, https://guide-humanitarian-law.org/content/article/3/private-military-companies/.

OAU Convention for the Elimination of Mercenarism in Africa, Libreville, 3rd July 1977', International Humanitarian Law Databases, https://ihl-databases.icrc.org/en/ihl-treaties/oau-mercenarism-1977.

Olivier, Mathieu (2022), Café, cash et alcool: au cœur du système Wagner, de Douala à Bangui, in: Jeune Afrique, 12 August 2022, https://www.jeuneafrique.com/1369001/politique/cafe-cash-et-alcool-au-coeur-du-systeme-wagner-de-douala-a-bangui/.

Ramani, Samuel (2023), Russia in Africa: Resurgent Great Power or Bellicose Pretender? London.

Riordan, Kevin (2021), International Convention against the recruitment, use, financing and training of mercenaries', General Assembly resolution 44/34, New York, 4 December 1989 https://legal.un.org/avl/ha/icruftm/icruftm.html.

Singer, Peter W. (2001/2002), Corporate Warriors: The rise of the privatized military industry and its ramifications for international security, in: International Security, 26/3, pp. 186–220.

Syrian Center for Media and Freedom of Expression (SCM), Wagner in Syria: Complaint filed with European Court of Human Rights following the dismissal of the case in Russia, 9 June 2022 https://www.fidh.org/IMG/pdf/wagner-cedh-q_a-en.pdf.

Yoshua, Yaffa (2023), Inside the Wagner Group's Uprising, in: The New Yorker, July 31, 2023,

Contributors

M.A. Kostiantyn Fedorenko, PhD candidate at *Zentrum für Osteuropäische und internationale Studien* (ZOIS) Berlin

M.A Julia Friedrich, research fellow at Global Public Policy Institute, Berlin

Prof. Dr Andreas Heinemann-Grüder, Centre for Advanced Security, Strategic and Integration Studies (CASSIS) and professor of Political Science at the University of Bonn

Dr Vyacheslav Likhachev, Ukraine Human Rights Associate at Fortify Rights; former Senior Fellow at UN Human Rights Monitoring Mission

B.A. Theresa Lütkefend, Non-resident fellow at Global Public Policy Institute, Berlin

Dr Nikolay Mitrokhin, Associate research fellow at *Forschungsstelle Osteuropa* at University of Bremen

Dr Natalia Savelyeva, Resident Fellow at the Center for European Policy Analysis, University of Wisconsin-Madison

Dr Anton Shekhovtsov, Director of the Centre for Democratic Integrity, Vienna

Colonel Leonid Poliakov, former First Deputy Minister of Defense of Ukraine

Dr Andreas Umland, Analyst at the Stockholm Centre for Eastern European Studies (SCEEUS) at the Swedish Institute of International Affairs

SOVIET AND POST-SOVIET POLITICS AND SOCIETY
Edited by Dr. Andreas Umland | ISSN 1614-3515

1 *Андреас Умланд (ред.)* | Воплощение Европейской конвенции по правам человека в России. Философские, юридические и эмпирические исследования | ISBN 3-89821-387-0

2 *Christian Wipperfürth* | Russland – ein vertrauenswürdiger Partner? Grundlagen, Hintergründe und Praxis gegenwärtiger russischer Außenpolitik | Mit einem Vorwort von Heinz Timmermann | ISBN 3-89821-401-X

3 *Manja Hussner* | Die Übernahme internationalen Rechts in die russische und deutsche Rechtsordnung. Eine vergleichende Analyse zur Völkerrechtsfreundlichkeit der Verfassungen der Russländischen Föderation und der Bundesrepublik Deutschland | Mit einem Vorwort von Rainer Arnold | ISBN 3-89821-438-9

4 *Matthew Tejada* | Bulgaria's Democratic Consolidation and the Kozloduy Nuclear Power Plant (KNPP). The Unattainability of Closure | With a foreword by Richard J. Crampton | ISBN 3-89821-439-7

5 *Марк Григорьевич Меерович* | Квадратные метры, определяющие сознание. Государственная жилищная политика в СССР. 1921 – 1941 гг | ISBN 3-89821-474-5

6 *Andrei P. Tsygankov, Pavel A. Tsygankov (Eds.)* | New Directions in Russian International Studies | ISBN 3-89821-422-2

7 *Марк Григорьевич Меерович* | Как власть народ к труду приучала. Жилище в СССР – средство управления людьми. 1917 – 1941 гг. | С предисловием Елены Осокиной | ISBN 3-89821-495-8

8 *David J. Galbreath* | Nation-Building and Minority Politics in Post-Socialist States. Interests, Influence and Identities in Estonia and Latvia | With a foreword by David J. Smith | ISBN 3-89821-467-2

9 *Алексей Юрьевич Безугольный* | Народы Кавказа в Вооруженных силах СССР в годы Великой Отечественной войны 1941-1945 гг. | С предисловием Николая Бугая | ISBN 3-89821-475-3

10 *Вячеслав Лихачев и Владимир Прибыловский (ред.)* | Русское Национальное Единство, 1990-2000. В 2-х томах | ISBN 3-89821-523-7

11 *Николай Бугай (ред.)* | Народы стран Балтии в условиях сталинизма (1940-е – 1950-е годы). Документированная история | ISBN 3-89821-525-3

12 *Ingmar Bredies (Hrsg.)* | Zur Anatomie der Orange Revolution in der Ukraine. Wechsel des Elitenregimes oder Triumph des Parlamentarismus? | ISBN 3-89821-524-5

13 *Anastasia V. Mitrofanova* | The Politicization of Russian Orthodoxy. Actors and Ideas | With a foreword by William C. Gay | ISBN 3-89821-481-8

14 *Nathan D. Larson* | Alexander Solzhenitsyn and the Russo-Jewish Question | ISBN 3-89821-483-4

15 *Guido Houben* | Kulturpolitik und Ethnizität. Staatliche Kunstförderung im Russland der neunziger Jahre | Mit einem Vorwort von Gert Weisskirchen | ISBN 3-89821-542-3

16 *Leonid Luks* | Der russische „Sonderweg"? Aufsätze zur neuesten Geschichte Russlands im europäischen Kontext | ISBN 3-89821-496-6

17 *Евгений Мороз* | История «Мёртвой воды» – от страшной сказки к большой политике. Политическое неоязычество в постсоветской России | ISBN 3-89821-551-2

18 *Александр Верховский и Галина Кожевникова (ред.)* | Этническая и религиозная интолерантность в российских СМИ. Результаты мониторинга 2001-2004 гг. | ISBN 3-89821-569-5

19 *Christian Ganzer* | Sowjetisches Erbe und ukrainische Nation. Das Museum der Geschichte des Zaporoger Kosakentums auf der Insel Chortycja | Mit einem Vorwort von Frank Golczewski | ISBN 3-89821-504-0

20 *Эльза-Баир Гучинова* | Помнить нельзя забыть. Антропология депортационной травмы калмыков | С предисловием Кэролайн Хамфри | ISBN 3-89821-506-7

21 *Юлия Лидерман* | Мотивы «проверки» и «испытания» в постсоветской культуре. Советское прошлое в российском кинематографе 1990-х годов | С предисловием Евгения Марголита | ISBN 3-89821-511-3

22 *Tanya Lokshina, Ray Thomas, Mary Mayer (Eds.)* | The Imposition of a Fake Political Settlement in the Northern Caucasus. The 2003 Chechen Presidential Election | ISBN 3-89821-436-2

23 *Timothy McCajor Hall, Rosie Read (Eds.)* | Changes in the Heart of Europe. Recent Ethnographies of Czechs, Slovaks, Roma, and Sorbs | With an afterword by Zdeněk Salzmann | ISBN 3-89821-606-5

24 Christian Autengruber | Die politischen Parteien in Bulgarien und Rumänien. Eine vergleichende Analyse seit Beginn der 90er Jahre | Mit einem Vorwort von Dorothée de Nève | ISBN 3-89821-476-1

25 Annette Freyberg-Inan with Radu Cristescu | The Ghosts in Our Classrooms, or: John Dewey Meets Ceauşescu. The Promise and the Failures of Civic Education in Romania | ISBN 3-89821-416-8

26 John B. Dunlop | The 2002 Dubrovka and 2004 Beslan Hostage Crises. A Critique of Russian Counter-Terrorism | With a foreword by Donald N. Jensen | ISBN 3-89821-608-X

27 Peter Koller | Das touristische Potenzial von Kam"janec'–Podil's'kyj. Eine fremdenverkehrsgeographische Untersuchung der Zukunftsperspektiven und Maßnahmenplanung zur Destinationsentwicklung des „ukrainischen Rothenburg" | Mit einem Vorwort von Kristiane Klemm | ISBN 3-89821-640-3

28 Françoise Daucé, Elisabeth Sieca-Kozlowski (Eds.) | Dedovshchina in the Post-Soviet Military. Hazing of Russian Army Conscripts in a Comparative Perspective | With a foreword by Dale Herspring | ISBN 3-89821-616-0

29 Florian Strasser | Zivilgesellschaftliche Einflüsse auf die Orange Revolution. Die gewaltlose Massenbewegung und die ukrainische Wahlkrise 2004 | Mit einem Vorwort von Egbert Jahn | ISBN 3-89821-648-9

30 Rebecca S. Katz | The Georgian Regime Crisis of 2003-2004. A Case Study in Post-Soviet Media Representation of Politics, Crime and Corruption | ISBN 3-89821-413-3

31 Vladimir Kantor | Willkür oder Freiheit. Beiträge zur russischen Geschichtsphilosophie | Ediert von Dagmar Herrmann sowie mit einem Vorwort versehen von Leonid Luks | ISBN 3-89821-589-X

32 Laura A. Victoir | The Russian Land Estate Today. A Case Study of Cultural Politics in Post-Soviet Russia | With a foreword by Priscilla Roosevelt | ISBN 3-89821-426-5

33 Ivan Katchanovski | Cleft Countries. Regional Political Divisions and Cultures in Post-Soviet Ukraine and Moldova | With a foreword by Francis Fukuyama | ISBN 3-89821-558-X

34 Florian Mühlfried | Postsowjetische Feiern. Das Georgische Bankett im Wandel | Mit einem Vorwort von Kevin Tuite | ISBN 3-89821-601-2

35 Roger Griffin, Werner Loh, Andreas Umland (Eds.) | Fascism Past and Present, West and East. An International Debate on Concepts and Cases in the Comparative Study of the Extreme Right | With an afterword by Walter Laqueur | ISBN 3-89821-674-8

36 Sebastian Schlegel | Der „Weiße Archipel". Sowjetische Atomstädte 1945-1991 | Mit einem Geleitwort von Thomas Bohn | ISBN 3-89821-679-9

37 Vyacheslav Likhachev | Political Anti-Semitism in Post-Soviet Russia. Actors and Ideas in 1991-2003 | Edited and translated from Russian by Eugene Veklerov | ISBN 3-89821-529-6

38 Josette Baer (Ed.) | Preparing Liberty in Central Europe. Political Texts from the Spring of Nations 1848 to the Spring of Prague 1968 | With a foreword by Zdeněk V. David | ISBN 3-89821-546-2

39 Михаил Лукьянов | Российский консерватизм и реформа, 1907-1914 | С предисловием Марка Д. Стейнберга | ISBN 3-89821-503-2

40 Nicola Melloni | Market Without Economy. The 1998 Russian Financial Crisis | With a foreword by Eiji Furukawa | ISBN 3-89821-407-9

41 Dmitrij Chmelnizki | Die Architektur Stalins | Bd. 1: Studien zu Ideologie und Stil | Bd. 2: Bilddokumentation | Mit einem Vorwort von Bruno Flierl | ISBN 3-89821-515-6

42 Katja Yafimava | Post-Soviet Russian-Belarussian Relationships. The Role of Gas Transit Pipelines | With a foreword by Jonathan P. Stern | ISBN 3-89821-655-1

43 Boris Chavkin | Verflechtungen der deutschen und russischen Zeitgeschichte. Aufsätze und Archivfunde zu den Beziehungen Deutschlands und der Sowjetunion von 1917 bis 1991 | Ediert von Markus Edlinger sowie mit einem Vorwort versehen von Leonid Luks | ISBN 3-89821-756-6

44 Anastasija Grynenko in Zusammenarbeit mit Claudia Dathe | Die Terminologie des Gerichtswesens der Ukraine und Deutschlands im Vergleich. Eine übersetzungswissenschaftliche Analyse juristischer Fachbegriffe im Deutschen, Ukrainischen und Russischen | Mit einem Vorwort von Ulrich Hartmann | ISBN 3-89821-691-8

45 Anton Burkov | The Impact of the European Convention on Human Rights on Russian Law. Legislation and Application in 1996-2006 | With a foreword by Françoise Hampson | ISBN 978-3-89821-639-5

46 Stina Torjesen, Indra Overland (Eds.) | International Election Observers in Post-Soviet Azerbaijan. Geopolitical Pawns or Agents of Change? | ISBN 978-3-89821-743-9

47 Taras Kuzio | Ukraine – Crimea – Russia. Triangle of Conflict | ISBN 978-3-89821-761-3

48 Claudia Šabić | „Ich erinnere mich nicht, aber L'viv!" Zur Funktion kultureller Faktoren für die Institutionalisierung und Entwicklung einer ukrainischen Region | Mit einem Vorwort von Melanie Tatur | ISBN 978-3-89821-752-0

49 *Marlies Bilz* | Tatarstan in der Transformation. Nationaler Diskurs und Politische Praxis 1988-1994 | Mit einem Vorwort von Frank Golczewski | ISBN 978-3-89821-722-4

50 *Марлен Ларюэль (ред.)* | Современные интерпретации русского национализма | ISBN 978-3-89821-795-8

51 *Sonja Schüler* | Die ethnische Dimension der Armut. Roma im postsozialistischen Rumänien | Mit einem Vorwort von Anton Sterbling | ISBN 978-3-89821-776-7

52 *Галина Кожевникова* | Радикальный национализм в России и противодействие ему. Сборник докладов Центра «Сова» за 2004-2007 гг. | С предисловием Александра Верховского | ISBN 978-3-89821-721-7

53 *Галина Кожевникова и Владимир Прибыловский* | Российская власть в биографиях I. Высшие должностные лица РФ в 2004 г. | ISBN 978-3-89821-796-5

54 *Галина Кожевникова и Владимир Прибыловский* | Российская власть в биографиях II. Члены Правительства РФ в 2004 г. | ISBN 978-3-89821-797-2

55 *Галина Кожевникова и Владимир Прибыловский* | Российская власть в биографиях III. Руководители федеральных служб и агентств РФ в 2004 г. | ISBN 978-3-89821-798-9

56 *Ileana Petroniu* | Privatisierung in Transformationsökonomien. Determinanten der Restrukturierungs-Bereitschaft am Beispiel Polens, Rumäniens und der Ukraine | Mit einem Vorwort von Rainer W. Schäfer | ISBN 978-3-89821-790-3

57 *Christian Wipperfürth* | Russland und seine GUS-Nachbarn. Hintergründe, aktuelle Entwicklungen und Konflikte in einer ressourcenreichen Region| ISBN 978-3-89821-801-6

58 *Togzhan Kassenova* | From Antagonism to Partnership. The Uneasy Path of the U.S.-Russian Cooperative Threat Reduction | With a foreword by Christoph Bluth | ISBN 978-3-89821-707-1

59 *Alexander Höllwerth* | Das sakrale eurasische Imperium des Aleksandr Dugin. Eine Diskursanalyse zum postsowjetischen russischen Rechtsextremismus | Mit einem Vorwort von Dirk Uffelmann | ISBN 978-3-89821-813-9

60 *Олег Рябов* | «Россия-Матушка». Национализм, гендер и война в России XX века | С предисловием Елены Гощило | ISBN 978-3-89821-487-2

61 *Ivan Maistrenko* | Borot'bism. A Chapter in the History of the Ukrainian Revolution | With a new Introduction by Chris Ford | Translated by George S. N. Luckyj with the assistance of Ivan L. Rudnytsky | Second, Revised and Expanded Edition ISBN 978-3-8382-1107-7

62 *Maryna Romanets* | Anamorphosic Texts and Reconfigured Visions. Improvised Traditions in Contemporary Ukrainian and Irish Literature | ISBN 978-3-89821-576-3

63 *Paul D'Anieri and Taras Kuzio (Eds.)* | Aspects of the Orange Revolution I. Democratization and Elections in Post-Communist Ukraine | ISBN 978-3-89821-698-2

64 *Bohdan Harasymiw in collaboration with Oleh S. Ilnytzkyj (Eds.)* | Aspects of the Orange Revolution II. Information and Manipulation Strategies in the 2004 Ukrainian Presidential Elections | ISBN 978-3-89821-699-9

65 *Ingmar Bredies, Andreas Umland and Valentin Yakushik (Eds.)* | Aspects of the Orange Revolution III. The Context and Dynamics of the 2004 Ukrainian Presidential Elections | ISBN 978-3-89821-803-0

66 *Ingmar Bredies, Andreas Umland and Valentin Yakushik (Eds.)* | Aspects of the Orange Revolution IV. Foreign Assistance and Civic Action in the 2004 Ukrainian Presidential Elections | ISBN 978-3-89821-808-5

67 *Ingmar Bredies, Andreas Umland and Valentin Yakushik (Eds.)* | Aspects of the Orange Revolution V. Institutional Observation Reports on the 2004 Ukrainian Presidential Elections | ISBN 978-3-89821-809-2

68 *Taras Kuzio (Ed.)* | Aspects of the Orange Revolution VI. Post-Communist Democratic Revolutions in Comparative Perspective | ISBN 978-3-89821-820-7

69 *Tim Bohse* | Autoritarismus statt Selbstverwaltung. Die Transformation der kommunalen Politik in der Stadt Kaliningrad 1990-2005 | Mit einem Geleitwort von Stefan Troebst | ISBN 978-3-89821-782-8

70 *David Rupp* | Die Rußländische Föderation und die russischsprachige Minderheit in Lettland. Eine Fallstudie zur Anwaltspolitik Moskaus gegenüber den russophonen Minderheiten im „Nahen Ausland" von 1991 bis 2002 | Mit einem Vorwort von Helmut Wagner | ISBN 978-3-89821-778-1

71 *Taras Kuzio* | Theoretical and Comparative Perspectives on Nationalism. New Directions in Cross-Cultural and Post-Communist Studies | With a foreword by Paul Robert Magocsi | ISBN 978-3-89821-815-3

72 *Christine Teichmann* | Die Hochschultransformation im heutigen Osteuropa. Kontinuität und Wandel bei der Entwicklung des postkommunistischen Universitätswesens | Mit einem Vorwort von Oskar Anweiler | ISBN 978-3-89821-842-9

73　*Julia Kusznir* | Der politische Einfluss von Wirtschaftseliten in russischen Regionen. Eine Analyse am Beispiel der Erdöl- und Erdgasindustrie, 1992-2005 | Mit einem Vorwort von Wolfgang Eichwede | ISBN 978-3-89821-821-4

74　*Alena Vysotskaya* | Russland, Belarus und die EU-Osterweiterung. Zur Minderheitenfrage und zum Problem der Freizügigkeit des Personenverkehrs | Mit einem Vorwort von Katlijn Malfliet | ISBN 978-3-89821-822-1

75　*Heiko Pleines (Hrsg.)* | Corporate Governance in post-sozialistischen Volkswirtschaften | ISBN 978-3-89821-766-8

76　*Stefan Ihrig* | Wer sind die Moldawier? Rumänismus versus Moldowanismus in Historiographie und Schulbüchern der Republik Moldova, 1991-2006 | Mit einem Vorwort von Holm Sundhaussen | ISBN 978-3-89821-466-7

77　*Galina Kozhevnikova in collaboration with Alexander Verkhovsky and Eugene Veklerov* | Ultra-Nationalism and Hate Crimes in Contemporary Russia. The 2004-2006 Annual Reports of Moscow's SOVA Center | With a foreword by Stephen D. Shenfield | ISBN 978-3-89821-868-9

78　*Florian Küchler* | The Role of the European Union in Moldova's Transnistria Conflict | With a foreword by Christopher Hill | ISBN 978-3-89821-850-4

79　*Bernd Rechel* | The Long Way Back to Europe. Minority Protection in Bulgaria | With a foreword by Richard Crampton | ISBN 978-3-89821-863-4

80　*Peter W. Rodgers* | Nation, Region and History in Post-Communist Transitions. Identity Politics in Ukraine, 1991-2006 | With a foreword by Vera Tolz | ISBN 978-3-89821-903-7

81　*Stephanie Solywoda* | The Life and Work of Semen L. Frank. A Study of Russian Religious Philosophy | With a foreword by Philip Walters | ISBN 978-3-89821-457-5

82　*Vera Sokolova* | Cultural Politics of Ethnicity. Discourses on Roma in Communist Czechoslovakia | ISBN 978-3-89821-864-1

83　*Natalya Shevchik Ketenci* | Kazakhstani Enterprises in Transition. The Role of Historical Regional Development in Kazakhstan's Post-Soviet Economic Transformation | ISBN 978-3-89821-831-3

84　*Martin Malek, Anna Schor-Tschudnowskaja (Hgg.)* | Europa im Tschetschenienkrieg. Zwischen politischer Ohnmacht und Gleichgültigkeit | Mit einem Vorwort von Lipchan Basajewa | ISBN 978-3-89821-676-0

85　*Stefan Meister* | Das postsowjetische Universitätswesen zwischen nationalem und internationalem Wandel. Die Entwicklung der regionalen Hochschule in Russland als Gradmesser der Systemtransformation | Mit einem Vorwort von Joan DeBardeleben | ISBN 978-3-89821-891-7

86　*Konstantin Sheiko in collaboration with Stephen Brown* | Nationalist Imaginings of the Russian Past. Anatolii Fomenko and the Rise of Alternative History in Post-Communist Russia | With a foreword by Donald Ostrowski | ISBN 978-3-89821-915-0

87　*Sabine Jenni* | Wie stark ist das „Einige Russland"? Zur Parteibindung der Eliten und zum Wahlerfolg der Machtpartei im Dezember 2007 | Mit einem Vorwort von Klaus Armingeon | ISBN 978-3-89821-961-7

88　*Thomas Borén* | Meeting-Places of Transformation. Urban Identity, Spatial Representations and Local Politics in Post-Soviet St Petersburg | ISBN 978-3-89821-739-2

89　*Aygul Ashirova* | Stalinismus und Stalin-Kult in Zentralasien. Turkmenistan 1924-1953 | Mit einem Vorwort von Leonid Luks | ISBN 978-3-89821-987-7

90　*Leonid Luks* | Freiheit oder imperiale Größe? Essays zu einem russischen Dilemma | ISBN 978-3-8382-0011-8

91　*Christopher Gilley* | The 'Change of Signposts' in the Ukrainian Emigration. A Contribution to the History of Sovietophilism in the 1920s | With a foreword by Frank Golczewski | ISBN 978-3-89821-965-5

92　*Philipp Casula, Jeronim Perovic (Eds.)* | Identities and Politics During the Putin Presidency. The Discursive Foundations of Russia's Stability | With a foreword by Heiko Haumann | ISBN 978-3-8382-0015-6

93　*Marcel Viëtor* | Europa und die Frage nach seinen Grenzen im Osten. Zur Konstruktion europäischer Identität' in Geschichte und Gegenwart | Mit einem Vorwort von Albrecht Lehmann | ISBN 978-3-8382-0045-3

94　*Ben Hellman, Andrei Rogachevskii* | Filming the Unfilmable. Casper Wrede's 'One Day in the Life of Ivan Denisovich' | Second, Revised and Expanded Edition | ISBN 978-3-8382-0044-6

95　*Eva Fuchslocher* | Vaterland, Sprache, Glaube. Orthodoxie und Nationenbildung am Beispiel Georgiens | Mit einem Vorwort von Christina von Braun | ISBN 978-3-89821-884-9

96　*Vladimir Kantor* | Das Westlertum und der Weg Russlands. Zur Entwicklung der russischen Literatur und Philosophie | Ediert von Dagmar Herrmann | Mit einem Beitrag von Nikolaus Lobkowicz | ISBN 978-3-8382-0102-3

97　*Kamran Musayev* | Die postsowjetische Transformation im Baltikum und Südkaukasus. Eine vergleichende Untersuchung der politischen Entwicklung Lettlands und Aserbaidschans 1985-2009 | Mit einem Vorwort von Leonid Luks | Ediert von Sandro Henschel | ISBN 978-3-8382-0103-0

98 *Tatiana Zhurzhenko* | Borderlands into Bordered Lands. Geopolitics of Identity in Post-Soviet Ukraine | With a foreword by Dieter Segert | ISBN 978-3-8382-0042-2

99 *Кирилл Галушко, Лидия Смола (ред.)* | Пределы падения – варианты украинского будущего. Аналитико-прогностические исследования | ISBN 978-3-8382-0148-1

100 *Michael Minkenberg (Ed.)* | Historical Legacies and the Radical Right in Post-Cold War Central and Eastern Europe | With an afterword by Sabrina P. Ramet | ISBN 978-3-8382-0124-5

101 *David-Emil Wickström* | Rocking St. Petersburg. Transcultural Flows and Identity Politics in the St. Petersburg Popular Music Scene | With a foreword by Yngvar B. Steinholt | Second, Revised and Expanded Edition | ISBN 978-3-8382-0100-9

102 *Eva Zabka* | Eine neue „Zeit der Wirren"? Der spät- und postsowjetische Systemwandel 1985-2000 im Spiegel russischer gesellschaftspolitischer Diskurse | Mit einem Vorwort von Margareta Mommsen | ISBN 978-3-8382-0161-0

103 *Ulrike Ziemer* | Ethnic Belonging, Gender and Cultural Practices. Youth Identitites in Contemporary Russia | With a foreword by Anoop Nayak | ISBN 978-3-8382-0152-8

104 *Ksenia Chepikova* | ‚Finiges Russland' - eine zweite KPdSU? Aspekte der Identitätskonstruktion einer postsowjetischen „Partei der Macht" | Mit einem Vorwort von Torsten Oppelland | ISBN 978-3-8382-0311-9

105 *Леонид Люкс* | Западничество или евразийство? Демократия или идеократия? Сборник статей об исторических дилеммах России | С предисловием Владимира Кантора | ISBN 978-3-8382-0211-2

106 *Anna Dost* | Das russische Verfassungsrecht auf dem Weg zum Föderalismus und zurück. Zum Konflikt von Rechtsnormen und -wirklichkeit in der Russländischen Föderation von 1991 bis 2009 | Mit einem Vorwort von Alexander Blankenagel | ISBN 978-3-8382-0292-1

107 *Philipp Herzog* | Sozialistische Völkerfreundschaft, nationaler Widerstand oder harmloser Zeitvertreib? Zur politischen Funktion der Volkskunst im sowjetischen Estland | Mit einem Vorwort von Andreas Kappeler | ISBN 978-3-8382-0216-7

108 *Marlène Laruelle (Ed.)* | Russian Nationalism, Foreign Policy, and Identity Debates in Putin's Russia. New Ideological Patterns after the Orange Revolution | ISBN 978-3-8382-0325-6

109 *Michail Logvinov* | Russlands Kampf gegen den internationalen Terrorismus. Eine kritische Bestandsaufnahme des Bekämpfungsansatzes | Mit einem Geleitwort von Hans-Henning Schröder und einem Vorwort von Eckhard Jesse | ISBN 978-3-8382-0329-4

110 *John B. Dunlop* | The Moscow Bombings of September 1999. Examinations of Russian Terrorist Attacks at the Onset of Vladimir Putin's Rule | Second, Revised and Expanded Edition | ISBN 978-3-8382-0388-1

111 *Андрей А. Ковалёв* | Свидетельство из-за кулис российской политики I. Можно ли делать добро из зла? (Воспоминания и размышления о последних советских и первых послесоветских годах) | With a foreword by Peter Reddaway | ISBN 978-3-8382-0302-7

112 *Андрей А. Ковалёв* | Свидетельство из-за кулис российской политики II. Угроза для себя и окружающих (Наблюдения и предостережения относительно происходящего после 2000 г.) | ISBN 978-3-8382-0303-4

113 *Bernd Kappenberg* | Zeichen setzen für Europa. Der Gebrauch europäischer lateinischer Sonderzeichen in der deutschen Öffentlichkeit | Mit einem Vorwort von Peter Schlobinski | ISBN 978-3-89821-749-1

114 *Ivo Mijnssen* | The Quest for an Ideal Youth in Putin's Russia I. Back to Our Future! History, Modernity, and Patriotism according to Nashi, 2005-2013 | With a foreword by Jeronim Perović | Second, Revised and Expanded Edition | ISBN 978-3-8382-0368-3

115 *Jussi Lassila* | The Quest for an Ideal Youth in Putin's Russia II. The Search for Distinctive Conformism in the Political Communication of Nashi, 2005-2009 | With a foreword by Kirill Postoutenko | Second, Revised and Expanded Edition | ISBN 978-3-8382-0415-4

116 *Valerio Trabandt* | Neue Nachbarn, gute Nachbarschaft? Die EU als internationaler Akteur am Beispiel ihrer Demokratieförderung in Belarus und der Ukraine 2004-2009 | Mit einem Vorwort von Jutta Joachim | ISBN 978-3-8382-0437-6

117 *Fabian Pfeiffer* | Estlands Außen- und Sicherheitspolitik I. Der estnische Atlantizismus nach der wiedererlangten Unabhängigkeit 1991-2004 | Mit einem Vorwort von Helmut Hubel | ISBN 978-3-8382-0127-6

118 *Jana Podßuweit* | Estlands Außen- und Sicherheitspolitik II. Handlungsoptionen eines Kleinstaates im Rahmen seiner EU-Mitgliedschaft (2004-2008) | Mit einem Vorwort von Helmut Hubel | ISBN 978-3-8382-0440-6

119 *Karin Pointner* | Estlands Außen- und Sicherheitspolitik III. Eine gedächtnispolitische Analyse estnischer Entwicklungskooperation 2006-2010 | Mit einem Vorwort von Karin Liebhart | ISBN 978-3-8382-0435-2

120 *Ruslana Vovk* | Die Offenheit der ukrainischen Verfassung für das Völkerrecht und die europäische Integration | Mit einem Vorwort von Alexander Blankenagel | ISBN 978-3-8382-0481-9

121 *Mykhaylo Banakh* | Die Relevanz der Zivilgesellschaft bei den postkommunistischen Transformationsprozessen in mittel- und osteuropäischen Ländern. Das Beispiel der spät- und postsowjetischen Ukraine 1986-2009 | Mit einem Vorwort von Gerhard Simon | ISBN 978-3-8382-0499-4

122 *Michael Moser* | Language Policy and the Discourse on Languages in Ukraine under President Viktor Yanukovych (25 February 2010–28 October 2012) | ISBN 978-3-8382-0497-0 (Paperback edition) | ISBN 978-3-8382-0507-6 (Hardcover edition)

123 *Nicole Krome* | Russischer Netzwerkkapitalismus Restrukturierungsprozesse in der Russischen Föderation am Beispiel des Luftfahrtunternehmens „Aviastar" | Mit einem Vorwort von Petra Stykow | ISBN 978-3-8382-0534-2

124 *David R. Marples* | 'Our Glorious Past'. Lukashenka's Belarus and the Great Patriotic War | ISBN 978-3-8382-0574-8 (Paperback edition) | ISBN 978-3-8382-0675-2 (Hardcover edition)

125 *Ulf Walther* | Russlands „neuer Adel". Die Macht des Geheimdienstes von Gorbatschow bis Putin | Mit einem Vorwort von Hans-Georg Wieck | ISBN 978-3-8382-0584-7

126 *Simon Geissbühler (Hrsg.)* | Kiew – Revolution 3.0. Der Euromaidan 2013/14 und die Zukunftsperspektiven der Ukraine | ISBN 978-3-8382-0581-6 (Paperback edition) | ISBN 978-3-8382-0681-3 (Hardcover edition)

127 *Andrey Makarychev* | Russia and the EU in a Multipolar World. Discourses, Identities, Norms | With a foreword by Klaus Segbers | ISBN 978-3-8382-0629-5

128 *Roland Scharff* | Kasachstan als postsowjetischer Wohlfahrtsstaat. Die Transformation des sozialen Schutzsystems | Mit einem Vorwort von Joachim Ahrens | ISBN 978-3-8382-0622-6

129 *Katja Grupp* | Bild Lücke Deutschland. Kaliningrader Studierende sprechen über Deutschland | Mit einem Vorwort von Martin Schulz | ISBN 978-3-8382-0552-6

130 *Konstantin Sheiko, Stephen Brown* | History as Therapy. Alternative History and Nationalist Imaginings in Russia, 1991-2014 | ISBN 978-3-8382-0665-3

131 *Elisa Kriza* | Alexander Solzhenitsyn: Cold War Icon, Gulag Author, Russian Nationalist? A Study of the Western Reception of his Literary Writings, Historical Interpretations, and Political Ideas | With a foreword by Andrei Rogatchevski | ISBN 978-3-8382-0589-2 (Paperback edition) | ISBN 978-3-8382-0690-5 (Hardcover edition)

132 *Serghei Golunov* | The Elephant in the Room. Corruption and Cheating in Russian Universities | ISBN 978-3-8382-0570-0

133 *Manja Hussner, Rainer Arnold (Hgg.)* | Verfassungsgerichtsbarkeit in Zentralasien I. Sammlung von Verfassungstexten | ISBN 978-3-8382-0595-3

134 *Nikolay Mitrokhin* | Die „Russische Partei". Die Bewegung der russischen Nationalisten in der UdSSR 1953-1985 | Aus dem Russischen übertragen von einem Übersetzerteam unter der Leitung von Larisa Schippel | ISBN 978-3-8382-0024-8

135 *Manja Hussner, Rainer Arnold (Hgg.)* | Verfassungsgerichtsbarkeit in Zentralasien II. Sammlung von Verfassungstexten | ISBN 978-3-8382-0597-7

136 *Manfred Zeller* | Das sowjetische Fieber. Fußballfans im poststalinistischen Vielvölkerreich | Mit einem Vorwort von Nikolaus Katzer | ISBN 978-3-8382-0757-5

137 *Kristin Schreiter* | Stellung und Entwicklungspotential zivilgesellschaftlicher Gruppen in Russland. Menschenrechtsorganisationen im Vergleich | ISBN 978-3-8382-0673-8

138 *David R. Marples, Frederick V. Mills (Eds.)* | Ukraine's Euromaidan. Analyses of a Civil Revolution | ISBN 978-3-8382-0660-8

139 *Bernd Kappenberg* | Setting Signs for Europe. Why Diacritics Matter for European Integration | With a foreword by Peter Schlobinski | ISBN 978-3-8382-0663-9

140 *René Lenz* | Internationalisierung, Kooperation und Transfer. Externe bildungspolitische Akteure in der Russischen Föderation | Mit einem Vorwort von Frank Ettrich | ISBN 978-3-8382-0751-3

141 *Juri Plusnin, Yana Zausaeva, Natalia Zhidkevich, Artemy Pozanenko* | Wandering Workers. Moros, Dehavlor, Way of Life, and Political Status of Domestic Russian Labor Migrants | Translated by Julia Kazantseva | ISBN 978-3-8382-0653-0

142 *David J. Smith (Eds.)* | Latvia – A Work in Progress? 100 Years of State- and Nation-Building | ISBN 978-3-8382-0648-6

143 *Инна Чувычкина (ред.)* | Экспортные нефте- и газопроводы на постсоветском пространстве. Анализ трубопроводной политики в свете теории международных отношений | ISBN 978-3-8382-0822-0

144 Johann Zajaczkowski | Russland – eine pragmatische Großmacht? Eine rollentheoretische Untersuchung russischer Außenpolitik am Beispiel der Zusammenarbeit mit den USA nach 9/11 und des Georgienkrieges von 2008 | Mit einem Vorwort von Siegfried Schieder | ISBN 978-3-8382-0837-4

145 Boris Popivanov | Changing Images of the Left in Bulgaria. The Challenge of Post-Communism in the Early 21st Century | ISBN 978-3-8382-0667-7

146 Lenka Krátká | A History of the Czechoslovak Ocean Shipping Company 1948-1989. How a Small, Landlocked Country Ran Maritime Business During the Cold War | ISBN 978-3-8382-0666-0

147 Alexander Sergunin | Explaining Russian Foreign Policy Behavior. Theory and Practice | ISBN 978-3-8382-0752-0

148 Darya Malyutina | Migrant Friendships in a Super-Diverse City. Russian-Speakers and their Social Relationships in London in the 21st Century | With a foreword by Claire Dwyer | ISBN 978-3-8382-0652-3

149 Alexander Sergunin, Valery Konyshev | Russia in the Arctic. Hard or Soft Power? | ISBN 978-3-8382-0753-7

150 John J. Maresca | Helsinki Revisited. A Key U.S. Negotiator's Memoirs on the Development of the CSCE into the OSCE | With a foreword by Hafiz Pashayev | ISBN 978-3-8382-0852-7

151 Jardar Østbø | The New Third Rome. Readings of a Russian Nationalist Myth | With a foreword by Pål Kolstø | ISBN 978-3-8382-0870-1

152 Simon Kordonsky | Socio-Economic Foundations of the Russian Post-Soviet Regime. The Resource-Based Economy and Estate-Based Social Structure of Contemporary Russia | With a foreword by Svetlana Barsukova | ISBN 978-3-8382-0775-9

153 Duncan Leitch | Assisting Reform in Post-Communist Ukraine 2000–2012. The Illusions of Donors and the Disillusion of Beneficiaries | With a foreword by Kataryna Wolczuk | ISBN 978-3-8382-0844-2

154 Abel Polese | Limits of a Post-Soviet State. How Informality Replaces, Renegotiates, and Reshapes Governance in Contemporary Ukraine | With a foreword by Colin Williams | ISBN 978-3-8382-0845-9

155 Mikhail Suslov (Ed.) | Digital Orthodoxy in the Post-Soviet World. The Russian Orthodox Church and Web 2.0 | With a foreword by Father Cyril Hovorun | ISBN 978-3-8382-0871-8

156 Leonid Luks | Zwei „Sonderwege"? Russisch-deutsche Parallelen und Kontraste (1917-2014). Vergleichende Essays | ISBN 978-3-8382-0823-7

157 Vladimir V. Karacharovskiy, Ovsey I. Shkaratan, Gordey A. Yastrebov | Towards a New Russian Work Culture. Can Western Companies and Expatriates Change Russian Society? | With a foreword by Elena N. Danilova | Translated by Julia Kazantseva | ISBN 978-3-8382-0902-9

158 Edmund Griffiths | Aleksandr Prokhanov and Post-Soviet Esotericism | ISBN 978-3-8382-0963-0

159 Timm Beichelt, Susann Worschech (Eds.) | Transnational Ukraine? Networks and Ties that Influence(d) Contemporary Ukraine | ISBN 978-3-8382-0944-9

160 Mieste Hotopp-Riecke | Die Tataren der Krim zwischen Assimilation und Selbstbehauptung. Der Aufbau des krimtatarischen Bildungswesens nach Deportation und Heimkehr (1990-2005) | Mit einem Vorwort von Swetlana Czerwonnaja | ISBN 978-3-89821-940-2

161 Olga Bertelsen (Ed.) | Revolution and War in Contemporary Ukraine. The Challenge of Change | ISBN 978-3-8382-1016-2

162 Natalya Ryabinska | Ukraine's Post-Communist Mass Media. Between Capture and Commercialization | With a foreword by Marta Dyczok | ISBN 978-3-8382-1011-7

163 Alexandra Cotofana, James M. Nyce (Eds.) | Religion and Magic in Socialist and Post-Socialist Contexts. Historic and Ethnographic Case Studies of Orthodoxy, Heterodoxy, and Alternative Spirituality | With a foreword by Patrick L. Michelson | ISBN 978-3-8382-0989-0

164 Nozima Akhrarkhodjaeva | The Instrumentalisation of Mass Media in Electoral Authoritarian Regimes. Evidence from Russia's Presidential Election Campaigns of 2000 and 2008 | ISBN 978-3-8382-1013-1

165 Yulia Krasheninnikova | Informal Healthcare in Contemporary Russia. Sociographic Essays on the Post-Soviet Infrastructure for Alternative Healing Practices | ISBN 978-3-8382-0970-8

166 Peter Kaiser | Das Schachbrett der Macht. Die Handlungsspielräume eines sowjetischen Funktionärs unter Stalin am Beispiel des Generalsekretärs des Komsomol Aleksandr Kosarev (1929-1938) | Mit einem Vorwort von Dietmar Neutatz | ISBN 978-3-8382-1052-0

167 Oksana Kim | The Effects and Implications of Kazakhstan's Adoption of International Financial Reporting Standards. A Resource Dependence Perspective | With a foreword by Svetlana Vlady | ISBN 978-3-8382-0987-6

168 *Anna Sanina* | Patriotic Education in Contemporary Russia. Sociological Studies in the Making of the Post-Soviet Citizen | With a foreword by Anna Oldfield | ISBN 978-3-8382-0993-7

169 *Rudolf Wolters* | Spezialist in Sibirien Faksimile der 1933 erschienenen ersten Ausgabe | Mit einem Vorwort von Dmitrij Chmelnizki | ISBN 978-3-8382-0515-1

170 *Michal Vít, Magdalena M. Baran (Eds.)* | Transregional versus National Perspectives on Contemporary Central European History. Studies on the Building of Nation-States and Their Cooperation in the 20th and 21st Century | With a foreword by Petr Vágner | ISBN 978-3-8382-1015-5

171 *Philip Gamaghelyan* | Conflict Resolution Beyond the International Relations Paradigm. Evolving Designs as a Transformative Practice in Nagorno-Karabakh and Syria | With a foreword by Susan Allen | ISBN 978-3-8382-1057-5

172 *Maria Shagina* | Joining a Prestigious Club. Cooperation with Europarties and Its Impact on Party Development in Georgia, Moldova, and Ukraine 2004–2015 | With a foreword by Kataryna Wolczuk | ISBN 978-3-8382-1084-1

173 *Alexandra Cotofana, James M. Nyce (Eds.)* | Religion and Magic in Socialist and Post-Socialist Contexts II. Baltic, Eastern European, and Post-USSR Case Studies | With a foreword by Anita Stasulane | ISBN 978-3-8382-0990-6

174 *Barbara Kunz* | Kind Words, Cruise Missiles, and Everything in Between. The Use of Power Resources in U.S. Policies towards Poland, Ukraine, and Belarus 1989–2008 | With a foreword by William Hill | ISBN 978-3-8382-1065-0

175 *Eduard Klein* | Bildungskorruption in Russland und der Ukraine. Eine komparative Analyse der Performanz staatlicher Antikorruptionsmaßnahmen im Hochschulsektor am Beispiel universitärer Aufnahmeprüfungen | Mit einem Vorwort von Heiko Pleines | ISBN 978-3-8382-0995-1

176 *Markus Soldner* | Politischer Kapitalismus im postsowjetischen Russland. Die politische, wirtschaftliche und mediale Transformation in den 1990er Jahren | Mit einem Vorwort von Wolfgang Ismayr | ISBN 978-3-8382-1222-7

177 *Anton Oleinik* | Building Ukraine from Within. A Sociological, Institutional, and Economic Analysis of a Nation-State in the Making | ISBN 978-3-8382-1150-3

178 *Peter Rollberg, Marlene Laruelle (Eds.)* | Mass Media in the Post-Soviet World. Market Forces, State Actors, and Political Manipulation in the Informational Environment after Communism | ISBN 978-3-8382-1116-9

179 *Mikhail Minakov* | Development and Dystopia. Studies in Post-Soviet Ukraine and Eastern Europe | With a foreword by Alexander Etkind | ISBN 978-3-8382-1112-1

180 *Aijan Sharshenova* | The European Union's Democracy Promotion in Central Asia. A Study of Political Interests, Influence, and Development in Kazakhstan and Kyrgyzstan in 2007–2013 | With a foreword by Gordon Crawford | ISBN 978-3-8382-1151-0

181 *Andrey Makarychev, Alexandra Yatsyk (Eds.)* | Boris Nemtsov and Russian Politics. Power and Resistance | With a foreword by Zhanna Nemtsova | ISBN 978-3-8382-1122-0

182 *Sophie Falsini* | The Euromaidan's Effect on Civil Society. Why and How Ukrainian Social Capital Increased after the Revolution of Dignity | With a foreword by Susann Worschech | ISBN 978-3-8382-1131-2

183 *Valentyna Romanova, Andreas Umland (Eds.)* | Ukraine's Decentralization. Challenges and Implications of the Local Governance Reform after the Euromaidan Revolution | ISBN 978-3-8382-1162-6

184 *Leonid Luks* | A Fateful Triangle. Essays on Contemporary Russian, German and Polish History | ISBN 978-3-8382-1143-5

185 *John B. Dunlop* | The February 2015 Assassination of Boris Nemtsov and the Flawed Trial of his Alleged Killers. An Exploration of Russia's "Crime of the 21st Century" | ISBN 978-3-8382-1188-6

186 *Vasile Rotaru* | Russia, the EU, and the Eastern Partnership. Building Bridges or Digging Trenches? | ISBN 978-3-8382-1134-3

187 *Marina Lebedeva* | Russian Studies of International Relations. From the Soviet Past to the Post-Cold-War Present | With a foreword by Andrei P. Tsygankov | ISBN 978-3-8382-0051-0

188 *Tomasz Stępniewski, George Soroka (Eds.)* | Ukraine after Maidan. Revisiting Domestic and Regional Security | ISBN 978-3-8382-1075-9

189 *Petar Cholakov* | Ethnic Entrepreneurs Unmasked. Political Institutions and Ethnic Conflicts in Contemporary Bulgaria | ISBN 978-3-8382-1189-3

190 *A. Salem, G. Hazeldine, D. Morgan (Eds.)* | Higher Education in Post-Communist States. Comparative and Sociological Perspectives | ISBN 978-3-8382-1183-1

191 *Igor Torbakov* | After Empire. Nationalist Imagination and Symbolic Politics in Russia and Eurasia in the Twentieth and Twenty-First Century | With a foreword by Serhii Plokhy | ISBN 978-3-8382-1217-5

192 *Aleksandr Burakovskiy* | Jewish-Ukrainian Relations in Late and Post-Soviet Ukraine. Articles, Lectures and Essays from 1986 to 2016 | ISBN 978-3-8382-1210-4

193 *Natalia Shapovalova, Olga Burlyuk (Eds.)* | Civil Society in Post-Euromaidan Ukraine. From Revolution to Consolidation | With a foreword by Richard Youngs | ISBN 978-3-8382-1216-6

194 *Franz Preissler* | Positionsverteidigung, Imperialismus oder Irredentismus? Russland und die „Russischsprachigen", 1991–2015 | ISBN 978-3-8382-1262-3

195 *Marian Madeła* | Der Reformprozess in der Ukraine 2014-2017. Eine Fallstudie zur Reform der öffentlichen Verwaltung | Mit einem Vorwort von Martin Malek | ISBN 978-3-8382-1266-1

196 *Anke Giesen* | „Wie kann denn der Sieger ein Verbrecher sein?" Eine diskursanalytische Untersuchung der russlandweiten Debatte über Konzept und Verstaatlichungsprozess der Lagergedenkstätte „Perm'-36" im Ural | ISBN 978-3-8382-1284-5

197 *Victoria Leukavets* | The Integration Policies of Belarus and Ukraine vis-à-vis the EU and Russia. A Comparative Analysis Through the Prism of a Two-Level Game Approach | ISBN 978-3-8382-1247-0

198 *Oksana Kim* | The Development and Challenges of Russian Corporate Governance I. The Roles and Functions of Boards of Directors | With a foreword by Sheila M. Puffer | ISBN 978-3-8382-1287-6

199 *Thomas D. Grant* | International Law and the Post-Soviet Space I. Essays on Chechnya and the Baltic States | With a foreword by Stephen M. Schwebel | ISBN 978-3-8382-1279-1

200 *Thomas D. Grant* | International Law and the Post-Soviet Space II. Essays on Ukraine, Intervention, and Non-Proliferation | ISBN 978-3-8382-1280-7

201 *Slavomír Michálek, Michal Štefansky* | The Age of Fear. The Cold War and Its Influence on Czechoslovakia 1945–1968 | ISBN 978-3-8382-1285-2

202 *Iulia-Sabina Joja* | Romania's Strategic Culture 1990–2014. Continuity and Change in a Post-Communist Country's Evolution of National Interests and Security Policies | With a foreword by Heiko Biehl | ISBN 978-3-8382-1286-9

203 *Andrei Rogatchevski, Yngvar B. Steinholt, Arve Hansen, David-Emil Wickström* | War of Songs. Popular Music and Recent Russia-Ukraine Relations | With a foreword by Artemy Troitsky | ISBN 978-3-8382-1173-2

204 *Maria Lipman (Ed.)* | Russian Voices on Post-Crimea Russia. An Almanac of Counterpoint Essays from 2015–2018 | ISBN 978-3-8382-1251-7

205 *Ksenia Maksimovtsova* | Language Conflicts in Contemporary Estonia, Latvia, and Ukraine. A Comparative Exploration of Discourses in Post-Soviet Russian-Language Digital Media | With a foreword by Ammon Cheskin | ISBN 978-3-8382-1282-1

206 *Michal Vít* | The EU's Impact on Identity Formation in East-Central Europe between 2004 and 2013. Perceptions of the Nation and Europe in Political Parties of the Czech Republic, Poland, and Slovakia | With a foreword by Andrea Pető | ISBN 978-3-8382-1275-3

207 *Per A. Rudling* | Tarnished Heroes. The Organization of Ukrainian Nationalists in the Memory Politics of Post-Soviet Ukraine | ISBN 978-3-8382-0999-9

208 *Kaja Gadowska, Peter Solomon (Eds.)* | Legal Change in Post-Communist States. Progress, Reversions, Explanations | ISBN 978-3-8382-1312-5

209 *Paweł Kowal, Georges Mink, Iwona Reichardt (Eds.)* | Three Revolutions: Mobilization and Change in Contemporary Ukraine I. Theoretical Aspects and Analyses on Religion, Memory, and Identity | ISBN 978-3-8382-1321-7

210 *Paweł Kowal, Georges Mink, Adam Reichardt, Iwona Reichardt (Eds.)* | Three Revolutions: Mobilization and Change in Contemporary Ukraine II. An Oral History of the Revolution on Granite, Orange Revolution, and Revolution of Dignity | ISBN 978-3-8382-1323-1

211 *Li Bennich-Björkman, Sergiy Kurbatov (Eds.)* | When the Future Came. The Collapse of the USSR and the Emergence of National Memory in Post-Soviet History Textbooks | ISBN 978-3-8382-1335-4

212 *Olga R. Gulina* | Migration as a (Geo-)Political Challenge in the Post-Soviet Space. Border Regimes, Policy Choices, Visa Agendas | With a foreword by Nils Muižnieks | ISBN 978-3-8382-1338-5

213 *Sanna Turoma, Kaarina Aitamurto, Slobodanka Vladiv-Glover (Eds.)* | Religion, Expression, and Patriotism in Russia. Essays on Post-Soviet Society and the State. ISBN 978-3-8382-1346-0

214 *Vasif Huseynov* | Geopolitical Rivalries in the "Common Neighborhood". Russia's Conflict with the West, Soft Power, and Neoclassical Realism | With a foreword by Nicholas Ross Smith | ISBN 978-3-8382-1277-7

215 *Mikhail Suslov* | Geopolitical Imagination. Ideology and Utopia in Post-Soviet Russia | With a foreword by Mark Bassin | ISBN 978-3-8382-1361-3

216 *Alexander Etkind, Mikhail Minakov (Eds.)* | Ideology after Union. Political Doctrines, Discourses, and Debates in Post-Soviet Societies | ISBN 978-3-8382-1388-0

217 *Jakob Mischke, Oleksandr Zabirko (Hgg.)* | Protestbewegungen im langen Schatten des Kreml. Aufbruch und Resignation in Russland und der Ukraine | ISBN 978-3-8382-0926-5

218 *Oksana Huss* | How Corruption and Anti-Corruption Policies Sustain Hybrid Regimes. Strategies of Political Domination under Ukraine's Presidents in 1994-2014 | With a foreword by Tobias Debiel and Andrea Gawrich | ISBN 978-3-8382-1430-6

219 *Dmitry Travin, Vladimir Gel'man, Otar Marganiya* | The Russian Path. Ideas, Interests, Institutions, Illusions | With a foreword by Vladimir Ryzhkov | ISBN 978-3-8382-1421-4

220 *Gergana Dimova* | Political Uncertainty. A Comparative Exploration | With a foreword by Todor Yalamov and Rumena Filipova | ISBN 978-3-8382-1385-9

221 *Torben Waschke* | Russland in Transition. Geopolitik zwischen Raum, Identität und Machtinteressen | Mit einem Vorwort von Andreas Dittmann | ISBN 978-3-8382-1480-1

222 *Steven Jobbitt, Zsolt Bottlik, Marton Berki (Eds.)* | Power and Identity in the Post-Soviet Realm. Geographies of Ethnicity and Nationality after 1991 | ISBN 978-3-8382-1399-6

223 *Daria Buteiko* | Erinnerungsort. Ort des Gedenkens, der Erholung oder der Einkehr? Kommunismus-Erinnerung am Beispiel der Gedenkstätte Berliner Mauer sowie des Soloveckij-Klosters und -Museumsparks | ISBN 978-3-8382-1367-5

224 *Olga Bertelsen (Ed.)* | Russian Active Measures. Yesterday, Today, Tomorrow | With a foreword by Jan Goldman | ISBN 978-3-8382-1529-7

225 *David Mandel* | "Optimizing" Higher Education in Russia. University Teachers and their Union "Universitetskaya solidarnost'" | ISBN 978-3-8382-1519-8

226 *Mikhail Minakov, Gwendolyn Sasse, Daria Isachenko (Eds.)* | Post-Soviet Secessionism. Nation-Building and State-Failure after Communism | ISBN 978-3-8382-1538-9

227 *Jakob Hauter (Ed.)* | Civil War? Interstate War? Hybrid War? Dimensions and Interpretations of the Donbas Conflict in 2014–2020 | With a foreword by Andrew Wilson | ISBN 978-3-8382-1383-5

228 *Tima T. Moldogaziev, Gene A. Brewer, J. Edward Kellough (Eds.)* | Public Policy and Politics in Georgia. Lessons from Post-Soviet Transition | With a foreword by Dan Durning | ISBN 978-3-8382-1535-8

229 *Oxana Schmies (Ed.)* | NATO's Enlargement and Russia. A Strategic Challenge in the Past and Future | With a foreword by Vladimir Kara-Murza | ISBN 978-3-8382-1478-8

230 *Christopher Ford* | Ukapisme – Une Gauche perdue. Le marxisme anti-colonial dans la révolution ukrainienne 1917-1925 | Avec une préface de Vincent Présumey | ISBN 978-3-8382-0899-2

231 *Anna Kutkina* | Between Lenin and Bandera. Decommunization and Multivocality in Post-Euromaidan Ukraine | With a foreword by Juri Mykkänen | ISBN 978-3-8382-1506-8

232 *Lincoln E. Flake* | Defending the Faith. The Russian Orthodox Church and the Demise of Religious Pluralism | With a foreword by Peter Martland | ISBN 978-3-8382-1378-1

233 *Nikoloz Samkharadze* | Russia's Recognition of the Independence of Abkhazia and South Ossetia. Analysis of a Deviant Case in Moscow's Foreign Policy | With a foreword by Neil MacFarlane | ISBN 978-3-8382-1414-6

234 *Arve Hansen* | Urban Protest. A Spatial Perspective on Kyiv, Minsk, and Moscow | With a foreword by Julie Wilhelmsen | ISBN 978-3-8382-1495-5

235 *Eleonora Narvselius, Julie Fedor (Eds.)* | Diversity in the East-Central European Borderlands. Memories, Cityscapes, People | ISBN 978-3-8382-1523-5

236 *Regina Elsner* | The Russian Orthodox Church and Modernity. A Historical and Theological Investigation into Eastern Christianity between Unity and Plurality | With a foreword by Mikhail Suslov | ISBN 978-3-8382-1568-6

237 *Bo Petersson* | The Putin Predicament. Problems of Legitimacy and Succession in Russia | With a foreword by J. Paul Goode | ISBN 978-3-8382-1050-6

238 *Jonathan Otto Pohl* | The Years of Great Silence. The Deportation, Special Settlement, and Mobilization into the Labor Army of Ethnic Germans in the USSR, 1941–1955 | ISBN 978-3-8382-1630-0

239 *Mikhail Minakov (Ed.)* | Inventing Majorities. Ideological Creativity in Post-Soviet Societies | ISBN 978-3-8382-1641-6

240 *Robert M. Cutler* | Soviet and Post-Soviet Foreign Policies I. East-South Relations and the Political Economy of the Communist Bloc, 1971–1991 | With a foreword by Roger E. Kanet | ISBN 978-3-8382-1654-6

241 *Izabella Agardi* | On the Verge of History. Life Stories of Rural Women from Serbia, Romania, and Hungary, 1920–2020 | With a foreword by Andrea Pető | ISBN 978-3-8382-1602-7

242 *Sebastian Schäffer (Ed.)* | Ukraine in Central and Eastern Europe. Kyiv's Foreign Affairs and the International Relations of the Post-Communist Region | With a foreword by Pavlo Klimkin and Andreas Umland| ISBN 978-3-8382-1615-7

243 *Volodymyr Dubrovskyi, Kalman Mizsei, Mychailo Wynnyckyj (Eds.)* | Eight Years after the Revolution of Dignity. What Has Changed in Ukraine during 2013–2021? | With a foreword by Yaroslav Hrytsak | ISBN 978-3-8382-1560-0

244 *Rumena Filipova* | Constructing the Limits of Europe Identity and Foreign Policy in Poland, Bulgaria, and Russia since 1989 | With forewords by Harald Wydra and Gergana Yankova-Dimova | ISBN 978-3-8382-1649-2

245 *Oleksandra Keudel* | How Patronal Networks Shape Opportunities for Local Citizen Participation in a Hybrid Regime A Comparative Analysis of Five Cities in Ukraine | With a foreword by Sabine Kropp | ISBN 978-3-8382-1671-3

246 *Jan Claas Behrends, Thomas Lindenberger, Pavel Kolar (Eds.)* | Violence after Stalin Institutions, Practices, and Everyday Life in the Soviet Bloc 1953–1989 | ISBN 978-3-8382-1637-9

247 *Leonid Luks* | Macht und Ohnmacht der Utopien Essays zur Geschichte Russlands im 20. und 21. Jahrhundert | ISBN 978-3-8382-1677-5

248 *Iuliia Barshadska* | Brüssel zwischen Kyjiw und Moskau Das auswärtige Handeln der Europäischen Union im ukrainisch-russischen Konflikt 2014-2019 | Mit einem Vorwort von Olaf Leiße | ISBN 978-3-8382-1667-6

249 *Valentyna Romanova* | Decentralisation and Multilevel Elections in Ukraine Reform Dynamics and Party Politics in 2010–2021 | With a foreword by Kimitaka Matsuzato | ISBN 978-3-8382-1700-0

250 *Alexander Motyl* | National Questions. Theoretical Reflections on Nations and Nationalism in Eastern Europe | ISBN 978-3-8382-1675-1

251 *Marc Dietrich* | A Cosmopolitan Model for Peacebuilding. The Ukrainian Cases of Crimea and the Donbas | With a foreword by Rémi Baudouï | ISBN 978-3-8382-1687-4

252 *Eduard Baidaus* | An Unsettled Nation. Moldova in the Geopolitics of Russia, Romania, and Ukraine | With forewords by John-Paul Himka and David R. Marples | ISBN 978-3-8382-1582-2

253 *Igor Okunev, Petr Oskolkov (Eds.)* | Transforming the Administrative Matryoshka. The Reform of Autonomous Okrugs in the Russian Federation, 2003–2008 | With a foreword by Vladimir Zorin | ISBN 978-3-8382-1721-5

254 *Winfried Schneider-Deters* | Ukraine's Fateful Years 2013–2019. Vol. I: The Popular Uprising in Winter 2013/2014 | ISBN 978-3-8382-1725-3

255 *Winfried Schneider-Deters* | Ukraine's Fateful Years 2013–2019. Vol. II: The Annexation of Crimea and the War in Donbas | ISBN 978-3-8382-1726-0

256 *Robert M. Cutler* | Soviet and Post-Soviet Russian Foreign Policies II. East-West Relations in Europe and the Political Economy of the Communist Bloc, 1971–1991 | With a foreword by Roger E. Kanet | ISBN 978-3-8382-1727-7

257 *Robert M. Cutler* | Soviet and Post-Soviet Russian Foreign Policies III. East-West Relations in Europe and Eurasia in the Post-Cold War Transition, 1991–2001 | With a foreword by Roger E. Kanet | ISBN 978-3-8382-1728-4

258 *Paweł Kowal, Iwona Reichardt, Kateryna Pryshchepa (Eds.)* | Three Revolutions: Mobilization and Change in Contemporary Ukraine III. Archival Records and Historical Sources on the 1990 Revolution on Granite | ISBN 978-3-8382-1376-7

259 *Mikhail Minakov (Ed.)* | Philosophy Unchained. Developments in Post-Soviet Philosophical Thought. | With a foreword by Christopher Donohue | ISBN 978-3-8382-1768-0

260 *David Dalton* | The Ukrainian Oligarchy After the Euromaidan. How Ukraine's Political Economy Regime Survived the Crisis | With a foreword by Andrew Wilson | ISBN 978-3-8382-1740-6

261 *Andreas Heinemann-Grüder (Ed.)* | Who Are the Fighters? Irregular Armed Groups in the Russian-Ukrainian War since 2014 | ISBN 978-3-8382-1777-2

262 *Taras Kuzio (Ed.)* | Russian Disinformation and Western Scholarship. Bias and Prejudice in Journalistic, Expert, and Academic Analyses of East European, Russian and Eurasian Affairs | ISBN 978-3-8382-1685-0

263 *Darius Furmonavicius* | LithuaniaTransforms the West. Lithuania's Liberation from Soviet Occupation and the Enlargement of NATO (1988–2022) | With a foreword by Vytautas Landsbergis | ISBN 978-3-8382-1779-6

264 *Dirk Dalberg* | Politisches Denken im tschechoslowakischen Dissens. Egon Bondy, Miroslav Kusý, Milan Šimečka und Petr Uhl (1968-1989) | ISBN 978-3-8382-1318-5

265 *Леонид Люкс* | К столетию «философского парохода». Мыслители «первой» русской эмиграции о русской революции и о тоталитарных соблазнах XX века | ISBN 978-3-8382-1775-8

266 *Daviti Mtchedlishvili* | The EU and the South Caucasus. European Neighborhood Policies between Eclecticism and Pragmatism, 1991-2021 | With a foreword by Nicholas Ross Smith | ISBN 978-3-8382-1735-2

267 *Bohdan Harasymiw* | Post-Euromaidan Ukraine. Domestic Power Struggles and War of National Survival in 2014–2022 | ISBN 978-3-8382-1798-7

268 *Nadiia Koval, Denys Tereshchenko (Eds.)* | Russian Cultural Diplomacy under Putin. Rossotrudnichestvo, the "Russkiy Mir" Foundation, and the Gorchakov Fund in 2007–2022 | ISBN 978-3-8382-1801-4

269 *Izabela Kazejak* | Jews in Post-War Wrocław and L'viv. Official Policies and Local Responses in Comparative Perspective, 1945-1970s | ISBN 978-3-8382-1802-1

270 *Jakob Hauter* | Russia's Overlooked Invasion. The Causes of the 2014 Outbreak of War in Ukraine's Donbas | With a foreword by Hiroaki Kuromiya | ISBN 978-3-8382-1803-8

271 *Anton Shekhovtsov* | Russian Political Warfare. Essays on Kremlin Propaganda in Europe and the Neighbourhood, 2020-2023 | With a foreword by Nathalie Loiseau | ISBN 978-3-8382-1821-2

272 *Андреа Пето* | Насилие и Молчание. Красная армия в Венгрии во Второй Мировой войне | ISBN 978-3-8382-1636-2

273 *Winfried Schneider-Deters* | Russia's War in Ukraine. Debates on Peace, Fascism, and War Crimes, 2022–2023 | With a foreword by Klaus Gestwa | ISBN 978-3-8382-1876-2

274 *Rasmus Nilsson* | Uncanny Allies. Russia and Belarus on the Edge, 2012-2024 | ISBN 978-3-8382-1288-3

275 *Anton Grushetskyi, Volodymyr Paniotto* | War and the Transformation of Ukrainian Society (2022–23). Empirical Evidence | ISBN 978-3-8382-1944-8

276 *Christian Kaunert, Alex MacKenzie, Adrien Nonjon (eds.)* | In the Eye of the Storm. Origins, Ideology, and Controversies of the Azov Brigade, 2014–23 | ISBN 978-3-8382-1750-5

277 *Gian Marco Moisé* | The House Always Wins. The Corrupt Strategies that Shaped Kazakh Oil Politics and Business in the Nazarbayev Era | With a foreword by Alena Ledeneva | ISBN 978-3-8382-1917-2

278 *Mikhail Minakov* | The Post-Soviet Human | Philosophical Reflections on Social History after the End of Communism | ISBN 978-3-8382-1943-1

279 *Natalia Kudriavtseva, Debra A. Friedman (eds.)* | Language and Power in Ukraine and Kazakhstan. Essays on Education, Ideology, Literature, Practice, and the Media | With a foreword by Laada Bilaniuk | ISBN 978-3-8382-1949-3

280 *Paweł Kowal, Georges Mink, Iwona Reichardt (eds.)* | The End of the Soviet World? Essays on Post-Communist Political and Social Change | With a foreword by Richardt Butterwick-Pawlikowski | ISBN 978-3-8382-1961-5

281 *Kateryna Zarembo, Michèle Knodt, Maksym Yakovlyev (eds.)* | Teaching IR in Wartime. Experiences of University Lecturers during Russia's Full-Scale Invasion of Ukraine | ISBN 978-3-8382-1954-7

282 *Oleksii Kresin* | The UN General Assembly Resolutions. Their Nature and Significance in the Context of the Russian Federation's War against Ukraine | With a preface by William E. Butler | ISBN 978-3-8382-1967-7

***ibidem**.eu*